Deutsche Wiederholungsgrammatik

Deutsche Wiederholungsgrammatik

A Morpho-Syntactic Review of German

Frank E. Donahue

The University of Texas at Austin

Yale University Press

New Haven & London

PUBLISHER: Mary Jane Peluso
DEVELOPMENT EDITOR: Brie Kluytenaar
PROJECT EDITOR: Timothy Shea
MANUSCRIPT EDITOR: Karen Hohner
PRODUCTION EDITOR: Ann-Marie Imbornoni
PRODUCTION CONTROLLER: Karen Stickler

Designed by James J. Johnson and set in Minion and Syntax types by Integrated Publishing Solutions.

Printed in the United States of America.

Library of Congress Cataloging-in-Publication Data
Donahue, Frank E.
Deutsche Wiederholungsgrammatik : a morpho-syntactic review of German / Frank E. Donahue
p. cm.
Includes bibliographical references and index.
ISBN 978-0-300-12468-2 (pbk. : alk. paper) 1. German language—Grammar. 2. German language—Textbooks for foreign speakers—English. I. Title.
PF3112.D654 2009
438.2′421—dc22 2007043538

A catalogue record for this book is available from the British Library.

The paper in this book meets the guidelines for permanence and durability of the Committee on Production Guidelines for Book Longevity of the Council on Library Resources.

10 9 8 7

This book is dedicated to the memory of my father.
A father makes all the difference.

Contents

Preface

For the past twenty years there has been much fluctuation in the field of foreign language education at the postsecondary level. There have been, essentially, two schools of thought. Teachers who believe that learning a foreign language should be conducted along the lines of the first language (native language) have striven to develop holistic, "osmotic" approaches that are deemed to be more natural and allegedly less anxiety-producing than more traditional forms of language instruction. According to this position, if students can make themselves understood and can comprehend what they read and what is said to them, they are deemed to be successful language learners. Grammatical accuracy is not emphasized to any great extent because it is believed to get in the way of communicative thought and to be inherently stressful. Of course, this need not be the case at all. Not surprisingly, students from such programs often have limited control of the fundamentals of German grammar. Other teachers, for many reasons, see learning a foreign language as quite different from learning one's native tongue or a second language, which is acquired in an environment much different from the one experienced by a foreign language learner. These teachers believe in structuring and sequencing instruction very carefully, proceeding from general to specific, and contrasting the foreign language with the students' native language in order to help them discover similarities and differences. Grammatical accuracy is valued and efforts are made to develop it as well as overall proficiency in the language right from the first day of instruction.

Students who have had a strong grounding in German grammar in their earlier German courses will find that this book provides a smooth review that enables them to fine-tune their accuracy. Those students who are unfamiliar with grammatical concepts and terminology, or who have not learned such things as principal parts of verbs, noun genders and plurals, and case affiliations, stand to gain the most from using this review grammar but may naturally have more work to do as they progress through the material. The various exercises in the book have been designed expressly to assist students in forming a firm foundation.

Deutsche Wiederholungsgrammatik was written to be used primarily in a course dedicated to a rigorous review of German grammar. When so used, it is recommended that the chapter sequence be followed. Students in other advanced German courses that focus on conversation, culture, or literature may use the book as a resource and simply skip around to parts of the chapters that interest them or which their instructor has assigned for out-of-class review. The index at the back of the book will prove useful in locating various points of grammar.

The grammar presentations and explanations are simple, straightforward, and in plain language. Numerous example sentences highlight the differences and similarities between German and English and will help make abstract grammar principles more concrete and "real" for some students. The exercise types employed in this book have been successful in developing accuracy for decades and have withstood the test of time, despite the comings and goings of various methods and approaches to foreign language teaching. While most of the exercises are designed to refine the students' grammatical accuracy, additional ones are included that will allow the students to use the target grammar in more open, communicative exercises.

Some exercises consist of discrete items, that is, items that are not related contextually to the previous or following lines. While this would be inappropriate in the communicative approach that is often followed in beginning foreign language textbooks, it is quite appropriate for grammar exercises. Decisions that students make about the grammar are based on the sentence in which the target grammatical point appears. The sentence itself is the contextual unit; previous and following sentences are irrelevant to this particular decision-making process.

Other exercises employ English as cues or as directions for what students are to write or say. While some teachers believe that the student's native language is the foe of the target foreign language and should be avoided at all costs, others believe that when used judiciously, it can be a great facilitator. Indeed, the proficiency approach relies heavily on English in setting up situations for students to use German communicatively. That has been a guiding principle in this book. There has never been, contrary to popular belief, any real convincing evidence that the use of the student's native language inherently affects learning adversely. Competent students have always been able to go between the native and foreign languages effectively, without translating word-for-word. In fact, it is a skill all serious students of the language should develop.

Deutsche Wiederholungsgrammatik has been field-tested ten times over three years and revised each time in view of student comments and the author's observations in class in order to make the textbook as efficient and successful as possible.

Suggestions for Using *Deutsche Wiederholungsgrammatik*

This book has been designed primarily for use in a junior/senior-level course that reviews German grammar intensively. Its focus is on helping students control German syntax (word order) and morphology (forms) more accurately. It may also be used in other courses as an adjunct text for independent review. The grammar presentations include discussions, example sentences to illustrate rules and concepts, and advice for studying. Grammatical terms are defined when first used and, since many students are not familiar with grammatical terminology, explained in simple language. The vocabulary used throughout the book consists of words that, for the most part, students will have learned in the first four semesters of study. The new vocabulary load is kept light deliberately so as to not interfere or compete with the focus on grammar.

The approach taken is that understanding the rules and grammatical relationships is the first step in the review process. Usually, several examples are given for each new concept. These are translated when translations would be helpful. The exercises that follow start off simply and progress from 1) mechanical to 2) controlled communicative application of the rules to 3) more open-ended, creative, or free use of the rules. An Answer Key—indicated by the symbol [✓]—is provided for the simpler exercises for which there is a "right" answer for each item. For the other exercises, students' answers may vary in word choice, word order, or tense selection, and these are meant to be done in class with the instructor, who can offer correction and feedback as needed. Exercises that invite students to be more creative may be done as group and partner work to promote greater student participation.

The book consists of twenty-four chapters divided into four distinct phases that can easily be covered in a semester if time is managed efficiently. Exercises for which answers are contained in the Answer Key are intended to be done and checked outside of class. The other exercises to be covered in class should be prepared beforehand to maximize efficient use of class time. Experience has shown that certain aspects of German grammar require more practice than others. Chapters that have a Part One and Part Two are best treated over two class sessions. Several chapters contain supplementary exercises that can be done outside of class after the chapter is completed. Answers for these are found in the Answer Key.

When preparing for class consider using the following strategy:

1. Read over the assigned grammar presentation slowly. Study the example sentences carefully to see how they follow the rules. If there is something in the presentation that should be memorized, take the time to do it before going on to any exercises. It will generally take 20–30 minutes to read over and absorb the grammar presentation. If your attention span seems to be wavering, take a break. If not, continue on.
2. Complete the Theory Review exercise. It runs through the grammar presentation chronologically and challenges you to complete sentences that reiterate the rules and concepts. This exercise will be covered in class with your instructor. He or she will help you better understand things if you discover any mistakes. If you are feeling a bit fatigued at this point or notice that your attention is wavering, this would be a logical time to take a break and come back to the remaining exercises when your mind is rested and refreshed.
3. Complete the Focus on Form exercise(s). This section focuses purely on grammatical forms or syntactic patterns. Since there is only one correct answer for these items, this section will usually not be done in class, so check your accuracy in the Answer Key. It is best to do this checking after each exercise rather than at the end of an entire section. It's most important to discover any errors as soon as possible, otherwise you will repeat them in all subsequent exercises. If you discover that you have not understood something, return to the grammar presentation and review the problem area. If you

still have lingering questions, mark the items you missed so you can ask your instructor about them in class.

4. The remaining sections continue to challenge you to come up with the correct forms, but as you move from one exercise to the next, the opportunity to come up with answers or responses that differ from those of the other students increases. As these are covered in class, your instructor will invite you to try your answer out. The Focus on Meaning section usually asks you to fill in blanks with words that make good sense. The Focus on Meaning and Form section does exactly what the name suggests: it challenges you to respond meaningfully and logically and with correct forms. The You Determine the Message and Form exercises ask you to respond to general questions of a more personal nature, and responses from student to student will vary greatly. Your instructor will no doubt invite several students to respond or encourage students to volunteer answers. The **Partnerarbeit** exercises will allow you to have some extended speaking practice with a partner. Some chapters have supplementary exercises for students who would like to have more practice than limited class time allows. Answers for these are in the Answer Key. Consider saving these exercises for reviewing for exams.
5. While some students prefer to study alone, many can profit from getting together with a fellow student to go over things periodically. Give this a try. It could prove to be very helpful.

Understanding the rules and concepts is the most important part of improving your grammatical accuracy. This enables you to make self-corrections and to make intelligent observations about what native speakers of German say and how they say it. On the other hand, mastering forms generally requires a good bit of memorization. If you were a second language learner in a German-speaking environment, you would learn the forms effortlessly because you would be bombarded by them for 12–15 hours a day. As a foreign language learner, however, your contact with the language is extremely minimal. Memorization is one way to try to compensate for this huge difference in language exposure. You will need to master the principal parts of verbs to be accurate with verb forms. Likewise, you will need to memorize noun genders and case affiliations to be accurate with case endings and various case forms. If you do not already know them, you will need to memorize prepositions, their meanings, and their case affiliations. Memorization is a first step. Sufficient practice is the next, and the more intensive the practice, the more effective it usually is. With enough practice your control can become automatic; that is, you can produce the target grammatical structures without thinking about it. To get the most practice, have all of your exercises completed before class so all of them can be covered thoroughly.

Acknowledgments

I wish to thank Mary Jane Peluso, Brie Kluytenaar, Timothy Shea, Ann-Marie Imbornoni, Karen Stickler, and James Johnson of Yale University Press for their contributions in bringing this book to press. I am most indebted to my editor, Karen Hohner, whose editorial expertise is without limit. I could not have wished for a better or more enjoyable editor with whom to work. Needless to say, she helped bring this book to a higher level.

I also wish to thank those who reviewed the manuscript prior to acceptance for their constructive comments: Marilya Veteto Reese, Northern Arizona University; Christian Hallstein, Carnegie Mellon University; Carmen Nikazm, Ohio State University; Glenn Levine, University of California, Irvine; and Randall Lund, Brigham Young University.

I am indebted to the many students at the University of Texas who have used this book as it was developed and field-tested and who have taken the time to make suggestions for improvement, especially Alan McKendree and Erik Malkemus. I am also most grateful for the assistance and native language expertise rendered to me by my colleagues at The University of Texas at Austin: Daniela Richter, Judith Hammer, Anja Moehring, and Professors Susanne Hafner and Hans Boas.

Phase I

Fundamentals of Verbs

Chapter 1 Present Tense

A verb is a word that denotes an action, like *I* ***am driving*** *my car to work,* or a state, like *The sky* **is** *cloudy today.* Verbs have *tenses* that signal when an activity took place or when a state or condition existed, and *moods,* which signal whether one is speaking factually, hypothetically, or commanding others to do something. In this chapter we will see how verbs operate in the present tense.

The Infinitive and Verb Endings

The *infinitive* is the base form of the verb and the first of the principal parts. Remove the infinitive ending (-**en** or -**n**) and you are left with the *stem,* where meaning resides. To the stem, add the verb endings that match up with the subject. This is known as subject-verb agreement.

Standard Present-Tense Endings

singular	*plural*	*formal/polite*
ich: stem + **-e**	**wir**: stem + **-en**	
du: stem + **-st**	**ihr**: stem + **-t**	**Sie**: stem + **-en**
er/sie/es: stem + **-t**	**sie**: stem + **-en**	

Regular (Weak) Verbs

Regular verbs (also known as "weak" verbs) have *regular stems*—they *never* change. Some verbs that are irregular in past tenses are regular in the present, for example, **finden**, **kommen**, **singen**.

Present Tense of Regular Verbs

machen

singular	*plural*	*formal/polite*
ich **mache**	wir **machen**	
du **machst**	ihr **macht**	Sie **machen**
er/sie/es **macht**	sie **machen**	

Verbs with *d*- and *t*-Stems

Verbs with stems ending in **d** or **t** add an **e** before any -**t** or -**st** ending. This is done to facilitate pronunciation and to make the verb ending stand out clearly from the stem.

findest **findet** **arbeitest** **arbeitet**

Present Tense of Regular Verbs with *d*- and *t*-Stems

warten

singular	*plural*	*formal/polite*
ich warte	wir warten	
du wart**est**	ihr wart**et**	Sie warten
er/sie/es wart**et**	sie warten	

finden

singular	*plural*	*formal/polite*
ich finde	wir finden	
du find**est**	ihr find**et**	Sie finden
er/sie/es find**et**	sie finden	

Verbs with *n*-Stems

Verbs with stems ending in -**n** sometimes add **e** before -**t** and -**st** endings, but not always.

öffn*e*st **öffn*e*t** BUT: **lernst** **lernt**

Some frequently used regular verbs:

angeln	freuen	leben	planen	segeln	töten
arbeiten	fühlen	legen	rauchen	setzen	trennen
baden	grillen	lernen	reisen	speichern	wandern
basteln	handeln	löschen	sagen	spielen	weinen
bauen	holen	machen	schämen	spüren	wischen
brauchen	hören	malen	schicken	stecken	zahlen
danken	husten	mogeln	schmecken	stellen	zählen
decken	kaufen	ordnen	schminken	stören	zeichnen
feiern	klären	packen	schmücken	suchen	zeigen
filmen	kosten	pflanzen	schütteln	surfen	zweifeln
fischen					

Verbs Ending in *-ieren*

Verbs ending in -**ieren** are regular verbs of French origin. They are usually also cognates and easy to understand.

abonnieren	fotografieren	programmieren	realisieren
amüsieren	passieren	radieren	spekulieren
argumentieren	polieren	rasieren	studieren
diskutieren	probieren	reagieren	synchronisieren

Impersonal Verbs Relating to Weather

The following regular verbs normally have **es** or a noun denoting a thing as the subject:

blitzen (Es blitzt.)	donnern (Es donnert.)	hageln (Es hagelt.)
nieseln (Es nieselt.)	regnen (Es regnet.)	schneien (Es schneit.)

In following chapters you will see how the addition of prefixes to these verbs affects meaning and sentence word order. Mastering the basic verbs above now will facilitate mastering verbs with separable and inseparable prefixes later.

Irregular (Strong) Verbs

Verbs that have vowel changes or other irregularities in their stems are *irregular* (strong) verbs. Verbs that are irregular in the present tense have irregular stems in the **du**- and **er/sie/es**-forms only. Examples:

Present Tense of Irregular (Strong) Verbs

sehen (e → ie)

singular	*plural*	*formal/polite*
ich sehe	wir sehen	
du **siehst**	ihr seht	Sie sehen
er/sie/es **sieht**	sie sehen	

essen (e → i)

singular	*plural*	*formal/polite*
ich esse	wir essen	
du **isst**	ihr esst	Sie essen
er/sie/es isst	sie essen	

fahren (a → ä)

singular	*plural*	*formal/polite*
ich fahre	wir fahren	
du **fährst**	ihr fahrt	Sie fahren
er/sie/es **fährt**	sie fahren	

laufen (au → äu)

singular	*plural*	*formal/polite*
ich laufe	wir laufen	
du **läufst**	ihr lauft	Sie laufen
er/sie/es **läuft**	sie laufen	

stoßen (o → ö)

singular	*plural*	*formal/polite*
ich stoße	wir stoßen	
du **stößt**	ihr stoßt	Sie stoßen
er/sie/es **stößt**	sie stoßen	

NOTE: An umlaut signals a shift in sound.

S-Stem Verbs

Verbs that have stems ending in **s, ss, ß, z, tz** (all are sibilants) simply add a **-t** to the **du**-form of the verb, not the usual -**st**, since the **s**-sound is supplied already by the stem.

blasen:	du **bläst**	genießen:	du **genießt**	heizen:	du **heizt**
reisen:	du **reist**	grüßen:	du **grüßt**	hetzen:	du **hetzt**
lesen:	du **liest**	schließen:	du **schließt**	sitzen:	du **sitzt**
essen:	du **isst**	schmeißen:	du **schmeißt**	setzen:	du **setzt**

Especially Irregular Verbs

Verbs that have stems with changes involving consonants as well as vowels, or that have radical changes to the stem and sometimes endings are known as *especially irregular verbs.* These must be memorized as they are encountered. Two of these are **nehmen** (consonant + vowel changes) and **wissen** (radical stem and ending changes).

Present Tense of Especially Irregular Verbs

nehmen

singular	*plural*	*formal/polite*
ich nehme	wir nehmen	
du **nimmst**	ihr nehmt	Sie nehmen
er/sie/es **nimmt**	sie nehmen	

wissen

singular	*plural*	*formal/polite*
ich **weiß**	wir wissen	
du **weißt**	ihr wisst	Sie wissen
er/sie/es **weiß**	sie wissen	

Haben, sein, werden

The following three verbs are the most commonly used verbs in German, in large part because they are used extensively to construct other tenses, the passive, and the subjunctive. They are verbs in their own right, however, not just helping verbs. Each is especially irregular, meaning that it must be memorized.

haben

singular	*plural*	*formal/polite*
ich habe	wir haben	
du **hast**	ihr habt	Sie haben
er/sie/es **hat**	sie haben	

sein

singular	*plural*	*formal/polite*
ich **bin**	wir **sind**	
du **bist**	ihr **seid**	Sie **sind**
er/sie/es **ist**	sie **sind**	

Remember that the final -**d** in **sind** and **seid** is devoiced, meaning the -**d** sounds like a -**t**.

werden

singular	*plural*	*formal/polite*
ich werde	wir werden	
du **wirst**	ihr werdet	Sie werden
er/sie/es **wird**	sie werden	

Present Tense = a *Simple* Tense = *One* Verb Form

Where English has progressive and emphatic forms involving two or more verb forms, German employs only one verb form: Sie **liest**. = *She **reads/is reading/does read**.* This means that the present tense in German is a simple tense.

Using a present time expression in German can approximate the progressive in English: Sie **liest** gerade/jetzt. = *She is reading now.* Using **doch** with the present can approximate the emphatic: Sie **liest** doch. = *She **does read**.*

Using the Present Tense to Form a Future

Present Tense + Future Time Expression → Colloquial Future

As in English, the present-tense forms can have a future meaning if used with a future time expression:

Morgen sind wir in Frankfurt.
***Tomorrow we're/we'll be** in Frankfurt.*

Zwei Tage später fahren wir nach Stuttgart.
***Two days later we're traveling/we'll be traveling** to Stuttgart.*

Present Tense + *schon, seit,* or *erst* → Continuous Present

To signal that an activity began in the past and continues to the present, uninterrupted, use **schon** (*already*), **seit** (*since*), or **erst** (*just*) + the present tense. Sometimes **schon** and **seit**, and **erst** and **seit** are combined.

Ich **spiele schon drei Jahre** Klavier. OR: Ich **spiele schon seit drei Jahren** Klavier.
------------------------ *I **have been playing** the piano **for three years.*** ------------------------

Ich **spiele seit 1995** Violine. OR: Ich **spiele schon seit 1995** Violine.
----------------- *I **have been playing** the violin **since 1995.*** ----------------

Ich **spiele erst drei Monate** Gitarre. OR: Ich **spiele erst seit drei Monaten** Gitarre.
------------------- *I **have been playing** the guitar **for just three months.*** -------------------

Ich **spiele erst seit Juni** Trompete.
*I **have been playing** the trumpet **just since June.***

Some Easily Confused Verbs

Some German verbs are challenging for native speakers of English because of confusion with English cognates, spelling, pronunciation, or because English does not make the same kinds of distinctions that are made in German. Some of these are:

Lernen vs. *studieren*

The verb **lernen** means *to study,* as when doing homework, or *to learn something:*

Abends **lerne** ich, dann gehe ich aus.
*I **study** in the evening, then I go out.*

The verb **studieren** means *to study* in the sense of being enrolled in a degree program at a university: **Ich studiere in Irland.** It can also be used to indicate your major: **Ich studiere Deutsch.** It may also be used to indicate that you are reading over something very carefully:

Wir **studieren** den Vertrag, bevor wir ihn unterschreiben.
*We **are studying/reading over** the contract before we sign it.*

Wissen vs. *kennen*

The verb **wissen,** *to know,* refers to cognitive or *factual* knowledge:

Ich **weiß** das/alles/etwas/nichts.
*I **know** that/everything/something/nothing.*

Ich **weiß** diese Antworten/Fakten/Daten.
*I **know** these answers/facts/dates.*

Wissen frequently precedes a clause signaling factual knowledge:

Ich **weiß**, dass du mich völlig verstehst.
*I **know** that you understand me completely.*

Wir **wissen** nicht, ob Hans jetzt zu Hause ist.
*We **don't know** if Hans is at home now.*

The verb **kennen**, *to know,* signals a *familiarity* with a person, place, or thing:

Ich **kenne** diesen Mann/die Stadt Berlin/diese Sinfonie.
*I **know/am familiar** with this man/the city of Berlin/this symphony.*

Werden vs. *bekommen*

The verb **werden** means *to become, to get,* as in:

Ich möchte Arzt **werden**.	OR:	Ich **werde** jetzt müde.
*I would like to **become** a doctor.*	OR:	*I am **getting/becoming** tired.*

The verb **bekommen** does NOT mean *become.* It means *to receive, to get* and is always used with a direct object:

Ich **bekomme** kein Geld mehr von den Eltern.
*I **am** not **receiving/getting** any more money from my parents.*

Word Order

Forming Statements

In statements the inflected verb (the verb with an ending that agrees with the subject) is anchored in second position, or "slot 2." In a statement only one chunk of information may precede the verb, which must remain in "slot 2."

That unit is often the subject:	**Der Student lernt** fleißig.
That unit may be another word:	**Jetzt höre** ich Musik.
That unit may be a noun phrase:	**Eines Tages kommt** mein Prinz.
That unit may be a prepositional phrase:	**In zwanzig Minuten bin** ich fertig.

Forming Questions

Questions for which a *yes/no* answer is expected always begin with the verb followed by the subject:

Sind Sie Student(in)? **Machst du** das jetzt? **Spielen wir** heute Karten?

Questions that elicit specific information begin with a question word, followed by the verb, then the subject:

Wann kommst du nach Hause? **Wie kocht man** das? **Warum lügst du** immer?

Exercises

Theory Review

1. Fill in the blanks with the correct information.

1. The ____________________ is the base form of the verb, what you find when you consult a dictionary.

2. The meaning of the verb is located in the ____________________.

3. The ending of an infinitive is typically ____________ or ____________.

4. Verbs whose stems never change are called ____________________ verbs.

5. Verbs that do have a stem change are ____________________ verbs.

6. Verbs take certain standard endings attached to the ____________________ that "agree" with the noun or pronoun subject.

7. In the present tense, if there is a stem change, which forms will show them?

   ____________________ and ____________________ forms.

8. If a verb stem ends in a **-d** or **-t**, an extra ____________ will be added to certain endings.

9. The endings that have this extra **e** are ____________ and ____________, found on **du**-, **er/sie/es**-, and **ihr**-forms.

10. Verbs whose infinitives end in ____________________ are typically French imports.

11. Are these regular or irregular verbs? ____________________

12. Impersonal verbs have a noun or the pronoun ____________________ as the subject. These are verbs that can only be used with subjects that are things, not persons.

13. One such category of verbs that are impersonal verbs are ____________________ verbs.

14. When a verb is irregular, it displays ____________________ changes in the **du**- and **er/sie/es**-forms.

15. When we talk about stem changes, we normally mean that a ____________________ shifts/changes.

16. List six verbs that have stem changes in the present:

    ____________________ ____________________ ____________________

    ____________________ ____________________ ____________________

17. Verbs whose stems end in a sibilant ("hissy") sound have what kind of ending for the **du**- form?

    ______________________ Why?

18. If a stem change involves a consonant as well as a vowel, or the stem is radically different from the infinitive stem, we call this verb ______________________ ______________________

19. Name three such verbs:

    ______________________ ______________________ ______________________

20. The present tense is a ______________________ tense because it consists of only *one* verb form.

21. The present tense may have the effect of the ______________________ if it is used with a time expression that points to a time yet to come.

22. The present-tense verb may be used with **schon, seit,** and **erst** to form the ______________________

    ______________________ Explain what this is.

23. Fill in the blanks in the sentences with the correct verb:

    Ich hoffe, dass ich etwas Geld von meinen Eltern ______________________.

    Ich möchte später Arzt/Ärztin ______________________.

    Ich ______________________ nicht, ob das wahr ist.

    Ich ______________________ diese Stadt ziemlich gut.

    Ich muss für meine Deutschprüfung ______________________.

    Meine Schwester will ein ganzes Jahr in Deutschland ______________________.

24. The three verbs that are "cornerstone" verbs in German, used by themselves and also as helping verbs for future and past tenses, the passive, and the subjunctive are:

    ______________________ ______________________ ______________________

25. In a statement the verb is always anchored in ______________________ position.

26. The subject of a statement may be in slot ____________ or slot ____________.

27. If the statement begins with something other than the subject, the subject is in slot

    ____________.

28. A **ja/nein-Frage** always begins with the ______________________.

29. A question that elicits specific information always begins with a ______________________

    ______________________.

30. That is followed by the ______________________, then the subject.

Focus on Form [✓]*

2. Write out full *du*- and *ihr*-forms of the following verbs.

	du	*ihr*
1. fragen	______	______
2. nehmen	______	______
3. fahren	______	______
4. laufen	______	______
5. arbeiten	______	______
6. lernen	______	______
7. wenden	______	______
8. sprechen	______	______
9. warten	______	______
10. kommen	______	______
11. geben	______	______
12. sagen	______	______
13. sein	______	______
14. haben	______	______
15. werden	______	______

Focus on Meaning and Form [✓]

3. Write in German that . . .

1. you are buying a shirt *Ich kaufe ein Hemd.*
2. the movie runs this week ______
3. you believe that ______
4. she's calling her mother ______

* For activities that are accompanied by the [✓] symbol, you can check your answers in the Answer Key in the back of the book.

5. you are opening the windows ______

6. I am tired (I'm a friend). ______

7. you have lots of friends ______

8. you are coming, too. ______

9. you are going to read for awhile ______

10. we are getting fat ______

11. you are getting too thin ______

12. Maria is going soon ______

4. Formulate questions to ask me, a friend, . . .

1. if I am getting sick ______

2. if we are driving to Munich ______

3. if Martina has any plans for this evening ______

4. if they are going home now ______

5. what I'm doing here ______

6. when the Spring Break ends ______

7. where I'll be staying this summer ______

5. Formulate questions to find out from me, a friend, . . .

1. where the book is ______

2. where we're going this evening ______

3. where I live ______

4. what I'm doing later ______

5. when I'll be at home ______

6. why I always do that ______

7. who my new girlfriend is ______

8. how you (use indefinite pronoun) do that ______

You Determine the Message and Form

6. Stellen Sie einem neuen Bekannten/einer neuen Bekannten fünf Fragen, um ihn/sie besser kennen zu lernen.

7. Stellen Sie dem Lehrer/der Lehrerin fünf Fragen.

Partnerarbeit

Preparing for an Oral Narration

8. Simple strategy for expanding a simple narration. For each sentence given, follow up with two more sentences that are linked by meaning to it. They can be a further elaboration on that sentence or a comment about the event mentioned in it. Note the example given for the first sentence.

Thema: Was ich jeden Tag mache

Ich schlafe bis sieben Uhr.

Ich bleibe eine Weile im Bett und werde wach.

Zehn Minuten später stehe ich auf.

Ich gehe ins Badezimmer und wasche mich.

Ich ziehe mich schnell an.

Dann mache ich mein Frühstück.

Um neun Uhr fahre ich zur Uni.

Im Laufe des Tages habe ich zwei oder drei Kurse an der Uni.

Um vier Uhr bin ich wieder zu Hause.

Um fünf Uhr mache ich ein Schläfchen für eine halbe Stunde.

Um sechs koche ich mein Abendessen.

Danach mache ich einen kleinen Spaziergang.

Dann lerne ich ein paar Stunden lang.

Um elf Uhr bin ich wirklich müde.

Gegen Mitternacht gehe ich ins Bett.

Oral Narration in Class

9. Using as many different verbs as possible, describe to your partner another person's (your roommate, a family member, a friend, a typical student) daily routine chronologically. Unlike in the previous exercise, you'll be using third-person verb forms this time. For stylistic variation, be sure to start some sentences with inverted word order, that is, with something other than the subject. Keep everything in the present tense and say anything that comes to mind.

Chapter 2 Present Perfect

Review of the Present Tense

The German *present tense* is used to express the following:

1. a current action or state:

   Ich **studiere** jetzt in Argentinien
   I'm studying now in Argentina.

2. a future action or state when accompanied by a future time expression:

   Wir **fliegen** kommenden Sommer nach Deutschland.
   We'll be flying this coming summer to Germany.

3. a current action or state that began in the past and continues unbroken to the present when **schon** (*already*), **seit** (*since, for*), **schon seit** (*already since, already for*), **erst** (*for just*), or **erst seit** (*just since*) are used:

Ich **studiere schon** ein Semester lang. Ich **studiere seit** einem Semester. Ich **studiere schon seit** einem Semester.	*I've been studying for one semester.*
Ich **studiere erst** ein Semester lang. Ich **studiere erst seit** einem Semester.	*I've been studying for just one semester.*

Two Main Past Tenses in German

The main vehicles for expressing completed past actions or states are the *simple past* and *present perfect* tenses. As far as meaning is concerned, the two are almost equal and can often be used interchangeably:

Ich **war** als Kind oft krank. = Ich **bin** oft als Kind krank **gewesen.**
I was often sick as a child.

Ingrid **machte** das nicht. = Ingrid **hat** das nicht **gemacht.**
Ingrid did not do that. OR: *Ingrid has not done that.*

We will focus in this chapter on the present perfect, since it is the dominant spoken past tense and therefore the most useful for communicative purposes; in the following chapter the focus will turn to the simple past.

Present Perfect: The Conversational/Spoken Past

The present perfect is employed primarily for informal oral reporting of past actions and states, particularly in conversation, which consists of back-and-forth speaking. Even when conversation turns to narration, the present perfect can still be, and often is, employed. (You can switch to simple past for extended narratives, but switch back to present perfect once the narrative is over.) The present perfect is also the "primary past-tense-vehicle" when writing letters or e-mail messages, which generally have a conversational tone to them.

The present perfect is a *compound,* not a simple, construction, which means that more than one verb is involved. The present perfect consists of a helping verb—**haben** or **sein**—and a past participle. It is called *present* perfect because the helping verb is conjugated in the *present tense,* and present *perfect* because a *past participle* is required.

Variable #1: The Helping Verbs *haben* and *sein*

All verbs that are transitive (can be used with a direct object) require **haben.**

Ich **habe** meine Hausaufgaben für morgen gemacht.
I did my homework for tomorrow. OR: *I have done my homework for tomorrow.*

Hast du ein Glas Bier getrunken?
Did you drink a glass of beer? OR: *Have you drunk a glass of beer?*

For verbs to require **sein,** two conditions must be met:

1. the verb must be *intransitive* (cannot accommodate a direct object);
2. the verb must signal a *change in condition* or *change of position* (A → B movement)

change in condition:	Mensch, es **ist** eiskalt **geworden**! *Man, it got ice-cold.* *Man, it has gotten ice-cold.*
change of position:	Wir **sind** in zwei Stunden von München nach Bremen **geflogen.** *We flew from Munich to Bremen in two hours.* *We have flown from Munich to Bremen in two hours.*

Otherwise, **haben** is required. Exceptions:

1. **bleiben** takes **sein** — **ist geblieben:** Ich **bin** den ganzen Vormittag hier **geblieben.**
2. **sein** takes itself — **ist gewesen:** Wir **sind** gestern bei Schneiders **gewesen.**

Variable #2: Past Participles*

Regular Verbs: *ge* + Stem + -[*e*]*t*

Regular verbs generally form their past participles by adding **ge-** before the **stem** and adding -[**e**]**t** after it:

gearbeit**et**	**ge**koch**t**	**ge**sag**t**	**ge**such**t**
gefrag**t**	**ge**mach**t**	**ge**spiel**t**	**ge**wart**et**

Irregular Verbs: *ge* + Stem + *-en*

Irregular verbs generally form their past participles by adding **ge-** before the **irregular stem** and -(**e**)**n** after it:

* Past participles of verbs with inseparable and separable prefixes are treated in Chapters 6 and 7, respectively.

geblieb**en**	gefund**en**	geseh**en**	gestoß**en**
gefahr**en**	gegang**en**	gesproch**en**	geta**n**
geflog**en**	gelauf**en**		

Verbs Ending in *-ieren:* Stem + *t* (= no *ge-* prefix)

Verbs that end in **-ieren** are regular verbs of French origin. They do not employ **ge-**, and they always end in **-t**:

amüsier**t**	finanzier**t**	produzier**t**	studier**t**
diskutier**t**	organisier**t**	protestier**t**	

Mixed Verbs

Mixed verbs are "hybrids" because they have properties of both regular and irregular verbs. They display a stem change in the past participle, just like irregular verbs, but use the -(**e**)**t** ending of regular verbs:

bringen, **gebracht**	kennen, **gekannt**
denken, **gedacht**	nennen, **genannt**
brennen, **gebrannt**	wissen, **gewusst**

English has mixed verbs, too, so do not think of them as being unique to German. Take the verb *think.* If it were regular, the principal parts would be *think, thinked, (have) thinked.* If it were irregular, the principal parts would be: *think, thank, (have) thunk.* Of course, it's a mixed verb: *think, thought, (have) thought.*

Haben, sein, werden

These three verbs are the main helping/auxiliary verbs in German. They are, however, verbs in their own right. Note the past participles of these verbs and note their own helping verbs:

haben: (**hat**) **gehabt**	sein: (**ist**) **gewesen**	werden: (**ist**) **geworden**
Ich **habe** viel Glück **gehabt**.	Susanne **ist** krank **gewesen**.	Wir **sind** hungrig **geworden**.

Word Order

The helping verb **haben** or **sein** agrees with the subject of the sentence and occupies "normal" verb position for the sentence type being generated. The main verb changes into a past participle and migrates to the end of the sentence:

statements:	Ich **habe** meine Übungen **geschrieben**.
	Wir **sind** etwas früher nach Hause **gegangen**.
	Gestern **haben** sie bis spät in die Nacht **gearbeitet**.
questions:	**Bist** du nach Belgien geflogen?
	Habt ihr eure Hausaufgaben **gemacht**?
	Sind Sie lange hier **geblieben**?

See Section 3 of the Appendix if you are unsure of the past participles of irregular and mixed verbs that come into play in the following exercises.

Exercises

Theory Review

1. Fill in the blanks with the correct information.

1. The ______________________ is the tense used to *talk* about events and states in the past.
2. This tense is also used when writing ______________________, since the tone of these is conversational.
3. This tense is a ______________________ tense because it consists of two verb components.
4. By contrast, a verb tense that consists of only one verb form is a ______________________ tense.
5. There are two verb components. The first one usually encountered is a(n) ______________________ verb.
6. There are two of these possible: ______________________ or ______________________.
7. This verb must agree with the ______________________.
8. The verb ______________________ is used as the helping verb with all transitive verbs.
9. Transitive verbs are verbs that may be used with a ______________________ ______________________.
10. By contrast, an ______________________ verb may not be used with a direct object.
11. If a verb is intransitive, does it automatically take **sein** as its helping verb? ____________
12. There must also be a change in ______________________ or ______________________.
13. Does that mean that a verb that is intransitive but does *not* signal a change in condition or position takes **haben** as its helping verb? ____________
14. The other verb component is the ______________________ ______________________.
15. If the verb is regular, you add a _____________ prefix to the stem and then a _____________ -ending.
16. If the verb is irregular, you add a _____________ prefix to the stem and then a _____________ -ending.
17. Does that mean that the past participle of any verb that has a stem change always ends in **-en**? ____________
18. Verbs with infinitives ending in **-ieren** are ______________________ verbs. Their stems never change.

19. One therefore expects the past participle to end in ____________.

20. Do past participles of **-ieren** verbs also take a **ge-** prefix? ____________

21. Verbs that have qualities of irregular verbs (stem changes) and regular verbs (participial **t**-endings) are hybrid verbs known as ______________________ verbs.

22. If these hybrid verbs are transitive, they take ______________________ as their helping verb.

23. If these hybrid verbs are intransitive and signal a change of condition or position, they take ______________________ as their helping verb.

24. What, then, determines whether the verb is transitive or intransitive? The __________________ of the verb.

25. Can you tell just by looking at the infinitive if a verb is regular or irregular? ____________

26. The helping verb for **haben** is ______________________.

27. The helping verb for **sein** is ______________________.

28. The helping verb for **werden** is ______________________.

29. Where is the past participle located in a sentence in the present perfect?

____

30. Where is the helping verb located? ______________________

Focus on Form [✓]

2. Fill in the blanks with the correct form of *haben* or *sein*.

A

1. Wir ______________________ gestern Abend für eine Prüfung gelernt.
2. Karl ______________________ niemals nach Australien gereist.
3. Letztes Jahr ______________________ ich in Deutschland gearbeitet.
4. Es ______________________ mir zu warm im Zimmer geworden.
5. An der Uni ______________________ ich Geographie studiert.
6. Das ______________________ mir wirklich Spaß gemacht.
7. Wir ______________________ mit der U-Bahn zur Arbeit gefahren.
8. Vati ______________________ Anja etwas Geld gegeben.
9. Ich ______________________ den ganzen Abend zu Hause geblieben.
10. Susi __________________ zu viel Bier getrunken und __________________ krank geworden.

B

1. Ich ______________________ Christine in Bremen gesehen.
2. Es ______________________ lange geregnet.
3. ______________________ du das nicht gehört?
4. Mutti ______________________ uns einen Apfel gegeben.
5. Sabine ______________________ heute nicht zur Schule gegangen.
6. ______________________ du gesagt, dass du ihn heiraten würdest?
7. Heute Morgen ______________________ ich die Zeitung nicht gekauft.
8. Das Messer ______________________ vom Tisch auf den Boden gefallen.
9. Das Flugzeug ______________________ mitten in der Luft explodiert.
10. Wo ______________________ er denn gewesen? Er ______________________ plötzlich verschwunden.

Focus on Meaning and Form

3. Fill in the blanks with any past participle that makes good sense.

A

1. Ich habe gestern Abend für eine Prüfung ______________________.
2. Auf der Party haben wir Musik ______________________ und dazu haben wir ______________________.
3. Ich bin mehrmals nach China ______________________.
4. Letzten Sommer habe ich bei einer deutschen Firma ______________________.
5. Es war mir zu warm im Zimmer. Also habe ich das Fenster ______________________.
6. Die Studenten haben dieses Thema im Seminar sehr lebhaft ______________________.
7. An der Uni habe ich Chemie ______________________.
8. Der Hund hat mich ______________________.
9. Wir sind von Brasilien nach Rom ______________________.
10. Max hat mir etwas Geld ______________________.

B

1. In der Kirche haben wir einige Hymnen ______________________.
2. Ich bin den ganzen Abend in meinem Zimmer ______________________.
3. Meine beste Freundin ist Krankenschwester ______________________.
4. Peter hat nicht genug Wasser ______________________ und ist schnell durstig

   ______________________.
5. Ich habe meine Schlüssel in der Küche ______________________.
6. Ich wollte es nicht machen, aber sie hat mich dazu ______________________.
7. Wir haben immer als Kinder viel Gemüse ______________________.
8. Ich habe Christine in Mainz ______________________.
9. Das Feuer hat lange ______________________.
10. Wir haben Irene früher ______________________ aber wir haben sie schon lange nicht

    ______________________.

C

1. Wo hast du das gehört? Ich habe das nicht ______________________.
2. Vati hat uns Schokolade ______________________.
3. Ich habe immer ______________________, du wolltest Arzt werden.
4. Sabine ist gestern um acht Uhr zur Schule ______________________.
5. Wir haben viel zu lange in der Schlange ______________________.
6. Was?! Was hast du ______________________?
7. Was hast du auf der Reise ______________________? Hattest du zufällig etwas zu Hause

   ______________________?
8. Es tut mir leid, aber ich habe Sie nicht ______________________. Wiederholen Sie das noch einmal, bitte.
9. Hast du ihm schon ______________________, dass du ihn nicht heiraten würdest?
10. Heute Morgen habe ich die Zeitung ______________________.

D

1. Karla hat mich in der Mensa ______________________ und wir haben miteinander ______________________.
2. Sie hat mich gefragt, aber ich habe ihr nicht ______________________.
3. Meine Eltern haben 1980 ______________________. Ich bin ihr erstes Kind.
4. Das Brötchen ist vom Tisch auf den Boden ______________________.
5. Ich habe meine Kleidung auf das Bett ______________________.
6. Das Schiff ist mitten im Hafen ____________. Glücklicherweise ist niemand ____________.
7. Ich habe mich auf die Bank ______________________. Ich war müde.
8. Wo warst du denn gestern Abend? Bist du zu Hause ______________________? Wir haben dich nicht gesehen.
9. Wir sind sehr hungrig, denn wir haben nichts ______________________.
10. Wie hast du dieses Gedicht ______________________? War es zu sentimental?

E

1. Wir haben unsere Seminararbeiten ______________________. Der Professor liest sie jetzt.
2. Beethoven hat diese Sinfonie ______________________.
3. Hast du den verlorenen Schlüssel wieder ______________________?
4. Martin hat Anja einen langen Brief ______________________.
5. Habt ihr Deutsch mit unserer Austauschstudentin aus Hamburg ______________________?
6. Als Kind habe ich viele Modellflugzeuge ______________________.
7. Letztes Jahr hatte ich 1 000 Euro auf meinem Sparkonto. Jetzt habe ich 2 000. Ich habe also 1 000 Euro ______________________.

You Determine the Message and Form

4. Schreiben Sie Antworten auf diese allgemeinen Fragen.

1. Was haben Sie neulich geschrieben?

   ____

2. Wohin sind Sie in letzter Zeit gegangen oder gefahren?

   ____

3. Sind Sie dieses Jahr irgendwohin geflogen?

   ____

4. Was haben Sie heute zum Frühstück getrunken?

___

5. Wen haben Sie heute oder gestern getroffen, und wo?

___

6. Haben Sie sich den Arm oder das Bein gebrochen?

___

7. Wem haben Sie diese Woche geholfen? Und wer hat Ihnen neulich geholfen?

___

8. Mit wem haben Sie heute an der Uni gesprochen?

___

9. Mit wem haben Sie heute oder gestern telefoniert?

___

10. Wer ist neulich gestorben? Wie alt war diese Person?

___

11. Was haben Sie zum Mittagessen gegessen?

___

12. Was haben Sie jemandem vor kurzem geliehen?

___

13. Was haben Sie heute gelesen?

___

14. Was haben Sie heute oder gestern im Fernsehen gesehen?

___

15. Wie sind Sie heute zur Uni gekommen?

___

16. Was hat Ihnen neulich gefallen oder nicht gefallen?

___

17. Haben Sie heute etwas zu Hause gelassen?

___

18. Wie lange haben Sie gestern Nacht geschlafen?

___

19. Wie haben Sie dieses Semester bis jetzt gefunden?

___

20. Wann haben Sie dieses Jahr Ferien gehabt?

___

Partnerarbeit

5. Select one of the themes below and tell your partner what you did in a spontaneous paragraph (= roughly a dozen sentences) in the conversational past, that is, the present perfect. Think chronologically, and this will prove to be a relatively easy task.

1. Was ich heute schon gemacht habe
2. Was ich gestern Abend gemacht habe
3. Was ich letztes Wochenende (Freitag bis Sonntag) gemacht habe
4. Was ich während der letzten Semesterferien gemacht habe

Review of the Present Perfect

Fill in the blanks with logical verb forms in the present perfect. This exercise will probe your accuracy with helping verbs and past participles. Various answers are possible. Let the context of the individual sentences be your guide.

1. Ich ____________ ein Jahr in München an der Universität ____________.
2. Obwohl er zwei Stunden darüber ____________ ____________, konnte er eigentlich nichts schaffen.
3. Ach, es ____________ wirklich sehr kalt ____________. Ich brauche einen wärmeren Mantel.
4. Wir ____________ den ganzen Abend zu Hause ____________ und haben nur ____________.
5. Donald Trump ____________ das Projekt ____________.
6. Die Arbeiter ____________ gegen die längeren Arbeitsstunden ____________.
7. Sabine und ich ____________ diese philosophische Frage ____________.
8. Was ____________ du zur Party ____________?
9. Ich ____________ das nicht ____________. Hast du das von einem Freund gelernt?
10. Wie viel Geld ____________ du gestern Abend bei dir ____________, als du ausgegangen bist?
11. Wir haben dich letzte Woche nicht gesehen. ____________ du krank ____________?
12. Hans ____________ seiner Mutter einen langen Brief ____________.
13. Letzten Sommer ____________ ich bei einer Firma in der Innenstadt ____________.
14. ____________ du mit dem Zug nach Paris ____________, oder ____________ du dahin ____________?

15. Ich ________________ die ganze Woche zu Hause ________________, weil ich eine ansteckende Krankheit hatte.

16. Heute haben wir eine große Prüfung. Ich ________________ also dafür sehr fleißig ________________.

17. Im Urlaub ________________ wir nach Südamerika ________________.

18. Ich ________________ sehr krank ________________, nachdem eine Biene mich gestochen hatte.

19. ________________ du dein Auto zur Arbeit ________________, oder ________________ du mit dem Bus ________________?

20. Da ich zufällig in der Nähe war, ________________ ich meine Großeltern ________________.

21. Gestern hatte ich Geburtstag, aber niemand ________________ mir eine Karte ________________.

22. Warum ________________ du das ________________? Das war wirklich blöd von dir!

23. Zwei Bomben ________________ mitten in der Nacht im Hauptbahnhof ________________.

24. Die Kinder ________________ ihre Bilderbücher ________________ und die farbreichen Bilder angesehen.

25. Ich ________________ lange an diesem Problem ________________, aber ich ________________ keine Lösung ________________.

26. Wie lange ________________ du auf mich ________________? Es tut mir Leid, dass es so lange ________________ ________________.

27. ________________ ihr etwas Interessantes in der Zeitung ________________?

28. ________________ du mit Lufthansa nach Deutschland ________________?

29. Nach der Schule ________________ wir immer Fußball ________________.

30. Statt unsere Hausaufgaben zu machen, ________________ wir ins Kino ________________.

Chapter 3 Simple Past and Past Perfect

The Past/Simple Past

The *simple past* is used primarily for *written past narration* and factual accounts and descriptions. It may also be used for oral news reporting and storytelling, including telling jokes. You'll encounter the simple past as the main "past-tense vehicle" in printed media: newspapers, magazines, and books. As a student you would use the simple past instead of the present perfect in composing written narratives, term papers, and essays, when composing a **Lebenslauf**, and when giving an oral report that contains narrative and/or historical elements.

The *simple* past is so called because only *one verb form* is involved; *simple* = one verb form.

Wir **machten** es besser.	Gestern **spielten** wir Fußball.	Heute **ging** ich nicht zur Schule.
We did it better.	*Yesterday we played soccer.*	*Today I didn't go to school.*

The key to remember: Use the simple past primarily for written narratives and reporting past events in a more formal context. For that reason, simple past verb forms with **du**, **ihr**, and **Sie** are not common. The present perfect is used with these forms instead, since they are used primarily when speaking.

Regular Verbs

Regular verbs (also known as *weak verbs*) form the simple past by adding the so-called -**te** set of endings to the stem:

mach**te**, sag**te**, frag**te**, glaub**te**, arbeite**te**, warte**te**

Simple Past of Regular (Weak) Verbs

machen

singular	*plural*	*formal/polite*
ich mach**te**	wir mach**ten**	
du mach**test**	ihr mach**tet**	Sie mach**ten**
er/sie/es mach**te**	sie mach**ten**	

Irregular Verbs

Irregular verbs (also known as *strong verbs*) and especially irregular verbs must display a *stem vowel change* in the simple past. The endings are the customary ones you learned for the present tense, except that the **ich** and **er/sie/es**-forms are "naked," that is, they have no ending whatsoever: **kam, ging, sprach, tat, las, fuhr, half, blieb, flog, aß.**

Simple Past of Irregular (Strong) Verbs

sprechen

singular	*plural*	*formal/polite*
ich **sprach**	wir sprachen	
du sprachst	ihr spracht	Sie sprachen
er/sie/es **sprach**	sie sprachen	

Mixed Verbs

Mixed verbs are "hybrids" because they display a stem change in the simple past, just like irregular verbs, but they use the regular verbs' -**te** set of endings. They form their past participles like regular verbs with a -[**e**]**t** ending while retaining the stem change encountered in the simple past. Note the stem changes (irregular) and -**t** endings (regular):

bringen, **brachte**, gebracht
denken, **dachte**, gedacht
brennen, **brannte**, gebrannt
kennen, **kannte**, gekannt
nennen, **nannte**, genannt
wissen, **wusste**, gewusst

Simple Past of Mixed Verbs

bringen

singular	*plural*	*formal/polite*
ich brachte	wir brach**ten**	
du brach**test**	ihr brach**tet**	Sie brach**ten**
er/sie/es brachte	sie brach**ten**	

Haben, sein, werden

Master the simple past of these auxiliary verbs, each of which is also a stand-alone verb:

haben: hat, **hatte**, gehabt
sein: ist, **war**, (ist) gewesen
werden: wird, **wurde**, (ist) geworden

Simple Past of *haben, sein,* and *werden*

haben

singular	*plural*	*formal/polite*
ich **hatte**	wir **hatten**	
du **hattest**	ihr **hattet**	Sie **hatten**
er/sie/es **hatte**	sie **hatten**	

sein

singular	*plural*	*formal/polite*
ich **war**	wir **waren**	
du **warst**	ihr **wart**	Sie **waren**
er/sie/es **war**	sie **waren**	

werden

singular	*plural*	*formal/polite*
ich **wurde**	wir **wurden**	
du **wurdest**	ihr **wurdet**	Sie **wurden**
er/sie/es **wurde**	sie **wurden**	

The Past Perfect: *hatte/war* + Past Participle

The past perfect is used to show that one past action was completed prior to another past action. The first action is therefore "more past" than the second one, so a "more-than-past-tense" is required. This is the *past perfect* tense, sometimes referred to as the *pluperfect,* or in German, the **Plusquamperfekt** (which is taken directly from Latin and means *more than past*). This tense is called *past* perfect because the helping verb is conjugated in the *simple past:* **hatte** or **war.** It is called past *perfect* because a *past participle* is required.

Nachdem ich meine Hausaufgaben **gemacht hatte,** habe ich mein Abendessen gegessen.
After I ***had done*** *my homework I ate my dinner.*

Bevor ich nach Hause gegangen bin, **war** ich einkaufen **gegangen**.
Before I went home I ***had gone*** *shopping.*

Grammatically sensitive, well-educated speakers of German use the past perfect when it is called for, especially in sentences employing **nachdem** and **bevor.** In colloquial (= informal) speech the past perfect might not always be employed. The present perfect is sometimes used colloquially instead, with time expressions doing the work of establishing the sequence of events:

Zuerst habe ich mich gewaschen, **dann** bin ich ins Bett gegangen.
First *I washed up,* ***then*** *I went to bed.*

The Principal Parts of Verbs: The *Key to Success* with Tense Accuracy

The foundation for accuracy with verb forms is mastery of the principal parts of verbs. These consist of the infinitive, the simple past form, and the past participle. When learning these—and you do need to memorize them—include the third-person singular present-tense form, which may involve a stem change. Examples:

regular: **machen: macht, machte, gemacht**
irregular: **fliegen: fliegt, flog, ist geflogen**

CRITICALLY IMPORTANT: Not only are these principal parts absolutely essential for accuracy in forming tenses, they will be indispensable for the accurate production of other verb constructions such as the passive and subjunctive that will be treated in later chapters. Invest a lot of time in learning these NOW so that mastery of their forms is assured. If you have to guess at these forms, your accuracy with tenses and other verb constructions will be poor.

NOTE: When a verb is used with **sein** in the present and past perfect, **ist** is shown with the past participle to make that clear. Seeing **ist/hat** with the past participle indicates that the verb may be used as a transitive *or* intransitive verb, depending on meaning and other elements in the sentence. Participles standing alone are **haben**-verbs.

Principal Parts of Irregular (Strong) and Mixed Verbs

infinitive	*present*	*past*	*past participle*	*English meaning*
backen	bäckt	buk	gebacken	*to bake*
beißen	beißt	biss	gebissen	*to bite*
biegen	biegt	bog	gebogen	*to bend*
bieten	bietet	bot	geboten	*to offer*
binden	bindet	band	gebunden	*to bind/tie*
bitten	bittet	bat	gebeten	*to ask/request*
bleiben	bleibt	blieb	*ist* geblieben	*to stay/remain*
brechen	bricht	brach	gebrochen	*to break*
brennen	brennt	brannte	gebrannt	*to burn*
bringen	bringt	brachte	gebracht	*to bring*
denken	denkt	dachte	gedacht	*to think*
essen	isst	aß	gegessen	*to eat*
fahren	fährt	fuhr	*ist/hat* gefahren	*to travel/drive a vehicle*
fallen	fällt	fiel	*ist* gefallen	*to fall*
fangen	fängt	fing	gefangen	*to catch*
finden	findet	fand	gefunden	*to find*
fliegen	fliegt	flog	*ist/hat* geflogen	*to fly*
fliehen	flieht	floh	*ist* geflohen	*to flee*
fressen	frisst	fraß	gefressen	*to eat (by an animal)*
frieren	friert	fror	*ist/hat* gefroren	*to freeze*

Principal Parts of Irregular (Strong) and Mixed Verbs—*Continued*

infinitive	*present*	*past*	*past participle*	*English meaning*
geben	gibt	gab	gegeben	*to give*
gehen	geht	ging	*ist* gegangen	*to go*
gießen	gießt	goss	gegossen	*to pour*
greifen	greift	griff	gegriffen	*to grasp/grab/seize*
haben	hat	hatte	gehabt	*to have*
halten	hält	hielt	gehalten	*to hold*
hängen	hängt	hing	gehangen	*to hang (intransitive)*
heben	hebt	hob	gehoben	*to lift/heft*
heißen	heißt	hieß	geheißen	*to be called (by name)*
helfen	hilft	half	geholfen	*to help*
kennen	kennt	kannte	gekannt	*to know/be familiar with*
klingen	klingt	klang	geklungen	*to sound*
kommen	kommt	kam	*ist* gekommen	*to come*
laden	lädt	lud	geladen	*to load*
lassen	lässt	ließ	gelassen	*to allow/let; to have done*
laufen	läuft	lief	*ist* gelaufen	*to run*
leiden	leidet	litt	gelitten	*to suffer*
leihen	leiht	lieh	geliehen	*to lend*
lesen	liest	las	gelesen	*to read*
liegen	liegt	lag	gelegen	*to lie/recline*
lügen	lügt	log	gelogen	*to lie/tell a lie*
messen	misst	maß	gemessen	*to measure*
nehmen	nimmt	nahm	genommen	*to take*
nennen	nennt	nannte	genannt	*to name*
reiten	reitet	ritt	*ist/hat* geritten	*to ride*
rennen	rennt	rannte	*ist* gerannt	*to race/run*
riechen	riecht	roch	gerochen	*to smell*
rufen	ruft	rief	gerufen	*to call*
saufen	säuft	soff	gesoffen	*to drink to excess or like an animal*
schaffen	schafft	schuf	geschaffen	*to create*
scheiden	scheidet	schied	geschieden	*to separate*
scheinen	scheint	schien	geschienen	*to seem/appear; to shine*
schieben	schiebt	schob	geschoben	*to shove*
schießen	schießt	schoss	geschossen	*to shoot*
schlafen	schläft	schlief	geschlafen	*to sleep*

infinitive	*present*	*past*	*past participle*	*English meaning*
schlagen	schlägt	schlug	geschlagen	*to strike/hit*
schließen	schließt	schloss	geschlossen	*to close*
schmeißen	schmeißt	schmiss	geschmissen	*to throw/fling*
schmelzen	schmilzt	schmolz	*ist/hat* geschmolzen	*to melt*
schneiden	schneidet	schnitt	geschnitten	*to cut*
schreiben	schreibt	schrieb	geschrieben	*to write*
schreien	schreit	schrie	geschrien	*to scream/cry*
schreiten	schreitet	schritt	*ist* geschritten	*to stride*
schweigen	schweigt	schwieg	geschwiegen	*to be silent*
schwimmen	schwimmt	schwamm	*ist* geschwommen	*to swim*
sehen	sieht	sah	gesehen	*to see*
sein	ist	war	*ist* gewesen	*to be*
senden	sendet	sandte	gesandt	*to send*
singen	singt	sang	gesungen	*to sing*
sinken	sinkt	sank	*ist* gesunken	*to sink*
sitzen	sitzt	saß	gesessen	*to sit (state of sitting)*
sprechen	spricht	sprach	gesprochen	*to speak*
stehen	steht	stand	gestanden	*to stand*
stehlen	stiehlt	stahl	gestohlen	*to steal*
steigen	steigt	stieg	*ist* gestiegen	*to climb*
sterben	stirbt	starb	*ist* gestorben	*to die*
stinken	stinkt	stank	gestunken	*to stink*
stoßen	stößt	stieß	gestoßen	*to push*
streichen	streicht	strich	gestrichen	*to stroke/pet; to spread*
streiten	streitet	stritt	gestritten	*to argue*
tragen	trägt	trug	getragen	*to carry*
treffen	trifft	traf	getroffen	*to meet; to hit*
treiben	treibt	trieb	getrieben	*to drive; to propel*
treten	tritt	trat	*ist/hat* getreten	*to step/kick*
trinken	trinkt	trank	getrunken	*to drink*
tun	tut	tat	getan	*to do*
wachsen	wächst	wuchs	*ist* gewachsen	*to grow*
waschen	wäscht	wusch	gewaschen	*to wash*
wenden	wendet	wandte	gewandt	*to turn*
werden	wird	wurde	*ist* geworden	*to become*
werfen	wirft	warf	geworfen	*to throw*
wissen	weiß	wusste	gewusst	*to know (factually)*
ziehen	zieht	zog	*ist/hat* gezogen	*to move/pull*
zwingen	zwingt	zwang	gezwungen	*to force*

Exercises

Theory Review

1. Fill in the blanks with the correct information.

1. The present perfect is the normal conversational past tense. The normal written past tense, used for narration, is the ______________ ______________.
2. The present perfect, or spoken past, consists of two verb forms and is a ______________ tense.
3. The written past consists of ______________ verb form and is therefore a ______________ past tense.
4. This tense is the main tense used in ______________ and other print media where reporting events is central.
5. For *regular* verbs simply take the stem and add the ______________ set of endings.
6. *Irregular* verbs *must* show a stem ______________ in the simple past.
7. This change will at the very least involve a ______________ change.
8. The simple past endings used with irregular verbs are the standard verb endings except that the ______________ and ______________ forms have no ending whatsoever. All you have is a stem.
9. These forms are considered to be " ______________."
10. Because the simple past is primarily a *written* narrative tense, the ______________, ______________, and ______________ forms are seldom used.
11. Mixed verbs are ______________ verbs because they have characteristics of both regular and irregular verbs.

12. What is the regular verb characteristic of mixed verbs? ______________________

13. What is the irregular verb characteristic of mixed verbs? ______________________

14. Does English have mixed verbs? ________

15. **Haben, sein,** and **werden** are perhaps the most important and most used verbs in German. The simple past form of **haben** is ____________, of **sein** ____________, and of **werden** ____________.

16. If a past action occurred before another past action, it is farther back in the past, and is therefore "more than past." The name of this "more than past" tense is ______________ ______________.

17. There are two verb components to this tense, so it is a ______________ tense.

18. In this "more than past" tense there is a helping verb, either a form of ______________ or a form of ______________.

19. The second verb component is a ______________ ______________.

20. In terms of word order, this tense is identical to the ____________ ____________.

21. When the subordinating conjunctions ______________ or ______________ are used, the past perfect usually comes into play.

22. The most important thing to learn to be accurate with verb forms in the present, simple past, present and past perfect, and future is the ______________ ______________ of verbs. The importance of these cannot be overstated.

23. If you did not grow up speaking German, you will have to ______________ them. Spend as much time as needed to master the elementary verbs listed in this chapter. Prioritize: Learn the ones you know you have encountered frequently first. When those are mastered, work on the less commonly encountered ones.

Focus on Form [✓]

2. Tense transformations. Rewrite each sentence in the following tenses.

1. Karl **wartet** auf seine Freundin.

   simple past: ______________________

   present perfect: ______________________

   past perfect: ______________________

2. Maria **liest** die Zeitung.

   simple past: ______________________

   present perfect: ______________________

   past perfect: ______________________

3. Ich **komme** nicht.

   simple past: ______________________

   present perfect: ______________________

   past perfect: ______________________

4. Wir **gehen** zur Uni.

   simple past: ______________________

   present perfect: ______________________

   past perfect: ______________________

5. Martin **fliegt** nach Rom.

   simple past: ______________________

   present perfect: ______________________

   past perfect: ______________________

6. Wir **essen** gern Wiener Schnitzel mit Spätzle.

   simple past: ______________________

   present perfect: ______________________

   past perfect: ______________________

7. Ich **trinke** ein Glas Bier.

   simple past: ______________________

   present perfect: ______________________

   past perfect: ______________________

8. Es **ist** kalt.

   simple past: ______________________________

   present perfect: ______________________________

   past perfect: ______________________________

9. Ihr **habt** Pech.

   simple past: ______________________________

   present perfect: ______________________________

   past perfect: ______________________________

10. Die Kinder **werden** krank.

   simple past: ______________________________

   present perfect: ______________________________

   past perfect: ______________________________

11. Ich **schreibe** meinen Eltern einen Brief.

   simple past: ______________________________

   present perfect: ______________________________

   past perfect: ______________________________

12. Frau Bruns **fährt** mit dem Taxi in die Stadt.

   simple past: ______________________________

   present perfect: ______________________________

   past perfect: ______________________________

13. Ich **bin** zu Hause.

   simple past: ______________________________

   present perfect: ______________________________

   past perfect: ______________________________

14. Thomas **spricht** immer zu schnell.

   simple past: ______________________________

   present perfect: ______________________________

   past perfect: ______________________________

15. Es **wird** heiß.

   simple past: ______________________________

   present perfect: ______________________________

   past perfect: ______________________________

16. Wir **treffen** unsere Freunde vor dem Kino.

simple past: ______________________________

present perfect: ______________________________

past perfect: ______________________________

17. Ich **antworte** ihnen nicht.

simple past: ______________________________

present perfect: ______________________________

past perfect: ______________________________

18. **Lernt** ihr es für die Prüfung?

simple past: ______________________________

present perfect: ______________________________

past perfect: ______________________________

19. Mutti **denkt** immer logisch.

simple past: ______________________________

present perfect: ______________________________

past perfect: ______________________________

20. Vati **rasiert** sich jeden Morgen.

simple past: ______________________________

present perfect: ______________________________

past perfect: ______________________________

3. Past perfect exercise. Form sentences logically with the past perfect for the sentence fragments given. Use *ich* as the subject for all of these.

1. Nachdem / mich duschen, ... mein Frühstück essen

____

2. Nachdem / mir die Hände waschen, ... ein Handtuch suchen

____

3. Nachdem / Zeitung lesen, ... zur Uni fahren

____

4. Bevor / Musik hören, ... Hausaufgaben machen

____

5. Bevor / ins Bett gehen, ... eine Weile einen Roman lesen

____

Focus on Meaning and Form

4. Fill in the blanks with a *simple past* verb form that makes good sense. More than one answer is possible for many of these.

A

1. Ich ______________________ gestern Abend für eine Prüfung.
2. Auf der Party ______________________ wir viel Musik.
3. Ich ______________________ mehrmals in Europa.
4. Letzten Sommer ______________________ ich bei einer französischen Firma.
5. Es ______________________ mir zu kalt im Haus.
6. Die Studenten ______________________ dieses Thema im Seminar sehr lebhaft.
7. An der Uni ______________________ ich Geschichte und Philosophie.
8. Der Hund ______________________ mich.
9. Wir ______________________ von Hamburg nach Bremen.
10. Max ______________________ mir etwas Geld.

B

1. In der Kirche ______________________ wir einige Hymnen.
2. Ich ______________________ den ganzen Abend in meinem Zimmer.
   Ich ______________________ nicht aus.
3. Meine beste Freundin ______________________ gestern am Ende der Party echt besoffen.
4. Peter ______________________ zu viel Wein und ______________________ zu viel Käse.
5. Wir ______________________ als Kinder immer viele Hausaufgaben.
6. Ich ______________________ Hannelore in Mainz.
7. Das Feuer ____________________ lange im Kamin und das Zimmer ____________________ langsam warm.
8. Ich ______________________ das gar nicht. Wo hast du das gehört?
9. Vati ______________________ uns Schokolade zu Ostern.
10. Karl ______________________ sich eine neue Hose.

C

1. Ich ____________________ immer, dass du Advokat werden wolltest.

2. Sabine ____________________ gestern um acht Uhr zur Arbeit.

3. Wir ____________________ sehr lange in der Schlange im Postamt.

4. Was?! Was ____________________ er? Ich kann das kaum glauben.

5. Was ____________________ du, als du in Japan wohntest?

6. Wann ____________________ du, dass du Pilot werden wolltest?

7. Heute Morgen _______________ ich die Zeitung und _______________ eine Tasse Kaffee.

8. Ich _______________ meine Freundin an der Bushaltestelle. Wir _______________ zusammen zur Uni.

9. Das Essen ______________ vom Teller auf den Boden und der Hund ______________ es.

10. Ich ____________ meine Kleidung auf das Bett und da ____________ sie den ganzen Tag.

D

1. Ich ____________________ das Bild zwischen die Fenster. Es hängt immer noch da.

2. Das Schiff ____________________ im Mittelmeer. Es ____________________ keine Überlebenden.

3. Ich ____________________ mich auf die Bank. Ich war müde. Ich ____________________ eine Weile da.

4. Wo ____________________ du denn? Ich warte schon lange auf dich.

5. Ich ____________________ dieses Gedicht nicht. Ich ____________________ es zu abstrakt und verwirrend.

6. Beethoven ____________________ diese Sinfonie.

7. ____________________ die Wikinger vor Kolumbus in Amerika?

8. Martin Luther ____________________ der „Vater der Reformation".

9. Klaus ____________________ der Lehrerin nicht.

10. Als Junge ____________________ ich viele Modellflugzeuge und Modellschiffe.

11. Gestern ____________________ ich 300 Euro, aber heute nicht mehr. Ich habe mein Geld alles ausgegeben.

5. Use the verbs and phrases listed below to compose a narrative, this time in the *simple past*, about what you did yesterday. Write a simple sentence for each verb, adding whatever details you wish.

sich waschen ____________________

schnell frühstücken ____________________

ein Stück Toast essen ____________________

eine Tasse Kaffee trinken ____________________

die Zeitung lesen ____________________

zur Bushaltestelle laufen ____________________

fünf Minuten auf den Bus warten ____________________

zur Uni fahren ____________________

zwei Kurse haben ____________________

dann in die Bibliothek gehen ____________________

einige Bücher suchen ____________________

zwei gute Bücher finden ____________________

Freunde in der Mensa treffen ____________________

nach Hause gehen ____________________

Sport treiben ____________________

eine Weile Fußball spielen ____________________

das Abendessen machen ____________________

Fisch, Reis und Erbsen essen ____________________

ein paar Stunden lernen ____________________

Nachbarn kurz besuchen ____________________

die Nachrichten im Fernsehen sehen ____________________

sich das Gesicht waschen ____________________

sich die Zähne putzen ____________________

ins Bett gehen ____________________

gut schlafen ____________________

Partnerarbeit

6. With your partner in class co-write a short paragraph in the *simple past* on any one of these familiar topic questions. You should mention approximately two dozen things this time, so generate sentences that form a "string" of activities like: *I read the paper, ate breakfast, drank some coffee, and went to work. Then I . . .*

1. Was ich heute Morgen schon machte
2. Was ich gestern Abend machte
3. Was ich letztes Wochenende machte
4. Was ich während der letzten Semesterpause machte

Review of the Simple Past and Past Perfect

Fill in the blanks with logical verb forms in the simple past and past perfect. Various answers are possible. Let the context of the sentences and the general theme be your guides.

Ich machte meine Hausafgaben für diesen Kurs:

Ich ____________________ mein Buch in meinem Schlafzimmer und ____________________ es unter dem Bett. Neben dem Buch ____________________ meine Socken und Schuhe und ein Roman. Nachdem ich mich an meinen Schreibtisch in der Ecke ____________________ ____________________, ____________________ ich das Buch auf Seite 23. Ich ____________________ die ersten Seiten, bis ich alles gut ____________________, dann machte ich die Übungen. Ich ____________________ die Fragen und ____________________ meine Antworten darauf ins Buch. Am Ende jeder Übung ____________________ ich die Lösungen im Answer Key an und ____________________ meine Fehler. Glücklicherweise ____________________ es nicht viele. Dann ____________________ ich die nächsten Übungen, bis ich mit allen fertig ____________________.

Ich machte mich für den Tag fertig:

Ich ____________________ um acht Uhr auf und ____________________ ins Badezimmer, wo ich mich ____________________. Ich ____________________ mir das Gesicht und ____________________ mir die Haare, dann ____________________ ich mich an. Ich ____________________ leider kein sauberes Hemd, aber es ____________________ mir nichts aus. Ich ____________________ in die Küche und ____________________ Wasser für Tee. Ich ____________________ ein Stück Brot in die Hand und ____________________

Erdnussbutter darauf und ______________ es. Ich ______________ ein Glas Milch dazu. Dann ______________ ich eine Vitaminpille ein und ______________ eine Weile am Tisch, während ich die Zeitung ______________. Dann ______________ ich ein bisschen fern, weil ich den Wetterbericht für heute noch nicht ______________. Gleich danach ______________ ich das Geschirr und ______________ etwas im Kühlschrank für mein Mitagessen. Ich ______________ mir meine Schlüssel, ______________ die Haustür, ______________ das Auto und ______________ auf dem Weg zur Uni. Nach zehn Minuten ______________ ich eine Panne. Ich ______________ das Auto und ______________ mit dem Bus den Rest des Weges zur Uni. Ich ______________ mehr als ein bisschen böse, dass der junge Tag schon so schlecht ______________.

Mein Tag an der Uni:

Also, heute ______________ eigentlich nichts Besonderes. Ich ______________ drei Kurse und die Professoren ______________ unglaublich theoretisch und langweilig, wie immer. Gegen Mittag ______________ ich in die Mensa, ______________ mir eine Kola und ______________ das Mittagessen, das ich von zu Hause ______________ ______________. Nach dem Mittagessen ______________ ich während der letzten Vorlesung sehr müde und ______________ langsam ein. Der Student hinter mir ______________ mich ______________, bevor der Professor mich ______________. Ich ______________ ihm am Ende der Vorlesung für seine Aufmerksamkeit. Ich ______________ um zwei Uhr einen Termin bei einer Lehrassistentin, aber ich ______________ ihn völlig. Da der Tag so schief ______________, ______________ ich, dass ich nach Hause gehen sollte. Ich ______________ die Werkstatt an und sie ______________ mein Auto weg. Ich ______________ den Bus nach Hause und ______________ mich aufs Bett, sobald ich zu Hause ______________. Ich ______________ ein Schläfchen und ______________ eine halbe Stunde später auf. Ich ______________ mich besser, viel energischer, und ______________ den Anfang das Abends mit einer Flasche Bier. Also, jetzt ______________ alles viel besser.

Chapter 4 Future and Future Perfect

The Future: *werden* + Infinitive

The future tense may be expressed by using a present-tense verb with a time expression that implies the future:

Ich **mache** das **bald.**
I'm doing that soon.
I'll be doing that soon.

Wir **kommen später.**
We're coming later.
We'll be coming later.

Gehst du **morgen** dahin?
Are you going there tomorrow?
Will you be going there tomorrow?

When no future time expression is used, or when the context does not already clearly point to the future, use **werden** + an *infinitive* to establish future time:

Ich **werde** das nicht **machen.**
I will not/won't do that.
I will not be doing that.

Peter **wird** bestimmt nicht **kommen.**
Peter will definitely not come.
Peter will definitely not be coming.

Note that the form of **werden**, the helping verb for the future, is conjugated in the present tense, is located in the usual verb position, and must agree with the subject. The main/finite verb moves to the end of the sentence and goes into the neutral infinitive form. Thus, the word order pattern is the same as for the present perfect and past perfect.

werden

singular	*plural*	*formal/polite*
ich **werde**	wir **werden**	
du **wirst**	ihr **werdet**	Sie **werden**
er/sie/es **wird**	sie **werden**	

The **werden** + infinitive construction may be used in conjunction with a future time expression, just as in English:

Wir **werden später am Abend** zu Hause **sein.**
We will be home later in the evening.

Remember, when there are two or more verbs being used in conjunction with each other, the verb construction is said to be *compound*, as opposed to *simple*. In compound constructions the helping verb agrees with the subject, is in the normal verb position, and "boots" the main verb to the end of the clause, where it morphs into a neutral form (that is, a form that does not agree with the subject), either an infinitive in the case of the future, or a past participle in the cases of the present and past perfect.

The Future Perfect in English: *will* + Past Infinitive

The future perfect tense is used to talk about a past event from some point in the future, as in these examples in English:

By tomorrow (the point in the future) I **will have completed** the report (past action).
We **will have graduated** before next year.
The group **will** certainly **have sung** the song by the end of the concert.
I **will have earned** a million dollars before I am forty.

The Future Perfect in German: *werden* + Past Infinitive

In German the future perfect is constructed by using **werden** as the helping verb to establish the point in the future and a *past infinitive* to establish that an action has been completed by then.

Past Infinitive = Past Participle + *haben* or *sein*

The past infinitive consists of a past participle and **haben** or **sein**, working together as a bound unit. Note that you must be sensitive to the **haben-sein** distinction.

gemacht **haben** gegessen **haben** gefahren **sein** geblieben **sein**

Now study these example sentences, noting again the use of **werden** as the helping verb and the past infinitive at the end of the sentence.

Wird der Mechaniker mein Wagen *bis dann* **repariert haben?**
Will the mechanic have repaired my car by then?

Karl **wird** die Aufgabe *bis nächsten Montag* bestimmt **erledigt haben.**
Karl will have certainly finished the assignment by next Monday.

Ich **werde** *bis heute Abend* das zerbrochene Fenster **ersetzt haben.**
I will have replaced the broken window by this evening.

Bis irgendwann im nächsten Sommer **werden** Schmidts nach Köln **gefahren sein.**
By sometime next summer the Schmidts will have traveled to Cologne.

Bis 2010 **wird** er zehn Jahre lang im Gefängnis **gewesen sein.**
By 2010 he will have been in prison for ten years.

Während des Winters **wird** es wohl mehrmals **gefroren haben.**
During the winter it will probably have frozen several times.

As you can see, the difference between the future and future perfect is the kind of infinitive that is used. The helping verb **werden** is the common denominator for both tenses.

Note also that there is almost always some time expression (the accusative preposition **bis** [*until, by*] is very common) used that will set a time limit or specific point of time in the future.

Exercises

Theory Review

1. Fill in the blanks with the correct information.

1. The ______________________ tense may be used to effect a future meaning if it is used in conjunction with a time expression that signals a time in the future *or* when context already makes it clear that the future is implied.
2. When there is no time expression to indicate the future, then it falls to the ______________________ to signal it.
3. This "pure" future tense employs the helping verb ______________________.
4. This verb must agree with the ______________________ and goes into the "normal" verb position.
5. The other future tense verb component is an ______________________ of the main, or finite, verb.
6. This verb form is located at the ______________________ of the sentence.
7. Since this verb form does not agree with the subject, it is a ______________________ verb form.
8. Since there are two verb components, the future tense is a ______________________ verb construction.
9. The word order for the future is identical to the ______________________ and ______________________ perfect.
10. The future perfect is used to express a ______________________ action, viewed as such from some point in the future.
11. This point in the future is often expressed as a time expression employing the preposition ______________________.
12. The helping verb for this tense is ______________________, just as in the regular future tense.
13. Instead of just an infinitive at the end of the sentence, a ______________________ ______________________ is employed.
14. This verb component is a compound unit that consists of a ______________________ ______________________ plus either ______________________ or ______________________ in infinitive form.
15. The past infinitive of **machen** is, therefore, ______________________.
16. The past infinitive of **gehen** is, therefore, ______________________.
17. Is the future perfect a commonly used tense? ______________________
18. Does that mean you can conveniently forget about it? ______________________

Focus on Form [✓]

2. Fill in the blanks with the correct form of *werden* to express the future.

1. Ich ______________________ dir immer treu sein.
2. ______________________ du mir helfen?
3. ______________________ es bald regnen?
4. Warum ______________________ wir heute nicht in die Stadt gehen?
5. Ihr ______________________ krank werden, wenn ihr das trinkt.
6. Herr und Frau Mohr ______________________ im Sommer in England sein.
7. ______________________ du ihn heiraten oder nicht?
8. Ich ______________________ dieses Dokument nicht unterschreiben.
9. Klaus ______________________ mir kein Geld leihen.
10. Warum ______________________ ihr nicht zur Party kommen?

3. Express each sentence into the future with *werden* + infinitive.

A

1. Karl wartet auf seine Freundin.

   ____

2. Maria liest die Zeitung.

   ____

3. Ich komme später mit meinem Freund.

   ____

4. Gehst du zur Uni?

   ____

5. Martin und Beate fliegen nach Rom.

   ____

6. Wir bestellen Wiener Schnitzel mit Spätzle.

   ____

7. Trinkt ihr ein Glas Bier?

   ____

8. Es wird kalt.

   ____

9. Ich habe Pech.

   ____

10. Tina ist überrascht.

   ____

B

1. Ich telefoniere mit meinen Eltern.

___

2. Die Frau bleibt zwei Wochen in Heidelberg.

___

3. Ich bin um sieben Uhr wieder zu Hause.

___

4. Thomas spricht immer lange über Politik.

___

5. Es wird bestimmt heiß.

___

6. Wir treffen unsere Freunde vor dem Theater.

___

7. Ich stelle dem Lehrer eine Frage.

___

8. Klaus schreibt morgen eine Prüfung.

___

9. Mutti denkt immer an die Vergangenheit.

___

10. Vati rasiert sich.

___

4. Write the past infinitive for each of the following.

wissen ___	werfen ___
waschen ___	geben ___
essen ___	trinken ___
sterben ___	kommen ___
sehen ___	schwimmen ___
schreiben ___	laufen ___
gehen ___	fahren ___

5. Change the following sentences from the present perfect to the future perfect.

1. Ich habe Mutti eine schöne Bluse gekauft.

____

2. Wir haben diesen Roman für den Literaturkurs gelesen.

____

3. Die Musikstudenten haben zusammen eine Sinfonie für den Semesterabschluss komponiert.

____

4. Die Kirche hat den Obdachlosen einen Platz zum Schlafen gegeben.

____

5. Herr Mayer hat bestimmt sein letztes Geld auf das Fußballspiel gewettet.

____

Focus on Meaning and Form

6. Fill in the blanks with an infinitive that makes good sense to form the future.

1. Trockenes Holz wird sehr leicht ____________.
2. Was wird dir der Weihnachtsmann dieses Jahr ____________?
3. In welches Restaurant wirst du ____________? *Ginos Ristorante* oder *Zum Goldenen Adler*?
4. Also, was werden wir ____________, eine Pizza oder ein Jägerschnitzel?
5. Ich werde dieses Jahr nach Kanada ____________.
6. Die Sekretärin wird den Brief bald ____________.
7. Es soll später sehr kalt werden. Wird es in der Nacht ____________?
8. Hoffentlich werde ich dieses Jahr keine Grippe ____________.
9. Ich werde meinen Kindern bei ihren Hausaufgaben ____________.
10. Wann werdet ihr mit der Zeitung fertig ____________?

7. Use the *werden* + infinitive construction in the following exercise.

1. Was werden Sie nach dem Studium machen? (3 Sätze)

____

____

____

____

____

____

2. Was wird Ihre Familie während des Urlaubs machen? (3 Sätze)

____

____

____

____

____

____

3. Was wird wahrscheinlich bald passieren? (3 Sätze)

____

____

____

____

____

____

8. Future perfect. Complete the sentences logically with a past infinitive.

1. In fünf Jahren wird Benzin ______________________.
2. Hoffentlich werde ich in drei Jahren ______________________.
3. Im Jahre 2020 wird man ______________________.
4. Wenn ich 50 Jahre alt bin, werde ich ______________________.
5. Innerhalb von drei Jahren werde ich ______________________.
6. Bis Ende der Woche werden wir ______________________.
7. Vor dem Ende des Jahres werden die Studenten ______________________.
8. Bis fünf Uhr werden wir alle ______________________.

You Determine the Message and Form

9. Schreiben Sie zusammen mit einem Partner, was Ihnen wahrscheinlich geschehen sein wird, bis Sie 35 Jahre alt sind.

Ich werde bestimmt einen Job gefunden haben und ...

Chapter 5 Imperative Mood: Commands

A *mood* is a *mode* of language use, and there are three of them: the *indicative,* used for speaking and writing about reality; the *subjunctive,* used to speak and write about non-reality; and the *imperative,* used to issue commands. Commands, also known as imperatives, are sentences used to tell another person to do something. When written, they no longer require an exclamation point, which they did require until 2005, when various language reforms became mandatory in Germany. Exclamation points may still be used, however, as in English, to signal agitation, excitement, or enthusiasm when the command is given.

Formal Commands

The formal command consists of the infinitive followed by **Sie**:

Bleiben Sie hier.	**Warten Sie** dort drüben.
Stay here.	*Wait over there.*

The **wir**-command (technically a request phrased in the subjunctive) consists of the infinitive followed by **wir**:

Bleiben wir hier.	**Warten wir** dort drüben.
Let's stay here.	*Let's wait over there.*

Plural Informal Commands

Informal plural commands consist simply of the **ihr**-form of the verb minus **ihr**:

Arbeitet fleißiger.	**Geht** jetzt nach Hause.	**Kommt** etwas früher.
Work harder.	*Go home now.*	*Come a bit earlier.*

Singular Informal Commands

The informal singular command (the so-called **du**-command) can be arrived at in this fail-safe way:

1. Generate the complete **du**-form of the verb:	**du wartest**	**du läufst**
2. Eliminate **du**:	**wartest**	**läufst**
3. Eliminate the **-st** ending:	**warte**	**läuf**
4. Eliminate any umlaut not found in the infinitive:	**warte**	**lauf**
5. What you're left with is the command form:	**Warte**	**Lauf**

Other examples:

du sagst – **Sag**	du tust – **Tu**	du wartest – **Warte**	du öffnest – **Öffne**
du sprichst – **Sprich**	du siehst – **Sieh**	du wendest – **Wende**	du schreibst – **Schreib**
du nimmst – **Nimm**	du fährst – **Fahr**	du kommst – **Komm**	du zählst – **Zähl**
du liest – **Lies**	du läufst – **Lauf**	du gehst – **Geh**	du fragst – **Frag**

NOTE: Informal singular commands may display an **-e** ending. This ending is optional for verbs that have no stem changes in the present tense (**sage**, **finde**, **suche**, **mache**, etc.) but is required of verbs whose stems end in **-ig** (**erledige**, **erkundige**, **beruhige**, etc.). The **-e** ending is not displayed on a command form that shows a stem vowel change.

Commands with *haben, sein, werden*

Sein has irregular forms for all of its commands:

Seien Sie ruhig.	**Sei** ruhig.	**Seid** ruhig.
Be quiet.	*Be quiet.*	*Be quiet.*

Haben has an irregular singular command form, Hab:

Haben Sie keine Angst.	**Hab** keine Angst.	**Habt** keine Angst.
Don't be afraid.	*Don't be afraid.*	*Don't be afraid.*
(Literally: *Have no fear.*)		

Werden has regular command forms:

Werden Sie bitte nicht böse auf mich.	**Werde** vorsichtiger.	**Werdet** ernster.
Don't get angry at me.	*Get/Become more careful.*	*Get/Become more serious.*

Infinitival Commands

Infinitives may be used alone to form commands directed to the public or groups of people.

Ruhig **sein**, bitte.	Nicht laut **sprechen**, bitte.	Nicht **rauchen**, bitte.
Quiet please.	*No loud talking please.*	*No smoking please.*

Infinitival commands will sometimes be used to repeat a conventionally given command if the command was not initially understood or needs to be repeated. Study the progression:

1. Conventionally given command or request:	**Warten Sie hier, bitte.**
2. Request for command to be repeated:	**Wie bitte?**
3. Simpler infinitival command given:	**Hier warten, bitte.**

Infinitival commands occur typically among friends, in classrooms, in the military, and when given over public-address systems.

Flavoring Particles with Commands

Flavoring particles are monosyllabic words that add an emotional dimension to a command.

- **Doch** adds a sense of urgency (anger, frustration, exasperation):
  Mach das **doch** und halte den Mund!
  Just do it and shut up.
  Hör doch damit auf!
  Come on, stop it.
- **Mal** adds a sense of impatience to the command:
  Sei mal etwas ruhiger!
  Just be a bit quieter!/Come on, be a bit quieter!
- **Nur** adds a threatening dimension to a command:
  Versuch's **nur** und du wirst es bereuen.
  Just try it and you'll regret it.

Requests with *bitte*

If you use **bitte** (*please*) with a command, you change it to a request. If you put **bitte** at the end of the request and it follows a complement (adverb, object, separable prefix, etc.), set it off with a comma:

Kommen Sie **bitte** mit.	**Bitte** kommen Sie mit.	Kommen Sie mit, **bitte**.
Gib mir **bitte** das Buch.	**Bitte** gib mir das Buch.	Gib mir das Buch, **bitte**.
Arbeite **bitte** schneller.	**Bitte** arbeite schneller.	Arbeite schneller, **bitte**.

Suggestions with *wir*

To get another person to join you in doing something, formulate a suggestion by using an infinitive followed by **wir**. While this is technically in the subjunctive mood and therefore not an imperative, it has the look, sound, and feel of a command, so it is logical, from a communicative standpoint, to include these examples here.

Gehen wir jetzt nach Hause.	**Warten wir** hier.	**Essen wir** etwas.
Let's go home now.	*Let's wait here.*	*Let's eat something.*

Word Order with Commands, Requests, and Suggestions

For all of these sentence types, the verb is in first position followed by the subject (except for informal commands) and any complements:

commands:	**Arbeiten Sie** fleißiger. **Macht** das schneller. **Bleib** hier!
requests:	**Sprechen Sie** lauter, bitte. **Kommt** bitte etwas früher an. **Schreib** das, bitte.
suggestions:	**Gehen wir** ins Kino. **Spielen wir** Karten. **Seien wir** vorsichtig.

Exercises

Theory Review

1. Fill in the blanks with the correct information.

1. To get another person to do what you tell him or her to do, you formulate a ________________.
2. Another term for such a sentence is ______________________.
3. To give a command to a stranger, older person, a person in authority, or a person with a title, that is, someone worthy of respect, simply use the infinitive followed by ______________________.
4. To give a command to one or more persons when you intend to join them in the activity, one simply uses the infinitive followed by ______________________.
5. To give a command to a person you know very well (family member, relative, close friend, boyfriend, girlfriend, lover, etc.), arriving at the correct command form is a bit more involved. First generate the full ____________-form of the verb. Next, drop the pronoun ____________. Then drop the **du**-form verb ending, which is ___________. Lastly, drop any _______________ that was not in the infinitive. What remains is the command form.
6. With verbs whose stems end in **-ig**, an ________ is added, ostensibly to facilitate pronunciation.
7. To give a command to two or more people whom you know well, simply use the ____________-form of the verb, but drop ____________.
8. A command can be softened by using ______________________, thus changing the command to a ______________________.
9. When giving commands to large groups, especially when a microphone, bullhorn, or public-address system is employed, just an ______________________ will suffice, with no pronoun.
10. This type of command may also be used to ______________________ a conventionally given command, especially when there may be confusion or disregard. It is also common in military settings.
11. One forms a suggestion by using an infinitive followed by ______________________ and then any other sentence complements.
12. Adding particles to commands will add an emotional flavor. Use ______________________ to signal urgency or frustration; use ______________________ to signal impatience; and use ______________________ to make a command threatening.
13. Under the new spelling and punctuation guidelines, the correct punctuation for a command is a ______________________.
14. An ______________________ ______________________ may be used instead to signal that immediate compliance is expected.

Focus on Form [✓]

2. Write out the *informal* command forms of the following verbs, singular and plural.

	singular	*plural*
1. fragen		
2. nehmen		
3. fahren		
4. laufen		
5. arbeiten		
6. lernen		
7. wenden		
8. sprechen		
9. warten		
10. kommen		
11. geben		
12. sagen		
13. sein		
14. haben		
15. werden		

Focus on Meaning and Form [✓]

3. Write various commands. Tell me, a friend, to . . .

1. work hard ______
2. walk/run quickly ______
3. read it now ______
4. take that ______
5. write well ______
6. do that carefully ______
7. sleep well ______
8. eat more vegetables ______
9. drink less beer ______
10. travel/drive safely ______
11. drive more slowly ______
12. be quiet ______

You Determine the Message and Form

4. Situational commands. Give commands appropriate to the following situations.

1. Give a young child whom you are babysitting five commands.

2. You've discovered a second child hiding under a bed. Now give *two* children the same commands.

3. Suggest five things you and several friends could all do together.

4. You are a teacher in a **Gymnasium**. Give five likely commands to your students. (They're 14 years old.)

5. Formulate five polite/formal requests to your instructor.

6. Formulate five infinitival commands given in public to a large group of people. They can be verbal commands or ones typically found on a sign.

Review of Commands

Write commands as directed.

1. Tell me, *a friend,* to do the following:

   bring the book here ______

   carry this into the room ______

   close the door ______

   sleep longer ______

   come here ______

   do it now ______

   drink a little more ______

   eat everything ______

   give it to you ______

   go home ______

   hang it on the wall ______

   tie it quickly ______

   get the newspaper ______

   not smoke ______

   sit down ______

   not cry ______

2. Tell your *friends* to . . .

   help you ______

   lend you some money ______

   read this magazine ______

   shove this into the corner ______

   stay there ______

   take everything away ______

   throw their jackets on[to] the sofa ______

   wash up ______

   look for it over there ______

   show you the way back ______

3. Tell *an older person* to . . .

be careful ______________________________

drive home safely ______________________________

meet you at six o'clock ______________________________

please speak more clearly ______________________________

tell you the truth ______________________________

write you a note ______________________________

buy herself something nice ______________________________

send you a postcard ______________________________

place this on the table ______________________________

Chapter 6 Verbs with Inseparable Prefixes

Prefixes are words or syllables that are attached to the front of a word, that is, *pre*fixed, in order to affect or alter the meaning of the core verb.

Verbs with inseparable prefixes have, as the term indicates, prefixes that remain fixed or attached to the verb stem at all times. Verbs with inseparable prefixes are stressed on the main verb stem, not the prefix, for example, **be*such*en**, **ver*steh*en**, **wieder*hol*en**. Inseparable prefixes are essentially syllables; they may affect the meaning of the main verb to which they are attached only marginally, or quite radically. This means that you will need to memorize their meanings in each case.

Common Verbs with Inseparable Prefixes

- **Be**- makes the verb automatically transitive and may affect the meaning of the core verb.

beantworten *to answer*	beantwortet, beantwortete, beantwortet
befehlen *to order, command*	befiehlt, befahl, befohlen
beginnen *to begin*	beginnt, begann, begonnen
begreifen *to comprehend, grasp*	begreift, begriff, begriffen
begrüßen *to greet*	begrüßt, begrüßte, begrüßt
bekommen *to receive*	bekommt, bekam, bekommen
beruhigen *to calm [down]*	beruhigt, beruhigte, beruhigt
besprechen *to discuss*	bespricht, besprach, besprochen
besuchen *to visit*	besucht, besuchte, besucht
beweisen *to prove*	beweist, bewies, bewiesen

- **Emp**- colors the meaning of the core verb variously.

empfangen *to receive, welcome*	empfängt, empfing, empfangen
empfehlen *to recommend*	empfiehlt, empfahl, empfohlen
empfinden *to feel*	empfindet, empfand, empfunden

- **Ent**- signals a removal, detachment, or separation of some kind.

entdecken *to discover, find*	entdeckt, entdeckte, entdeckt
sich **entfalten** *to unfold*	entfaltet, entfaltete, entfaltet
entkommen *to escape*	entkommt, entkam, *ist* entkommen
entwickeln *to develop*	entwickelt, entwickelte, entwickelt

- **Er-** signals *to make.*

erfinden *to invent*	erfindet, erfand, erfunden
erledigen *to complete, finish*	erledigt, erledigte, erledigt
erleichtern *to ease, make easy*	erleichtert, erleichterte, erleichtert
ermöglichen *to make possible*	ermöglicht, ermöglichte, ermöglicht
ersetzen *to replace*	ersetzt, ersetzte, ersetzt
erzählen *to tell a story*	erzählt, erzählte, erzählt

- **Ge-** colors the meaning of the core verb variously.

gefallen *to please*	gefällt, gefiel, gefallen
gehören *to belong to*	gehört, gehörte, gehört
gelingen *to succeed*	gelingt, gelang, *ist* gelungen
genießen *to enjoy*	genießt, genoss, genossen
geschehen *to happen*	geschieht, geschah, *ist* geschehen
gewinnen *to win*	gewinnt, gewann, gewonnen

- **Hinter-** signals *behind* and sometimes a deception.

hinterlassen *to leave behind*	hinterlässt, hinterließ, hinterlassen

- **Miss-** signals that something is amiss, false, or incorrect.

missdeuten *to misinterpret*	missdeutet, missdeutete, missdeutet
misshandeln *to mistreat, abuse*	misshandelt, misshandelte, misshandelt
misstrauen *to mistrust*	misstraut, misstraute, misstraut
missverstehen *to misunderstand*	missversteht, missverstand, missverstanden

- **Ver-** can signal that an error has been made, that something is being consumed, that something is being pushed away, or, like **er-**, that something is being made or altered in some way.

sich **verändern** *to change (appearance)*	verändert, veränderte, verändert
verbergen *to hide, conceal*	verbirgt, verbarg, verborgen
verbessern *to improve*	verbessert, verbesserte, verbessert
verbrauchen *to consume, use up*	verbraucht, verbrauchte, verbraucht
verbrennen *to burn up*	verbrennt, verbrannte, *ist/hat* verbrannt
verbringen *to spend time*	verbringt, verbrachte, verbracht
sich **verfahren** *to get lost driving*	verfährt, verfuhr, verfahren
verfaulen *to spoil, rot, decompose*	verfault, verfaulte, *ist* verfault
vergessen *to forget*	vergisst, vergaß, vergessen
vergleichen *to compare*	vergleicht, verglich, verglichen
sich **verlaufen** *to get lost walking*	verläuft, verlief, verlaufen
verlieren *to lose*	verliert, verlor, verloren
verlegen *to misplace*	verlegt, verlegte, verlegt
vermeiden *to avoid*	vermeidet, vermied, vermieden
vernichten *to annihilate*	vernichtet, vernichtete, vernichtet
verschwinden *to disappear*	verschwindet, verschwand, *ist* verschwunden
versprechen *to promise*	verspricht, versprach, versprochen
vertreiben *to drive off, repel*	vertreibt, vertrieb, vertrieben
verursachen *to cause*	verursacht, verursachte, verursacht
verwöhnen *to spoil (children)*	verwöhnt, verwöhnte, verwöhnt
verzeihen *to forgive, pardon*	verzeiht, verzieh, verziehen

- **Zer**- signals *to pieces, to shreds* and denotes the end or destruction of something.

zerbrechen *to break into pieces*	zerbricht, zerbrach, zerbrochen
zerfallen *to fall to pieces*	zerfällt, zerfiel, *ist* zerfallen
zerreißen *to tear to pieces*	zerreißt, zerriss, zerrissen
zerschneiden *to cut to pieces*	zerschneidet, zerschnitt, zerschnitten
zerstören *to destroy*	zerstört, zerstörte, zerstört

Present and Simple Past

Since the prefix remains attached to the stem at all times, formation of the present and simple past tenses follows normal expectations for regular and irregular verb forms and for word order.

present:

Wir **begrüßen** unsere Gäste.
We are greeting our guests.

Der Mechaniker **ersetzt** den Ventilator.
The mechanic is replacing the fan.

Verbringst du viel Zeit in den Alpen?
Do you spend a lot of time in the Alps?

Der Kellner **empfiehlt** diesen Wein.
The waiter recommends this wine.

Wem **gehört** dieser Wagen?
To whom does this car belong? (Whose car is this?)

Leider **misstraue** ich ihr.
Unfortunately, I mistrust her.

simple past:

Die Studenten **beantworteten** die Fragen des Professors völlig richtig.
The students answered the professor's questions completely accurately.

Kolumbus **entdeckte** Amerika im Jahre 1492.
Columbus discovered America in 1492.

Mein Onkel **erzählte** zum tausendsten Mal seine alten Kriegsgeschichten.
My uncle retold his old war stories for the thousandth time.

Der tödliche Unfall **geschah** in Spanien.
The deadly accident happened in Spain.

Wir **verbesserten** unsere Arbeit.
We improved our work.

Das Glas **zerbrach** wegen des schnellen Temperaturwechsels.
The glass broke due to the quick change in temperature.

Present Perfect

Selection of the Helping Verb

The present perfect is formed in the usual manner by using either **haben** or **sein** as the helping verb along with a past participle at the end of the sentence. **Haben** is the helping verb for all transitive verbs and **sein** is the helping verb for all intransitive verbs that also signal a change in position or state. You must know the meaning of the verb in order to make the right choice.

Formation of the Past Participle: Prefix + Stem + -[*e*]*t*/-*en*

The past participle is formed simply by adding a -[**e**]**t** ending if the verb is regular, or an **-en** ending if the verb is irregular. *There is no* ***ge-*** *prefix.*

regular verbs:	**be**ruhig**t**, **er**ledig**t**, **er**zähl**t**, **ver**brauch**t**, **zer**stört
irregular verbs:	**be**griff**en**, **emp**fohl**en**, **miss**verstand**en**, **ver**glich**en**, **zer**riss**en**

Word Order in the Present Perfect

The helping verb **haben** or **sein** goes into normal verb position for the sentence type used and the past participle is located at the end of the sentence, as expected.

regular verbs:

Wir **haben** unsere Verwandten in Emden **besucht**.
We visited our relatives in Emden.

Der Gast **hat** die Serviette **entfaltet**.
The guest unfolded the napkin.

Die Finanzen meines Großvaters **haben** mein Studium **ermöglicht**.
My grandfather's finances made my study (at the university) possible.

Der Mann **hat** den Hund furchtbar **misshandelt**.
The man abused the dog terribly.

Wieviel Benzin **hat** dein Auto während der langen Reise **verbraucht**?
How much gasoline did your car consume during the long trip?

Das Holz **ist** zu Asche **verbrannt**.
The wood burned to ashes.

irregular verbs:

Was für Geschenke **hast** du zu Weihnachten **bekommen**?
What kind of gifts did you receive for Christmas?

Habt ihr das mit dem Chef **besprochen**?
Have you discussed that with the boss?

Der Präsident **hat** die ausländischen Minister freundlich aber formell **empfangen**.
The president received the foreign ministers in a friendly but formal manner.

Ich **habe** deine Erdbeertorte wirklich **genossen**.
I really enjoyed your strawberry torte.

Was **ist** denn eigentlich **geschehen**?
What actually happened?

Wie **hast** du ihn **missverstanden**?
How did you misunderstand him?

Die Piraten **haben** den Schatz irgendwo an der Küste Kaliforniens **verborgen**.
The pirates hid the treasure somewhere on the coast of California.

Past Perfect

The past perfect is formed exactly like the present perfect tense, except that forms of **hatten** and **waren** are used as helping verbs:

Die Kinder **hatten** sich **beruhigt**, bevor sie schlafen gegangen sind.
The children had calmed down before they went to sleep.

Die Soldaten **waren** mitten in der Nacht mit einem Hubschrauber aus dem Gefecht **entkommen**.
The soldiers had escaped from the engagement by helicopter in the middle of the night.

Diese Erklärung **hatte** es **ermöglicht**, eine Lösung zu finden.
This explanation had made it possible to find a solution.

Hatte der Film allen Mädchen **gefallen**?
Had all the girls enjoyed the film?
(Literally: *Had the film been pleasing to all the girls?*)

Future

The future is formed by using **werden** as the helping verb with an infinitive at the end of the sentence.

Werden wir die Kinder irgendwann bei Oma **hinterlassen**?
Will we leave the children [behind] with grandma sometime?

Wirst du die Farbe der Wände in deinem Zimmer **verändern**?
Will you change the color of the walls in your room?

Vorsicht, oder du **wirst** dich in der Fußgängerzone **verlaufen**.
Careful or you'll lose your way in the pedestrian zone.

Tina **wird** ihm bestimmt **versprechen**, dass sie ihn heiratet.
Tina will definitely promise him that she'll marry him.

Commands and Suggestions

Commands formed with verbs with inseparable prefixes are straightforward and follow normal expectations:

familiar singular	*familiar plural*	*polite/formal*
Beantworte die Frage.	**Beantwortet** die Frage.	**Beantworten Sie** die Frage.
Besprich es mit uns.	**Besprecht** es mit uns.	**Besprechen Sie** es mit uns.
Verbessere den Satz.	**Verbessert** den Satz.	**Verbessern Sie** den Satz.
Verfahr dich nicht.	**Verfahrt** euch nicht.	**Verfahren Sie** sich nicht.
Verleg die Papiere nicht.	**Verlegt** die Papiere nicht.	**Verlegen Sie** die Papiere nicht.
Zerreiß den Scheck.	**Zerreißt** den Scheck.	**Zerreißen Sie** den Scheck.

Suggestions are formed similarly to commands:

Beantworten wir die Fragen.	**Verbessern wir** die Aufsätze.	**Verlegen wir** die Papiere nicht.
Besprechen wir den Text.	**Verfahren wir** uns nicht.	**Zerreißen wir** diese Dokumente.

Exercises

Theory Review

1. Fill in the blanks with the correct information.

1. Words or syllables attached to the beginning of a word are called ____________________.
2. The addition of a prefix to a word ____________________ the meaning of that word, perhaps mildly, perhaps drastically.
3. Prefixes that remain attached to a verb stem at all times are known as ____________________ prefixes.
4. Some of these prefixes are: __________, __________, __________, __________, __________.
5. Do these typically look like words? __________
6. Is it usually easy for students of German to determine the meaning of a verb with an inseparable prefix? __________
7. Is the primary stress of such verbs on the prefix or the stem of the core verb? Stress is on the ____________________.
8. Formation of the present and simple past tenses is straightforward. Knowledge of the ____________________ parts of the core verb will ensure accuracy.
9. When forming the present and past perfect, the selection of **haben** or **sein** as the helping verb will be determined by the ____________________ of the verb.
10. The most startling aspect of the past participle's formation is that there is no __________ prefix. The inseparable prefix will not "make room" to accommodate one.
11. Remember that a verb that never undergoes a stem change will have a past participle that ends in __________.
12. Except for a few mixed verbs, a verb that does undergo a stem change has a past participle that ends in __________.
13. Are there any inherent differences in word order with inseparable-prefix verbs in the various tenses, other than the fact that there is no **ge-** prefix on past participles? __________
14. Is the formation of the various command forms essentially the same as for the core verbs to which the prefixes are attached? __________.

Focus on Form [✓]

2. Generate sentences in the present tense from the fragments.

1. Wir / begrüßen / unsere Verwandten

   ____

2. Die Kandidaten / besprechen / ihre Ideen

   ____

3. Die Kellnerin / empfehlen / das Jägerschnitzel

   ____

4. Diese Landkarte / erleichtern / die Planung / unserer Reise

   ____

5. Ersetzen / du / die Batterien?

   ____

6. Opa / erzählen / uns / immer / von dem Krieg

   ____

7. Gefallen / es / dir?

   ____

8. Wem / gehören / das?

   ____

9. Er / hinterlassen / seine Familie / in Bosnien

   ____

10. Du / missdeuten / alles

    ____

11. Karl / verlaufen / sich / immer / in der Stadt

    ____

12. Das / versprechen / er / jedem Mädchen

___

3. Change the following sentences from the present to the simple past.

1. Die Partisanen misshandeln ihre Gefangenen.

___

2. Wir misstrauen dem ausländischen Verteidigungsminister.

___

3. Wo verbirgt man das gestohlene Geld?

___

4. Dieses Auto verbraucht viel Benzin.

___

5. Ich verbringe den ganzen Sommer in Bulgarien.

___

6. Die Mutter vergleicht ihre Tochter mit ihrem Sohn.

___

7. Die Armee vernichtet den Feind in zwei großen Schlachten.

___

8. Der Plan entwickelt sich schnell.

___

9. Was geschieht während deines Aufenthalts in der Schweiz?

___

10. Ich besuche meine Tante in Frankfurt.

___

4. Indicate whether *haben* or *sein* is the correct helping verb in the present perfect for these verbs and then indicate the correct past participle.

Example: verbergen → *hat verborgen*

begrüßen __________________

beantworten __________________

bekommen __________________

besprechen __________________

besuchen __________________

empfangen __________________

empfehlen __________________

entfalten __________________

erleichtern __________________

ersetzen __________________

erzählen __________________

gefallen __________________

gehören __________________

geschehen __________________

hinterlassen __________________

missdeuten __________________

misshandeln __________________

misstrauen __________________

verlaufen __________________

verbergen __________________

verbrauchen __________________

verbringen __________________

vergleichen __________________

versprechen __________________

5. Form sentences in the present perfect from the fragments.

1. Ich / beantworten / die Frage / nicht

   ____

2. Begreifen / du / seine Aussagen?

   ____

3. Was / bekommen / du / zum Geburtstag?

   ____

4. Entdecken / die Wikinger / Amerika?

   ____

5. Ihre Hilfe / ermöglichen / den Erfolg / dieses Unternehmens

   ____

6. Wir / genießen / das Abendessen / bei euch

   ____

7. Oma und Opa / verwöhnen / ihre Enkelkinder

   ____

8. Ihr / missverstehen / mich / furchtbar

9. Warum / verändern / du / dein Aussehen / so drastisch?

10. Wieso / verschwinden / du / plötzlich?

6. Form sentences in the past perfect from the fragments.

1. Jeder Student / verbessern / seinen Aufsatz

2. Ein Virus / verursachen / diese Krankheit

3. Sie / zerreißen / das Bild / ihres ehemaligen Freundes

4. Der Koch / zerschneiden / das Gemüse und das Fleisch

5. Das Feuer / zerstören / zwei Gebäude

7. Change the following sentences from the present to the future.

1. Beantwortest du die Frage nicht?

2. Wann erledigen wir unsere Leseaufgabe?

3. Das erleichtert viel für uns.

4. Die Schuhe gefallen Christiane sehr.

5. Ihr genießt das ohne Zweifel.

8. Paraphrasing. The simple past (written past) and the present perfect (spoken past) are equivalent in meaning. Express the same sentence in the present perfect tense.

1. Wir beantworteten alle Fragen.

____

2. Der Professor empfahl mir diese zwei Kurse.

____

3. Al Gore erfand das Internet!

____

4. Ich beruhigte mich.

____

5. Diese Idee entwickelte sich ganz langsam in meinem Gehirn.

____

6. So ein Spiel gefiel uns sehr.

____

7. Das geschah blitzschnell und ohne Warnung.

____

8. Er missverstand mich einfach.

____

9. Wir erkannten Ilse nicht, denn sie hatte sich sehr verändert.

____

10. Deine Faulheit verursachte deine akademischen Schwierigkeiten.

____

Focus on Meaning and Form

9. Statements. Tell me that . . .

1. you grasp the theory

____

2. you greeted the president

____

3. they will receive the guests in the garden

____

4. he replaced your computer with a new one

____

5. it happened years ago

____

6. you belong to a club

____

7. I misinterpreted your statement

____

8. you misunderstood me

____

9. we had consumed all the wine

____

10. the dog drove off the birds

____

10. Questions. Remember that questions are normally asked orally. Questions about the past are usually formed in the present perfect. Ask me . . .

1. if I will discuss it with you later

____

2. what I recommend

____

3. if I have finished the plan

____

4. if I mistrust you

____

5. where I misplaced my car keys

____

6. if I misunderstood her

____

7. if I lost the key

____

8. if I used up/consumed the water

____

9. if it was a success

____

10. if we were avoiding the assignment

____

11. Commands. Tell me to . . .

1. discuss this with the boss

____

2. recommend something

____

3. tear up your love letter

____

4. spend more time at home

____

5. promise her everything

____

You Determine the Message and Form

12. Write commands as directed.

1. Generate three commands to a stranger with these verbs. Supply whatever vocabulary is needed.

   besprechen ______________________________

   erzählen ______________________________

   vergleichen ______________________________

2. Generate three commands to a brother or sister with these verbs. Add whatever is needed.

   erledigen ______________________________

   misshandeln ______________________________

   verlegen ______________________________

3. Generate three commands to two or three children with these verbs. Add whatever is needed.

   beantworten ______________________________

   beruhigen ______________________________

   verschwinden ______________________________

Partnerarbeit

13. Arbeiten Sie mit einem Partner/einer Partnerin und beantworten Sie die folgenden Fragen mündlich.

A

1. Was hast du neulich zerbrochen, zerrissen oder zerstört? War das absichtlich oder unabsichtlich?
2. Wem hast du vor kurzem etwas versprochen? Was hast du dieser Person eigentlich versprochen?
3. Was verlegst du oft? Wo verlegst du das?
4. Wo hast du dich verlaufen oder verfahren?
5. Was hast du vor jemandem in letzter Zeit verborgen? Warum?

B

1. Wen hast du neulich missverstanden?
2. Was ist letztes Jahr in deinem Leben geschehen?
3. Gehörst du zu einem Verein oder einer Organisation oder einer Kirche?
4. Was erleichtert es dir, wenn du ein großes Problem hat?
5. Was hast du in den letzten paar Wochen erledigt?

C

1. Ich habe Hunger und gehe mit dir in ein italienisches Restaurant. Was empfiehlst du?
2. Wen besuchst du bald? Wo wohnt diese Person?
3. Mit wem hast du etwas Wichtiges besprochen?
4. Was hast du das letzte Mal von deinem Freund oder deiner Freundin zum Geburtstag bekommen?
5. Was hast du in diesem Kurs noch nicht völlig begriffen?

Chapter 7 Verbs with Separable Prefixes

Verbs with separable prefixes have prefixes that separate from the core verb and move to the end of the sentence. Unlike inseparable prefixes, which do not look like words, separable prefixes *do* look like words and therefore are more literal in meaning and thus easier to learn, remember, and use correctly.

Pronunciation note: Verbs with separable prefixes have their main stress on the prefix, which usually looks like a preposition or an adverb, e.g., ***an*kommen**, ***aus*machen**, ***mit*arbeiten**, ***zu*hören**, ***um*steigen**.

Learn the meanings and the principal parts of the following verbs, especially the formation of past participles. Note how the prefixes separate from the core verb to allow the insertion of a **ge**- prefix. The list may seem a bit overpowering at first glance, but these verbs are merely variations of the basic verbs you have reviewed and learned previously. If you have mastered those verbs' principal parts, this becomes then essentially a vocabulary exercise.

Common Verbs with Separable Prefixes

- **Ab-** *off, away, down*

abfahren *to drive off*	fährt ... ab, fuhr ... ab, *ist* abgefahren
abholen *to pick up*	holt ... ab, holte ... ab, abgeholt
abnehmen *to take off weight*	nimmt ... ab, nahm ... ab, abgenommen
abschließen *to lock, complete*	schließt ... ab, schloss ... ab, abgeschlossen
abschneiden *to cut off*	schneidet ... ab, schnitt ... ab, abgeschnitten
abschreiben *to copy*	schreibt ... ab, schrieb ... ab, abgeschrieben

- **An-** *on, at, to*

anfangen *to begin*	fängt ... an, fing ... an, angefangen
anhören *to listen to*	hört ... an, hörte ... an, angehört
ankommen *to arrive*	kommt ... an, kam ... an, *ist* angekommen
anmachen *to turn on*	macht ... an, machte ... an, angemacht
anrufen *to call up* (phone)	ruft ... an, rief ... an, angerufen
ansehen *to look at, watch*	sieht ... an, sah ... an, angesehen

- **Auf-** *up, open, on*

aufheben *to lift up*	hebt ... auf, hob ... auf, aufgeboben
aufhören *to stop, cease*	hört ... auf, hörte ... auf, aufgehört
aufmachen *to open [up]*	macht ... auf, machte ... auf, aufgemacht
aufpassen *to pay attention*	passt ... auf, passte ... auf, aufgepasst
aufräumen *to straighten up*	räumt ... auf, räumte ... auf, aufgeräumt
aufstehen *to stand/get up*	steht ... auf, stand ... auf, *ist* aufgestanden
aufwachen *to wake up*	wacht ... auf, wachte ... auf, *ist* aufgewacht

- **Aus-** *out, off*

ausbrechen *to break out*	bricht ... aus, brach ... aus, *ist* ausgebrochen
ausgeben *to spend*	gibt ... aus, gab ... aus, ausgegeben
ausgehen *to go out*	geht ... aus, ging ... aus, *ist* ausgegangen
auslachen *to mock, make fun of*	lacht ... aus, lachte ... aus, ausgelacht
ausmachen *to turn out, turn off*	macht ... aus, machte ... aus, ausgemacht
aussehen *to look, appear*	sieht ... aus, sah ... aus, ausgesehen
austauschen *to exchange*	tauscht ... aus, tauschte ... aus, ausgetauscht
ausziehen *to pull off, undress*	zieht ... aus, zog ... aus, ausgezogen

- **Ein-** *in, into*

einführen *to introduce*	führt ... ein, führte ... ein, eingeführt
einkaufen *to shop*	kauft ... ein, kaufte ... ein, eingekauft
einladen *to invite*	lädt ... ein, lud ... ein, eingeladen
eintreten *to enter, step into*	tritt ... ein, trat ... ein, *ist* eingetreten

- **Fern-** *distant, far off*

fernsehen *to watch TV*	sieht ... fern, sah ... fern, ferngesehen

- **Fort-** *away, forth*

fortfahren *to depart* (by vehicle)	fährt ... fort, fuhr ... fort, *ist* fortgefahren
fortgehen *to depart* (on foot)	geht ... fort, ging ... fort, *ist* fortgegangen
fortsetzen *to continue, set forth*	setzt ... fort, setzte ... fort, fortgesetzt

- **Los-** *loose* (a detachment of some kind is indicated)

loslassen *to let go, let loose*	lässt ... los, ließ ... los, losgelassen
loslösen *to detach*	löst ... los, löste ... los, losgelöst
losschneiden *to cut loose*	schneidet ... los, schnitt ... los, losgeschnitten
loswerden *to get rid of*	wird ... los, wurde ... los, *ist* losgeworden

- **Mit-** *with, along [with]*

mitbringen *to bring along*	bringt ... mit, brachte ... mit, mitgebracht
mitgehen *to go along*	geht ... mit, ging ... mit, *ist* mitgegangen
mitkommen *to come along*	kommt ... mit, kam ... mit, *ist* mitgekommen
mitmachen *to participate*	macht ... mit, machte ... mit, mitgemacht
mitspielen *to play with*	spielt ... mit, spielte ... mit, mitgespielt
mitteilen *to inform, tell*	teilt ... mit, teilte ... mit, mitgeteilt

- **Nach-** *after, behind*

nacherzählen *to retell*	erzählt ... nach, erzählte ... nach, nacherzählt
nachgeben *to give in*	gibt ... nach, gab ... nach, nachgegeben
nachschlagen *to look up*	schlägt ... nach, schlug ... nach, nachgeschlagen

- **Um-** *around, over, about*

umdrehen *to turn around*	dreht ... um, drehte ... um, umgedreht
umkippen *to tip over*	kippt ... um, kippte ... um, *ist/hat* umgekippt
umsteigen *to transfer* (train, bus)	steigt ... um, stieg ... um, *ist* umgestiegen
umziehen *to move* (one's residence)	zieht ... um, zog ... um, *ist* umgezogen

- **Vor-** *before, ahead of time (pre-)*

vorbereiten *to prepare*	bereitet ... vor, bereitete ... vor, vorbereitet
vorgehen *to run fast* (clock)	geht ... vor, ging ... vor, *ist* vorgegangen
vorhaben *to intend*	hat ... vor, hatte ... vor, vorgehabt
vorlesen *to lecture, read aloud*	liest ... vor, las ... vor, vorgelesen
vorschlagen *to suggest*	schlägt ... vor, schlug ... vor, vorgeschlagen
vorstellen *to introduce*	stellt ... vor, stellte ... vor, vorgestellt

- **Vorbei-** *by, past*

vorbeifahren *to drive by*	fährt ... vorbei, fuhr ... vorbei, *ist* vorbeigefahren
vorbeikommen *to come by*	kommt ... vorbei, kam ... vorbei, *ist* vorbeigekommen
vorbeilaufen *to run by*	läuft ... vorbei, lief ... vorbei, *ist* vorbeigelaufen

- **Weg-** *away*

wegfahren *to drive away*	fährt ... weg, fuhr ... weg, *ist* weggefahren
weggehen *to go away*	geht ... weg, ging ... weg, *ist* weggegangen
weglaufen *to run away*	läuft ... weg, lief ... weg, *ist* weggelaufen
wegstellen *to put away*	stellt ... weg, stellte ... weg, weggestellt
wegwerfen *to throw away*	wirft ... weg, warf ... weg, weggeworfen

- **Weiter-** *further, farther, additionally, continually*

weiterfahren *to travel farther*	fährt ... weiter, fuhr ... weiter, *ist* weitergefahren
weitergehen *to go farther*	geht ... weiter, ging ... weiter, *ist* weitergegangen
weiterlesen *to read further*	liest ... weiter, las ... weiter, weitergelesen
weitermachen *to carry on*	macht ... weiter, machte ... weiter, weitergemacht

- **Zu-** *to, toward, closed, shut off*

zuhören *to listen to*	hört ... zu, hörte ... zu, zugehört
zumachen *to close*	macht ... zu, machte ... zu, zugemacht
zunehmen *to gain/put on weight*	nimmt ... zu, nahm ... zu, zugenommen
zuwinken *to wave to/at*	winkt ... zu, winkte ... zu, zugewinkt

- **Zurück-** *back*

zurückbleiben *to stay behind*	bleibt ... zurück, blieb ... zurück, *ist* zurückgeblieben
zurückbringen *to bring back*	bringt ... zurück, brachte ... zurück, zurückgebracht
zurückgehen *to go back*	geht ... zurück, ging ... zurück, *ist* zurückgegangen
zurückkommen *to come back*	kommt ... zurück, kam ... zurück, *ist* zurückgekommen
zurückwerfen *to throw back*	wirft ... zurück, warf ... zurück, zurückgeworfen

- **Zusammen-** *together*

zusammenarbeiten *to work together, collaborate*	arbeitet ... zusammen, arbeitete ... zusammen, zusammengearbeitet
zusammenbinden *to tie/bind together*	bindet ... zusammen, band ... zusammen, zusammengebunden
zusammenbrechen *to collapse*	bricht ... zusammen, brach ... zusammen, *ist* zusammengebrochen
zusammenbringen *to bring together, join*	bringt ... zusammen, brachte ... zusammen, zusammengebracht
zusammenkommen *to come together, assemble*	kommt ... zusammen, kam ... zusammen, *ist* zusammengekommen
zusammenstellen *to put/place together*	stellt ... zusammen, stellte ... zusammen, zusammengestellt

Present and Simple Past

In the present and simple past tenses separable prefixes break off from the main verb and migrate to the end of the sentence where verb complements are normally located.

present:

Hans **schneidet** ein Stück Brot **ab**.
Hans is cutting off a piece of bread.

Am Freitagabend **gehen** wir immer **aus**.
We always go out on Friday evening.

Ich **wache** jeden Morgen um sechs Uhr **auf**.
I wake up every morning at six o'clock.

Wen **lädst** du zur Party **ein**?
Whom are you inviting to the party?

simple past:

Harald **teilte** mir **mit**, dass er bald eine neue Arbeitsstelle suchen wird.
Harald informed me that he will be looking for a new position soon.

Karola **fuhr** nach Hause **zurück**.
Karola drove back home.

Das Glas Milch **kippte** plötzlich **um**.
The glass of milk suddenly tipped over.

Unsere Freunde **kamen** kurz nach acht **vorbei**.
Our friends came by shortly after eight.

Wir **setzten** unsere Konversation leise und geheim **fort**.
We continued our conversation quietly and secretly.

NOTE: In subordinate clauses containing a verb with a separable prefix in the present or simple past, the verb and the prefix join up as one word at the end of the clause:

Ich verstehe nicht, was er uns **vorschlägt**.
I don't understand what he is suggesting to us.

Ich hörte nicht, was er **vorschlug**.
I didn't hear what he suggested.

Present Perfect

Selection of Helping Verb

As you have learned, the present perfect is formed by using either **haben** or **sein** as the helping verb along with a past participle at the end of the sentence. Remember that **haben** is the helping verb for all transitive verbs and **sein** is the helping verb for intransitive verbs that signal a change in position or condition.

Formation of the Past Participle: Prefix + *-ge-* + Verb Stem + -[*e*]*t*/*-en*

The past participle is formed by inserting a -**ge**- between the prefix and the verb stem. The past participle will end in -**t** or -**et** if the verb is regular and -**en** if the verb is irregular. Note: This means that in the past participle the prefix is still separated from the verb stem by -**ge**-.

regular verbs:	auf**ge**macht, an**ge**hört, fort**ge**setzt, mit**ge**teilt, um**ge**kippt, vor**ge**stellt
irregular verbs:	aus**ge**gangen, an**ge**rufen, vorbei**ge**kommen, zusammen**ge**brochen

An exception to this is when the separable prefix is affixed to a verb that also contains an inseparable prefix. No participial **ge**- can be added because of the presence of the inseparable prefix:

nacherzählen → **nacherzählt** vorbereiten → **vorbereitet**

Word Order

The helping verb **haben** or **sein** goes into normal verb position for the sentence type and the past participle is located at the end of the sentence.

regular verbs:

Ich **habe** das Buch auf Seite 231 **aufgemacht**.
I opened the book to page 321.

Die Kinder **haben** stundenlang Rockmusik **angehört**.
The children listened to rock music for hours on end.

Toni und Anke **haben** ihr Gespräch am nächsten Tag **fortgesetzt**.
Toni and Anke continued their discussion the next day.

Warum **hast** du mir nichts davon **mitgeteilt**?
Why didn't you inform me/tell me anything about it?

Der alte Mann **ist** mit seinem wackeligen Stuhl plötzlich **umgekippt**.
The old man tipped over suddenly along with his wobbly chair.

Ich glaube, ihr **habt** uns euren Vater schon einmal **vorgestellt**.
I think you've introduced your father to us once before.

irregular verbs: Wir **sind** gegen neun Uhr mit unseren Freunden **ausgegangen.**
We went out with our friends at around nine o'clock.

Warum **hast** du deine Großeltern zu Weihnachten nicht **angerufen**?
Why didn't you call your grandparents at/for Christmas?

Bist du mehrmals auf der langen Reise mit der Bahn **umgestiegen**?
Did you change trains several times on the long trip?

Seid ihr gestern Nachmittag oder gestern Abend **vorbeigekommen**?
Did you come by yesterday afternoon or yesterday evening?

Ich **habe** meine kaputte Armbanduhr **weggeworfen.**
I threw my broken watch away.

Das Gebäude war schwach gebaut und **ist** während des Erdbebens **zusammengebrochen.**
The building was poorly constructed and collapsed during the earthquake.

Past Perfect

The past perfect is formed exactly like the present perfect tense except that forms of **hatten** and **waren** are used as helping verbs:

Nachdem wir nach London **geflogen waren**, sind wir mit dem Eurostar nach Frankreich gefahren.
After we had flown to London, we traveled to France with the Eurostar°. *high-speed Chunnel train*

Warst du wirklich so früh am Morgen **aufgestanden**?
Had you really gotten up so early in the morning?

Wir **hatten** unsere Sachen noch nicht **weggestellt**, als das Feuer ausbrach.
We had not yet put away our things when the fire broke out.

Bernd **hatte** die Handschrift seines Vaters ganz genau **abgeschrieben.**
Bernd had copied his father's handwriting precisely.

Future

The future is formed by using **werden** as the helping verb with an infinitive at the end of the sentence.

Wann **wirst** du dein Studium **abschließen**?
When will you complete your studies?

Werden wir dieses Wochenende irgendeinen Film **ansehen**?
Will we watch a film this weekend?
Are we going to watch a film this weekend?

Später **werde** ich mein Büro **aufräumen.**
I'll straighten up my office later.

Wann **wird** die Lehrerin das neue Kapitel **einführen**?
When will the teacher introduce the new chapter?

Werdet ihr etwas zur Party **mitbringen**?
Will you be bringing something [along] to the party?

Commands and Requests

Commands formed with verbs with separable prefixes are straightforward and follow normal expectations.

familiar singular	*familiar plural*	*polite/formal*
Nimm es **weg.**	**Nehmt** es **weg.**	**Nehmen Sie** es **weg.**
Fang damit **an.**	**Fangt** damit **an.**	**Fangen Sie** damit **an.**
Mach mir die Tür **auf.**	**Macht** mir die Tür **auf.**	**Machen Sie** mir die Tür **auf.**
Zieh dich **an.**	**Zieht** euch **an.**	**Ziehen Sie** sich **an.**
Lade meinen Freund **ein.**	**Ladet** meinen Freund **ein.**	**Laden Sie** meinen Freund **ein.**
Lass es **los.**	**Lasst** es **los.**	**Lassen Sie** es **los.**
Bring etwas **mit.**	**Bringt** etwas **mit.**	**Bringen Sie** etwas **mit.**
Kipp es nicht **um.**	**Kippt** es nicht **um.**	**Kippen Sie** es nicht **um.**

Suggestions are formed similarly to commands:

Gehen wir alle **mit.**	**Spielen wir mit.**	**Bereiten wir** uns darauf **vor.**
Steigen wir in Köln **um.**	**Hören wir** ihm gut **zu.**	**Werfen wir** die Dosen **weg.**

Exercises

Theory Review

1. Fill in the blanks with the correct information.

1. Verb prefixes that look like words, not merely syllables, are generally ______________________ prefixes.
2. The type of word these prefixes resemble most is the ______________________.
3. Do these prefixes therefore have meaning in their own right? ____________
4. Does this make the meaning of verbs with these prefixes relatively easy to determine? ________
5. Is the primary stress on the prefix or on the stem of the core verb? Stress is on the __________.
6. Does the prefix separate from the core verb in the present and simple past tenses? __________
7. In these tenses the prefix moves to the ________________ of the sentence.
8. When forming the present and past perfect, the selection of **haben** or **sein** as the helping verb will be determined by the ________________ of the verb.
9. As you learned in the previous chapter, verbs with inseparable prefixes did not employ a ________________ prefix on the past participle.
10. Do verbs with separable prefixes employ this prefix? ____________
11. Where is this prefix placed? ________________
12. Remember that a verb that never undergoes a stem change will have a past participle that ends in ____________.

13. A verb that does undergo a stem change will have a past participle that ends in ____________.
14. Are there any inherent differences in word order with separable-prefix verbs in the various tenses, other than the fact that the prefix is moveable? ____________
15. When formulating commands and requests, whether formal or informal, singular or plural, the last unit heard is the ________________.
16. Under the new spelling guidelines, the correct punctuation at the end of the command is a ________________.

Focus on Form [✓]

2. Generate sentences in the present tense from the fragments.

A

1. Jeden Abend / fernsehen / ich / ein bisschen

___

2. Endlich / loswerden / wir / diesen Unsinn

___

3. Mitbringen / ihr / eure Instrumente?

___

4. Mitgehen / du / auch?

___

5. Jeder Student / vorbereiten / sich / auf das Examen

___

6. Meine Uhr / vorgehen / drei Minuten

___

7. Was / vorhaben / du?

___

8. Franz / abschließen / sein Studium / im Jahre 2010

___

9. Wann / anfangen / das Konzert?

___

10. Die Musikstudenten / anhören / die Sinfonie von Mahler.

___

B

1. Die Lehrer / aufpassen / immer / auf die Schüler

2. Ich / aufwachen / jeden Morgen / um sieben Uhr

3. Wie viel Geld / ausgeben / du / dafür?

4. Unsere Kinder / ausziehen / sich / immer / sehr langsam

5. Viele Eltern / einkaufen / am Samstagmorgen / von neun bis Mittag

6. Wie viele Gäste / einladen / ihr / zur Party?

7. Wir / wegstellen / unsere Sachen / jetzt

8. Warum / wegwerfen / du / deine alte Kleidung?

9. Warum / zurückbringen / du / es / nicht?

10. Die Mitglieder des Vereins / zusammenkommen / wegen der Tournee

3. Change the following sentences from the present to the simple past.

1. Man setzt das Spiel nach dem Gewitter fort.

2. Der Vater lässt seinen Sohn plötzlich los.

3. Alle machen mit.

4. Wir erzählen die Witze nach.

5. Andreas schlägt viele Wörter im Wörterbuch nach.

6. Das Kind dreht sich blitzschnell um.

___

7. Die Reisenden steigen in Berlin um.

___

8. Der Professor liest aus seinen Notizen vor.

___

9. Udo fährt sehr böse ab.

___

10. Klara nimmt zehn Kilo ab.

___

4. Indicate whether *haben* or *sein* is the correct helping verb in the present perfect for these verbs and then indicate the correct past participle.

Example: einsteigen → *ist eingestiegen*

abschneiden	___	loslassen	___
abschreiben	___	loswerden	___
anfangen	___	mitkommen	___
anrufen	___	nachbleiben	___
aufpassen	___	umdrehen	___
aufräumen	___	umziehen	___
austauschen	___	vorschlagen	___
ausziehen	___	vorstellen	___
einführen	___	vorbeikommen	___
einladen	___	wegwerfen	___
fernsehen	___	zuwinken	___
fortsetzen	___	zusammenarbeiten	___

5. Form sentences in the present perfect from the fragments.

1. Ich / loslösen / die zwei Karten / voneinander

___

2. Warum / mitkommen / er und seine Söhne?

___

3. Davon / mitteilen / sie / uns / nichts

___

4. Die Vase / umkippen / plötzlich

5. Als Kind / umziehen / ich / dreimal

6. Klara / abnehmen / zehn Kilo

7. Die Köchin / abschneiden / die Spargelspitzen

8. Warum / ankommen / du / so spät?

9. Alle Schüler / aufmachen / die Bücher

10. Der Junge / aufräumen / sein Zimmer

6. Form sentences in the past perfect from the fragments.

1. Um Mitternacht / ausmachen / ich / das Licht

2. Ausgehen / ihr / mit euren Freunden?

3. Der Beamte / eintreten / in sein Büro

4. Die Chefin / einführen / den neuen Plan

5. Eine Schülerin / abschreiben / während der Klausur

7. Change the following sentences from the present to the future.

1. Der Philosoph schlägt heute eine neue Interpretation der Theorie vor.

2. Wir stellen der Lehrerin unsere Eltern vor.

3. Karola kommt später am Abend vorbei.

4. Helmut geht schnell nach Hause zurück.

5. Wann kommst du zurück?

6. Die Kinder lachen den Lehrer bestimmt aus.

8. Paraphrasing. The simple past (written past) and the present perfect (spoken past) are equivalent in meaning. Express the same sentence in the present perfect tense.

1. Die Männer fuhren an unserem Haus vorbei.

2. Ohne ein einziges Wort zu sagen ging Hanna verärgert weg.

3. Die Kinder liefen von dem Fremden weg.

4. Im Hörsaal hörten die Studenten dem Professor sehr genau zu.

5. Das Kind machte die Tür langsam und vorsichtig auf.

6. Ich nahm ein bisschen zu viel ab.

7. Beim Abschied winkte sie mir ganz freundlich zu.

8. Wann kamst du zurück?

9. Der Angler warf den kleinen Fisch ins Wasser zurück.

10. Die Sekretärinnen arbeiteten sehr gut miteinander zusammen.

Focus on Meaning and Form

9. Statements. Tell me in German that . . .

1. you are picking me up at seven o'clock ______
2. you tied the two pieces together ______
3. the movie starts at eight o'clock ______
4. they completed their studies ______
5. you all watched a couple of movies ______
6. your mother got up at eight o'clock ______
7. my sister looks very tired ______
8. you are inviting lots of friends to the party ______
9. you are coming along, too ______
10. you are going to read on for a while ______
11. I am putting on lots of weight ______
12. you are finally losing weight ______
13. you are going back home soon ______

10. Questions. Ask me if I . . .

1. am copying your homework ______
2. am going out this weekend ______
3. have any plans for this evening ______
4. am driving back to Oldenburg ______
5. spent a lot of money ______
6. prepared supper ______
7. I'll be picking you up ______
8. am continuing the project ______
9. plan to carry on ______

11. Questions. Find out . . .

1. when I'll be arriving ______
2. why I turned the light off ______
3. when I woke up ______

4. whom I invited to the party ______

5. when I watched TV ______

6. why I let it go ______

7. why I didn't inform you about it ______

8. when the summer vacation begins ______

12. Commands. Tell me to . . .

1. put the parts of the plan together

______

2. collaborate better with my coworkers

______

3. listen to you carefully (i.e., *precisely*)

______

4. put these papers away ______

5. suggest something ______

You Determine the Message and Form

13. Write commands as directed.

1. Generate three commands to a stranger with these verbs. Add whatever is needed.

   ankommen ______

   vorschlagen ______

   zurückkommen ______

2. Generate three commands to a brother or sister with these verbs. Add whatever is needed.

   aufhören ______

   aufräumen ______

   loslassen ______

3. Generate three commands to two or three children with these verbs. Add whatever is needed.

   anmachen ______

   ausziehen ______

   weglaufen ______

Partnerarbeit

14. Prepare this exercise prior to your next instructional period. Use the verbs and phrases listed below to write a conversational narrative in the *present perfect* about what you did yesterday. Write a simple sentence for each verb, and yes, fabricate if you must to keep the chronology going. Try using several complements (objects, adverbs, etc.) per sentence and use inverted word order for some of the sentences. The main goal is to demonstrate you can use these verbs correctly. In class, work with a partner: read your narratives to each other and ask questions to find out more details about each other's activities.

aufwachen *Ich bin heute Morgen um sieben Uhr aufgewacht.*

verschlafen ______

müde sein ______

im Bett bleiben ______

aufstehen ______

sich duschen ______

sich anziehen ______

das Frühstück machen ______

essen und trinken ______

lesen ______

das Haus verlassen ______

die Haustür schließen ______

auf den Bus warten ______

zur Uni fahren ______

Kurse haben ______

in der Mensa sein ______

einen Kaffee bestellen ______

Freunde treffen ______

in die Bibliothek gehen ______

Bücher suchen ______

nichts Gutes finden ______

nach Hause fahren ____________________

Sport treiben ____________________

das Abendesssen vorbereiten ____________________

essen und trinken ____________________

für einen Test lernen ____________________

Hausaufgaben für morgen erledigen ____________________

Freunde anrufen ____________________

fernsehen ____________________

müde werden ____________________

sich ausziehen ____________________

sich waschen ____________________

einschlafen ____________________

gut schlafen ____________________

15. Arbeiten Sie mit einem Partner/einer Partnerin und beantworten Sie diese Fragen mündlich.

A

1. Wann gehst du wieder nach Hause zurück?
2. Wem hast du neulich sehr genau zugehört? Warum?
3. Was hast du in den letzten paar Tagen weggeworfen?
4. Wem hast du diese Woche etwas vorgeschlagen? Was war der Vorschlag?
5. Was hast du dieses Wochenende vor?

B

1. Wer ist mit dir das letzte Mal ins Kino gegangen? Welchen Film habt ihr gesehen? Wie hast du ihn gefunden?
2. Was wirst du bald loswerden? Warum?
3. Wie viele Stunden siehst du jeden Tag fern? Welche Sendungen findest du gut?
4. Welche elektronischen Geräte hast du heute an- oder ausgemacht?
5. Mit wem bist du das letzte Mal ausgegangen? Wohin?

C

1. Wie viel Geld hast du dieses Semester für deine Bücher ausgegeben?
2. Wann bist du heute aufgewacht und aufgestanden?
3. Was hast du neulich aufgeräumt?
4. Was hast du neulich angesehen oder angehört?
5. Mit welchem Projekt wirst du bald anfangen?

Gruppenarbeit

16. Simple past narration. Join with two other students and use the sentence fragments to form a simple oral narrative in the simple past. The fragments are in outline form and clustered in groups of three or four so you can generate a long sentence that contains three or four actions, for example: I got up at 6:30, was tired, and lay in bed for about 30 minutes.

Follow the phrases line by line and from left to right. See if you can combine the sentences you generate into longer multidimensional ones by using conjunctions and time markers to link them together. This will give your narrative better "flow."

um halb sieben aufwachen • müde sein • 30 Minuten im Bett liegen • um sieben aufstehen
sich das Gesicht waschen • wach werden • sich rasieren/mir die Haare kämmen/bürsten
warme Kleidung suchen • sich schnell anziehen • heute einen Pulli tragen
das Frühstück machen • Schinken, Eier und Kartoffeln essen • Saft und Kaffee trinken
um acht zur Uni fahren • den Bus nehmen • mit Verspätung an der Uni ankommen
ein paar Vorlesungen haben • Professor langweilig finden • heute eine Deutschprüfung haben
in die Mensa gehen • Essen bestellen • Freunde treffen • mit ihnen zusammenreden
in die Bibliothek gehen • ein paar Bücher suchen • eine Stunde da verbringen
um vier nach Hause zurückfahren • ein Schläfchen machen • dann eine Weile spazieren gehen
das Abendessen vorbereiten • Pasta kochen • Fleischbälle kochen • Wein dazu trinken
ein paar Stunden lernen • Hausaufgaben haben/machen • mit einer Semesterarbeit anfangen
müde werden • heute sehr viel arbeiten • ein bisschen fernsehen
ins Badezimmer gehen • sich ausziehen • sich waschen • sich die Zähne putzen
den Wecker für sieben Uhr stellen • ins Bett springen • ein bisschen in einem Roman lesen
sehr schläfrig werden • das Licht endlich ausmachen • Augen zumachen
schnell einschlafen • tief schlafen • süße Träume haben

Chapter 8 Modal Auxiliaries

Part One

Modal verbs are helping verbs that express the attitude or disposition of the subject toward the action or state indicated by the finite (main) verb. That is, modal verbs signal how the subject "feels" about or is attitudinally disposed toward what's happening.

müssen:	attitude: necessity	*have to; must*
sollen:	attitude: obligation	*supposed to; obligated to; expected to*
wollen:	attitude: desire	*want to; wish to; desire to*
können:	attitude: ability	*can, able to, know how to*
dürfen:	attitude: permission	*may; allowed to; permitted to*
mögen:	attitude: liking	*like; like to*

Present Tense of Modal Verbs

Study the present-tense forms of the modal verbs below and note their especially irregular **ich**- and **er/sie/es**-forms:

Forms of Modal Verbs: Present Tense

	können			**dürfen**	
ich **kann**	wir **können**		ich **darf**	wir **dürfen**	
du **kannst**	ihr **könnt**	Sie **können**	du **darst**	ihr **dürft**	Sie **dürfen**
er/sie/es **kann**	sie **können**		er/sie/es **darf**	sie **dürfen**	
	sollen			**wollen**	
ich **soll**	wir **sollen**		ich **will**	wir **wollen**	
du **sollst**	ihr **sollt**	Sie **sollen**	du **willst**	ihr **wollt**	Sie **wollen**
er/sie/es **soll**	sie **sollen**		er/sie/es **will**	sie **wollen**	
	müssen			**mögen**	
ich **muss**	wir **müssen**		ich **mag**	wir **mögen**	
du **musst**	ihr **müsst**	Sie **müssen**	du **magst**	ihr **mögt**	Sie **mögen**
er/sie/es **muss**	sie **müssen**		er/sie/es **mag**	sie **mögen**	

Observe how the following sentences, though identical in structure, take on different meanings with different modal verbs:

Er **kann** das jetzt **machen**. *He **can do** that now.*	Er **will** das jetzt **machen**. *He **wants to do** that now.*	Er **soll** das jetzt **machen**. *He **is supposed to do** that now.*
Er **muss** das jetzt **machen**. *He **has to do** that now.*	Er **darf** das jetzt **machen**. *He **may do** that now.*	

Note the following about the forms of the modal verbs:

1. The **ich**- and **er/sie/es**-forms have no ending.
2. The present singular stems are usually different from the infinitive stem.
3. The plural forms follow the expected ending patterns.

Memorize these forms so they become second nature to you.

Word Order: Modal Verb + Infinitive at End

Modal verbs in the present require an infinitive to complete meaning in a sentence. The modal verb occupies normal verb position and the main verb morphs into an infinitive, a neutral verb form, and migrates to the end of the sentence:

Ich **kann** heute Abend **mitkommen**.
Darfst du jetzt hier **sein**?
Jeder Student **soll** das **wissen**.
Wann **wollen** wir morgen Abend **ausgehen**?
Ihr **müsst** schneller **arbeiten**, Leute.

Meanings of Modals

Müssen, sollen, können, and *dürfen*

- With **müssen** the subject has no real choice about the action:

  Ich **muss** das machen, oder ich bin so gut wie tot!
  *I **have to** do that or I'm as good as dead.*

- With **sollen** the subject is obligated or under pressure to perform an action; it does have a choice about the action, however. Guilt or failure will be the price paid if the action is not performed:

  Ich **soll** fleißig **lernen**, um gute Noten zu bekommen.
  *I **ought to** study hard to earn good grades.*

- In colloquial speech **können** is sometimes used instead of **dürfen**. As an educated speaker, however, avoid it. Remember this infamous, universal example:

  Kind: Mutti, **kann** ich ins Kino **gehen**?
  Mutter: Ja, du **kannst** in Kino **gehen**, denn du hast zwei gute Beine. Du **darfst** aber nicht ins Kino **gehen**, weil dein Zimmer wie ein Schweinestall aussieht!

Mögen and the *möchte*-Forms

Remember that **mögen** in the indicative is used now primarily as a transitive verb to indicate that one likes someone or something:

Mögen Sie süße Schokolade?
Do you like sweet chocolate?

Ich **mag** diese Bluse nicht.
I don't like this blouse.

However, the subjunctive of **mögen**, the **möchte**-form, is commonly used to indicate that one *would like something* or *would like to do something.* The present subjunctive forms of **mögen** are used just like the other modal verbs, that is, with the infinitive at the end of the sentence. It will be useful to review them now, even though the subjunctive is not the focal point of this chapter.

möchte-Forms		
ich **möchte**	wir **möchten**	
du **möchtest**	ihr **möchtet**	Sie **möchten**
er/sie/es **möchte**	sie **möchten**	

Ich **möchte** dieses Jahr in der Türkei Urlaub **machen.**
I'd like to take a vacation in Turkey this year.

Möchtest du mit mir **ausgehen**?
Would you like to go out with me?

Möchtet ihr ein Glas Wein **trinken**?
Would you like to drink a glass of wine?

Wir **möchten** bald nach Hause **gehen.**
We'd like to go home soon.

Gern haben = mögen

The idiom **gern haben** (*to like*), a substitute for **mögen**, should be used mainly with direct objects that are persons (or pets), not things. This idiom **gern haben** conveys an *affectionate* feeling for living things.

Inge **hat** Helmut **gern.**
Ich **habe** deine Familie **gern.**
Petra **hat** deinen Hund nicht **gern.**

LESS COMMON: Inge **hat** die Suppe **gern.**
BETTER: Inge **mag** die Suppe.

Using Modal Verbs with the Negators *nicht* and *kein*

In most cases, **nicht** negates the attitude expressed by the modal verb. Sometimes using **kein** with the object has the same effect:

nicht können	*not able to*	Ich kann das nicht machen, weil ich nicht begabt bin. *I can't do that because I'm not talented.*
nicht wollen	*do not want to*	Ich will nicht mit dir tanzen, weil du zwei linke Beine hast. *I don't want to dance with you because you have two left feet.*
nicht dürfen	*not permitted/allowed to* (used to scold)	Du darfst kein Bier trinken, weil du nur vierzehn Jahre alt bist. *You're not allowed to drink any beer because you're only fourteen.*
nicht sollen	*not supposed to* (used to advise someone strongly)	Du sollst nicht hier sein. Deine Eltern werden böse auf dich sein. *You're not supposed to be here. Your parents will be angry at you.*
nicht mögen	*don't like*	Ich mag dich nicht, weil du immer lügst. *I don't like you because you're always lying.*
nicht müssen	*don't have to* (NOT: *must not*)	Ich muss nicht zu Hause bleiben, also darf ich mit euch ausgehen. *I don't have to stay at home, so I can go out with you.*

Note the relative emphatic strength, in decreasing order, of the following:

Mach das nicht!	=	*Don't do it!*
Du **darfst** das nicht machen.	=	*You must not do that.* (= You are not allowed to.)
Du **sollst** das nicht machen.	=	*You are not to do that.* (= You are obligated not to do that.)

Simple Past of Modal Verbs

Observe how the simple past forms of the modal verbs resemble the simple past of mixed verbs. Both have the stem changes of irregular verbs but employ the **-te** set of endings of regular verbs:

Forms of Modal Verbs: Simple Past

	können			**dürfen**	
ich **konnte**	wir **konnten**		ich **durfte**	wir **durften**	
du **konntest**	ihr **konntet**	Sie **konnten**	du **durftest**	ihr **durftet**	Sie **durften**
er/sie/es **konnte**	sie **konnten**		er/sie/es **durfte**	sie **durften**	
	sollen			**wollen**	
ich **sollte**	wir **sollten**		ich **wollte**	wir **wollten**	
du **solltest**	ihr **solltet**	Sie **sollten**	du **wolltest**	ihr **wolltet**	Sie **wollten**
er/sie/es **sollte**	sie **sollten**		er/sie/es **wollte**	sie **wollten**	
	müssen			**mögen**	
ich **musste**	wir **mussten**		ich **mochte**	wir **mochten**	
du **musstest**	ihr **musstet**	Sie **mussten**	du **mochtest**	ihr **mochtet**	Sie **mochten**
er/sie/es **musste**	sie **mussten**		er/sie/es **mochte**	sie **mochten**	

NOTE: There are no umlauted forms in the past tense.

Word Order of Modals in the Simple Past

Modal verbs in the simple past require an infinitive to complete meaning in a sentence, just as in the present tense. The modal verb occupies normal verb position and the main verb changes to an infinitive and moves to the end of the sentence:

Ich **konnte** gestern Abend früh von der Arbeit nach Hause **kommen.**
Durftest du das wirklich nicht **machen**?

Die Kandidatin **sollte** das bestimmt **wissen**.
Wir **wollten** heute Morgen etwas früher **aufstehen**.
Musstet ihr so viele neue Schuhe **kaufen**?

Remember that **mögen** is used primarily as a transitive verb:

Als Kind **mochte** ich allerlei Süßigkeiten.
As a child I liked all kinds of sweets.

Exercises: Part One

Theory Review

1. Fill in the blanks with the correct information.

1. Modal verbs express ______________________ or dispositions toward an action or state.
2. The action or state is named by the other verb in the sentence. This verb is always in the form of an _________________, a neutral verb form, and this verb is located at the _______________ of the sentence.
3. Whose attitude or disposition is expressed by the modal verb? ______________________
4. Name the attitude (not the translation, which can vary) expressed by these modal verbs:

   mögen ______________________ wollen ______________________

   dürfen ______________________ sollen ______________________

   können ______________________ müssen ______________________
5. In the present tense the modal verbs have no ending whatsoever in the ____________ and ____________ forms.
6. Except for **sollen**, all modal verbs have highly ______________________ stems in the present tense.
7. In the simple past the modal verbs have the ______________________ set of endings. Except for **wollen** and **sollen**, the others have ______________________ changes.
8. A common feature of the simple past is the total absence of ______________________.

Focus on Form [✓]

2. For each sentence, add the correct form of the cued modal verb and rewrite it.

1. Wir erledigen das für Montag. (*necessity*)

 ____

2. Ich gehe mit euch ins Kino. (*permisssion*)

 ____

3. Hilfst du mir? (*ability*)

 ____

4. Wir lernen es auswendig für die Prüfung. (*obligation*)

 ____

5. Es regnet morgen früh. (*expectation*)

 ____

6. Warum heiratest du ihn nicht? (*desire*)

 ____

7. Der Kunde bezahlt die Rechnung. (*necessity*)

 ____

8. Fotografiert man im Museum? (*permission*)

 ____

9. Ich verstehe ein bisschen Italienisch. (*ability*)

 ____

10. Ich sage es niemandem. (*obligation*)

 ____

3. Change the following sentences to the simple past.

1. Alex kann gut Tennis spielen. ______________________________
2. Unsere Eltern wollen eine Reise nach Graz machen.

 ____

3. Man darf da kein Bier trinken. ______________________________

4. Musst du das für den Kurs lesen? ____________________
5. Darfst du am Wochenende ausgehen? ____________________
6. Moni will nicht länger hier bleiben. ____________________
7. Wir können ihnen leider nicht helfen. ____________________
8. Sollst du das für heute erledigen? ____________________
9. Anke muss in die Stadt fahren. ____________________
10. Wir wollen eine Flasche Wein bestellen. ____________________
11. Die Kinder sollen auf Ilse warten. ____________________
12. Ich mag das nicht. ____________________
13. Kannst du nicht später mitkommen? ____________________
14. Franz will dich anrufen. ____________________

Focus on Meaning and Form

4. Express in good German:

A

1. It was supposed to snow on the weekend. ____________________
2. I don't know how to fix that. ____________________
3. May I have a piece of cake? ____________________
4. You simply have to eat something! ____________________
5. Didn't you want to play cards? ____________________
6. What are we supposed to do? ____________________
7. I can play a musical instrument. ____________________
8. People are not permitted to smoke in restaurants in many cities.
____
9. You didn't have to eat everything. ____________________
10. Hans would like to visit you sometime next week.
____

B

1. You may not go out with your friends tonight.

____

2. I couldn't eat that; it was awful. _______________
3. We didn't have to finish the assignment. _______________
4. Don't you want to listen to music? _______________
5. They aren't supposed to have any money. _______________
6. I don't like you. _______________
7. We weren't allowed to watch any television. _______________
8. I couldn't hide it. _______________
9. The weather is expected to be good this weekend. _______________
10. She didn't like the film. _______________

You Determine the Message and Form

5. Beantworten Sie diese Fragen.

1. Was soll man machen, wenn man ...

   fit bleiben will? _______________

   gesund bleiben will? _______________

   gute Noten haben will? _______________

   reich werden will? _______________

2. Was muss man machen, ...

   um in diesem Kurs erfolgreich zu sein? _______________

   um von Amerika nach Deutschland zu reisen? _______________

   um genug körperliche Energie zu haben? _______________

3. Was darf man normalerweise ...

   im Kino nicht machen? _______________

   im Klassenzimmer nicht machen? _______________

   bei einer Prüfung nicht machen? _______________

4. Was kann man machen, wenn ...

   das Auto kaputt ist? _______________

   es zu warm im Zimmer ist? _______________

   es zu dunkel ist? _______________

   man hungrig und durstig ist? _______________

Partnerarbeit

6. Arbeiten Sie mit einem Partner/einer Partnerin und beantworten Sie diese Fragen.

A

1. Was kannst du ziemlich gut machen oder leider nur schlecht machen?
2. Was darfst du nicht machen, wo du jetzt wohnst?
3. Kannst du jetzt ein Instrument spielen? Konntest du als Kind eins spielen?
4. Was solltest du gestern Abend für diesen Kurs machen?

B

1. Wie soll das Wetter am Wochenende sein?
2. Was wolltest du letztes Wochenende machen? Konntest du es machen? Wie war es?
3. Was solltest du neulich machen? Konntest du es machen? Wolltest du es machen?
4. Was möchtest du heute Abend machen, wenn du Zeit hast?
5. Was willst oder musst du bald kaufen?

C

1. Welche Dinge durftest du als Kind oder Teenager nicht machen? Warum nicht?
2. Was darf man mit 18 Jahren machen? Mit 21 Jahren?
3. Was wolltest du als kleines Kind immer haben? Als Teenager?
4. Welches Essen mochtest du als Kind? Welches mochtest du nicht?
5. Welche Fremdsprachen wolltest du immer lernen? Konntest du sie lernen? Welche Spiele mochtest du als Kind?

Part Two

Modal Verbs in Compound Tenses: Present Perfect, Past Perfect, and Future

When modal verbs require **haben** or **werden** to form tenses, a double-infinitive construction is automatically triggered:

Modal Verb + Helping Verb + Infinitive → Double Infinitive

present perfect:	Ich **habe** den Film **sehen wollen.**
past perfect:	Ich **hatte** den Film **sehen wollen.**
future:	Ich **werde** den Film **sehen wollen.**

The verb **haben** is helping the modal verb, not the main verb; all modal verbs require **haben** for the present perfect and past perfect tenses, never **sein**:

Wir **haben** als Kinder jeden Tag zur Schule **gehen müssen.**
When we were kids we had to go to school every day.

Ich **habe** letzten Sommer nach Europa **reisen können.**
I was able to travel to Europe last summer.

Hast du das ganze Wochenende zu Hause **bleiben sollen**?
Were you obliged to stay home the whole weekend?

Wirst du mit uns in den Park **gehen dürfen**?
Will you be able (that is, permitted) to go to the park with us?

Wann **werdet** ihr eure Hausaufgaben **machen müssen**?
When will you have to do your homework?

Remember, the simple past and present perfect tenses mean exactly the same thing. Since the simple past, normally reserved for written narration, is simpler to construct with modal verbs, it is frequently used in spoken German:

Ich **wollte** diesen Roman **lesen.** = Ich **habe** diesen Roman **lesen wollen.** = *I wanted to read this novel.*

Omitting an Obvious Main Verb

When the action verb (dependent infinitive) is obvious from context or has already been mentioned, it may be omitted:

obvious:	Ich **möchte** diesen Sommer nach Deutschland [fahren/reisen/fliegen].
already mentioned:	Hans: **Kannst** du mir zwanzig Euro **leihen**?
	Beate: Leider **kann** ich das nicht [machen].

When the main verb (dependent infinitive) is not mentioned explicitly in the present perfect and past perfect, no double infinitive is possible. Instead a "**ge** + stem + **t**" past participle is used:

gekonnt	**gemusst**	**gewollt**	**gesollt**	**gedurft**	**gemocht**

Silke:	Hast du immer nach Amerika fahren wollen?
Otto:	Ja, das **habe** ich immer **gewollt.**
Silke:	**Hast** du es nicht **gekonnt**?
Otto:	Ich **habe** es **gekonnt** aber leider nicht **gedurft.**

Brauchen + *zu* + Infinitive = *müssen* + Infinitive

The pseudo-modal verb **brauchen** is sometimes used colloquially as a substitute for **müssen.** Since **brauchen** is *not* a modal verb, it may not use a dependent infinitive alone. It needs a "boost" from **zu:**

Ich **muss** schneller **arbeiten.** = Ich **brauche** schneller ***zu*** **arbeiten.**
Ich **habe** schneller **arbeiten müssen.** = Ich **habe** schneller ***zu*** **arbeiten brauchen.**

While this is technically grammatically correct, it strikes many native speakers as odd-sounding. As a result, **brauchen** is often used colloquially as if it were a modal verb:

Du **brauchst** es nicht **machen.**

ADVICE: Use **müssen** + infinitive. There can be no dispute about its correctness. Use **brauchen** as a normal transitive verb.

Principal Parts of Modal Verbs

dürfen	darf	durfte	gedurft	*to be allowed/permitted to*
können	kann	konnte	gekonnt	*to be able to*
mögen	mag	mochte	gemocht	*to like [to]*
müssen	muss	musste	gemusst	*to have to, must*
sollen	soll	sollte	gesollt	*to be obligated to*
wollen	will	wollte	gewollt	*to want/wish/desire to*

Exercises: Part Two

Theory Review

1. Fill in the blanks with the correct information.

1. Once you use a modal verb in a compound tense or compound verb construction, that is, when there is a main verb and a helping verb besides the modal verb, a ________________ -infinitive construction results.
2. In the present perfect and past perfect, the helping verb is assisting the modal verb, and all modal verbs require ________________ as the helping verb. The infinitive of the main verb has no bearing on this.
3. In the future tense, the helping verb is always ________________.
4. Again, in the present perfect, past perfect, and future tenses, a ________________ -infinitive construction is required when there is a main verb, a modal verb, and a helping verb.
5. If the main verb has been mentioned previously or if it is perfectly obvious what verb that is, it may be ________________, a common occurrence in conversational German.
6. When that happens, no double-infinitive construction is possible. The past participle of the modal verb will then be formed as follows: ____________ + modal verb stem + ____________ ending.

Focus on Form [✓]

2. Rewrite the following sentences in the various tenses.

1. Ich kann das kaufen.
   simple past: ______________________
   pres. perf.: ______________________
   past perf.: ______________________
   future: ______________________
2. Maria will zur Party kommen.
   simple past: ______________________
   pres. perf.: ______________________
   past perf.: ______________________
   future: ______________________
3. Wir müssen diese Aufgabe fehlerfrei erledigen.
   simple past: ______________________
   pres. perf.: ______________________
   past perf.: ______________________
   future: ______________________
4. Hans darf das nicht kaufen.
   simple past: ______________________
   pres. perf.: ______________________
   past perf.: ______________________
   future: ______________________

3. Add the cued modal verb to the sentences. Do not change tenses.

1. Wir lernten Griechisch. (*desire*)
   ____
2. Gehst du mit uns ins Kino? (*permission*)
   ____
3. Unsere Eltern fuhren nach München. (*necessity*)
   ____
4. Karl machte das Abendessen fertig. (*obligation*)
   ____
5. Wir haben unsere Hausaufgaben nicht gemacht. (*ability*)
   ____
6. Maria ist mit Freunden ausgegangen. (*permission*)
   ____

7. Ich hatte meine Großeltern besucht. (*desire*)

8. Ich werde heute zu Hause bleiben. (*necessity*)

9. Das Wetter war gut. (*expectation*)

10. Wir machen dieses Jahr Urlaub in Florida. (*ability*)

Focus on Meaning and Form

4. Express the following in German. Use the present perfect for past actions.

1. Were you able to read the book?

2. I always wanted to do that.

3. I had to work late.

4. She was not permitted to do that.

5. You will have to wait awhile.

6. I wasn't able to help them.

7. I couldn't pay the bill.

8. I'll probably be able to go along.

9. I didn't like the film.

10. We were allowed to go out last night.

Partnerarbeit

5. Arbeiten Sie mit einem Partner/einer Partnerin und beantworten Sie diese Fragen.

1. Was hast du am Wochenende machen können?
2. Was wirst du für morgen oder übermorgen machen müssen?
3. Was wirst du kommendes Wochenende machen wollen?
4. Was wirst du in den Frühlingsferien machen können?
5. Wem hast du vor kurzem helfen sollen?
6. Was hast du als Kind nicht machen dürfen?
7. Was hast du als Teenager nicht machen wollen?

Phase II

Fundamentals of Case

Chapter 9 Nouns and Case

Part One

Nouns are words used to name a person, place, or thing. Nouns have two major dimensions: *gender* (masculine, feminine, and neuter) and *number* (singular or plural).

Gender in German

German makes use of both natural and grammatical genders. Natural gender is used for living things, male and female. Grammatical gender is used for inanimate things, which means that they may be masculine, feminine, or neuter. Some nouns designating living things are neuter, but the reasons for that are grammatical and not biological.

Masculine Nouns

The following noun categories are masculine:

- male persons: **Mann, Herr, Vater, Sohn, Bruder, Onkel, Opa, Junge, Bursche**
- male animals: **Hund, Kater, Tiger, Löwe**
- occupations: **Arbeiter, Lehrer, Student, Professor, Direktor, Arzt, Anwalt, Sekretär**
- nationalities: **Amerikaner, Deutscher, Engländer, Kanadier, Spanier, Franzose, Russe**
- makes of cars: **Volkswagen, Audi, Mercedes, Porsche, Opel, Ford**
- days of the week: **Montag, Dienstag, Mittwoch, Donnerstag, Freitag, Samstag/Sonnabend, Sonntag**
- parts of days: **Morgen, Vormittag, Mittag, Nachmittag, Abend** (BUT: ***die* Nacht**)
- months: **Januar, Februar, März, April, Mai, Juni, Juli, August, September, Oktober, November, Dezember**
- seasons: **Frühling, Sommer, Herbst, Winter**
- weather terms: **Regen, Schnee, Hagel, Nebel**
- directions: **Norden, Süden, Osten, Westen**
- nouns ending in **-en: Wagen, Garten, Hafen, Rücken, Ofen, Norden, Süden, Westen, Osten**
- most nouns ending in **-er: Rechner, Computer, Wecker, Hammer, Kopfhörer** (BUT: ***die* Mutter**)
- nouns ending in **-ich** or **-ig: Teppich, Honig, Essig, König**
- nouns ending in **-ang: Gang, Eingang, Ausgang, Klang, Fischfang, Rang, Vorrang, Vorhang, Zwang**
- Rhine river and its tributaries: **Rhein, Main, Neckar, Lech, Inn**

Feminine Nouns

The following noun categories are feminine:

- female persons: **Frau, Dame, Mutter, Tochter, Schwester, Oma, Tante, Kusine**
- female animals: **Hündin, Katze, Maus, Ratte**
- occupations: **Lehrerin, Studentin, Professorin, Direktorin, Ärztin, Anwältin, Sekretärin**
- nationalities: **Amerikanerin, Deutsche, Engländerin, Kanadierin, Französin, Russin**
- German rivers: **Elbe, Weser, Donau, Mosel, Ruhr**

Most nouns ending in these common endings and suffixes are feminine:

-e:	**Sprache, Hose, Lampe, Blume, Vase, Kreide, Decke, Ecke, Leine, Maschine, Garage**
-ei:	**Prügelei, Kanzlei, Polizei, Konditorei, Bücherei, Fleischerei, Schweinerei**
-enz:	**Existenz, Kompetenz, Residenz, Intelligenz**
-ie:	**Biologie, Chemie, Philosophie, Psychologie, Demokratie, Theorie**
-in:	**Mexikanerin, Schweizerin, Chefin, Forscherin, Präsidentin, Dolmetscherin**
-ik:	**Republik, Musik, Politik, Fabrik, Grammatik, Germanistik**
-ion:	**Religion, Revolution, Kaution, Nation, Union, Explosion**
-heit:	**Freiheit, Dummheit, Gleichheit, Dunkelheit, Krankheit**
-keit:	**Freundlichkeit, Feindlichkeit, Heiligkeit, Schwierigkeit, Süßigkeit**
-schaft:	**Freundschaft, Feindschaft, Nachbarschaft, Gesellschaft, Brüderschaft**
-tät:	**Qualität, Quantität, Universität, Spezialität, Aktivität, Brutalität**
-ung:	**Haltung, Handlung, Bildung, Landung, Entdeckung, Erfindung**
-ur:	**Natur, Struktur, Fraktur, Figur, Klausur, Reparatur** (BUT: ***das*** **Futur**)

Neuter Nouns

The following noun categories are **neuter**:

- small, immature persons and animals: **Baby, Kind, Mädchen, Lämmchen, Hündchen, Kätzchen**
- nouns ending in these common suffixes, both of which signal smallness and/or immaturity. These are sometimes referred to as diminutives:

-chen:	**Märchen, Kindchen, Männchen, Hündchen, Kätzchen, Schweinchen, Mäuschen**
-lein:	**Büchlein, Fischlein, Fräulein, Vögelein, Kindlein**
-el or **-l:**	**Mädel; Kindl, Dirndl**

- many nouns with the prefix **Ge-: Gemüse, Gebäude, Gepäck, Gedicht, Gespräch, Gehalt, Gesicht**
- most metals: **Eisen, Gold, Silber, Aluminium, Blei, Blech, Kupfer, Chrom** (BUT: ***der*** **Stahl**)
- most countries: **Deutschland, Irland, England, Italien, Spanien, Frankreich, Schweden, Norwegen**
- gerunds: **Schwimmen, Laufen, Spielen, Angeln, Wandern, Fliegen, Schreiben, Lesen, Weinen**
- letters of the alphabet: **A, B, C,** etc.
- fractions: **Drittel, Viertel, Fünftel, Sechstel, Zehntel, Zwanzigstel, Hundertstel, Tausendstel**

Weak Nouns/N-Nouns

Weak nouns—nowadays often referred to as "special nouns" or "**n**-nouns"—are masculine nouns that resemble feminine nouns insofar as many end in **-e** in the nominative singular, as do many feminine nouns, and they add **-n** or **-en** to the stem in other cases (**-e**, **-n**, and **-en** are essentially standard feminine noun endings). Examples:

Franzose	**Kollege**	**Neffe**
Junge	**Kunde**	**Russe**
Knabe	**Name**	**Zimmerkollege**

Other weak/**n**-nouns, loan words from French, end in a **t**-, **nt**-, or **st**-sound that is spelled with a final -**d**, -**t**, -**nt**, or -**st**. They are stressed on the last syllable, as are most French loan words:

Kamerad	**Agent**	**Präsident**	**Journalist**
Soldat	**Patient**	**Student**	**Polizist**

Some others end in -**r** (**Herr, Nachbar**) or **ts**-sounds (**Herz, Prinz**). Make note of them as they come up in this and future chapters.

Note how the **n**-sound is added to the noun in the singular once it is no longer in the nominative case:

nominative:	**Der Kunde** hat immer recht.
accusative:	Der Verkäufer hat **den Kunde*n*** schnell bedient.
dative:	Er hat **dem Kunde*n*** zwei Euro zurückgegeben.
genitive:	Ich habe den Namen **des Kunde*n*** vergessen.

. . . and in the plural:

nominative:	**Die Kunde*n*** haben viel gekauft.
accusative:	Ich habe **alle Kunde*n*** begrüßt.
dative:	Ich habe **diesen Kunde*n*** geholfen.
genitive:	Wie sind die Namen **dieser Kunde*n***?

Some weak nouns add both a weak -**n** and a strong -**s** to the genitive form:

der Name → des Name**ns** der Glaube → des Glaube**ns** das Herz → des Herz**ens**

Since the singular ending may be slightly different from the plural ending, it is customary in most dictionaries to show two endings after weak nouns; the first is usually the genitive singular ending, and the second is the plural:

der Herr, -**n**, -**en** der Name, -**ns**, -**n** der Student, -**en**, -**en**

Compound Nouns

Compound nouns take their gender from the last noun component, and the last component also determines how the plural is formed. Semantically, the last part of the compound identifies the basic identity of the noun, that is, essentially what the noun is, and the previous part(s) are descriptive. Hence, a noun like **Semesterarbeit** is feminine: **das Semester + die Arbeit →** ***die*** **Semesterarbeit**, and the plural is **Semesterarbeite*n*** (**die Arbeit**, -***en***).

The foundation for case accuracy with nouns and all words used in association with them is gender accuracy. Close to 50 percent of all mistakes learners make with case endings can be traced to uncertainty about noun gender, which automatically compromises case-ending accuracy. Knowing genders is to case accuracy what knowing the principle parts is to accuracy with verbs.

Noun Plurals

Plural endings are typically: -**e** (**Monat*e***), -**er** (**Arbeit*er***), -**en** (**Universität*en***), -**n** (**Frage*n***), and -**s** (**Auto*s***), with umlauts sometimes added. Some nouns add no ending in the plural and look just like the singular form (**Wagen**), and some add just an umlaut (**Mütter**). That means that there are quite a few possible endings, with or without umlauts, making accuracy with noun plural forms potentially quite challenging for native speakers of English and other languages that employ only natural gender with simpler rules for plural formation.

Monosyllabic Nouns

Monosyllabic nouns usually add -**e** (**Brief → Brief*e***) in the plural. Some neuter nouns add -**er** (**Kind → Kind*er***) instead. Umlauts are sometimes added as well (**Ton → Töne**, **Gut → Güter**, **Loch → Löcher**, **Buch → Bücher**).

Polysyllabic Nouns

Masculine and neuter polysyllabic (consisting of two or more syllables) nouns form plurals by adding no endings or by adding an -**e**. Sometimes umlauts are added as well.

no endings:	**Wagen, Fenster, Spaten**
-**e** ending:	**Institute, Romane, Monate, Geräte**
umlaut + -**e**:	**Anwälte, Verträge, Züge**

Feminine polysyllabics have plurals that typically end in an **n**-sound, adding either -**n** or -**en**: **Tomaten**, **Bananen**, **Schwestern**, **Strukturen**, **Nationen**. Notable exceptions are **Mutter →** ***Mütter,*** **Tochter →** ***Töchter.***

Loan Words

English loan words in German usually form the plural by adding an -**s**, as in English: **Hotel*s***, **Auto*s***. Note, though, that some loan words from English ending in -**y** form plurals differently from English nouns: **Babys**, **Hobbys**.

French loan words are usually feminine and employ feminine suffixes like -**ie**, -**ik**, -**ion**, -**tät**, and -**ur**. Their plurals are formed by adding -**n** or -**en**:

Fantasie → Fantasien	**Figur → Figuren**	**Quantität → Quantitäten**
Plastik → Plastiken	**Nation → Nationen**	

Neuter nouns of Latin origin that end in -**ium** form their plurals by changing to -**ien:**

Studium → Studien	**Stipendium → Stipendien**	**Gymnasium → Gymnasien**

The rules for noun plurals can be dizzying. Until you develop an innate feel for noun gender in German, which usually takes several years and residence abroad for a year or more, it is advisable to target each noun individually, memorizing the gender and plural forms. In an unnatural, academic environment you must memorize certain things to compensate for the fact that you do not have thousands of hours of exposure to German in a "natural language acquisition environment." Memorizing vocabulary (meaning, gender, plural forms) is really the only practical, effective, and efficient way to achieve accuracy with nouns when exposure time is minimal. You will become fluent with the vocabulary items you encounter frequently and regularly in written and spoken German and use often in speaking and writing.

Exercises: Part One

Theory Review

1. Fill in the blanks with the correct information.

1. Words used to name or identify persons, places, and things are ______________________.

2. Viewed in isolation, nouns have two dimensions: ______________________ and ______________________.

3. ______________________ refers to whether the noun is masculine, feminine, or neuter.

4. ______________________ refers to whether the noun is singular or plural.

5. ______________________ gender is used with persons and animals. They are either male/masculine or female/feminine.

6. ______________________ gender is used with inanimate objects, which means they may be masculine, feminine, or neuter.

7. Nouns that end in ____________, ____________, ____________ or ____________ are masculine.

8. Nouns that end in ____________, ____________, ____________, ____________, or ____________, to mention a few, are feminine.

9. Nouns ending with the suffixes ____________, ____________, or ____________ are neuter.

10. Name the gender normally associated with the following categories of nouns:

days	______________	most metals	______________
directions	______________	nationalities	______________
gerunds	______________	nouns ending in **-in**	______________
letters of the alphabet	______________	nouns with the prefix **Ge-**	______________
makes of cars	______________	occupations	______________
mathematical fractions	______________	Rhine and tributaries	______________
months	______________	seasons	______________
most countries	______________	small/immature living things	______________
most German rivers	______________		

11. Masculine nouns that have features of feminine nouns are known as ______________________ nouns, ______________________ nouns, or ______________________-nouns.

12. These masculine nouns often end in ____________; also ____________, ____________, ____________, or ____________.

13. The latter group generally has its primary word stress on the ______________________ syllable and they are usually ______________________ loan words.

14. A ______________________ noun consists of two or more nouns joined together.

15. The gender of this type of noun is determined by the gender of the ______________________ noun component.

16. The plural form of this type of noun is determined by the plural form of the ________________ component.

17. Some of the possible endings used to form noun plurals are: ____________, ____________, ____________, ____________, ____________.

18. Some nouns form plurals by adding an ______________________ with or without an ending.

19. Nouns borrowed from English usually have an ____________-ending in the plural.

20. For native speakers of English, noun genders and noun plurals normally need to be , ______________________, at least during the first few years of language study, until a real **Sprachgefühl** is developed, which normally requires a substantial amount of time spent abroad.

Focus on Form [✓]

Noun Gender

2. Indicate the gender of each of the following nouns by supplying the correct form of the definite article.

___________ Franzose ___________ Präsident ___________ Assistentin

___________ Antwort ___________ Essen ___________ B

___________ Patient ___________ Kunde ___________ Operation

___________ Warnung ___________ Grammatik ___________ Dienstag

___________ Woche ___________ Herbst ___________ Abend

___________ Jahr ___________ Wochenende ___________ Mai

___________ Problemchen ___________ Auto ___________ Wagen

___________ Kind ___________ Spezialität ___________ Freundlichkeit

___________ Ärztin ___________ Straße ___________ Chemie

___________ Polizei ___________ Krankheit ___________ Freundschaft

___________ Mädchen ___________ Regen ___________ Ausländer

___________ Gold	___________ Trinken	___________ Konditorei
___________ Stipendium	___________ Morgen	___________ Russe
___________ VW	___________ Westen	___________ Porsche

3. Indicate the gender of the following compound nouns.

___________ Gummistiefel	___________ Hosentasche
___________ Lederschuh	___________ Regenmantel
___________ Semesterpause	___________ Sommersemester
___________ Strickjacke	___________ Taschenrechner
___________ Trainingsanzug	___________ Winterkleidung

Noun Plurals

4. Write the plural form for each of the following common nouns.

Frage	___________	Arzt	___________	Polizist	___________
Vorlesung	___________	Fabrik	___________	Tag	___________
Wagen	___________	Schwester	___________	Party	___________
Universität	___________	Krankheit	___________	Meinung	___________
Vater	___________	Mutter	___________	Kind	___________
Hotel	___________	Gast	___________	Buch	___________
Hund	___________	Mann	___________	Satz	___________
Rad	___________	Jahr	___________	Hand	___________
Frau	___________	Mädchen	___________	Vertrag	___________
Gefängnis	___________	Bus	___________	Familie	___________
Studentin	___________	Freund	___________	Schuh	___________
Haus	___________	Chance	___________	Nummer	___________
Paket	___________	Roman	___________	Arbeiter	___________
Ausweis	___________	Stipendium	___________	Thema	___________
Scheck	___________	Herz	___________	Gymnasium	___________

Compound Nouns

5. Write down twelve compound nouns with the definite article and the plural form.

Example: ***die Lederhose, Lederhosen***

______________________________ ______________________________

______________________________ ______________________________

______________________________ ______________________________

______________________________ ______________________________

______________________________ ______________________________

______________________________ ______________________________

Part Two

Fundamentals of Case

Cases are simply sets of distinctive noun-related language forms. There are four cases, or sets of forms in German: nominative, accusative, dative, and genitive. These cases, or sets, are used to *signal the function of a word or phrase in a sentence.*

To make the abstract more concrete, think of there being four boxes, one for each of the four cases. Inside each box are all the possible forms for that case. If you know which case is required, you reach into that box and pull out the forms you need and then plug them into the sentence. Before you can come up with the correct forms, however, you must absolutely know which case is required. Even if you have mastery of gender in German, if you guess at case, you will make errors, probably many. And obviously, if you guess at both gender *and* case, you'll reach into the wrong boxes, and accuracy will suffer proportionately. Take the time NOW to be sure you know which case to use for which sentence function, for example, subject, object, indirect object. The following chapters will elaborate on all of these in different ways and provide practice in some depth with the relevant forms. You will also find a summary of all the case endings in the Appendix.

Nominative Case

The nominative case/set forms are used to designate:

1. The **subject** of the sentence. The subject may be *active* (= actor/doer), *passive* (being acted upon), or *statal* (inactive and being identified or described).

active: **Der Student** liest die Zeitung.
passive: **Die Prüfung** wird heute von allen Schülern gemacht.
statal: **Das Buch** ist sehr interessant.

2. The **predicate noun**, the noun that *identifies or names the subject;* it is separated from the subject by the predicate (verb).

Das ist ein **Hund.**	Das ist ein **Pferd.**
Das ist eine **Katze.**	Das sind **Heinz** und **Inge.**

3. The **predicate adjective**, the adjective that *describes or modifies the subject;* it is separated from the subject by the predicate (verb).

Der Film ist **interessant.**
Die Oper war **langweilig.**
Das Rockkonzert war **toll.**

4. **Direct address.** This boils down to persons' names for the most part, and less frequently to *titles* when used to gain someone's attention. Note the use of the comma.

Julia, komm mal her.	Guten Tag, **Herr Doktor**!
Hallo, **Herr Meyer**!	**Du**, sei ruhig.

Accusative Case

The accusative forms are used to designate:

1. The **direct object**, *that which the subject acts upon* (= controls, manipulates, affects in some direct way).

Fritz liest **einen Roman.**
Wir besuchen **Verwandte.**
Ich liebe **meine Tochter.**

2. Certain **prepositional phrases**; the following six prepositions require the use of the accusative after them:

bis	*till, to*	bis nächstes Jahr	bis kommenden Freitag	bis Juli
durch	*through*	durch die Stadt	durch das Fenster	durch Feuer
für	*for*	für meinen Freund	für alle Personen	für nichts
gegen	*against*	gegen einen Baum	gegen den Stuhl	gegen ein Uhr
ohne	*without*	ohne meine Brille	ohne einen Pass	ohne dich
um	*around*	um den See	um die Stadt	um uns

3. **Noun phrases** (noun + article or adjective) denoting *specific time, duration of time,* and *specific measure.*

specific time:	dieses Wochenende	nächstes Semester	letztes Jahr
duration of time:	eine Woche [lang]	zwei Monate [lang]	drei Stunden
specific measure:	ein Kilo	20 Meter	eine halbes Glas

Dative Case

The **dative** forms are used to designate:

1. The **indirect object**, the person/thing *to whom* the direct object is given, sent, said, written.

Ich schreibe **dem Chef** einen Zettel.	Er gab **jedem Kind** Schokolade.
Wir kaufen **unserer Mutter** Blumen zum Muttertag.	Jens erzählte **den zwei Polizisten** alles.

2. The **beneficiary**, the person/thing *for whom* the subject acts.

Mach **mir** die Tür auf.	Du hast es **ihnen** ganz klar gemacht.

3. Certain verbs that take **dative objects** (these dative objects are actually beneficiaries). Some common ones are:

ähneln	*to resemble*	Die Tochter **ähnelt der Mutter**.
antworten	*to answer*	**Antworten** Sie **mir**, bitte.
danken	*to thank*	Du sollst **ihr** für das Geschenk **danken**.
folgen	*to follow*	Der Hund **folgt dem Kind** überall hin.
gefallen	*to please*	Das **gefällt ihnen** nicht.
gehören	*to belong to*	**Wem gehört** das?
geschehen	*to happen*	**Ihm** ist nichts **geschehen**.
glauben	*to believe*	Kannst du **ihnen glauben**?
helfen	*to help*	**Hilf der alten Frau** über die Straße.
trauen	*to trust*	Ihr könnt **diesen Leuten** ruhig **trauen**.

4. Certain **prepositional phrases**; the following nine prepositions require the use of the dative after them:

aus	*out of, from*	Die Kinder liefen **aus dem Zimmer**.
außer	*besides*	**Außer ihm** ist nur Helmut da.
bei	*at*	Ist Petra **bei euch**?
mit	*with*	Arbeitest du **mit mir**?
nach	*after, to*	Komm **nach dem Abendessen nach Hause**.
seit	*since, for*	Ich studiere erst **seit einem Monat**.
von	*from*	Ist der Brief **von deiner Freundin**?
zu	*to*	Wir laufen jetzt **zur** (**zu** + **der**) **Bibliothek**.
gegenüber	*opposite*	Sie saß **ihnen gegenüber**. AUCH: Sie saß **gegenüber ihnen.**

There is another group of nine prepositions that may take either accusative or dative objects. They are:

an	*to, on*	Ich hänge das Bild **an die Wand**. → Das Bild hängt **an der Wand**.
auf	*on, onto*	Ich lege es **auf den Tisch**. → Es liegt **auf dem Tisch**.
hinter	*behind*	Stell das **hinter die Tür**. → Es steht **hinter der Tür**.
vor	*in front of*	Stell die Blumen **vor das Bild**. → Die Blumen stehen **vor dem Bild**.
über	*over, above*	Häng die Lampe **über den Tisch**. → Die Lampe hängt **über dem Tisch**.
unter	*under, below*	Roll das **unter das Bett**. → Es liegt **unter dem Bett**.
in	*in, into*	Geh **in das Zimmer**. → Bleib **in dem Zimmer**.
neben	*next to*	Stell das **neben das Sofa**. → Das steht **neben dem Sofa**.
zwischen	*between*	Stell es **zwischen die Bilder**. → Es steht **zwischen den Bildern**.

All of these prepositions will be treated in much more depth in Chapters 15 and 16.

Genitive Case

The genitive forms are used to designate:

1. A **possessor**:

   Das ist das Auto **meines Vaters.** Wo ist die Telefonnummer **meiner Chefin**?
   Note that the phrase naming the possessor normally *follows* the thing that is possessed.

2. A **relationship**, usually some kind of *belonging to* the preceding noun, that is, being a part of something. This is technically referred to as the "partitive genitive."

   der Titel **des Romans** das Ende **der Woche** der Anfang **des Semesters**

3. Certain **prepositional phrases**; the following four prepositions are the most common ones that require the genitive:

(an)statt	*instead of*	Ich habe eine Zeitschrift **statt der Zeitung** gelesen.
trotz	*in spite of*	**Trotz des Wetters** spielten die Kinder draußen.
während	*during*	**Während der Woche** gehe ich drei- oder viermal joggen.
wegen	*because of, due to*	**Wegen seiner Krankheit** ist er nicht zur Arbeit gekommen.

   Less common ones are:

diesseits	*this side of*	**Diesseits des Flusses** liegt die Stadt Buda.
jenseits	*that side of*	**Jenseits des Flusses** liegt die Stadt Pest.
innerhalb	*inside of, within*	Das Gefängnis befand sich **innerhalb der Festung**.
außerhalb	*outside of, beyond*	Ein Vorort liegt **außerhalb einer größeren Stadt**.

4. **Noun phrases** indicating *indefinite* or vague time:

   Eines Abends ging er weg, ohne etwas zu sagen. **Eines Tages** kommt mein Prinz.

In the following chapters you will work intensively with case functions and case forms. For now, be sure you have learned all of the main case affiliations above so that you will know immediately which case is required.

Exercises: Part Two

Theory Review

1. Fill in the blanks with the correct information.

1. Sets of forms that signal the role of nouns and pronouns in a sentences are known as

   ______________________.

2. In German there are ______________________ of them.

3. The names of these are ______________________, ______________________,

   ______________________, and ______________________.

Basic Case Affiliations [✓]

2. Name the case associated with the following sentence unit(s).

active subject ____________________

an/auf, hinter/vor, über/unter, in, neben, zwischen ____________________

aus, außer, bei, mit, nach, seit, von, zu, gegenüber ____________________

beneficiary ____________________

bis, durch, für, ohne, um ____________________

direct address ____________________

direct object ____________________

duration of time ____________________

helfen, glauben, antworten, trauen ____________________

indirect object ____________________

noun phrase of non-specific time ____________________

noun phrase of specific measure ____________________

noun phrase of specific time ____________________

noun phrase of vague time ____________________

part *of a whole* ____________________

passive subject ____________________

possessor/owner ____________________

predicate adjective ____________________

predicate noun ____________________

statal subject ____________________

trotz, wegen, während, (an)statt ____________________

3. Name the case(s) associated with the following prepositions.

an	____________________	auf	____________________
aus	____________________	außer	____________________
bei	____________________	durch	____________________
für	____________________	gegen	____________________
hinter	____________________	in	____________________

mit	______	nach	______
neben	______	ohne	______
seit	______	über	______
um	______	unter	______
von	______	vor	______
zu	______	zwischen	______

4. Indicate whether the following verbs take an accusative or dative object.

abschneiden	______	glauben	______
ansehen	______	helfen	______
antworten	______	missverstehen	______
aufräumen	______	mitbringen	______
ausziehen	______	sehen	______
beantworten	______	tragen	______
danken	______	trauen	______
einladen	______	verbrauchen	______
empfehlen	______	vergleichen	______
ersetztten	______	vorbereiten	______
folgen	______	vorstellen	______
fortsetzen	______	wegstellen	______
gehören	______	zerschneiden	______
genießen	______	zurückgeben	______
geschehen	______	zurückwerfen	______

Supplementary Exercises

1. Indicate the gender of the following nouns and explain the reason for that gender.

Abend	Figur	Herbst	Mosel	Qualität	Süden
Ärztin	Fischlein	Journalist	Nation	Residenz	Süßigkeit
Bildung	Freiheit	Junge	Nebel	Rhein	Theorie
Blei	Freitag	Juni	Norwegen	Russin	Vase
Drittel	Gesellschaft	Kater	Ofen	Schweinchen	Wandern
Essig	Gewitter	Katze	Polizei	Spanier	
Fabrik	Hammer	Kollege	Porsche	Student	

2. Indicate the cases associated with each of the following concepts or words.

auf	direct object	**in**	specif. measure	**um**
außer	**für**	indirect object	specif. time	vague time
bei	**gegen**	part of a whole	**statt**	**wegen**
beneficiary	**gehören**	possessor	subject	**zu**
diesseits	**helfen**	predicate noun	**über**	**zwischen**

Chapter 10 Articles, *der*-Words, and *ein*-Words

Part One

The definite article is used to signal that the noun used with it is regarded as a specific one. In English we use the word *the*. In German we use **der**, **die**, and **das** and their variant forms.

Forms of the Definite Article

	masculine	*feminine*	*neuter*	*plural*
nominative:	**der**	**die**	**das**	**die**
accusative:	**den**	**die**	**das**	**die**
dative:	**dem**	**der**	**dem**	**den**
genitive:	**des**	**der**	**des**	**der**

Der-Words

Der-words are adjectives that are declined exactly like the definite article. They are:

all-	*all*	**Alle Kinder** wissen das.
beid-	*both*	**Beide Kinder** wissen das.
dies-	*this/these*	**Dieses Kind** weiß das. Und **diese Kinder** wissen das auch.
jed-	*each, every*	**Jedes Kind** weiß das.
jen-	*that*	**Jenes Kind** weiß das.
manch-	*many [a]*	**Manch ein Kind** weiß das. **Manche Kinder** wissen das.
solch-	*such*	**Solch ein Kind** weiß das. **Solche Kinder** wissen das.
welch-	*which*	**Welches Kind** weiß das? **Welche Kinder** wissen das?

Primary Case Sounds and the Master Paradigm

When one learns various language forms such as articles, adjectives, and pronouns, one typically learns them in print first, and, as a result, one thinks of case endings as "printed things." Remember, though, that writing came about after speaking, and what people wrote was a representation of speech, that is, of speech *sounds*. Think of case endings as grammatical language sounds first and printed endings second.

Primary case sounds are the sounds that are common for articles and **der**-words for each case and gender. Plural forms are the same for all, so gender differences effectively disappear in the plural. (There are secondary case sounds as well, but these will be discussed later.) For now, remember that these primary sounds are the sounds one interprets grammatically when one listens to another speaker, and when speaking, it is important to use these case sounds/endings accurately so that you will be understood clearly and easily. Knowledge of these primary case sounds will help you arrive at the correct form for virtually all words that are noun-related. Note the primary sounds located at the bottom of each column in the following chart.

Definite Article, *der*-Words, and Their Primary Case Sounds

	masculine	*feminine*	*neuter*	*plural*
nominative:	**der**	**die**	**das**	**die**
	dieser	diese	dieses	diese
	jeder	jede	jedes	alle
	jener	jene	jenes	jene
	welcher	welche	welches	welche
	mancher	manche	manches	manche
	solcher	solche	solches	solche
	——	——	——	beide
	r	**e**	**s**	**e**
accusative:	**den**	**die**	**das**	**die**
	diesen	diese	dieses	diese
	jeden	jede	jedes	alle
	jenen	jene	jenes	jene
	welchen	welche	welches	welche
	manchen	manche	manches	manche
	solchen	solche	solches	solche
	——	——	——	beide
	n	**e**	**s**	**e**
dative:	**dem**	**der**	**dem**	**den**
	diesem	dieser	diesem	diesen
	jedem	jeder	jedem	allen
	jenem	jener	jenem	jenen
	welchem	welcher	welchem	welchen
	manchem	mancher	manchem	manchen
	solchem	solcher	solchem	solchen
	——	——	——	beiden
	m	**r**	**m**	**n**
genitive:	**des**	**der**	**des**	**der**
	dieses	dieser	dieses	dieser
	jedes	jeder	jedes	jeder
	jenes	jener	jenes	jener
	welches	welcher	welches	welcher
	manches	mancher	manches	mancher
	solches	solcher	solches	solcher
	——	——	——	beider
	s	**r**	**s**	**r**

Noun Case Endings/Sounds

Generally, nouns in German do not bear case endings. In the dative plural and genitive singular, masculine, and neuter, however, there *are* case endings on the nouns. The dative noun ending or sound is -**n**, and the genitive sound is -**s**:

dative plural:	**Welchen Kinder*n*** hast du das gesagt? Ich habe **allen Freunde*n*** Weihnachtskarten geschickt.
genitive masculine:	Das ist die Adresse **meines Onkel*s***. Wie ist der Name **deines Sohn*es***?
genitive neuter:	Wer ist der Besitzer **dieses Auto*s***? Das Ende **des Semester*s*** macht uns allen immer viel Freude.

Traditionally, students have had to memorize charts of declensions for many different kinds of words such as definite articles, indefinite articles, **der**-words, **ein**-words, unpreceded adjectives, adjectives after **der**-words, adjectives after **ein**-words, interrogative pronouns, personal pronouns, impersonal pronouns, demonstrative pronouns, and relative pronouns. Which is easier: memorizing a dozen or more declensions or the master declension that stands behind and drives all of them?

Memorize the chart that follows, which consists solely of primary case sounds and required noun endings. We will add on to it as you review the other noun-related aspects of case in this and following chapters. Learning this will save much time, both now and later, and reduce inter-chart confusion. German has the unfortunate reputation for being a "hard" language to learn, but it doesn't have to be that way.

Primary Case Sounds: *der*-Words + Noun Endings

	masculine	*feminine*	*neuter*	*plural*
nominative:	**r**	**e**	**s**	**e**
accusative:	**n**	**e**	**s**	**e**
dative:	**m**	**r**	**m**	**n + n**
genitive:	**s + s**	**r**	**s + s**	**r**

REMINDER: Masculine and neuter nouns typically add an **s**-sound in the genitive singular. They may also sometimes exhibit an archaic, vestigial -**e** in monosyllabic nouns in the dative singular, for example, **dem Mann*e***, and in certain prepositional phrases, like **nach Haus*e***. Avoid using it otherwise. All dative plural nouns end in an **n**-sound except those English loan words that form plurals with -**s**.

Dies- and *jen*-

In colloquial German **dies**- can mean *this* or *that,* and in the plural, *these* and *those.* Only in formal writing will you perhaps need to use **dies**- + **jen**- together to present a strong contrast.

more colloquial:	Ich möchte **dieses Hemd** hier und **dieses Hemd** da kaufen.
more formal:	Ich möchte **dieses Hemd** hier und **jenes Hemd** da kaufen.

Dies- and *d e r / d i e / d a s*

Even when a strong contrast is needed, most speakers use the definite article as an emphatic pronoun rather than **jen-**: Ich möchte **diese Hose** (hier), und **d i e** (da).

The uninflected **dies**, both singular and plural, is sometimes used to begin a sentence and mean *this/these.* It's uninflected because it does not refer to any previously mentioned noun: ***Dies* ist mein Bruder**. It's far more common to use **das** to mean *this/these:*

Das ist meine Familie. **Das ist** mein Mann und **das sind** meine Kinder.

The bottom line: You will only seldom need to use the adjective **jen-** or the pronoun **dies**.

Manch-, solch-, welch-

These three **der**-words can be used by themselves, that is, without an article:

Welche Leute haben Kreditkarten?
Manche Leute haben Kreditkarten.
Solche Leute geben oft viel Geld zu Weihnachten aus.

These three words may also be used with **ein**. When so used, **ein** is inflected and follows the **der**-word. The **der**-words are used only in stem form. Note, too, that **solch-** can be reduced to **so**.

Ich habe **manch einen** Dummkopf gekannt.
Welch ein Idiot! (More common: **Was für ein** Idiot!)
Kennst du **solch eine** Person? (More common in conversation: Kennst du ***so* eine** Person?)

Consider **so** followed by a form of **ein** as a shortened form of **solch-**.

When to Use the Definite Article

In German, unlike English, the definite article is commonly used with the following:

- parts of the body and clothing (with a dative pronoun):

  Wasch dir **die** Hände. Zieh dir **die** Kleidung an!

- in many prepositional phrases denoting a destination or means of travel:

  an **den** See mit **dem** Auto mit **der** U-Bahn zu**r** Schule zu**m** Arzt

Most countries are neuter and do not use the definite article: **Deutschland** liegt in Europa. **China** liegt in Asien. Countries (and their abbreviations) that are feminine, masculine, or plural use the definite article *at all times,* and they employ **in** instead of **nach** with destinations:

Saddam Hussein war der Präsident von **dem Irak**.
Die Schweiz ist ein kleines Land.
Die Vereingten Staaten/Die USA *sind* ein großes Land.
Wilhelm Tell lebte **in der Schweiz**.
Benjamin Franklin lebte **in den USA**.

The definite article is *not* used when indicating a person's occupation, nationality, social status, or religion:

Er ist **Schweizer.** Sie ist **Chefin.** Ich bin **Student/Studentin.**
Er ist **Witwer.** Sie ist **Katholikin.** Ich bin **Kinderärztin.**

Nor is the article used when mentioning that one plays a musical instrument:

Ich spiele **Violine** und **Mandoline.** Spielst du **Gitarre**? Spielt er **Trompete**?

Exercises: Part One

Theory Review

1. Fill in the blanks with the correct information.

1. The ____________________ article is used with a noun to signal that the noun is referred to as a specific person, place, or thing.
2. Depending on the form of this article, one can determine the noun's ____________________, ____________________, and ____________________. Put another way, this is what you must be aware of in order to come up with the correct form of the article.
3. A group of adjectives following the same pattern of endings as the definite article is known as the __________-words.
4. Indicate the meaning of each of these words, presented in stem form:

   all- ____________________ **beide-** ____________________
   dies- ____________________ **jed-** ____________________
   jen- ____________________ **manch-** ____________________
   solch- ____________________ **welch-** ____________________
5. The master paradigm for the definite article and **der**-words consists of primary case ____________________.
6. The definite article and the **der**-words ____________________ provide the primary case sound.
7. Knowledge of these sounds makes it very easy to determine the printed ____________________ of these words.
8. Do German nouns have endings? __________
9. For the dative plural the noun must end in __________.
10. For the masculine and neuter genitive singular, the noun usually ends in __________. (Weak nouns/**n**-nouns are an exception.)
11. The **der**-word that can mean *this, that, these,* and *those* is ____________________.
12. The definite article is used in German with parts of the ____________________ and items of ____________________ plus a dative pronoun that indicates ownership.
13. The definite article is also used with modes of ____________________ and with some local destinations.
14. Most countries have ______________ gender. Is the definite article used with them? ________
15. Is the definite article used with countries that are masculine, feminine, or plural? __________
16. The definite article is not used in German when identifying a person's ____________________, ____________________, ____________________, or ____________________.
17. The definite article is not used when indicating that one plays a ____________________ ____________________.

Focus on Form [✓]

2. Definite article and *der*-words. Fill in the blanks with correct case endings. If no ending is required, leave the blank empty. Fill in any required noun endings as well.

A

1. Antworte d_______ Professorin.
2. Antworten Sie d_______ Chef sofort.
3. Arbeitest du für d_______ Mann hier oder d_______ Frau dort?
4. Hast du dies_______ Fisch gefangen?
5. Hast du dies_______ Auto kaufen wollen?
6. Weißt du, aus welch_______ Land ich komme?
7. Welch_______ Leute sind schon angekommen?
8. Dies_______ Dame kommt aus Italien.
9. Mit einem Teleskop kann ich fast all_______ Planeten und Sterne im Himmel sehen.
10. Dies_______ Studentin ist sehr tüchtig.

B

1. Das kommt nur mit d_______ Zeit.
2. Der Professor hat die Namen all_______ Student_______ in d_______ Kurs gelernt.
3. Die Farbe dies_______ Bluse gefällt mir nicht.
4. Die Lehrerin kennt die Fähigkeiten jed_______ Schüler_______.
5. Solch_______ Bilder hasse ich.
6. Dies_______ Häuser kosten viel zu viel.
7. D_______ Mappe ist aus Leder, nicht aus Plastik.
8. Hast du dies_______ Wintermantel gekauft?
9. Solch_______ Wagen fahren immer sehr schnell.
10. All_______ Frauen im Büro sind einfach toll!

C

1. Solch_______ Bücher wollen wir nicht lesen.
2. Ende dies_______ Woche kommen meine Eltern zu Besuch.
3. Er hat d_______ Frau nicht geantwortet.
4. Jed_______ Taxifahrer kennt all_______ Straßen in d_______ Stadt.
5. Onkel Werner kommt am Ende d_______ Monat_______ zu Besuch.
6. Fährst du mit d_______ Straßenbahn oder mit d_______ Bus zur Uni?
7. Jed_______ Fahrrad in dies_______ Geschäft ist preiswert.
8. Siehst du d_______ Segelschiff im Hafen?

9. Gefallen dir d_______ Meinungen dies_______ Politikerin nicht?
10. Findest du jed_______ Film von Steven Spielberg interessant?

D

1. Hast du Kekse für dies_______ Kind?
2. Bist du blind?! Hilf d_______ Dame da mit d_______ Koffer.
3. Ja, Hans, ich möchte dies_______ Wein doch trinken, aber nicht zum Frühstück!
4. Ich kenne dies_______ Uni noch nicht sehr gut.
5. Manch_______ Arbeiter streiken gegen d_______ Firma als Protest.
6. All_______ Kinder lieben Schokolade.
7. Kennst du d_______ Bruder dies_______ Frau?
8. Hast du all_______ Romane für d_______ Kurs gelesen?
9. Du musst jed_______ Wort auswendig lernen.
10. Willst du d_______ Zeitung hier oder d_______ Zeitschrift da lesen?

E

1. Man kann nicht all_______ Leute_______ helfen.
2. Sie kommen alle aus d_______ Haus und gehen zu Oma und Opa.
3. Sie spielt gut mit d_______ Kinder_______.
4. Manch_______ Leute würden das auch meinen. Ich aber nicht.
5. Kennst du d_______ Professor und d_______ Studenten im Kurs?
6. Während d_______ Semester_________ wohne ich zu Hause bei d_______ Eltern.
7. Während d_______ Tag_______ sieht man ihn nur selten.
8. Glauben Sie dies_______ Mann nicht?
9. In d_______ Wintermonaten wohnt er in Spanien.
10. Trotz d_______ Regen_______ will er spazieren gehen.

F

1. Welch_______ Zeitung wollte er kaufen?
2. Welch_______ Bier trinkst du am liebsten?
3. Welch_______ Auto möchtest du eines Tages haben?
4. Welch_______ Leute meinen Sie?
5. Welch_______ Bus fährt dahin?
6. Welch_______ Bus nimmst du zur Arbeit?
7. Mit welch_______ Bus kann man direkt zu_______ Bahnhof kommen?
8. Bei welch_______ Firma arbeitet Maria jetzt?
9. Welch_______ Hemd würdest du lieber kaufen? Dies_______ oder jen_______?
10. Welch______ Junge______ hast du d______ Telefonnummern all______ Mädchen gegeben?

Focus on Form (for in-class review)

3. Definite article and *der*-words. Fill in the blanks with correct case endings. If no ending is required, leave the blank empty. Supply any noun endings required.

A

1. Antworte d_______ Chefin.
2. Hast du einen Ball für dies_______ Spiel mitgebracht?
3. Muss man immer d_______ Wahrheit sagen?
4. Solch_______ Filme interessieren mich nicht.
5. Welch_______ Anzug wollte er kaufen?
6. All_______ Kinder in dies_______ Klasse spielen sehr gut miteinander zusammen.
7. Dies_______ Kollege ist sehr tüchtig.
8. Findest du jed_______ Roman von dies_______ Autorin interessant?
9. Trotz d_______ Hitze will Manfred im Garten arbeiten.
10. D_______ Kinder laufen jetzt aus d_______ Schule.

B

1. Ende d_______ Jahr_______ kommen meine Neffen zu Besuch.
2. Welch_______ Restaurant gefällt dir am meisten?
3. Würden Sie bitte dies_______ Frau helfen?
4. Die Farbe dies_______ Wagen_______ gefällt mir sehr.
5. Er hat d_______ Lehrerin gar nicht geantwortet.
6. D_______ Tochter spielt gut mit d_______ Tier_______.
7. Das glauben manch_______ Leute.
8. Hast du dies_______ Ei gekocht?
9. Ich kenne dies_______ Stadt noch nicht sehr gut.
10. Es sind nur achtzehn Tage bis zum Ende d_______ Semester_______!

C

1. Hast du dies_______ Kette kaufen wollen?
2. Solch_______ Leute vermeide ich immer.
3. Welch_______ Zug fährt nach Emden?
4. Dies_______ Lehrbücher sind viel zu teuer.
5. Fährst du mit d_______ U-Bahn zur Uni?
6. Jed_______ Kind liebt Süßigkeiten.
7. Während d_______ Woche arbeite ich bei dies_______ Firma.
8. Weißt du, aus welch_______ Stadt ich komme?
9. D_______ Regenschirm ist aus Nylon.
10. Kennst du d_______ Schwester dies_______ Jung_______?

D

1. Welch________ Freunde hast du eingeladen?
2. Dies________ Familie kommt aus Dänemark.
3. Hast du all________ Examen bestanden?
4. Trauen Sie dies________ Leut________ nicht?
5. Wo hast du dies________ Fernseher gekauft?
6. Was halten Sie von d________ Präsident________?
7. Mit welch________ Werkzeug________ repariert man ein Auto?
8. Ich würde sehr gern mit solch________ Kolleg________ (*pl.*) arbeiten.
9. D________ Hund hat d________ Briefträger gebissen.
10. Beid________ Kinder sind krank geworden.

Focus on Meaning and Form

4. Statements. Write that . . .

1. you answered every question ________________________________
2. Mr. Braun works in this building ________________________________
3. all students know that ________________________________
4. they don't like such people ________________________________
5. you knew that girl very well ________________________________

5. Questions. Ask me . . .

1. if I have read every word ________________________________
2. if each child has brought along enough money ________________________________
3. which address I'm looking for ________________________________
4. which wine I would like to order ________________________________
5. if I believe every politician ________________________________

6. Commands. Tell me to . . .

1. work each Saturday this semester ________________________________
2. memorize all of the names ________________________________
3. drink this beer but not that wine ________________________________
4. not believe every person ________________________________
5. pick up all of the kids after school ________________________________

Part Two

Ein-Words

The indefinite article **ein-**, its negator **kein** (= **nicht** + **ein**), and the **ein**-words (possessive adjectives) all follow the same pattern of case endings/sounds:

Forms of the Indefinite Article

	masculine	*feminine*	*neuter*	*plural*
nominative:	**ein**	**eine**	**ein**	**keine**
accusative:	**einen**	**eine**	**ein**	**keine**
dative:	**einem**	**einer**	**einem**	**keinen**
genitive:	**eines**	**einer**	**eines**	**keiner**

NOTE: **Ein** does not have plural forms, so **kein-** is shown to illustrate the plural endings.

Indefinite Article, *ein*-Words, and Their Primary Case Sounds

	masculine	*feminine*	*neuter*	*plural*
nominative:	**ein**	**eine**	**ein**	**keine**
	mein	meine	mein	meine
	dein	deine	dein	deine
	sein	seine	sein	seine
	ihr	ihre	ihr	ihre
	euer	eure	euer	eure
	Ihr	Ihre	Ihr	Ihre
	—	**e**	—	**e**
accusative:	**einen**	**eine**	**ein**	**keine**
	meinen	meine	mein	meine
	deinen	deine	dein	deine
	seinen	seine	sein	seine
	ihren	ihre	ihr	ihre
	euren	eure	euer	eure
	Ihren	Ihre	Ihr	Ihre
	n	**e**	—	**e**
dative:	**einem**	**einer**	**einem**	**keinen**
	meinem	meiner	meinem	meinen
	deinem	deiner	deinem	deinen
	seinem	seiner	seinem	seinen
	ihrem	ihrer	ihrem	ihren
	eurem	eurer	eurem	euren
	Ihrem	Ihrer	Ihrem	Ihren
	m	**r**	**m**	**n**
genitive:	**eines**	**einer**	**eines**	**keiner**
	meines	meiner	meines	meiner
	deines	deiner	deines	deiner
	seines	seiner	seines	seiner
	ihres	ihrer	ihres	ihrer
	eures	eurer	eures	eurer
	Ihres	Ihrer	Ihres	Ihrer
	s	**r**	**s**	**r**

The pattern of endings for **ein**-words is the same as for **der**-words except in three places, where no ending is given, just a stem form. We call these forms "naked." It will be conceptually easier to view them as *deficient,* since they fail to deliver the primary sound.

ein	*a, one*	Ich habe **einen Hund.**
kein	*not a, not any, no*	Ich habe **kein Geld** bei mir.
mein	*my*	**Mein Vater** heißt Bruno.
dein	*your*	Ist das **deine Mutter**?
sein	*his, its*	Er hat **seinen Führerschein** zu Hause gelassen.
ihr	*her, its*	Susanne geht mit **ihrem Hund** spazieren.
unser	*our*	**Unsere Freunde** machen jetzt Urlaub in Spanien.
euer	*your*	Habt ihr **eure Hausaufgaben** gemacht?
Ihr	*your*	Zeigen Sie mir bitte **Ihren Pass.**

Note that there are three ways to say *your* in German. The choice of word must agree with the subject of the sentence, **du, ihr,** or **Sie.**

- **Dein** is the informal singular form, related to the informal pronoun **du: Du** und **deine Freunde**
- **Euer** is the informal plural form, related to the informal pronoun **ihr: Ihr** und **eure Freunde**
- **Ihr** is the formal singular and plural form, related to the formal pronoun **Sie: Sie** und **Ihre Freunde**

Note, too, that **ihr** can mean *her* or *its* when referring to feminine nouns, or *their* when referring to plural nouns:

Karola hat **ihren** Kuli zu Hause gelassen.
***Karola** left **her** pen at home.*

Die Fußballmannschaft hat **ihren** ersten Sieg gefeiert.
***The soccer team** celebrated **its** first win.*

Die Kinder haben **ihre** Spielzeuge weggestellt.
***The kids** put **their** toys away.*

Sein can mean *his* when referring to a masculine noun, or *its* or *her* when referring to a neuter noun that designates a female person:

Karl hat **seinen** Wagen verkauft.
***Karl** sold **his** car.*

Das Mädchen hat **seine** Hausaufgaben nicht gemacht.
***The girl** did not do **her** homework.*

Das Land hat **seine** Grenzen gesichert.
***The country** secured **its** borders.*

The possessive adjective linked to the indefinite subject **man** is **sein:**

Man soll **seinen** Ausweis immer bei sich haben.
***One** should always have **one's** ID with one.*

Euer drops the second (internal) **e** when a case ending is added: **euren Wagen, eure Freunde.** In colloquial speech **unser** often drops its **e** when a case ending is added: **unsre Freunde.**

Was für (ein)

In the combination **was für** [**ein**] (*what kind of* [*a*]), **ein** is used and inflected in the singular. With nouns that normally do not use an article or in the plural, only **was für** is used:

nominative: **Was für ein Hund** ist das?
Was für Wein ist das?
Was für Leute würden so etwas machen?

accusative: **Was für einen Wagen** hast du?
Was für Bier trinkst du gern?
Was für Freunde hast du?

dative: **Mit was für einem Werkzeug** hast du die Maschine repariert?
Was für Leute*n* würde man mit diesem Geld helfen?

Master Paradigm for *ein*-Words

Primary Case Sounds: *ein*-Words + Noun Endings

	masculine	*feminine*	*neuter*	*plural*
nominative:	—	**e**	—	**e**
accusative:	**n**	**e**	—	**e**
dative:	**m**	**r**	**m**	**n + n**
genitive:	**s + s**	**r**	**s + s**	**r**

Synthesis of *der*-Words and *ein*-Words

The following paradigm combines the **der**- and **ein**-words and required noun endings.

Summary of Primary Case Sounds: *der*-Words or *ein*-Words + Noun Endings

	masculine	*feminine*	*neuter*	*plural*
nominative:	**r** *or* —	**e**	**s** *or* —	**e**
accusative:	**n**	**e**	**s** *or* —	**e**
dative:	**m**	**r**	**m**	**n + n**
genitive:	**s + s**	**r**	**s + s**	**r**

Exercises: Part Two

Theory Review

1. Fill in the blanks with the correct information.

1. The ______________________ article is used with a noun to signal that the noun is referred to in a *general* sense, that is, as a *type* or *kind* of thing.

2. The stem of this article is ______________________.

3. Does this article follow the same pattern of endings as the **der**-words? ____________

4. Differences occur in three places: ______________________ , ______________________, and ______________________.

5. Possessive adjectives follow the same pattern of endings as the indefinite article and are therefore often referred to as ____________ -words.

6. Indicate the possible meanings for these possessive adjectives:

mein	__________________	**unser**	__________________		
dein	__________________	**euer**	__________________	**Ihr**	__________________
sein	__________________	**ihr**	__________________		

7. The combination of **ein-** + **nicht** → the negator ______________________, also an **ein**-word.

8. Indicate which **ein**-words match up with these subject pronouns:

ich	__________________	**wir**	__________________		
du	__________________	**ihr**	__________________	**Sie**	__________________
er	__________________				
sie	__________________	**sie**	__________________		
es	__________________				

9. In the expression **was für ein** ..., the form of **ein** is determined by the ____________________ of the noun with which it is used, not by the preposition **für**. In this expression (what kind of [a]), **für** has no influence over **ein**.

Focus on Form [✓]

2. *Ein*-words. Fill in the blanks with correct case endings. If no ending is required, leave the blank empty. Fill in any required noun endings required as well.

A

1. Wer ist dein________ Lieblingsautorin?
2. Hast du mein________ Kinder gesehen?
3. Die Familie hat einmal in unser________ Haus gewohnt.
4. Möchtest du lieber ein________ Haus kaufen oder ein________ Wohnung mieten?
5. Folgen Sie mein________ Kollegen *(pl.)* ins Konferenzzimmer hinein.
6. Wir fahren mit unser________ Freund________ *(pl.)* nach Spanien.
7. Wir helfen ein________ Student________ bei sein________ Hausaufgaben.
8. Wir müssen kein________ Milch kaufen. Wir haben schon genug.
9. Wir treffen uns morgen mit sein________ Verwandten.
10. Wir werden unser________ Mitarbeiter *(pl.)* später sehen.

B

1. Was für ein________ Wagen kauft er?
2. Was für ein________ Haustier hast du?
3. Was für ein________ Buch liest du im Moment?
4. Was für ________ Kurse hast du mit Professor Allwissend?
5. Was für ein________ Idiot/Narr bist du!
6. Was für ein________ Kleid willst du heute Abend tragen?
7. Was für ein________ Mädchen würdest du so 'was denn sagen?
8. Was für ein________ Zeitschrift ist das? Eine Modezeitschrift?
9. Mit was für________ Verkehrsmitteln können wir nach München fahren?
10. Was für ________ Freunde hast du?

C

1. Ich möchte kein________ Auto kaufen.
2. Ein________ Flasche Bier würde mir jetzt gut schmecken.
3. Wohnst du in ein________ Haus oder ein________ Wohnung?
4. Ich kenne kein________ Studenten an dieser Uni.
5. Er trägt heute ein________ Anzug.
6. Und sie trägt ein________ Kostüm.
7. Wir würden sein________ Eltern nichts sagen.
8. Ist das der Titel ein________ Film________ oder ein________ Roman________?
9. Vielleicht kann ich das in mein________ Büro finden.
10. Hast du kein________ Fragen?

D

1. Ich muss zu mein________ Frauenärztin gehen.
2. Ist das nicht euer________ Hund?
3. Hast du dein________ Führerschein bei dir?
4. Karl hat eine Postkarte von sein________ Freundin bekommen.
5. Habt ihr eur________ Verwandten in der Schweiz besucht?
6. Was habt ihr mit eur________ Büchern gemacht?
7. Sie geht mit ihr________ Freund ins Kino.
8. Ich habe nichts gegen eur________ Idee.

9. Bist du mit ein________ Bus oder ein________ Straßenbahn gekommen?
10. Was hast du dein________ Mutter zum Geburtstag geschenkt? Und dein________ Vater? Und dein________ Geschwistern?

E

1. Wo kann man ein________ Restaurant in der Nähe finden?
2. Dein________ Kleid ist sehr schön.
3. Mein________ Tochter ist mit ihr________ Freundinnen ausgegangen.
4. Das ist ein Bild von unser________ Tante.
5. Wie ist der Name eur________ Oma?
6. Ein________ Paket von dein________ Schwester liegt auf dem Tisch dort.
7. Das Ende sein________ Film________ ist übersentimental und einfach unglaublich.
8. Das gefällt mein________ Kinder________ nicht. Schade.
9. Was würde dein________ Schwager gefallen?
10. Arbeitest du für ein________ Chef oder für ein________ Chefin?

F

1. Warum sind dein________ Katzen so faul?
2. Haben Sie kein________ Post für mein________ Familie?
3. Solch ein________ Person könnte ich sehr leicht hassen!
4. Wie werdet ihr das eur________ Eltern erklären?
5. Wegen sein________ Prüfung sind alle sein________ Studenten heute „krank" geworden.
6. Gehört dieser iPod dein________ Bruder?
7. Es gibt keine U-Bahn in unser________ Stadt.
8. Welche Kurse gefallen dir und dein________ Mitstudenten dieses Semester?
9. Wollt ihr heute Abend mit eur________ Freunden ausgehen?
10. Was für ein________ Vorschlag ist das? Das ist blöd!

G

1. Was für ________ Leute würden so 'was sagen?
2. Du sollst lieber zu mein________ Arzt gehen.
3. Hast du ein________ Kugelschreiber bei dir?
4. Ist das ein________ Frau an der Ecke, oder siehst du ein________ Mann da?

Focus on Form (for in-class review)

3. *Ein*-words. Fill in the blanks with correct case endings. If no ending is required, leave the blank empty. Fill in any required noun endings.

A

1. Gibt es ein_______ Kino in der Nähe?
2. Ich möchte kein_______ Hose kaufen.
3. Ich muss zu mein_______ Psychiater gehen.
4. Warum sind dein_______ Kinder immer so schlampig?
5. Was für ein_______ Hund hat er?
6. Wer ist dein_______ Lieblingsschauspieler?
7. Arbeitest du für ein_______ Mann oder für ein_______ Frau?
8. Hast du kein_______ Antwort auf mein_______ Frage?
9. Wir werden unser_______ Freunde am Wochenende sehen.
10. Ein_______ Glas Wein würde mir jetzt gut schmecken.

B

1. Hast du mein_______ Schlüssel (*pl.*) gesehen?
2. Ist das nicht dein_______ Katze?
3. Was für ein_______ Haus hast du?
4. Hat sie ihr_______ Pass nicht bei sich?
5. Hast du ein_______ Kuli bei dir?
6. Mein_______ Sohn ist mit sein_______ Freundin ausgegangen.
7. Möchten Sie lieber in ein_______ Haus oder in ein_______ Wohnung leben?
8. Solch ein_______ Mann kann ich nicht leiden!
9. Was für ein_______ Roman liest du gern?
10. Das ist ein_______ Bild von unser_______ Großmutter.

C

1. Karl hat ein_______ Geschenk von sein_______ Onkel bekommen.
2. Wie werdet ihr das eur_______ Lehrerin erklären?
3. Er trägt heute ein_______ Krawatte.

4. Habt ihr eur________ Fahrräder draußen im Regen gelassen?
5. Gehört der Wagen dir oder dein________ Eltern?
6. Sabine trägt ein________ Hosenanzug.
7. Was für ein________ Jacke willst du ihm kaufen?
8. Was habt ihr mit eur________ Freund________ *(pl.)* gemacht?
9. Wir fahren mit unser________ Eltern in den Urlaub.
10. Ich habe nichts gegen eur________ Vorschlag.

D

1. Wir müssen kein________ Geld sparen. Wir haben schon mehr als wir brauchen.
2. Auf was für ein________ Instrument klingt dieses Lied am schönsten?
3. Vielleicht kann ich das irgendwo in mein________ Schreibtisch finden.
4. Was würde dein________ Schwiegermutter gefallen?
5. Wollt ihr heute Abend mit eur________ Arbeitskollegen ausgehen?
6. Was für ein________ Plan ist das?
7. Wir möchten Käthe ein________ Ring geben.
8. Arbeitest du bei ein________ Firma in dieser Stadt?
9. Zeigen Sir mir bitte Ihr________ Führerschein.
10. Ich habe sein________ Adresse vergessen.

Focus on Meaning and Form

4. Statements. Write that . . .

1. you own a dog and a cat and many fish

____

2. we are supposed to read his book

____

3. one must always have one's driver's license with one

____

4. my friend Thomas visited his family

____

5. you have no friends in the city

____

5. Questions. Ask me . . .

1. if I see your friend Hans

____

2. if I'm coming with my sister

____

3. if my friends know her friends

____

4. if my mother knows his father

____

5. what kind of car I drive

____

6. Commands. Tell me to . . .

1. read your letter ______________________________
2. visit my grandfather in Hamburg ______________________________
3. buy your car ______________________________
4. believe our friends ______________________________
5. not forget her name ______________________________

Partnerarbeit

7. Arbeiten Sie mit einem Partner/einer Partnerin zusammen und besprechen Sie die folgenden Themen.

Ihre Familienmitglieder und was Sie mit ihnen machen
Ihre Freunde und was Sie mit ihnen machen, wenn Sie ausgehen
welche Dinge Sie in Ihrem Zimmer haben und was Sie damit machen
was Sie lesen, ansehen oder anhören möchten
was für ein Haus Sie haben und was für Zimmer es hat
Haustiere, die Sie jetzt haben oder früher hatten

8. Identifizieren Sie alles, was Sie heute von Kopf bis Fuß tragen und was Sie bei sich haben und beschreiben Sie alles. Benutzen Sie das unbestimmte Artikel so: *Ich trage ein Hemd. Es ist blau.*

9. Nennen Sie alles, was Sie im Klassenzimmer sehen, und beschreiben Sie die Sachen mit mehreren Adjektiven so: *Ich sehe eine Tafel, usw.*

10. Zeigen Sie Ihrem Partner/Ihrer Partnerin alles, was Sie bei sich haben, d.h., was Sie im Portmonnee, im Rucksack oder in der Tasche haben und was Sie heute zur Uni mitgebracht haben und beschreiben Sie die Sachen mit mehreren Adjektiven.

Supplementary Exercises

Der- and *ein*-Words Combined with Noun Endings [✓]

Fill in the blanks with correct case endings. When no ending is required, leave the blank empty.

A

1. Antworte d_______ Chefin.
2. Antworten Sie Ihr_______ Lehrer.
3. Arbeitest du für ein_______ Professor oder für ein_______ Forscherin?
4. Hast du ein_______ Pferd?
5. Hast du ein_______ Kater oder ein_______ Katze?
6. Aus welch_______ Land und aus welch_______ Stadt kommt er?
7. Welch_______ Gäste sind schon angekommen?
8. D_______ Frau kommt aus Italien.
9. In mein_______ Teleskop sehe ich ein_______ Gruppe Bergsteiger auf ein_______ Berg.
10. Ein_______ Putzfrau muss doch schwer arbeiten.

B

1. Das kommt nur mit d_______ Zeit.
2. Ich habe all_______ Kolleg_______ zur Party eingeladen.
3. Die Farbe ihr_______ Schuhe gefällt mir nicht.
4. Die Lehrerin kennt jed_______ Schüler.
5. Solch_______ Autos sind mir zu teuer.
6. Dies_______ Ohrringe kosten zu viel.
7. Ein_______ Jacke aus Leder kann teuer sein.
8. Ein_______ Hund bleibt immer treu.
9. Mein_______ Motorrad fährt sehr schnell.
10. Mein_______ Tochter ist einfach toll!

C

1. Solch_______ Zeitschriften wollen wir nicht lesen.
2. Ende dies_______ Woche kommen meine Geschwister zu Besuch.

3. Der Verkäufer hat mein_______ Mutter nicht geantwortet.

4. Unser_______ Onkel kennt fast all_______ Politiker in dies_______ Stadt.

5. Mein_______ Bruder kommt am Ende d_______ Semester_______ zu Besuch.

6. Fährst du mit d_______ U-Bahn oder mit d_______ Bus?

7. Hast du ein_______ Fahrrad?

8. Fährt er mit ein_______ Reisebus nach Mexiko?

9. Gefallen dir sein_______ Meinungen nicht?

10. Das ist ein_______ Film von Steven Spielberg. Findest du sein_______ Filme interessant?

D

1. Hast du etwas für dein_______ Kind?

2. Hilf d_______ Schülerin mit ihr_______ Aufgabe.

3. Ich trinke kein_______Wein. Wenigstens doch nicht zu_______ Frühstück.

4. Ich kenne dies_______ Gegend noch nicht sehr gut.

5. Manch_______ Arbeiter streiken gegen d_______ Firma aus Protest.

6. Fast all_______ Kinder lieben Schokolade.

7. Kennst du mein_______ Freund und sein_______ Freundin?

8. Lesen Sie all_______ Bücher für dies_______ Kurs.

9. Vergiss kein_______ Wort.

10. Willst du d_______ Zeitung hier oder d_______ Illustrierte da lesen?

E

1. Man kann nicht all_______ Leute_______ helfen.

2. Sie kommen alle aus d_______ Restaurant.

3. Sie spielt gut mit d_______ anderen Kinder_______.

4. Welch_______ Leute siehst du da?

5. Siehst du mein_______ Vetter dort?

6. Während d_______ Sommer_______ wohne ich zu Hause bei mein_______ Eltern.

7. Während d_______Tag_______ sieht man ihn nur selten.

8. Glauben Sie dies_______ Bekannten?

9. Während d_______ Wintermonate wohnt er in Griechenland.

10. Trotz d_______ Wetter_______ geht er spazieren.

F

1. Welch_______ Computer wollte er kaufen?
2. Welch_______ Bier trinkst du am liebsten?
3. Welch_______ Wörterbuch hast du?
4. Welch_______ Romane meinen Sie?
5. Welch_______ Zug ist das?
6. Welch_______ Bus nimmst du zur Arbeit?
7. Mit welch_______ Freund kommt er?
8. Bei welch_______ Firma arbeitet Hans?
9. Welch_______ Auto möchtest du kaufen?
10. Welch_______ Student_______ (*pl.*) hast du mein_______ Telefonnummer gegeben?

G

1. Wer ist die Autorin dies_______ Geschichten?
2. Wer sind die Lehrer und Lehrerinnen von d_______ Schüler_______?
3. Wer sind die Familien in dies_______ Häuser_______?
4. Möchtest du ein_______ Haus kaufen oder ein_______ Wohnung mieten?
5. Folgen Sie d_______ Assistentin in d_______ Büro hinein.
6. Wir fahren mit unser_______ Frau_______ (*pl.*) nach Paris.
7. Wir helfen jed_______ Jung_______ bei sein_______ Hausaufgaben.
8. Wir müssen kein_______ Eier kaufen.
9. Wir treffen uns morgen mit d_______ Anwältin.
10. Wir werden unser_______ Verwandten (*pl.*) später sehen.

H

1. Was für ein_______ Hund hat er?
2. Was für ein_______ Wagen ist das?
3. Was für ein_______ Buch liest du?
4. Was für _______ Werkzeuge meinen Sie?
5. Was für ein_______ Idiot bist du?
6. Was für ein_______ Hemd willst du tragen?
7. Was für ein_______ Kind würdest du so etwas schenken?

8. Was für ein_______ Halskette ist das?

9. Mit was für_______ Verkehrsmittel_______ kann man nach Lübeck fahren?

10. Was für _______ Getränke trinkst du gern, wenn du Durst hast?

I

1. Ich möchte ein_______ Frettchen haben.

2. Ein_______ Glas Limonde würde jetzt ganz gut schmecken.

3. Warst du heute Nachmittag in ein_______ Kaufhaus oder in ein_______ Buchhaltung?

4. Ich kenne all_______ Professoren ziemlich gut.

5. Er trägt heute ein_______ Anorak.

6. Moni trägt ein_______ hübsches Sommerkleid.

7. Wir würden kein_______ Leute_______ so etwas sagen.

8. Ist das der Titel d_______ Film_______ oder d_______ Roman_______?

9. So was kann man in d_______ Bibliothek finden.

10. Hast du noch ein_______ Frage?

J

1. Ich muss zu mein_______ Psychologin gehen.

2. Das ist nicht mein_______ Scheckheft.

3. Hast du dein_______ Führerschein dabei?

4. Karl hat ein Paket von sein_______ Tante in Emden bekommen.

5. Habt ihr eur_______ Verwandten *(pl.)* besucht?

6. Was hast du mit dies_______ Bücher_______ gemacht?

7. Sie geht mit ihr_______ Vater aus.

8. Ich habe nichts gegen dies_______ Idee.

9. Bist du mit d_______ Auto oder mit d_______ Straßenbahn gekommen?

10. Was hast du dein_______ Mutter geschenkt? Und dein_______ Vater? Und dein_______ Geschwister_______?

K

1. Wo kann man ein_______ Kino in der Nähe finden?

2. Jed_______ Kleid in dies_______ Geschäft ist sehr hübsch.

3. Mein________ Schwester ist mit ihr________ Freundinnen ausgegangen.
4. Das ist ein Bild von unser________ Opa.
5. Wie ist der Name eur________ Oma?
6. D______ Paket von dein________ Schwester liegt auf jen________ Tisch dort.
7. Das Ende manch ein________ Roman________ von dies________ Autor ist schwach oder unnatürlich.
8. Das gefällt jed________ Kind aber wahrscheinlich nicht sein________ Eltern.
9. Was gefällt eur________ Kinder________ besser?
10. Hast du ein________ Professor oder ein________ Professorin?

L

1. Warum spielen ihr________ Kinder so wild?
2. Haben Sie Post für dies________ Leute?
3. Solch________ ein________ Person könnte ich sehr leicht hassen!
4. Was sagt ihr eur________ Eltern?
5. Wegen d________ Prüfung sind wir all________ heute „krank" geworden.
6. Welch________ Person gehört dieser CD-Spieler?
7. Welch________ Züge fahren nach Bonn?
8. Welch________ Kurs gefällt dir dieses Semester am wenigsten?
9. Mit welch________ Freunde________ geht ihr heute Abend aus?
10. Mit welch________ Zug soll er ankommen?

M

1. Was für ein________ Idee ist das?!
2. Was für ________ Leute würden so 'was sagen?
3. Du solltest zu d________ Arzt gehen – er soll sehr gut sein.
4. Hast du ein________ Kugelschreiber bei dir?
5. Siehst du d________ Frau an der Ecke, oder ist das ein________ Mann?

Chapter 11 Adjective Endings

Part One

Adjectives are words that modify (describe or limit) nouns and pronouns. Keep the following basic notions in mind:

1. Adjectives are not normally capitalized unless they begin a sentence:

   Das sind **schöne** Kleider. **Schöne** Kleider sind oft teuer.

2. Adjectives denoting a nationality or religious affiliation are not capitalized:

   George Washington war der erste **amerikanische** Präsident.
   Ist Helene **katholisch**, **protestantisch**, **lutherisch** oder **jüdisch**?

3. When adjectives precede the nouns they modify, they bear case endings:

   Wir haben heute **schön*es* Wetter**.
   Herr Siebert fährt einen **groß*en* dick*en* Mercedes**.

4. Adjectives that follow the nouns they modify, for example, predicate adjectives, bear *no* ending:

   Das **Wetter** ist heute **schön**.

To arrive at the correct ending it is presumed you know the gender and case of the noun you'll be modifying. If you don't know the gender or the case of the noun, you will be merely guessing, and the odds are that you'll probably guess wrong. The importance of knowing noun genders as well as basic case affiliations cannot be overemphasized.

Primary and Secondary Case Endings/Sounds

There are two "sets" of adjective endings: primary endings and secondary endings. Since these endings are orthographic representations of sounds, we'll call them primary and secondary sounds, and each sound can be reduced to a single letter, making things simpler. (Traditional grammars refer to these as "strong" and "weak" endings. Since these labels have little pragmatic value for students, we will not use them.)

As far as determining the endings, it is practical to think of them in three groups or "scenarios":

1. the **der**-words and adjectives that follow them
2. the **ein**-words and adjectives that follow them
3. adjectives not preceded by **der**- or **ein**-words

To see more easily how secondary endings are used, it will be worthwhile to review the primary case sounds briefly.

Review of Primary Case Sounds

The definite article and **der**-words *always* display a primary sound:

Primary Case Sounds: *der*-Words + Noun Endings

	masculine	*feminine*	*neuter*	*plural*
nominative:	**r**	**e**	**s**	**e**
accusative:	**n**	**e**	**s**	**e**
dative:	**m**	**r**	**m**	**n + n**
genitive:	**s + s**	**r**	**s + s**	**r**

Ein-words display the primary sounds except for three instances, where they display no ending at all. We'll view the **ein**-words as "deficient" in these instances because they do not display the expected sound/ending, and we'll indicate that by using a dash:

Primary Case Sounds: *ein*-Words + Noun Endings

	masculine	*feminine*	*neuter*	*plural*
nominative:	—	**e**	—	**e**
accusative:	**n**	**e**	—	**e**
dative:	**m**	**r**	**m**	**n + n**
genitive:	**s + s**	**r**	**s + s**	**r**

If we integrate the **der**- and **ein**-word paradigms, we have this next paradigm, which you should be able to reproduce quickly whenever needed:

Summary of Primary Case Sounds:
***der*-Words or *ein*-Words + Noun Endings**

	masculine	*feminine*	*neuter*	*plural*
nominative:	**r** *or* —	**e**	**s** *or* —	**e**
accusative:	**n**	**e**	**s** *or* —	**e**
dative:	**m**	**r**	**m**	**n+n**
genitive:	**s+s**	**r**	**s+s**	**r**

Adjectives Following *der*-Words: Secondary Case Sounds

Until now, the sentences with which you have worked have not employed adjectives after **der**- and **ein**-words. Keep this fundamental rule in mind: When the ***der***- or ***ein***-word supplies the primary sound, any following adjectives display secondary sounds.

There are only two secondary sounds: **e** and **n.** Use **e** for all the nominative singulars and all the accusative singulars except the masculine, which has a primary **n**-sound. Use **n** in the masculine accusative and everywhere else.

If we integrate that information into the primary sound paradigm, using superscript letters to represent following secondary sounds, it looks like this:

Primary and Secondary Case Sounds:
***der*-Words and Following Adjectives**

	masculine	*feminine*	*neuter*	*plural*
nominative:	der alte Mann $\mathbf{r^e}$	die kleine Frau $\mathbf{e^e}$	das schöne Mädchen $\mathbf{s^e}$	die jungen Leute $\mathbf{e^n}$
accusative:	den alten Mann $\mathbf{n^n}$	die kleine Frau $\mathbf{e^e}$	das schöne Mädchen $\mathbf{s^e}$	die jungen Leute $\mathbf{e^n}$
dative:	dem alten Mann $\mathbf{m^n}$	der kleinen Frau $\mathbf{r^n}$	dem schönen Mädchen $\mathbf{m^n}$	den jungen Leuten $\mathbf{n^n + n}$
genitive:	des alten Mannes $\mathbf{s^n + s}$	der kleinen Frau $\mathbf{r^n}$	des schönen Mädchens $\mathbf{s^n + s}$	der jungen Leute $\mathbf{r^n}$

NOTE: You will remember that **n**-nouns, or weak nouns, had two possible endings: -**e** in the nominative singular (**Junge**) and -**n** or -**en** in all other cases, singular and plural (**Jungen**). These endings are, in fact, secondary case sounds and are referred to conventionally as "weak endings" and are the reason these nouns are frequently referred to as "weak nouns." The term "**n**-nouns" is a recent convention.

Adjectives Following *ein*-Words: The Notion of Compensation

Ein-words supply primary sounds except for the three instances already noted. When **ein**-words supply the primary sound, *any* adjectives that follow will display the secondary sound. *When* ***ein****-words fail to deliver the primary sound, any adjectives that follow will have to compensate by taking on that responsibility and supplying them.* In effect, the adjectives are *compensating* for the **ein**-words' "deficiencies."

Primary and Secondary Case Sounds:
***ein*-Words and Following Adjectives**

	masculine	*feminine*	*neuter*	*plural*
nominative:	ein alt**er** Mann ___^{r}	ein**e** klein**e** Frau $\mathbf{e^{e}}$	ein schön**es** Mädchen ___^{s}	kein**e** jung**en** Leute $\mathbf{e^{n}}$
accusative:	ein**en** alt**en** Mann $\mathbf{n^{n}}$	ein**e** klein**e** Frau $\mathbf{e^{e}}$	ein schön**es** Mädchen ___^{s}	kein**e** jung**en** Leute $\mathbf{e^{n}}$
dative:	ein**em** alt**en** Mann $\mathbf{m^{n}}$	ein**er** klein**en** Frau $\mathbf{r^{n}}$	ein**em** schön**en** Mädchen $\mathbf{m^{n}}$	kein**en** jung**en** Leut**en** $\mathbf{n^{n} + n}$
genitive:	ein**es** alt**en** Mann**es** $\mathbf{s^{n} + s}$	ein**er** klein**en** Frau $\mathbf{r^{n}}$	ein**es** schön**en** Mädchen**s** $\mathbf{s^{n} + s}$	kein**er** jung**en** Leute $\mathbf{r^{n}}$

Let's look at the three instances of "deficiency" to see what transpires:

masculine nominative:	Ein neu**er**, groß**er**, blau**er** Wagen stand vor unserem Haus.
neuter nominative:	Ein neu**es**, groß**es**, blau**es** Auto stand vor unserem Haus.
neuter accusative:	Ich habe ein neu**es,** groß**es**, blau**es** Auto gekauft.

Adjectives that precede a noun all take the same ending, or give the same sound. They will either all be secondary sounds/endings after a **der**- or **ein**-word that supplies the primary sound, or they will all have primary endings/sounds after an **ein**-word that is deficient.

Dies**e** gut**en** alt**en** Freunde wohnen in Bremen. (Secondary sounds always required after a **der**-word.)
Das ist ein groß**er** schwarz**er** Hund. (Primary sounds required because the **ein**-word is deficient.)
Wir wohnen in ein**em** alt**en** weiß**en** Haus. (Secondary sounds required after **ein**-words with primary sounds.)
Ich habe meine gut**en** alt**en** Freunde besucht. (Secondary sounds required after **ein**-words with primary sounds.)

Unpreceded Adjectives

When adjectives precede a noun, they must display an ending. *Any and all adjectives not preceded by a* ***der****- or* ***ein****-word must display the primary sound for the case, gender, and number of the noun,* unless the noun displays that ending, in which case the adjective will bear a secondary sound.

Here are some example sentences using masculine nouns, since their endings are the most distinctive:

nominative:	Frisch**er** brasilianisch**er** Kaffee schmeckt wunderbar.
accusative:	Ich trinke nur frisch**en** brasilianisch**en** Kaffee.
dative:	Ich mag keinen Zucker in frisch**em** brasilianisch**em** Kaffee.
genitive:	Der Duft frisch**en** brasilianisch**en** Kaffee*s* ist unbeschreiblich gut.

Note that in the genitive example above, the primary **s**-sound is displayed by the noun, so the adjectives display the secondary **n**-sound, and this secondary sound anticipates and *precedes* the noun ending. Though this is all perfectly logical, it does take some getting used to.

Primary Sounds: Unpreceded Adjectives

	masculine	*feminine*	*neuter*	*plural*
nominative:	schwarze**r** Kaffee **r**	kalt**e** Milch **e**	deutsche**s** Bier **s**	jung**e** Leute **e**
accusative:	schwarze**n** Kaffee **n**	kalt**e** Milch **e**	deutsche**s** Bier **s**	jung**e** Leute **e**
dative:	schwarze**m** Kaffee **m**	kalte**r** Milch **r**	deutsche**m** Bier **m**	junge**n** Leute**n** **n + n**
genitive:	schwarze**n** Kaffee**s** ^{n}+ **s**	kalte**r** Milch **r**	deutsche**n** Bier**es** ^{n}+ **s**	junge**r** Leute **r**

The Special Case of Adjectives with Vanishing Vowels or Consonants

Some adjectives drop the **e** at the end of the stem when an adjective ending is added:

teuer: Eva kauft sich viele **teure** Schuhe. (just like **euer**)
dunkel: Es war eine **dunkle** und windige Nacht.
miserabel: Gestern hatten wir **miserables** Wetter.

The adjective **hoch** drops the **c** when an adjective ending is added:

Das Gebäude ist **hoch**. vs. Das ist ein **hohes** Gebäude.

Synthesis of Primary and Secondary Sounds: The Complete Master Paradigm

If we integrate **der**- and **ein**-words with secondary and compensatory primary sounds and mandatory noun case endings, the paradigm now looks like this:

Synthesis of Primary and Secondary Case Sounds:
***der*-words, *ein*-words, Following Adjectives + Noun Endings**

	masculine	*feminine*	*neuter*	*plural*
nominative:	$\mathbf{r}^{e}$ *or* —^{r}	$\mathbf{e}^{e}$	$\mathbf{s}^{e}$ *or* —^{s}	$\mathbf{e}^{n}$
accusative:	$\mathbf{n}^{n}$	$\mathbf{e}^{e}$	$\mathbf{s}^{e}$ *or* —^{s}	$\mathbf{e}^{n}$
dative:	$\mathbf{m}^{n}$	$\mathbf{r}^{n}$	$\mathbf{m}^{n}$	$\mathbf{n}^{n} + \mathbf{n}$
genitive:	$\mathbf{s}^{n} + \mathbf{s}$	$\mathbf{r}^{n}$	$\mathbf{s}^{n} + \mathbf{s}$	$\mathbf{r}^{n}$

This is the fully developed paradigm for noun-related case endings/sounds. Study it carefully, understand it completely, and be able to reproduce it in one minute or less. Pay attention to formatting since it is quite significant.

Exercises: Part One

Theory Review

1. Fill in the blanks with the correct information.

1. When an adjective precedes a noun that it is modifying, it must display a case ______________.
2. If only an adjective precedes a noun, that is, if no article or **der**-word is used with the noun, the adjective is known as an ______________________ adjective.
3. When there is only an adjective before the noun, the adjective will always display a ______________________ case ending/sound. (Exceptions: genitive singular, masculine and neuter.)
4. If there are two or more of these unpreceded adjectives before a noun, will they bear the same primary ending/sound? ____________
5. If a definite article or **der**-word is used with an adjective before a noun, the definite article or **der**-word will display a ______________________ case ending/sound and the adjective will display a ______________________ ending/sound.
6. There are only two secondary case sounds: _________________ and ___________________.
7. In all nominative and accusative singulars (except masculine accusative) the secondary sound is ______________________.
8. In all other cases (accusative singular, all datives, all genitives, all plurals) the secondary sound is ______________________.
9. To repeat: Whenever a definite article or **der**-word is used with an adjective, the definite article or **der**-word displays a ______________________ case ending/sound, and the following adjective will display a ______________________ case ending/sound.
10. Do the indefinite article and **ein**-words (possessive adjectives + **kein**) always display primary case endings/sounds? ____________
11. In which instances does the **ein**-word family fail to display it? ______________________, ______________________, and ______________________.

12. What must any adjective used with the **ein**-word do in these situations?

____

13. What must any adjective used with the **ein**-word do when the **ein**-word does display a primary case ending/sound?

____

14. General rule of thumb: All adjectives in the same "string" will have the ____________ case ending/sound.

Focus on Form [✓]

2. Fill in the blanks with the correct adjective and noun endings. Leave blanks empty when no endings are required.

A

1. Ich habe kein_______ billig_______ Wagen.
2. Das war ihr_______ letzt_______ Brief.
3. Dein_______ grün_______ Mantel hängt dort drüben.
4. Sie fährt mit d_______ letzt_______ Zug.
5. Der Kellner serviert es ein_______ ander_______ Gast.
6. Haben Sie etwas für ein_______ arm_______ Mann?
7. Gibt es hier gut_______ Essen?
8. Hilf d_______ alt_______ Frau.
9. Ich meine d_______ ander_______ Mann da drüben.
10. Ich würde kein_______ ausländisch_______ Wagen *(sg.)* fahren.

B

1. Ich möchte d_______ ander_______ Mädchen kennen lernen.
2. Wie schnell kann dein_______ neu_______ Auto fahren?
3. Er schenkt d_______ klein_______ Kind ein Stück Kaugummi.
4. Das ist nichts für ein_______ krank_______ Kind.
5. Er wohnt nicht weit von dies_______ neu_______ Hotel.

6. Das ist ein_______ alt_______ Gebäude.

7. Kommen Sie in mein_______ neu_______ Büro.

8. Was für ein_______ alt_______ Gerät ist das?

9. Wir fahren mit ein_______ norwegisch_______ Schiff.

10. Ich kann dir ein_______ gut_______ Beispiel davon geben.

C

1. D_______ braun_______ Ledermappe kostet vierzig Euro.

2. Das ist ein_______ schön_______ Farbe für ein_______ Krawatte.

3. Das ist kein_______ schwer_______ Übung.

4. Der Brief ist von mein_______ klein_______ Schwester.

5. Reinhold kommt aus ein_______ klein_______ Stadt in Niedersachsen.

6. Ich lese ein_______ deutsch_______ Zeitschrift.

7. Fahr nicht schnell durch dies_______ fremd_______ Stadt.

8. Ich gebe es d_______ neu_______ Sekretärin.

9. Mein_______ neu_______ Uhr geht nach.

10. So ein_______ alt_______ romantisch_______ Stadt sieht man nicht oft.

D

1. Das Ende sein_______ neu_______ Film_______ war schockierend.

2. Er ist der Besitzer ein_______ groß_______ Fabrik in Berlin.

3. Er ist ein_______ Liebhaber klassisch_______ italienisch_______ Musik.

4. Er wohnt am Ende d_______ lang_______ Straße.

5. Sie ist die Tochter ein_______ berühmt_______ Politiker_______.

6. Wegen furchtbar_______ Wetter_______ mussten wir zu Hause bleiben.

7. Wo sind die Eltern dies_______ wild_______ laut_______ Kinder?

8. Verstehen Sie d_______ alt_______ Dame?

9. Was machen wir mit dies_______ kaputt_______ Maschine?

10. Wem gehört dies_______ weiß_______ Bluse?

E

1. Lieb________ Frau Schneider, ...
2. Der Professor gibt gut________ Beispiele.
3. Deutschland hat wenig________ hoh________ Gebäude.
4. Er schrieb schön________ Gedichte.
5. Frisch________ Brot schmeckt sehr gut.
6. Frisch________ Kaffee aus Kolumbien riecht wunderbar.
7. Trinkt er nur teur________ französisch________ Wein?
8. Dunkl________ Farben gefallen mir nicht.
9. Ich lese gern deutsch________ Romane.
10. In dieser Stadt gibt es schön________ Parks.

F

1. D________ erst________ Seiten sind immer schwer zu lesen.
2. Haben Sie kein________ deutsch________ Bücher hier?
3. Ich sehe gern italienisch________ Filme an.
4. In dieser Stadt sind zwei klein________ Häfen.
5. Man soll all________ arm________ Leute________ helfen, wenn's möglich ist.
6. Morgen bringe ich dir d________ ander________ restauriert________ Bild.
7. Niedrig________ Temperaturen statt dies________ hoh________ Temperaturen würden mir sehr gefallen.
8. Sie fängt mit d________ neu________ Arbeit an.
9. Unser________ neu________ Klassenkameraden sind schon angekommen.
10. Was sollen wir mit dies________ alt________ Klamotten° machen? *Kleidung*

G

1. Welch________ alt________ Freunde meinst du?
2. Wo sind mein________ golden________ Ohrringe?
3. Kalt________ Bier trinke ich gern an ein________ warm________ Abend.
4. Man soll krank________ Leute________ helfen.
5. Die Lehrerin korrigiert unsere Klausuren mit blutrot________ Tinte.
6. Sie trägt d________ klein________ Pakete ins Haus.

7. Trinken Sie gern warm_______ Milch, bevor Sie schlafen gehen?

8. Nur nett_______ freundlich_______ Leute werden auf der Party sein.

9. Seien Sie vorsichtig, mein lieb_______ Herr Wulf!

10. Wir sollen zu d_______ nächst_______ Tankstelle fahren.

H

1. Zeigen Sie mir d_______ neu_______ Landkarte, bitte.

2. Sie will d_______ grün_______ Kleid haben.

3. Hier ist ein Brief von ein_______ amerikanisch_______ Mädchen aus New York.

4. Ist das Ihr_______ neu_______ Segelboot mit drei groß_______ Masten, Herr Trump?

5. Er kauft kein_______ billig_______ Bier.

6. Welch_______ neu_______ Buch meinen Sie?

7. Hast du ein_______ neu_______ Ausweis bekommen?

8. Können Sie mir d_______ ander_______ Plan zeigen?

9. Verkauft ihr eur_______ alt_______ Wagen *(sg.)* nicht?

10. Welch_______ blond_______ Jungen *(pl.)* meinst du?

Focus on Form (for in-class review)

3. Adjectives after *der-* and *ein*-words as well as unpreceded adjectives. Fill in the blanks with correct endings. Leave blanks empty where no endings are required.

A

1. D_______ schwarz_______ Gürtel war mir zu teuer.

2. Der Anfang ihr_______ letzt_______ Roman_______ war spannend.

3. Französisch_______ Filme gefallen mir nicht.

4. Ich möchte d_______ ander_______Student_______ *(pl.)* kennen lernen.

5. Ich würde nur amerikanisch_______ Autos kaufen.

6. In dieser Stadt gibt es groß_______ interessant_______ Museen.

7. Solch_______ arm_______ Länder sieht man in der Dritt_______ Welt.

8. Wo isst man roh_______ Pferdefleisch?

9. Der Professor gibt lang_______ aber leicht_______ Examen.

10. Er ist Direktor ein_______ groß_______ Firma in Berlin.

B

1. Wo ist mein________ silbern________ Brille?
2. Er schenkt sein________ klein________ Nichte eine Tafel Schokolade.
3. Kalt________ Limonade trinke ich gern an ein________ heiß________ Nachmittag im Sommer.
4. Mein________ schwarz________ Jacke liegt auf dem Bett.
5. Der Brief ist von mein________ deutsch________ Familie.
6. Gustav Mahler komponierte eigenartig________ Sinfonien mit kompliziert________ Harmonien.
7. Man soll mehr für dies________ arm________ verloren________ Kinder tun.
8. Sie fährt mit d________ erst________ Bus.
9. Der Laden ist nicht weit von d________ italienisch________ Restaurant.
10. Er ist der Sohn ein________ berühmt________ Sportler________.

C

1. Verfault________ Fisch stinkt furchtbar.
2. Das ist ein________ sehr alt________ Rathaus.
3. Frisch________ Brot direkt aus dem Ofen riecht wunderbar.
4. Haben Sie etwas für ein________ arm________ Kind?
5. Trotz d________ sonnig________ Wetter________ sind wir zu Hause geblieben.
6. Hier hat man gut________ deutsch________ Bier.
7. Hilf d___ alt________ Leute________.
8. Ich schicke es all________ neu________ Kunden.
9. Sie fängt mit ein________ neu________ Leben an.
10. Was für ein________ alt________ Ding ist das?

Focus on Meaning and Form

4. Statements. Say that . . .

1. you have a new apartment, a new job, a new car, and a new boyfriend/girlfriend.

____

2. your last boss is also your new boss.

____

3. you are wearing a white shirt with a red tie, gray pants, a blue jacket, and black shoes.

____

4. one is supposed to help an old man/an old woman/old people.

____

5. you would like to get to know an intelligent, friendly, successful, rich, and good-looking young man/woman.

____

6. this clothing is not appropriate (= **nichts**) for a young girl.

____

7. you can give good, logical examples.

____

8. the letter is from your dear old aunt/your sick grandfather/your evil stepmother.

____

9. you like long, serious, overly emotional, Italian films.

____

10. your rich brother, the lawyer, just bought a big, fat, expensive, fast BMW.

____

5. Questions. Ask me, a new acquaintance, . . .

1. if my native country/homeland has tall mountains, many lakes, and large forests.

____

2. if there are many interesting things to do in this city on a rainy weekend.

____

3. what one is supposed to do with these old things.

____

4. if I would like to buy large or small gold earrings.

____

5. if I can show you an interesting plan for a new house.

____

6. Commands. Tell me, a friend, to . . .

1. come into your new office at the end of the hallway.

   ____

2. bring a bottle of good German wine and some expensive cheese.

   ____

3. drive a bit more slowly in this strange town.

   ____

4. buy only fresh bread, fresh vegetables, fresh meat, and fresh fish.

   ____

5. stop at the next gas station.

   ____

Partnerarbeit

7. Arbeiten Sie zusammen mit Ihrem Partner/Ihrer Partnerin und beantworten Sie diese Fragen mit vielen Adjektiven.

A

1. Was für einen Mann/eine Frau möchtest du eines Tages heiraten?
2. Was für ein Auto möchtest du kaufen? Beschreib es.
3. Welche Kleidung trägst du heute? Beschreib sie.

B

1. Was für Essen wirst du bald kaufen?
2. Beschreib, was du in deinem Schlafzimmer hast.
3. Was für Freunde hast du?

Part Two

Compound Adjectives: *derselbe/dieselbe/dasselbe; dieselben*

Consider **derselbe** and its variant forms to be nothing other than a compound adjective: the marriage of **der** (*the*) to the adjective **selb-** (*same*). Since **der** always supplies the primary sound, **selb-** always supplies a secondary sound:

nominative:	Das ist **derselbe** Wagen, nicht wahr?
accusative:	Ich habe **denselben** Wagen gesehen.
dative:	Karin saß in **demselben** Wagen.
genitive:	Was ist die Farbe **desselben** Wagens?

Plural Adjectives

The adjectives **andere**, **einige**, **mehrere**, **viele**, and **wenige** are plural adjectives that denote a vague quantity or number. They are neither **der**- nor **ein**-words, which means that any adjectives used with them will have the same ending. There's really nothing notable about these except that they are plural.

andere	*other*	**Andere alte Filme** von ihm sind besser.
einige	*some*	Ich habe **einige gute Freunde** in Holland.
mehrere	*several*	Wir sprachen mit **mehreren ausländischen Studenten** von dem Kurs.
viele	*many*	Bruno hat **viele konservative Meinungen.**
wenige	*few*	**Wenige junge Leute** haben solche Meinungen.

Adjectival Nouns

Very often the words **Mann**, **Frau**, and **Kind** are replaced by an adjective-turned-noun. These adjectives are *hybrids:* They are capitalized like nouns, but have endings like adjectives:

Ein Kleiner spielte auf dem Spielplatz.
A little boy played in the playground.

Hast du **diesen Kleinen** gesehen?
Did you see the little boy?

Hast du **mit der Kranken** gesprochen?
Did you speak with the sick woman?

Wie ist der Name **der Kranken**?
What's the name of the sick woman?

Abstractions are phrased as neuter adjectival nouns and normally used with a definite article:

Was ist **das Schlechte** daran?
What's the bad thing about it?

Das Gute kämpft immer gegen **das Böse**.
Good always struggles agains evil.

Das Schöne und **das Hässliche** passen nicht zusammen.
The beautiful and the ugly do not go well together.

Adjectives Following Uninflected Elements

When an adjective follows a word or expression, usually denoting a quantity, that is uninflected (has no case ending), it must provide the primary case sound required by the noun. Again, we see the compensatory role of adjectives at work.

etwas	*some*	Ich muss ***etwas*** **wärmere Kleidung** kaufen.
ein wenig	*a little*	Willst du noch ***ein wenig*** **schwarzen Kaffee** trinken?
ein paar	*a couple of*	Hast du ***ein paar*** **süße Kekse**?
genug	*enough*	Haben wir ***genug*** **kaltes Bier**?
viel	*much*	Kaufen wir ***viel*** **weißen Käse**.
wenig	*little*	Wir haben ***wenig*** **frisches Obst**.
mehr	*more*	Das Mädchen will **mehr interessante Liebesromane** lesen.
numbers		Ich möchte ***zwei oder drei*** **neue Bücher** suchen.

If a **der**- or **ein**-word is used along with an uninflected word or expression, the adjective reacts to the **der**- or **ein**-word and displays the appropriate ending:

Hast du **eine *etwas* kürzere Prüfung** gehabt?
Did you have a somewhat shorter test?

Jetzt lesen wir **einen *etwas* längeren Roman**.
Now we'll read a somewhat longer novel.

Adjectives after the Indefinite Pronouns *alles, etwas, nichts, viel, wenig*

The pronouns **alles**, **etwas**, **nichts**, **viel**, and **wenig** are neuter indefinite pronouns, so adjectives that follow them need to be neuter as well, and these adjectives need to be capitalized since they function as adjectival nouns. All of these except **alles**, a member of the **der**-word group, are indeclinable forms, so primary sounds/endings are needed:

Das ist wirklich **etwas Schönes**! (nominative)
That is really something bautiful!

Ich habe dir **wenig Neues** zu erzählen. (accusative)
I have something new to tell you about.

Im Westen **nichts Neues**. (nominative)
All quiet in the west. (All Quiet on the Western Front)

Viel Interessantes stand gestern in der Zeitung.
There was much that was interesting in the newspaper yesterday.

Alles is a variant form of **all**-, a **der**-word, so the **s** on the end of **alles** is a primary sound. That means that an adjective after **alles** exhibits a secondary sound:

Ich wünsche dir **alles Gute** zum Geburtstag.
I wish you all the best for your birthday.

Ich will **alles Neue** wissen.
I want to know everything new/all that is new.

Ich habe **alles mögliche** vesucht.
I've tried everything possible.

Wir haben **alles übrige** zu Hause gelassen.
We left everything else at home.

NOTE: **Möglich** (*possible*), **übrig** (*extra*), and **ander** (*other, else*) are not capitalized in this kind of expression. These pronouns are normally used either as a nominative subject or accusative object; when they are used with a preposition, one must remember to use the appropriate accusative or dative primary sound/ending on the adjective:

Kerstin arbeitete **an etwas Interessantem**.
Kerstin worked on something interesting.

Die Rede des Kanzlers handelte **von wenig Neuem**.
The chancellor's speech dealt with little that was new.

Die Diskussion führte **zu nichts Wichtigem.**
The discussion led to nothing important.

Er antwortete dem Lehrer **mit etwas Blödem**.
He answered the teacher with something stupid.

Remember, again, that **alles** is a **der**-word; when used after a preposition, it will bear a primary sound/ending and any adjective following it will display a secondary one:

Bernd redete **von allem anderen.**
Bernd spoke (chatted) about everything else.

Hast du **an alles andere** gedacht?
Have you thought of everything else?

Aus allem Bösen kann etwas Gutes noch aufspringen.
Something good can come of everything bad.

Sie haben immer **gegen alles Unehrliches** gekämpft.
They always fought against everything dishonest.

Participial Adjectives

Present and past participles may be employed as adjectives and will display whatever case endings are required.

Past Participles

In English, past participles are used "as is" as adjectives:

Have the police found the *stolen* car?
This is a *used* car.
That was an *unidentified* object.

In German, simply use a past participle and add the required adjective ending:

Hat die Polizei den **gestohlenen** Wagen gefunden?
Das ist ein **gebrauchter** Wagen.
Das war ein **unidentifiziertes** Objekt.

Present Participles

Present participles in English are adjectives derived from verbs. One simply adds *-ing* to the infinitive.

Listen to the *roaring* brook. Answer the *following* questions. Was that a *flying* pig?

To form a present participle in German, simply add a **-d** to the infinitive and then any required adjective ending:

Example: **folgen** + **d** + adjective ending

Lies die **folgenden** Beispiele.
Read the following examples.

Beantworte die **folgenden** Fragen.
Answer the following questions.

Pass auf den **folgenden** Bericht auf.
Pay attention to the following report.

NOTE: It is possible for a noun to be modified by both a past and a present participle:

Ich habe einmal ein **glänzendes unidentifiziertes fliegendes** Objekt gesehen.
I once saw a shining unidentified flying object.

Exercises: Part Two

Theory Review

1. Fill in the blanks with the correct information.

1. Words like **derselbe, dieselbe, dasselbe, dieselben** are actually ______________________ adjectives. The first component behaves like the ______________________ article and the second component behaves like a following ______________________.
2. These words consist of a ______________________ sound on the first component and a ______________________ sound on the second.
3. Are **einige, andere, wenige, viele,** and **mehrere der**-words? _________ **Ein**-words? _________
4. These adjectives share one thing in common: They are all ______________________.
5. Their endings/sounds will simply be those of any ______________________. Since they are normally used without a **der**-word, you can usually expect these adjectives to have ______________________ sounds/endings most of the time.
6. Of course, in the relatively rare instances where they may be used with a **der**-word, they will display ______________________ sounds/endings.
7. Adjectival nouns are nouns derived from an adjective. Since they are nouns, they will always be ______________________.
8. Since they are still "adjectival," they will display a case ______________________.
9. If an adjectival noun follows a **der**-word, it will display a ______________________ sound/ending.
10. If it follows an **ein**-word that does not display the primary sound/ending, the adjectival noun will ______________________ for that "deficiency."
11. Words like **etwas, viel, wenig, ein paar,** and **genug** are ______________________. They have no case ending. They are frequently used without any following adjectives.
12. The gender of these words is ______________________ when used as pronouns.
13. An adjectival noun is frequently used after them. Remember that it must be ______________________ because it is a noun.
14. An adjectival noun following an indefinite pronoun will display a neuter singular ending/sound. Its ______________________ will be determined by the role of the phrase it is in and it will display a ______________________ sound/ending.

15. The word **alles**, on the other hand, is special. It is a member of the ____________ -word family, and the *s* on the end is a primary case sound/ending. Any adjectival noun that follows will display a ______________________ case sound/ending.
16. Present and past ______________________ may function as adjectives. Their endings are determined in the usual manner.

Focus on Form [✓]

2. Supply the correct endings. Leave the blanks empty if no endings are required.

A

1. Alles ander_______ muss bis Freitag fertig sein.
2. Alles Gut_______ zum Geburtstag, Moni!
3. Das ist das Dumm_______ daran.
4. Das ist nichts Besonder_______ für Petra.
5. Das ist mir nichts Wichtig_______.
6. Das Nett_______ daran ist, dass Eva endlich zu Besuch kommt.
7. Das Schlecht_______ daran ist, dass ich kein Geld dafür habe.
8. Das Theaterstück hat wenig Gut_______ zu empfehlen.
9. Hast du nichts Neu_______ von Tante Helene gehört?
10. Hast du je etwas Ähnlich_______ gesehen?

B

1. Alles ander_______ muss bis morgen Nachmittag erledigt sein.
2. Das ist nichts Außergewöhnlich_______.
3. Für mich ist das etwas Besonder_______.
4. Dieses Geschäft hat nur drei neu_______ Angestellt_______.
5. Er hat wirklich nichts Interessant_______ gesagt.
6. Er ist ein_______ alt_______ Bekannt_______ von ein_______ gut_______ Freund von mir.
7. Ich möchte etwas Gut_______ sehen, bitte!
8. Ist das eine Geburtstagskarte von dein_______ Verwandt_______ in Amerika?
9. Ist sie Beamt_______?
10. Ist Jutta ein_______ Bekannt_______ oder ein_______ Freundin von dir?

C

1. Kann der Arzt dies_______ Krank_______ helfen?
2. Kannst du mir etwas Teur_______ zeigen?
3. Viel_______ Blind_______ führen ein bedeutungsvoll_______ Leben.
4. Wer ist d_______ Schön_______ da drüben?
5. Lass das jetzt ruhig. Wir können alles ander_______ später machen.
6. Ich möchte etwas Einfach_______ tragen.
7. „Im Westen nichts Neu_______" ist der Titel ein_______ Roman_______ über d_______ erst_______ Weltkrieg.
8. Sie hat nie etwas Interessant_______ zu sagen.
9. Wir werden alles möglich_______ für Sie tun, Frau Bruns.
10. Wir haben nichts Wichtig_______ gehört.

D

1. Einig_______ gut_______ Freunde von mir kommen heute Abend vorbei.
2. Der Reporter hat dem Bürgermeister viel_______ interessant_______ Fragen gestellt.
3. Wir haben mit mehrer_______ tschechisch_______ Studenten geredet.
4. Karl hat heute viel ausländisch_______ Post bekommen.
5. Haben wir genug frisch_______ Obst?
6. Wir haben ein paar alt_______ Bücher in der Bibliothek gefunden.
7. Ich möchte ihr ein_______ etwas teur_______ Ring kaufen.
8. Die Assistentin half mir bei einig_______ schwierig_______ Übungen.
9. Mehrer_______ sehr klein_______ Kinder spielten im Park.
10. Du hast immer viel_______ gut_______ Ideen und Vorschläge.

E

1. Frisch_______ gebacken_______ Brot schmeckt wunderbar!
2. Ich möchte gern zwei gebraten_______ Hähnchen kaufen.
3. Wo sind mein_______ schon gewaschen_______ Hemden?
4. In letzter Zeit gab es hoch steigend_______ Temperaturen.
5. Der Verletzt_______ hatte kein_______ gebrochen_______ Knochen.

6. Verflucht mal! Es ist immer d________selb________!
7. Es war doch d________selb________ Mann.
8. Ich habe auch mit d________selb________ Frau geredet.
9. Wir haben d________selb________ Film gesehen.
10. Ich bin auch d________selb________ Meinung.

Focus on Form (for in-class review)

3. Supply the correct endings. Leave the blanks empty if no endings are required.

A

1. Frisch gebacken________ Kuchen schmeckt lecker.
2. Wir werden einig________ gut________ Freunde in Hamburg besuchen.
3. Du hast immer viel________ interessant________ philosophisch________ Theorien zu diskutieren.
4. Ist Karl-Heinz ein________ Verwandt________ von dir?
5. Paul ist leider nicht d________selb________ Meinung.
6. Alles Gut________, Stefan!
7. Ich möchte gern zwei gekocht________ Eier zum Frühstück haben.
8. Das ist das Best________ daran, Konrad.
9. Für uns ist das nichts Besonder________.
10. Wir arbeiten mit mehrer________ ausgezeichnet________ Kollegen in dieser Abteilung.

B

1. Das ist nichts Außergewöhnlich________.
2. Neulich gab es niedrig sinkend________ Temperaturen.
3. Wer ist d________ Schön________ da drüben?
4. Der Jung________ hatte ein________ zum Tode gefroren________ Ente im Park gefunden.
5. Haben wir genug frisch________ Obst fur die Gäste?
6. Käthe will immer etwas ander________ machen.
7. Ich möchte Ihnen etwas Modisch________ zeigen.
8. Wir haben ein paar alt________ Sachen im Keller entdeckt.
9. Das Best________ daran ist, dass der Plan ganz logisch ist.
10. Es war doch d________selb________ Kind.

C

1. Ich möchte etwas Billig________ kaufen.
2. Wir möchten ihr ein_______ etwas besser_______ Kette kaufen.
3. Tina hat mit d_______selb_______ Polizisten gesprochen.
4. Der Chef hat nie etwas Intelligent________ zu sagen.
5. Hast du etwas Neu_______ in der Zeitung gelesen?
6. Ist er Beamt_______ bei der Post?
7. Mehrer_______ sehr klein_______ Hunde liefen die Straße entlang.
8. Wir haben d_______selb_______ Roman für den Englischkurs lesen müssen.
9. Wir werden alles möglich_______ machen.
10. Ich habe ein_______ gebraucht_______ Motorrad gekauft.

Focus on Meaning and Form

4. Statements. Express the following in German. Say that . . .

1. You'd like some Italian bread, cold milk, French wine, and green vegetables.

 ____

2. We have some good books, some rich friends, and some interesting things.

 ____

3. You know several intelligent people.

 ____

4. You now have lots of money, lots of new friends, and no new enemies.

 ____

5. We have read the same book, seen the same film, heard the same story, and had the same opinions about them.

 ____

 ____

6. The police spoke with the same man . . . the same woman . . . the same child . . . the same people.

 ____

 ____

7. He lived in the same house with the same people, studied at the same university, worked for the same boss, drove the same car, read the same paper, drank the same beer, and died on the same day!

8. The strong must help the weak.

9. The rich are obligated to give something to the poor.

10. After the war there remained only the living and the dead.

11. You like freshly baked bread, boiled eggs, and fried green tomatoes.

12. The police caught the man with the stolen money.

5. Commands. Tell me to . . .

1. greet the arriving guests

2. answer all the following questions

3. always do the unexpected instead of the expected.

6. Fill in the blanks with the cued adjectival nouns.

1. Ich sprach ______________________________. (*with the cute one → fem.*)
2. Und sie sprach ______________________________. (*with the tall one → masc.*)
3. ______________________________ ist endlich kaputt. (*That awful thing*)
4. ________________________ M&Ms sind lecker, aber ich finde ________________________ leckerer. (*Yellow; the red ones*)
5. Du hast ein nagelneues Auto, aber ich habe nur ______________________________ Auto. (*an old used*)
6. Ich habe ______________________________ in der Zeitung gelesen. (*nothing important*)
7. Thomas spielt immer mit ______________________________. (*something new*)
8. Ich möchte eine Zeitschrift kaufen, aber ich kann ______________________________ finden. (*nothing interesting*)
9. __________________________ daran ist, dass ich es nicht mehr machen muss. (*The good thing*)
10. ______________________________ bekommen gewöhnlich die besten Noten, und

    ______________________________ bekommen meistens die schlechten Noten. (*The hard-working ones; the lazy ones*)

Supplementary Exercises [✓]

The following exercises include unpreceded adjectives, adjectives after *der-* and *ein*-words, adjectives that follow indefinite pronouns, and participial adjectives. Fill in the blanks with the correct adjective and noun endings. Leave blanks empty when no endings are required.

A

1. Ich muss alles möglich_______ versuchen.
2. Du musst nichts ander_______ machen.
3. D_______ schwarz_______ Schuhe kosten achtzig Euro.
4. D_______ erst_______ Tage sind immer schwer bei der Arbeit.
5. Das Ende sein_______ letzt_______ Roman_______ war überraschend.
6. Einig_______ alt_______ Freunde treffen sich abends in der Kneipe.
7. Gebraten_______ Huhn ist lecker!
8. Ich habe kein_______ neu________ Auto.
9. Ich möchte d_______ ander________ Leute kennen lernen.
10. Kannst du dies________ Jung_______ glauben?

B

1. Lieb________ Herr Kramer, ...
2. Welch________ deutsch________ Lehrbuch meinst du?
3. Zeigen Sie mir d________ neu________ Bild, bitte.
4. Du hast immer viel________ vernünftig________ Meinungen.
5. Hast du je so etwas Komisch________ gesehen?
6. Ich bin nicht ander________ Meinung.
7. Ich kann dir kein________ logisch________ Erklärung dafür geben.
8. Ich würde ein_______ ausländisch_______ Auto kaufen, aber nur ein_______ japanisch_______.
9. In dieser Stadt gibt es schön________ groß________ Kirchen.
10. Ist Harald ein________ Verwandt________ von euch?

C

1. Solch________ ein________ romantisch________ Person kennt man nur selten.
2. Was sollen wir mit unser________ alt________ Computer machen?
3. Welch________ blond________ Mädchen meinst du?
4. Wem gehört dies________ kariert________ Rock?
5. Wir haben Ihnen alles Wichtig________ mitgeteilt.
6. Wir sollen zu d________ nächst________ Rastplatz fahren.
7. Alles Gut________ zum Geburtstag, Stefan!
8. Das ist ein________ hässlich________ Farbe für ein________ formell________ Kleid.
9. Das ist nichts Gewöhnlich________.
10. Das war ihr________ letzt________ Anruf.

D

1. Die Professorin gibt uns gut________ Erklärungen.
2. Der Student hat dem Professor viel________ schwer________ Fragen gestellt.
3. Frau Dorn ist die Besitzerin ein________ groß________ Firma in Frankfurt.
4. Haben Sie kein________ deutsch________ Bier hier?
5. Ich möchte gern zwei________ gekocht________ Eier essen.
6. Kannst du mir etwas Billig________ zeigen?
7. Ich will ein________ braun________ Jacke kaufen.

8. Wie schnell kann dein_______ neu_______ Boot segeln?

9. Wo sind mein_______ silbern_______ Ketten?

10. Das ist das Gut_______ daran.

E

1. Das ist kein_______ leicht_______ Übung.
2. Dein_______ schwarz_______ Regenschirm hängt dort drüben.
3. Die Schweiz hat viel_______ reich_______ Banken.
4. Er ist ein_______ verrückt_______ Fan dies_______ bayrisch_______ Fußballmannschaft.
5. Er gibt d_______ klein_______ Junge_______ ein Stück Schokolade.
6. Für mich ist das etwas Dumm_______.
7. Hier ist ein Brief von ein_______ russisch_______ Mädchen aus Moskau.
8. Ich sehe gern traurig_______ romantisch_______ Filme an.
9. Heiß_______ Kaffee trinke ich gern an ein_______ kalt_______ Wintertag.
10. Man kann oft alt_______ kaputt_______ Fahrräder wieder in Ordnung bringen.

F

1. Wir haben mit wenig_______ Leute_______ darüber gesprochen.
2. Wo sind unser_______ neu_______ Rucksäcke?
3. Das ist nichts Außergewöhnlich_______ für Petra.
4. Das ist aber nichts für ein_______ jung_______ Mädchen.
5. Der Brief ist von mein_______ alt_______ Onkel.
6. Diese Firma hat vierzig ausländisch_______ Gastarbeiter.
7. Er schrieb nur kurz_______ Briefe.
8. Das Büro der Direktorin ist am Ende d_______ lang_______ Korridor_______.
9. In dieser Stadt sind zwei berühmt_______ Museen.
10. In letzter Zeit hatten wir sehr kalt_______ Temperaturen.

G

1. Ist das Ihr_______ neu_______ Sternschiff, Kapitän Kirk?
2. Bettina hat viel holländisch_______ Schokolade zum Geburtstag bekommen.
3. Man soll d_______ Blind_______ immer helfen.

4. Sie fährt mit d_______ frühest_______ Bus zur Arbeit.
5. Kennst du d_______ Blond_______ *(masc.)* da drüben?
6. Das ist aber wirklich etwas Überraschend_______, was du da erzählst.
7. Der Kellner empfiehlt das all_______ Gästen.
8. Die Verletzt_______ hatte ein_______ gebrochen_______ Bein.
9. Die Lehrerin hat unser_______ letzt_______ Prüfung streng korrigiert.
10. Der Politiker hat wirklich nichts Neu_______ gesagt.

H

1. Ich kaufe kein_______ billig_______ Wein.
2. Er wohnt nicht weit von d_______ neu_______ Schule.
3. Frisch_______ Obst schmeckt sehr gut.
4. Ich will nur sehr frisch_______ Fisch essen.
5. Man soll d_______ arm_______ Obdachlos_______ wenigstens etwas zu Essen geben.
6. Reinhold kommt aus ein_______ klein_______ Dorf in Österreich.
7. Er ist der Sohn ein_______ berühmt_______ Historiker_______.
8. Wir wollen alles möglich_______ probieren.
9. Das ist ein_______ modern_______ Stadt.
10. Das Best_______ daran ist, dass wir ein bisschen Freizeit haben werden.

I

1. Sie ist ein_______ alt_______ Bekannt_______ von ein_______ gut_______ Freundin von mir.
2. Frisch_______ Brötchen direkt von d_______ deutsch_______ Bäckerei schmecken fantastisch.
3. Haben Sie etwas für ein_______ alt_______ krank_______ Soldat_______?
4. Ich lese manchmal ein_______ deutsch_______ Zeitung.
5. Ich möchte etwas Elegant_______ zum Empfang tragen.
6. Morgen gebe ich dir d_______ ander_______ Sachen.
7. Sie trägt d_______ schwer_______ Paket mit groß_______ Schwierigkeit.
8. Verflucht mal! Es sind immer d_______selb_______ falsch_______ Gerüchte.
9. Wegen des sonnig_______ Wetter_______ können wir heute nach draußen gehen.
10. Welch_______ neu_______ Auto meinen Sie?

J

1. Wir haben einig_______ interessant_______ Manuskripte im Museum gelesen.
2. Das Interessant_______ daran ist, dass dies_______ wichtig_______ Erfindung zu der Zeit nicht erfolgreich war.
3. Es war doch d_______selb_______ Junge.
4. Fahr nicht schnell durch dies_______ fremd_______ Nachbarschaft.
5. Hast du ein_______ neu_______ Pass bekommen?
6. Gibt es hier gut_______ Restaurants?
7. Ich möchte etwas Besser_______ sehen, bitte!
8. Ich möchte ihm ein_______ warm_______ Pulli kaufen.
9. Kommen Sie in mein_______ neu_______ Weinkeller.
10. Kühl_______ Temperaturen statt dies_______ unglaublich heiß_______ Sommertemperaturen würde ich sehr begrüßen.

K

1. Trinken Sie gern etwas Warm_______, bevor Sie schlafen gehen?
2. Trinkt er nur belgisch_______ Bier und kein_______ deutsch_______ Bier?
3. Wo ist die Mutter dies_______ unhöflich_______ Junge_______?
4. Dies_______ Universität hat viel Gut_______ zu empfehlen.
5. Mutti half mir bei mein_______ schwer_______ Hausaufgaben.
6. Hell_______ Farben gefallen mir sehr.
7. Glaub dies_______ Klein_______ nicht.
8. Ich schenke es mein_______ lieb_______ Nichte.
9. Ich habe auch mit d_______selb_______ Versicherungsagent_______ gesprochen.
10. Ist das eine Geburtstagskarte von dein_______ krank_______ Tante in Hamburg?

L

1. Können Sie mir d_______ ander_______ grau_______ Anzug zeigen?
2. Ich habe nur interessant_______ freundlich_______ Leute zur Party eingeladen.
3. Sie fängt mit d_______ neu_______ Job am Montag an.
4. Sie hat nie etwas Positiv_______ zu sagen.
5. Verstehst du d_______ weinend_______ Kind?

6. Was für ein________ altmodisch________ Maschine ist das? Das ist ein echt________ Museumsstück!

7. Hast du etwas Bös________ über dein________ lieb________ Tante Gertrud gesagt?

8. Ich sehe gern französisch________ Filme an.

9. Ich meine d________ ander________ Junge________ da drüben.

10. Ist er Beamt________?

M

1. Viel________ mutig________ Soldaten sind in der Schlacht gefallen.

2. Mein________ neu________ Uhr geht zwei Minuten vor.

3. Seien Sie vorsichtig, mein________ lieb________ Frau Keck!

4. Unser________ neu________ Chef ist heute angekommen.

5. Verkaufst du dein________ alt________ Rad?

6. Was sollen wir mit dies________ schmutzig________ Kleidung machen?

7. Wir fahren mit ein________ neu________ italienisch________ Luxusschiff.

8. Ich habe d________selb________ Bericht gelesen.

9. Wir werden alles möglich________ für euch machen.

10. Das ist aber einfach rein________ Unsinn!

Chapter 12 Comparative and Superlative Degrees

Adjectives and adverbs have three degrees: *positive, comparative,* and *superlative.* Adjectives and adverbs are used most frequently in the positive degree, with or without case endings:

Dieser Wagen ist **schnell.**	Das ist ein **schneller** Wagen.	Mein Wagen fährt **schnell.**
This car is fast.	*That's a fast car.*	*My car drives fast.*

Comparative Degree: Stem + *-er*

The comparative degree is used to indicate a greater amount of an attribute. To form the comparative degree of an adjective or adverb, extend the positive degree stem by adding **-er**: **schnell** → **schnell*er***, plus any case ending that may be required.

Dieser Wagen ist **schneller**.	Das ist ein **schnellerer** Wagen.	Mein Auto fährt **schneller**.
This car is faster.	*That's a faster car.*	*My car drives faster.*

NOTE: Some adjectives in English are used in the positive degree with the word *more* to form the comparative, for example, *more interesting, more demanding, more exciting, more potent, more abusive, more decisive.* German does not use **mehr** with an adjective or adverb to form the comparative, just the **-er** stem extension: **Dieses Auto ist *teurer*.**

Superlative Degree: Stem + *-(e)st*

The superlative degree is used to indicate the greatest amount of an attribute. To form the superlative degree, extend the stem of the adjective or adverb by adding -(**e**)**st**: **schnell** → **schnell*st*-**, plus any case ending that may be required. Note that the superlative degree is virtually always used in conjunction with the definite article:

Das ist **der schnellste** Wagen.
That's the fastest car.

Ich habe **den schnellsten** Wagen.
I have the fastest car.

Wir folgen **dem schnellsten** Wagen.
We're following the fastest car.

Wer ist der Fahrer **des schnellsten** Wagens?
Who is the driver of the fastest car?

Das ist **das interessanteste** Gedicht.
That's the most interesting poem.

Marthe hat uns **das interessanteste** Gedicht vorgelesen.
Marthe read the most interesting poem to us.

Gab es Symbole in **den interessantesten** Gedichten?
Were there [any] symbols in the most interesting poems?

Wie fandest du den Stil **des interessantesten** Gedichts?
What did you think of the style of the most interesting poem?

Superlative forms always display secondary case endings/sounds because they are always used with the definite article, which supplies the primary case ending/sound:

Die* meist*en Studenten müssen diese Kurse belegen.
Most students have to register for these courses.

Rainer hat die Prüfung mit ***der* niedrigst*en*** Note bestanden.
Rainer passed the test with the lowest grade.

Predicate Adjectives and Adverbs: *am* + Stem + *-sten*

When the adjective is used as a predicate adjective, it is used with the prepositional contraction **am** (**an** + **dem**) + stem + **-sten**.

Dieser Wagen ist ***am* schnell*sten*.**
This car is the fastest.

The same **am -sten** construction is used for a superlative adverb:

Mein Wagen fährt ***am* schnell*sten*.**
My car drives the fastest.

NOTE: The **am -sten** construction for the superlative form of the predicate adjective or adverb is, essentially, a neuter dative prepositional phrase: **an** + **dem** + adjective ending in **-en**. (Remember your dative sound sequence for the neuter: $\mathbf{m}^{\mathbf{n}}$. This is what's being followed here.)

Monosyllabic Adjectives and Adverbs

Expect most monosyllabic adjectives and adverbs to employ an umlaut in forming the comparative and superlative degrees:

alt → **ä**lter → am **ä**ltesten	*old, older, [the] oldest*
jung → j**ü**nger → am j**ü**ngsten	*young, younger, [the] youngest*
rot → r**ö**ter → am r**ö**testen	*red, redder, [the] reddest*

Polysyllabic adjectives sometimes add umlauts, too:

gesund, ges**ü**nder, am ges**ü**ndesten	*healthy, healthier, [the] healthiest*

Irregular Comparatives and Superlatives

Note the irregularities in the comparative and superlative for:

bald, **eher**, **am ehesten**	*soon, sooner, soonest*
dunkel, **dunkler**, am dunkelsten	*dark, darker, darkest*
gern(e), **lieber**, **am liebsten**	*like, like more/prefer, like most*
groß, größer, **am größten**	*big, bigger, biggest*
gut, **besser**, **am besten**	*good, better, best*
hoch, **höher**, am höchsten	*high, higher, highest*
leise, **leiser**, am leisesten	*quiet, quieter, quietest*
nah, **näher**, **am nächsten**	*near, nearer, nearest*
oft, **öfter**, **am öftesten**	*often, more often, most often*
teuer, **teurer**, am teuersten	*expensive, more expensive, most expensive*
viel, **mehr**, **am meisten**	*much, more, most*

Special Comparative and Superlative Constructions

There are a number of specialized constructions used with positive, comparative, and superlative degree adjectives and adverbs to effect particular meanings. Study the constructions that follow carefully, paying particular attention to their English equivalents.

Positive Degree + *so ... wie*

Ich bin **so fleißig wie** du.
I'm ***as hardworking as*** *you.*

Karl ist **so intelligent wie** Steffi.
Karl is ***as smart as*** *Steffi.*

Mein Vater ist **so stark wie** dein Vater.
My father is ***as strong as*** *your father.*

Ich bin **genauso/ebenso intelligent wie** du.
I'm ***just as intelligent as*** *you.*

Comparative Degree + *als*

Mein Vater ist **stärker als** dein Vater.
My father is ***stronger than*** *your father.*

Meine Schwester ist **noch fleißiger als** ich.
My sister is ***even more hardworking than*** *I.*

Etwas/viel + Comparative Degree

Dieser Roman ist **viel besser.**
This novel is ***much better.***

Dieses Auto ist **etwas teurer.**
This car is ***somewhat more expensive.***

Immer + Comparative Degree

Die Tage werden **immer länger** und die Nächte **immer kürzer.**
The days are getting ***longer and longer*** *and the nights* ***shorter and shorter.***

Je ..., desto ... + Comparative Degree

Je mehr, desto besser.
The more, the better.

Je mehr ich lerne, **desto intelligenter** werde ich.
The more *I study,* ***the smarter*** *I get.*

Am + aller ... -sten

Meine Mutter ist **am allerschönsten.**
My mother is *[**the**]* ***prettiest of all.***

Das schmeckt uns **am allerbesten.**
*That tastes [**the**]* ***best of all*** *to us.*

Anomalies with *viel* and *wenig*

Remember the following regarding the use of **viel** and **wenig**:

1. They are indeclinable in the singular: Ich habe **viel/wenig Geld.**
2. They require endings in the plural: Ich kenne **viel*e*/wenig*e* Leute** in der Stadt.
3. Comparative forms, however, are indeclinable: Ich habe **mehr/weniger Freunde** als du.

False Superlatives

Use **höchst** and **äußerst** with a positive degree adjective or adverb to create "false superlatives." They are "false" because there is no comparison of any kind and "superlative" because **höch*st*** and **äußer*st*** both have superlative **-st** sounds. They simply signal a very high degree of whatever attribute or quality the adjective or adverb describes.

höchst interessant = *highly interesting*	Ich finde diesen Roman **höchst interessant.**
äußerst wichtig = *extremely important*	Mir ist dieser Kurs **äußerst wichtig.**
äußerst schnell = *extremely fast*	Mein Porsche fährt **äußerst schnell.**

Adverbial Superlatives Ending in *-ens*

Superlative adverbs ending in **-ens** signal an extreme limit:

frühestens = *at the earliest*	Ich stehe morgens **frühestens** um sieben Uhr auf.
höchstens = *at [the] highest; most*	Das kostet **höchstens** 20 000 Euro.
meistens = *most of the time*	**Meistens** esse ich das nicht.
mindestens = *at [the] least*	Diese Stadt hat **mindestens** 200 000 Einwohner.
wenigstens = *at [the] least*	Ich habe **wenigstens** 2 000 Briefmarken gesammelt.
spätestens = *at the latest*	Du musst **spätestens** um Mitternacht hier sein.

NOTE: The adverbs **mindestens** and **wenigstens** may be used interchangeably.

Adjectival Nouns in the Comparative and Superlative

Adjectival nouns may be in the comparative and superlative degrees. Remember that adjectival nouns are capitalized and take whatever ending is required:

Hans ist ein guter Spieler, aber Karl ist **der Bessere.**
Hans is a good player, but Karl is the better [one/player].

Die Fleißigeren bekommen fast immer die besseren Noten.
The harder working [ones/students] almost always get the better grades.

Die Faulsten bekommen gewöhnlich die schlechtesten Noten.
The laziest [ones/students] usually get the worst grades.

Das ist aber **das Blödeste,** was ich je gehört habe!
That is really the dumbest [thing] I've ever heard of!

Das Beste daran ist der Preis.
The best [thing] about it is the price.

Exercises

Theory Review

1. Fill in the blanks with the correct information.

1. Adjectives and adverbs have ______________________ possible degrees.
2. The adjective in its "normal" form, as presented in a dictionary, is in the ____________________ degree.
3. When two things are compared to each other, the ______________________ degree is used.
4. To form this degree, add ____________ to the stem of the adjective or adverb.
5. After the stem is extended to produce a comparative, any necessary ______________________ ______________________ is added.
6. When three or more things are compared to each other, the ______________________ degree normally comes into play.
7. To form this degree, add ____________ to the stem, followed by any required case ending/sound.
8. A *predicate* adjective in the superlative degree is used with the dative prepositional contraction ____________.
9. Since this dative contraction contains a primary case sound/ending (**m**), the superlative adjective will end in the secondary ____________ -sound/ending.
10. Monosyllabic adjectives and adverbs usually add an ______________________ to the stressed vowel in the comparative and superlative degrees.
11. Some adjectives form irregular comparatives and superlatives. Can you predict these? ________
12. That means you must treat each of these as a unique word and ______________________ the irregular forms.
13. There are a few special constructions that employ the positive, comparative, and superlative degrees. Fill in the blank with the missing key elements for the different constructions:

    as intelligent as you = ____________ intelligent ____________ du

    bigger than a house = größer ____________ ein Haus

    much more expensive = ____________ teurer

    somewhat more interesting = ____________ interessanter

    faster and faster = ____________ schneller

    the less, the better = ____________ weniger, ____________ besser

    [the] best of all = am ____________ besten

14. To signal an extreme limit, add ____________________ to the superlative stem of an adverb.

    Example: ____________________

15. ____________________ nouns may also be used in the comparative and superlative. Their endings will be determined in the usual way.

Focus on Form [✓]

2. Supply the comparative and superlative predicate adjective/adverb forms.

	comparative	*superlative*
1. leise	____________________	____________________
2. dunkel	____________________	____________________
3. teuer	____________________	____________________
4. hoch	____________________	____________________
5. gut	____________________	____________________
6. viel	____________________	____________________
7. bald	____________________	____________________
8. gern	____________________	____________________
9. groß	____________________	____________________
10. stark	____________________	____________________
11. gesund	____________________	____________________
12. nah	____________________	____________________

3. Give the German equivalents of the following expressions.

1. quicker than ____
2. the quickest ____
3. as quick as ____
4. the fastest car ____
5. faster and faster ____
6. the faster, the better ____
7. extremely fast ____
8. seven o'clock at the earliest ____
9. five o'clock at the latest ____

10. The strong are supposed to help the weak.

____

11. The stronger are supposed to help the weaker.

____

12. The strongest are supposed help the weakest.

____

4. Fill in the blanks with the cued expressions.

A

1. ________________ er arbeitet, ________________ wird er. *(the more . . . the more tired)*
2. ____________________ Mal werde ich zu Hause bleiben. *([the] next)*
3. ____________________ haben ein Auto. *(most people)*
4. ____. *(the softer, the better)*
5. Das Gepäck wird ____________________. *(heavier and heavier)*
6. Die italienischen Filme sind ____. *(the longest and slowest)*
7. Diese Fotos sind ____________________. *(the sharpest)*
8. Er ist ____________________ du glaubst. *(bigger/taller than)*
9. Er läuft ____________________ ich. *(faster than)*
10. Er liest ____________________ ich. *(further than)*

B

1. Er sucht ____________________ Wohnung. *(a larger)*
2. Es ist ____________________ Gebäude in der Stadt. *(the tallest)*
3. Es ist ____________________ Rennwagen in ganz Italien. *(the fastest)*
4. Franz erzählt ____________________ Geschichten. *(the craziest)*
5. Haben Sie ____________________ Messer? *(a sharper)*
6. Heute ist nicht ____________________ gestern. *(as warm as)*
7. Hier ist das Wasser ____________________. *(the clearest)*
8. Ich brauche ____________________ Mantel. *(a warmer)*
9. Ich fahre mit ____________________ Zug. *(the next)*
10. Ich kenne ____________________ Mann. *(no more intelligent)*

C

1. Ich trinke ______________________ Tee. *(like to)*
2. Ihre Töchter werden ______________________. *(prettier and prettier)*
3. Im Dezember sind die Tage ______________________ und die Nächte ______________________. *(shortest; longest)*
4. Karl ist ______________________ sein Bruder. *(older than)*
5. Kühe sind ______________________ Tiere. *(the most stupid)*
6. Sie ist ____ ihre Mutter. *(even prettier than)*
7. Was trinken Sie ______________________? *(like to best)*
8. Wer arbeitet ______________________? *(extremely hard)*
9. Wir trinken ______________________ Wein. *(prefer to)*
10. Meine Familie ist ______________________. *([the] best of all)*

Focus on Meaning

5. Fill in the blanks with logical words, phrases, or expressions like those reviewed in this chapter. Try to avoid using the same word or expression more than once.

A

1. Je __________________ Bernd __________________, desto __________________ wird er.
2. Bei heißem Wetter trinke ich ______________________ Limonade oder kaltes Wasser statt Bier.
3. Dieses Haus ist zu groß und teuer für uns. Ich möchte etwas ______________________ und ______________________.
4. Es gibt keine ____________________ Person als Lene. Sie will immer alles mögliche für uns tun.
5. Meine Mutter ist am ______________________.
6. Nina lernt Latein ______________________ als ich.
7. Das war das ______________________ Mal, das wir ihn gesehen haben. Wir hatten ihn vorher nie gesehen.
8. Hier ist der ______________________ Ring im Geschäft. Er kostet natürlich ______________________, aber es gibt nichts ______________________.
9. Frau Meyer, jeden Tag werden Ihre Blumen noch ______________________.
10. Das war die ______________________ Geschichte, die ich je gehört habe.

B

1. Im Juni sind die Tage am ____________________ und die Nächte am ____________________.

2. Je ____________________ man isst, desto ____________________ wird man.

3. Wenn Liesl ihre Gitarre ____________________ spielt, klingt das Lied ____________________.

4. Klaus erzählt die ____________________ Witze.

5. Tina ist etwas ____________________ als ihre Schwester.

6. Dein Kätzchen wird immer ____________________, weil es so viel frisst.

7. Hast du einen ____________________ Hammer? Dieser ist zu leicht.

8. Hunde sind die ____________________ Haustiere.

9. Er ist so ____________________ wie sein Vater.

10. Heute Nacht soll es viel ____________________ werden. Vielleicht schneit es.

C

1. Diese Kamera ist am ____________________. Ich werde sie kaufen.

2. Hier ist das Leben am ____________________. Man könnte ewig hier bleiben!

3. Was trinken Sie am ____________________, wenn Sie im Restaurant essen?

4. Das ist nicht so ____________________ wie du glaubst.

5. Ich brauche eine ____________________ Hose. Diese Hose ist mir zu klein.

6. Welcher Computer ist am ____________________?

7. Hans spielt Schach viel ____________________ als ich. Ich verliere fast jedes Spiel.

8. Ich fahre mit dem ____________________ Bus nach Hause. Wenn ich ihn verpasse, muss ich ein Taxi rufen.

9. Wir trinken nur den ____________________ Wein.

10. Wir gehen ____________________ um Mitternacht ins Bett.

Focus on Meaning and Form

6. Statements. You and a classmate, Dieter, are engaging in a bragging contest. Tell him that . . .

1. your father's stronger than his father [is].

____

2. your mother's prettier than his mother [is].

____

3. your brother's bigger than his brother [is].

4. your sister is smarter than his sister [is].

5. your dog barks louder than his dog [barks].

6. your cat catches more birds than his cat [catches].

7. your father's car drives faster than his father's car [drives].

8. your clothes are more expensive than his.

9. you're a thousand times better than he [is].

10. this exercise is getting weirder and weirder. (*use* **komisch**)

Gruppenarbeit

7. Bilden Sie Gruppen aus drei oder vier Studenten und ...

1. Vergleichen Sie diese akademischen Fächer miteinander:

   Deutsch, Französisch und Spanisch
   Mathematik, Philosophie und Geschichte
   Biologie, Chemie, Physik
   Soziologie, Psychologie, Anthropologie

2. Vergleichen Sie diese Kategorien miteinander:

   drei verschiedene Städte
   das Klima in drei Ländern
   drei verschiedene Länder
   drei berühmte Leute/Sänger/Politiker/Filmstars

3. Vergleichen Sie fünf Gegenstände (Dinge) im Klassenzimmer miteinander.

4. Vergleichen Sie mindestens zwei von den folgenden Kategorien miteinander:

   zwei männliche Politiker
   zwei Politikerinnen
   zwei Fernsehsendungen
   zwei männliche Filmstars
   zwei weibliche Filmstars
   zwei Sportler

5. Vergleichen Sie wenigstens zwei von den folgenden Kategorien:

   Ihre Eltern (3–5 Sätze)
   Ihre zwei besten Freunde/Freundinnen (3–5 Sätze)
   zwei Haustiere (2–3 Sätze)
   zwei Autos (2–3 Sätze)
   zwei Unis (2–3 Sätze)
   zwei Filme (2–3 Sätze)

Chapter 13 Pronouns

Part One

Personal Pronouns

A *pronoun* is a word that takes the place of a noun. Personal pronouns refer to persons, places, and things, that is, to nouns previously mentioned, and to address persons. They have variant forms for the nominative, dative, and accusative cases. There are no genitive personal pronouns. Note the forms:

Forms of the Personal Pronoun

	singular					*plural*			*formal*
nominative:	ich	du	er	sie	es	wir	ihr	sie	Sie
accusative:	mich	dich	ihn	sie	es	uns	euch	sie	Sie
dative:	mir	dir	ihm	ihr	ihm	uns	euch	ihnen	Ihnen

Grammatical Gender with Pronouns

A personal pronoun is used to refer to a noun that has already been mentioned; it must agree with the noun in both gender and number. The case of the pronoun will depend on its function in the sentence.

Das ist mein **Wagen**. **Er** ist neu. Ich habe **ihn** letzte Woche gekauft.
That's my ***car****.* ***It****'s new. I bought* ***it*** *last week.*

Das ist unsere **Schreibmaschine. Sie** ist ziemlich alt, aber ich mag **sie** immer noch.
That's our ***typewriter. It****'s pretty old but I still like* ***it****.*

Das ist unser **Boot. Es** ist ein Segelboot. Ich segele **es** meistens am Wochenende.
That's our ***boat. It****'s a sailboat. I sail* ***it*** *mostly on the weekend.*

Das sind meine **Freunde**. Ich habe **ihnen** einige Weihnachtsgeschenke geschickt und werde **sie** bald besuchen.
Those are our ***friends****. I sent* ***them*** *some Christmas presents and will visit* ***them*** *soon.*

When Natural Gender Overrides Grammatical Gender

Nouns with diminutive suffixes (-**chen** and -**lein**) are neuter. While strict grammarians insist that **es** is the correct pronoun to use for all nouns with diminutive endings, current everyday usage allows for natural gender to be used for persons. Thus:

Wer ist **das Mädchen** da? **Sie/Es** sieht sehr sportlich aus.
Who is the girl over there? She looks very athletic.

Use natural gender with **das Baby** and **das Kind** if you know the child's sex, otherwise use **es**.

NOTE: **Fräulein** is a noun that is now regarded as old-fashioned and socially out of favor with many well-educated young adults, and you are best advised to refrain from using it to avoid possibly giving offense. When referring to a young woman approximately 16 years old or older, use **junge Frau** instead. When addressing women, whether married or single, use **Frau**: **Frau Schmidt**.

Interrogative Pronouns *wer* and *was*

Wer and its various case forms elicit information about people.

If you want to find out the identity of the doer, use the nominative form **wer** (*who*):

Wer sind Sie? **Wer** ist das? **Wer** hat das Buch geschrieben?

If you want to find out which person is affected or acted upon by the subject of the sentence, use the accusative form **wen** (*whom*):

Wen meinst du? **Wen** triffst du später? **Wen** hast du besucht?

If you want to find out the identity of the indirect object or beneficiary, use the dative form **wem** (*to/for whom*):

Wem hast du den Brief geschrieben? **Wem** hast du neulich geholfen?

If you want to find out the owner of something, use the genitive form **wessen** (*whose*):

Wessen Auto ist das? **Wessen** Mäntel sind das?

If you use a preposition, use the correct form of **wer** as required by the preposition:

Mit wem bist du ins Kino gegangen?
With whom *did you go to the movies?*
Who[m] *did you go to the movies* ***with****?* (coll.)

Auf wen hast du so lange gewartet?
For whom *did you wait so long?*
Who[m] *did you wait so long* ***for****?* (coll.)

Über wen habt ihr geredet?
About whom *did you speak?*
Who[m] *did you speak* ***about****?* (coll.)

Bei wem warst du das ganze Wochenende?
At whose house *were you all weekend?*
Whose house *were you* ***at*** *all weekend?* (coll.)

The pronoun **was** (*what*) is used to refer to things. The form **was** may be nominative or accusative. There are no genitive or dative forms.

nominative:	**Was** ist das?	**Was** hat den Lärm gemacht?
accusative:	**Was** hast du gekauft?	**Was** hast du gesagt?

Demonstrative Pronoun *der/die/das*

When **der/die/das** is used as a demonstrative pronoun (an emphatic form of *he, she, it, this one, that one,* etc.), its forms are nearly identical to the definite article. Note, however, how the dative plural and all genitive forms differ:

Forms of the Demonstrative Pronoun

	masculine	*feminine*	*neuter*	*plural*
nominative:	der	die	das	die
accusative:	den	die	das	die
dative:	dem	der	dem	**denen**
genitive:	**dessen**	**deren**	**dessen**	**deren**

Very often **hier** and **da** are used to help distinguish between *this one* and *that one.*

Welches Auto willst du kaufen? Willst du **das hier** oder **das da**?
Which car do you want to buy? Do you want this one here or that one there?

You may use **der/die/das** as emphatic replacements for personal pronouns. When spoken, they are emphasized vocally. When written, spaces between the letters may sometimes be used to signal a very strong emphasis:

Mit denen [Leuten] kann man gar nicht reden.
You can't speak with them at all.

Mit dem [Auto] bin ich sehr zufrieden.
I'm very satisfied with that one.

Den [Mann] kann ich einfach nicht leiden.
I simply can't stand that one (that is, him).

Der [Frau] würde ich nichts leihen.
I wouldn't lend anything to that one (that is, her).

Da-compounds are often used as replacements for prepositional phrases that refer to a thing:

Ich bin **mit meinem Auto** sehr zufrieden. → Ich bin sehr zufrieden **damit**.
I'm very happy with my car. → I'm very happy with it.

For strong emphasis, however, one may use an emphatic pronoun:

Mit dem [Auto] bin ich sehr zufrieden.
I'm very satisfied with that one.

Dessen and *deren*

The genitive pronouns **dessen** and **deren** are used to mean *the latter's* and should be used when the possessive adjectives **sein** or **ihr** might lead to ambiguity:

Wir sind mit Tina, Paul und **dessen** Schwester ausgegangen. (= *with Paul's sister*)
Wir sind mit Paul, Tina und **deren** Schwester ausgegangen. (= *with Tina's sister*)
Wir sind mit Inge, Käthe und **deren** Bruder ausgegangen. (= *with Käthe's brother*)

Ein-Words as Pronouns

When **ein**-words are used as pronouns (instead of articles or possessive adjectives) they always provide a primary case sound:

Hast du einen Bleistift? —Ja, hier ist **einer**.
Do you have a pencil? —Yes, here's one.

Wo ist eine Gaststätte? —Da drüben ist **eine**.
Where is [there] an inn? —There's one over there.

Wo ist ein Restaurant? —Auf der anderen Straßenseite ist **ein(e)s**.
Where is [there] a restaurant? —There's one on the other side of the street.

Ist das deine Zeitschrift? —Ja, das ist **meine**.
Is that your magazine? —Yes, it's mine.

Ist das dein Kuli? —Ja, das ist **meiner**.
Is that your pen? —Yes, it's mine.

Hast du dein Geld bei dir? —Ja, ich habe **mein(e)s**.
Do you have your money with you? —Yes, I have mine.

Von + Dative to Signal *of mine, of yours,* etc.

Instead of using a genitive noun phrase to signal ownership or possession, the preposition **von** + the dative may be used, particularly in spoken German, and particularly with pronouns.

Ist das ein Freund **von dir/euch/Ihnen**?
Is that a friend of yours?

Das ist ein Kollege **von mir/ihm/ihr/ihnen/uns**.
That's a colleague of mine/his/hers/theirs/ours.

Indefinite Pronouns

Indefinite pronouns do not refer to any person specifically. They are used to refer to unknown persons or to make very general statements about people. In English, the pronouns *one, you,* and *they* may be used impersonally.

Man

The impersonal pronoun **man** (*one, you, they*) is used as the subject of the sentence with a third-person singular verb form (**er/sie/es**-form):

Was **macht man** eigentlich mit diesem Werkzeug?
What does one actually do with this tool? OR: *What do you do with this tool?*

Was sa**gt man** darüber?
What does one say about it? OR: *What do they say about it?*

The indefinite pronoun **man** uses **sein** as its possessive adjective:

Man soll **seine** Hausaufgaben täglich machen.
One is supposed to do one's homework every day.

The accusative and dative forms of **man** are **einen** and **einem**:

Wie würdest du **einem** helfen, wenn man plötzlich ohnmächtig würde?
How would you help [some]one, if one suddenly became unconscious?

Das wird **einen** bestimmt böse machen.
That will definitely make (some)one angry.

Jemand and *niemand*

These two pronouns **jemand** (*someone, somebody*) and **niemand** (*no one, nobody, not anyone*) have inflected forms that are less frequently used in conversation but often appear in more formal speech samples. Often **anders** is used with **jemand** and **niemand** and is rendered as *else:*

Hast du **jemand**[**en**] da gesehen? —Nein, ich habe **niemand**[**en**] gesehen.
Did you see someone there? —No, I saw no one./I didn't see anybody/anyone.

Hast du **jemand**[**em**] etwas davon erzählt? —Nein, ich habe **niemand**[**em**] davon erzählt.
Did you tell someone anything about it? —No, I told no one about it./No I didn't tell anybody about it.

Kommt noch **jemand anders**? —Nein, **niemand anders** kommt.
Is anyone else coming? —No, no one else is coming.

Irgend-

The use of **irgend**- signals *vagueness.* It is joined with another word to form a single, compound word.

irgendjemand	**irgendwelche**	**irgendwo**
irgendetwas	**irgendwie**	**irgendwohin**
irgendein	**irgendwann**	**irgendwoher**

Negative variants are: **nirgendwo** or **nirgends** (*nowhere*), **nirgendwoher** (*from nowhere*) and **nirgendwohin** (*to nowhere*).

Uses of the Pronoun *es*

Every sentence must have a subject. The pronoun **es** is frequently used to "stand in" for a subject when there is no specific subject and "start off" the sentence.

Es gibt and *es ist/es sind*

Use **es gibt** (*there is/there are*) + an accusative object to signal the general existence of things or **Was gibt es?/Was gibt's?** to ask a question about the existence of something:

Es gibt viele Studenten an dieser Uni.
There are many students at this university.

Es gibt immer viel Lärm bei dir.
There's always a lot of noise at your place.

Es gibt einen Dom in der Stadt.
There's a cathedral in the city.

Was gibt's zum Mittagessen, Mutti?
What's for lunch, Mom?

Use **es ist** or **es sind** (*there is/there are*) + nominative to signal the existence of a *precise* number of things:

Es ist nur eine Studentin im Hörsaal.
There is only one student in the lecture hall.

Es sind 50 000 Studenten an dieser Uni.
There are 50,000 students at this university.

Es as a "Slot Filler"

For stylistic reasons, one may begin a sentence with **es:**

Niemand ist hier. = **Es** ist niemand hier.
Die Studenten machen jetzt eine Prüfung. = **Es** machen die Studenten jetzt eine Prüfung.

Es and Following *dass*-Clauses or Infinitive Phrases

Very often the pronoun **es** will be used as an object. Alone, its meaning might be ambiguous or otherwise unclear. To make the full meaning of **es** clear, an explanatory clause or infinitive phrase will follow:

Ich kann **es** nicht verstehen, **dass Karl böse auf mich ist.**
Ich habe **es** sehr gern, **frühmorgens angeln zu gehen.**

Word Order with Objects

Keep this simple portable rule in mind when dealing with objects:

> Dative first, unless the accusative is a pronoun.

Study the examples to see how this rule holds up:

Gib **dem Mann** den Schlüssel.
Gib **ihm** den Schlüssel.
Gib ihn **dem Mann.**
Gib ihn **ihm.**

Gib **der Frau** die Postkarte.
Gib **ihr** die Postkarte.
Gib sie **der Frau.**
Gib sie **ihr.**

Gib **dem Kind** das Buch.
Gib **ihm** das Buch.
Gib es **dem Kind.**
Gib es **ihm.**

NOTE: Native speakers are not consciously aware of this rule, or many others, for that matter. They order objects intuitively as a result of thousands of hours of language modeling by adults when they were children. Rules are generally more helpful, if not essential, to non-native students of the language who do not have thousands of hours of listening time at their disposal and have to learn as much as possible in an often incredibly short period of time.

Exercises: Part One

Theory Review

1. Fill in the blanks with the correct information.

1. A personal ______________________ is a word used to refer to a previously mentioned person, place, or thing, that is, a noun.

2. There are personal pronouns for all of the cases in modern German except for the ______________________.

3. Pronouns must agree with their noun referents in ______________________ and ______________________.

4. The ______________________ of the pronoun will be determined by its role or use in the sentence.

5. Current usage allows for using the pronoun ______________________ when referring to nouns like **Mädchen** and **Fräulein**, which are grammatically neuter. In fact, using **es** may strike some native speakers as unnatural.

6. While personal pronouns refer to an already-mentioned noun, ______________________ pronouns are used to ask about a noun that has not yet been mentioned.

7. When inquiring about people, variant forms of the interrogative pronoun ______________________ are used.

8. The accusative form of this pronoun is ______________________ (*whom*); the dative form is ______________________ (*to whom*); and the genitive form is ______________________ (*whose*).

9. When inquiring about things, the interrogative pronoun ______________________ (*what*) is used.

10. This form may be either ______________________ or ______________________ case.

11. Does it have dative and genitive variant forms? ______________________

12. The definite article may be used alone as a ______________________ pronoun instead of the usual **er/sie/es** personal pronouns.

13. This occurs primarily in ______________________ and is used for emphasis.

14. That means that when spoken it must be orally ______________________.

15. When written, which is rather rare, the demonstrative pronoun is spelled with ______________________ between the letters.

16. The forms of demonstrative pronouns are the same as those for the definite article except for a few cases.

    In the dative plural, the form is ______________________, not **den**.

    In the genitive, the form is ______________________, not **des**, and ______________________, not **der**.

17. Note that these forms display both primary and secondary case ____________________.

18. To avoid potential confusion, the pronouns ________________ and ________________ are used to mean *the latter's.*

19. **Ein**-words may stand alone as pronouns, too. When used as pronouns, the **ein**-word must

    always display a ____________________ case sound/ending. That means that **ein**-words are never "deficient" when used as pronouns.

20. ____________________ pronouns do not refer to anyone or anything specific and are general or vague in meaning.

21. The indefinite pronoun ____________________ may mean *one, you,* or *they* in colloquial English.

22. The indefinite pronoun ____________________ means *someone* or *somebody.*

23. The indefinite pronoun ____________________ means *no one* or *nobody.*

24. When ____________________ is used with a pronoun, or any other kind of word for that matter, the degree of vagueness is intensified.

25. The pronoun **man** has variant forms. The accusative form is ____________________;

    the dative form is ____________________.

26. **Jemand** and **niemand** have inflected forms, but they are ____________________.

    jemand: accusative = ____________________; dative = ____________________

    niemand: accusative = ____________________; dative = ____________________

27. When making general statements about the existence of persons, places, or things, ________

    ________ means *there is* or *there are* followed by a(n) ____________________ object.

28. When making statements about the precise number of persons, places, or things, ________

    __________ means *there is* and __________ __________ means *there are.* Both are

    followed by a ____________________, not a direct object.

29. Whenever the pronoun **es** is used as an object and there is a need to know what **es** refers to, a

    ____________________-clause or an ____________________ phrase follows. (Both will be treated in upcoming chapters.)

30. When a sentence contains both a direct and an indirect object, the rule governing word order is:

    ____

    ____

Focus on Meaning and Form [✓]

2. Answer the following questions affirmatively. When answering, use a pronoun to refer to the italicized noun phrases.

1. Gibst du *Marie* den Schlüssel?
2. Zeigt er uns *das Bild*?
3. Gibt er *Franz* das Auto?
4. Zeigen Sie der Frau *die neuen Waren*?
5. Sagt er uns *seine Adresse*?
6. Kaufen wir *Mutti* diese Blumen?
7. Wirfst du Hans *den Ball?*
8. Schenkt er *seiner Freundin* Schokolade?
9. Gibst du ihr *das Geld*?
10. Sollen wir ihnen *den Brief* zeigen?
11. Schicken Sie *Irmgard* eine Einladung?
12. Gibt sie ihrem Mann *das Paket*?
13. Sagt sie dir *ihre Telefonnummer*?

14. Kaufst du mir *das Kleid*?

____

15. Erklären Sie ihnen *das Problem*?

____

3. Now try answering similar questions affirmatively with pronouns for both italicized objects. Observe correct word order for objects.

1. Gibst du *Marie den Schlüssel*? ________________________
2. Zeigt er *Bernd das Bild*? ________________________
3. Gibt er *Franz das Auto*? ________________________
4. Zeigen Sie *der Frau die neuen Waren*? ________________________
5. Sagt er *meinen Eltern seine Adresse*? ________________________
6. Kaufen wir *Mutti diese Blumen*? ________________________
7. Wirfst du *Hans den Ball*? ________________________
8. Bringt er *seiner Freundin Schokolade*? ________________________
9. Gibst du *dem Kind das Geld*? ________________________
10. Sollen wir *unseren Freunden den Brief* zeigen? ________________________
11. Schicken Sie *Irmgard eine Einladung*? ________________________
12. Gibt sie *ihrem Mann das Paket*? ________________________
13. Sagt sie *dem neuen Freund ihre Telefonnummer*? ________________________
14. Kaufst du *mir und Irene die Kleider*? ________________________
15. Erklären Sie *der Studentin das Problem*? ________________________

Focus on Meaning

4. Fill in the blanks with logical pronouns or other words reviewed in this chapter.

A

1. ____________ gibt viele Einwohner in dieser Stadt.
2. ____________ sind genau sieben Flaschen Wein auf dem Tisch.
3. ____________ Buch ist das? Gehört es dir?
4. ____________ hast du das gesagt? Der Sonja? Dem Klaus?
5. ____________ willst du im Krankenhaus besuchen?

6. __________ war das? Hast du das nicht gehört?

7. __________________ muss es gemacht haben, aber ich habe keine Ahnung, wer das sein könnte.

8. Bei __________ wohnst du jetzt, oder hast du schon ein eigenes Haus?

9. Das ist mein Computer. __________ ist neu.

10. Das sind gute Kollegen. Mit __________ kann man gut reden.

B

1. Die Kinder sind __________________ gelaufen und ich weiß nicht, wo sie jetzt sind.

2. Dieser Sessel ist sehr bequem, aber __________ ist mir ein bisschen zu teuer.

3. Du sollst __________ helfen, wenn man dringend Hilfe braucht.

4. Hast du auch einen Pass? —Ja, ich habe __________.

5. Hast du das Kind gesehen? —Nein, ich habe __________ nicht gesehen.

6. Hast du schon den Führerschein? —Ja, ich habe __________ schon seit einem Jahr.

7. Hier ist mein Wagen. Wo ist __________?

8. Ich habe mit __________ anders darüber gesprochen, nur mit dir.

9. Ich weiß nicht, __________ das ist. Ist das Heinrich oder Franz?

10. Ich werde __________________ zurückkommen, aber nur wenn ich etwas Zeit habe.

C

1. Ist das Karls Heft? —Ja, es ist __________.

2. Kennst du das Mädchen? —Nein, ich kenne __________ nicht.

3. Maria, Dieter und __________ Schwester haben wir zur Party eingeladen. (Dieters Schwester)

4. Mit __________ willst du sprechen?

5. Petra ist meine beste Freundin. __________ kann ich alles sagen.

6. Über __________ lachen Sie? Über mich oder über meine Freundin?

7. Wenn __________ Hunger hat, kann __________ in ein Restaurant gehen.

8. Wo ist mein Autoschlüssel? Ich kann __________ nicht finden.

9. __________ ist niemand außer mir hier.

10. Wir müssen das __________ erledigen. Kannst du einen Weg aus diesem Dilemma finden?

Focus on Meaning and Form

5. Express in German:

A

1. I have a new car. Do you have one, too?

2. Your dress is nice. Mine is not as pretty as yours.

3. That is a powerful tool. With this one [here] you can't do much.

4. We were playing with Hans, Franz, and his brother.

5. This is my hat. Where's yours?

6. Tina, Klara, and her sister visited me in the hospital.

7. One must never forget one's friends.

8. One can give one's old clothing to the poor.

9. I saw someone in the parking lot.

10. I didn't speak with anyone.

B

1. Somebody [or other] said that.

2. She went somewhere [or other].

3. He said something [or other], but I didn't hear it.

4. It was nowhere to be found.

5. What do you mean? I didn't go anywhere!

6. There's a knock at the door.

7. The phone's ringing. See who it is.

8. Call the fire department. There's a fire!

9. Those are nice belts. I'll take this one here and that one there, please.

10. I have a test tomorrow. It's not supposed to be too difficult.

C

1. Something [or other] is not right.

2. They are nice people. You (*indef.*) can talk reasonably with them.

3. What do you (*indef.*) do when that happens?

4. They (*indef.*) say you (*indef.*) have to get used to it.

5. There are many students at this university. Yes, there are 35,000.

6. I didn't do it. It was someone else.

7. Nonsense! You did it. It was no one else but you.

8. Too much wine makes a person sick.

9. I can't find it anywhere.

10. She seldom believes anyone.

Part Two

Reflexive Pronouns

Reflex = from the Latin: *to bend (flex) back (re-)*

In a sentence employing reflexive verbs/reflexive pronouns, the meaning of the sentence, flowing from left to right, "bends back" on itself by referring to the subject instead of continuing to progress straight ahead to the right. This happens when you reach the reflexive pronoun. (The reflexive pronouns exist only in the accusative and dative forms—they technically have no nominative form.) The reflexive pronoun functions as the direct or indirect object of the sentence, and *it is the same person/thing as the subject.* The net effect is that the reflexive pronoun refers to the subject.

direct object:

Ich schneide **mich** immer, wenn **ich mich** rasiere.
Wir schneiden **uns** immer, wenn **wir uns** rasieren.

Kannst **du dich** nicht schneller anziehen?
Könnt **ihr euch** nicht schneller anziehen?
Können **Sie sich** nicht schneller anziehen?

Karl erkältet **sich** oft im Winter.
Marlene erkältet **sich** oft im Winter.
Marlene und Karl erkälten **sich** oft im Winter.

indirect object:

Ich wasche **mir** die Hände.
Wir waschen **uns** die Hände.

Du sollst **dir** einen wärmeren Mantel anziehen.
Ihr sollt **euch** einen wärmeren Mantel anziehen.
Sie sollen **sich** einen wärmeren Mantel anziehen.

Udo hat **sich** das Bein gebrochen.
Hannelore hat **sich** das Bein gebrochen.
Hannelore und Uwe haben **sich** das Bein gebrochen.

As you can see in the chart below, the first- and second-person informal forms are identical to the personal pronoun forms. The third-person forms and second-person formal forms have **sich** for both dative and accusative. These forms differ from personal pronoun forms.

Forms of the Reflexive Pronoun

	singular					*plural*			*formal*
nominative:	ich	du	er	sie	es	wir	ihr	sie	Sie
accusative:	mich	dich	**sich**	**sich**	**sich**	uns	euch	**sich**	**sich**
dative:	mir	dir	**sich**	**sich**	**sich**	uns	euch	**sich**	**sich**

Verbs That May Be Used with a Reflexive Pronoun Object

There are a number of verbs that may be used with noun or personal pronoun objects *or* reflexive pronoun objects:

• **anziehen** *to dress*	Der Vater zieht seinen kleinen Sohn an. *The father is dressing his little son.*
	Man soll **sich** fürs Konzert formell anziehen. *One is expected to dress (oneself) formally for the concert.*
• **ausziehen** *to undress*	Die Mutter zog dem Kind die Pyjamas aus. *The mother is taking off the child's pyjamas* (that is, *pulling them off from the child*).
	Ich habe **mich** schnell ausgezogen und ging schlafen. *I undressed [myself] quickly and went to bed.*
• **bedienen** *to serve*	Der Kellner hat die Gäste sehr schnell bedient. *The waiter served the guests very quickly.*
	Bedienen **Sie sich** bitte, oder das Essen wird kalt werden. *Serve yourself/yourselves or the food will get cold.*
• **brechen** *to break*	Wie hast du deinen Schaukelstuhl gebrochen? *How did you break your rocking chair?*
	Wie hast **du dir** die Nase gebrochen? *How did you break your nose?*
• **duschen** *to shower*	**Du** sollst **dich** jeden Tag duschen. *You are supposed to shower [yourself] every day.*
• **erinnern** *to remind; remember*	Ich habe Vati an Muttis Geburtstag erinnert. *I reminded Dad about Mom's birthday.*
	Ich konnte **mich** nicht daran erinnern. *I couldn't remember it* (that is, *I couldn't remind myself of it*).
• **kaufen** *to buy*	Kauf mir etwas, bitte. *Buy me something, please.*
	Und kauf **dir** auch etwas. *And buy yourself something, too.*
• **legen** *to lay something flat/ horizontally; lay [oneself] down*	Leg das bitte nicht auf das Sofa. *Please don't lay that on the sofa.*
	Leg **dich** hin, wenn du wirklich so müde bist. *Lay [yourself] down, if you're really so tired.*
• **putzen** *to brush, scrub*	Du sollst alles putzen, bis es glänzt. *You're expected to scrub everything till it shines.*
	Putzt **euch** die Zähne, bevor ihr ins Bett geht. *Brush your teeth before you go to bed.*
• **rasieren** *to shave*	Der Tierarzt rasierte den Hund vor der Operation. *The veterinarian shaved the dog before the operation.*
	Der Tierarzt rasierte **sich**, bevor er zur Arbeit ging. *The veterinarian shaved [himself] before going to work.*

- **schneiden** *to cut* — Du sollst das Fleisch sorgfältig schneiden.
  You're supposed to cut the meat carefully.

  Vorsicht, oder **du** wirst **dich** schneiden.
  Careful, or you'll cut yourself.

- **schreiben** *to write* — Schreib mir ab und zu einen Brief.
  Write me a letter from time to time.

  Der Junge und das Mädchen schrieben **sich** Liebesbriefe.
  The boy and girl wrote love letters to each other.

- **sehen** *to see* — Die Mutter sieht sie [ihre Kinder] im Foto von der Familie.
  The mother sees them [her children] in the photo of the family.

  Die Mutter sieht **sich** im Foto von der Familie.
  The mother sees herself in the photo of the family.

- **setzen** *to set, set down, sit down, set oneself down* — Opa setzte den Kaffeetisch vor das Sofa.
  Grandpa set the table down in front of the sofa.

  Opa setzte **sich** auf das Sofa und saß eine Weile da.
  Grandpa sat [himself] down on the sofa and sat there for awhile.

- **stellen** *to put, place, position* — Stell das auf den Tisch.
  Place/Put it on the table.

  Stell **dich** zwischen Oma und Opa für das Foto.
  Place/Put yourself between Grandma and Grandpa for the photo.

- **vorstellen** *to present, introduce* — Meine Freundin hat mich ihren Eltern vorgestellt.
  My girlfriend introduced me to her parents.

  Ich habe **mich** den Eltern meiner Freundin vorgestellt.
  I introduced myself to my girlfriend's parents.

- **waschen** *to wash* — Wir sollen das Auto waschen.
  We're expected to wash the car.

  Wir sollen **uns** vor dem Abendessen waschen.
  We're supposed to wash up before supper.

There are also a number of verbs that are reflexive in German, but not in English. Many of these reflexive verbs employ prepositions idiomatically. Since there is not a close "fit" with English, spend some extra time learning these if you are not already comfortable with them. These verbs and idiomatic expressions are some of the most challenging aspects of learning German, at least for speakers of English. Since these expressions don't always occur frequently, and since you're not in a natural language acquisition environment, you have to make a real mental effort to learn them. Bottom line: Memorize, memorize, memorize, and review, review, review until they become second nature, that is, automatic.

Idioms Requiring Accusative Reflexive Pronouns

The following idiomatic expressions always involve accusative reflexive pronouns. The first English equivalent is the normal translation. The second one given is a much more literal meaning. This second equivalent may help you "see" the meaning of these idioms more easily.

- **sich amüsieren** *to have fun; to amuse oneself*

  Wir haben **uns** in Las Vegas sehr **amüsiert.**
  We had fun in Las Vegas (that is, *amused ourselves*).

- **sich ausruhen** *to rest up; to rest oneself*

  Ich bin unglaublich müde. Ich muss **mich ausruhen.**
  I'm unbelievably tired. I have to rest up.

- **sich beeilen** *to hurry up; to hurry oneself along*

  Beeile dich, oder du wirst zu spät ankommen.
  Hurry up, or you'll arrive too late.

- **sich beruhigen** *to calm down; to calm oneself*

  Es ist nicht so wichtig. **Beruhige dich.**
  It's no so important. Calm down.

- **sich entscheiden** *to decide; to bring onself to a decision*

  Ich muss **mich** bald **entscheiden.**
  I have to decide soon.

- **sich entschließen** *to decide; to unlock oneself mentally*

  Du musst **dich** bis Freitag **entschließen.**
  You have to decide by Friday.

- **sich entschuldigen** *to excuse oneself* (lit: *to remove guilt from oneself)*

  Ihr müsst **euch** sofort **entschuldigen.**
  You have to excuse yourselves immediately.

- **sich erkälten** *to catch a cold; to make onself sick with a cold*

  Ich habe **mich** letzten Winter schwer **erkältet.**
  I caught a bad cold last winter.

- **sich freuen** *to be happy; to make oneself happy*

  Meine Eltern haben **sich** sehr **gefreut**, dass sie nach Amerika reisen konnten.
  My parents were very happy that they could travel to America.

- **sich fürchten** *to fear; to make oneself fearful*

  Warum **fürchtest** du **dich**?
  Why are you so afraid?

- **sich irren** *to err; to make oneself erroneous*

  Wir **irren uns** bestimmt, wenn wir solchen Blödsinn glauben.
  We'll definitely be wrong if we believe such nonsense.

- **sich schämen** *to be ashamed; to shame oneself*

  Karl muss **sich** wirklich **schämen**, dass er sich so schlecht benommen hat.
  Karl has to be ashamed that he behaved so badly.

Idioms Requiring Dative Reflexive Pronouns

Some of the more challenging of these expressions will be those that require a dative reflexive pronoun. In virtually all cases, there is a noun or pronoun direct object being used with it.

- **sich** etwas **ansehen** *to examine something; to look at something carefully, take a good look at*

  Ich will **mir** dieses Bild **ansehen.**
  I want to take a good look at this picture.

- **sich** etwas **anschauen** *to examine something; to look at something carefully*

  Der Direktor will **sich** den Plan genauer **anschauen.**
  The director wants to examine the plan in more detail.

- **sich** etwas **anziehen** *to put on something; to dress oneself with*

  Wir haben **uns** heute dicke Pullis **angezogen.**
  We put on heavy sweaters today.

- **sich** etwas **brechen** *to break some part of the body*

  Wie hast du **dir** das Bein **gebrochen**?
  How did you break your leg?

- **sich** etwas **leisten** *to afford something [for oneself]*

  Konntet ihr **euch** wirklich ein neues Auto **leisten**?
  Were you really able to afford a new car?

- **sich** die Zähne **putzen** *to brush one's teeth*

  Die Kinder haben **sich** endlich die Zähne **geputzt.**
  The children finally brushed their teeth.

- **sich** etwas **rasieren** *to shave some part of the body*

  Die Frau **rasierte sich** die Beine.
  The woman shaved her legs.

- **sich** etwas **überlegen** *to consider; to think over (lay it over in your mind)*

  Ich muss es **mir überlegen**, ob ich zu Ilses Party gehen werde.
  I have to think [it] over whether I'll go to Ilse's party.

- **sich** etwas **vorstellen** *to imagine something; to place something before oneself (that is, before the mind's eye)*

  Wir können es **uns** nicht **vorstellen**, das jemand so etwas machen könnte!
  We can't imagine that someone could do such a thing.

- **sich** etwas **waschen** *to wash some part of the body*

  Du sollst **dir** die Hände vorm Abendessen **waschen.**
  You're expected to wash your hands before supper.

NOTE: Remember that for most idiomatic expressions, two-way prepositions most often require the accusative after them.

Word Order with Reflexive Pronouns

When using reflexive pronouns, remember the rule you learned before: *dative first, unless the accusative is a pronoun.*

Ich kann **mir das Auto** nicht leisten. BUT: Ich kann **es mir** nicht leisten.

When a demonstrative pronoun is the direct object, however, it has the force of a noun, and it will follow, not precede a dative reflexive:

Ich kann mir dieses Auto nicht leisten. → Ich kann **mir das** nicht leisten.
Wir sollen **uns diesen Wagen** nicht kaufen. → Wir sollen **uns den** nicht kaufen.

Reflexive Pronouns and Prepositions

Reflexive pronouns may also be used as objects of prepositions. Logic and meaning will dictate when to use them.

non-reflexive:	Sabine hat über ihre Zukunft gedacht. *Sabine thought about her future.*	Wir haben über den Witz gelacht. *We laughed at/about the joke.*
reflexive:	Sabine hat **über sich** gedacht. *Sabine thought about herself.*	Wir haben **über uns** gelacht. *We laughed at ourselves.*

Reciprocal Pronoun *einander*

The reciprocal pronoun **einander** (*one another*) is often used as a substitute for a plural reflexive pronoun.

Wir rufen **uns** oft an.
Wir rufen **einander** oft an.
*We call **one another/each other** often.*

Sie schreiben **sich** Briefe.
Sie schreiben **einander** Briefe.
*They write **one another/each other** letters.*

Einander may be joined directly to a preposition:

Sie haben schon lange nicht mehr **voneinander** gehört.
*They haven't heard **from one another/ from each other** in a long time.*

Sie telefonieren oft **miteinander**.
*They often telephone **one another/each other**.*

Diese zwei Länder haben oft **gegeneinander** gekämpft.
*These two countries have often fought **against one another/against each other**.*

Uses of the Intensifier *selbst/selber*

The intensifiers **selbst** and **selber** may be used interchangeably. They normally intensify the subject, and are usually placed after a direct object or predicate noun.

Klaus hat seinen Wagen **selbst/selber** repariert.
He fixed the car himself.

Hast du das Abendessen **selbst/selber** gemacht?
Did you make supper yourself?

Es ist die Chefin **selbst/selber.**
It's the boss herself.

Die Leute haben die Arbeit **selbst/selber** erledigt.
The people finished the task themselves.

When **selbst** or **selber** follows a reflexive pronoun, it intensifies it.

> Der dumme Karl hat **sich selbst** noch einmal in den Finger geschnitten.
> *Crazy Karl cut himself in the finger again.*

When **selbst** precedes a subject in slot one, however, it means *even:*

> **Selbst ich** habe das gewusst.
> *Even I knew that.*
>
> **Selbst Hans** kann besser als ich tanzen.
> *Even Hans can dance better than I.*

Exercises: Part Two

Theory Review

1. Fill in the blanks with the correct information.

1. When an accusative or dative pronoun refers to the subject of the sentence, it is called a ______________________ pronoun.
2. It is called that because the meaning of the sentence is momentarily ______________________ to the subject instead of continuing on to the next complement in the sentence.
3. These pronouns are identical to the forms of personal pronouns except for the third-person ______________________ and ______________________ forms.
4. In all cases where the reflexive pronoun is different from the personal pronoun, regardless of gender or number, the correct form is ______________________.
5. There are many verbs that can be used with or without reflexive pronouns. What determines whether a reflexive pronoun is required is the ______________________ of the sentence.
6. There are a number of German verbs that, unlike their English equivalents, are used with a reflexive pronoun. These must be ______________________.
7. Most of the time the case of the reflexive pronoun will be ______________________ because the reflexive pronoun is functioning in the sentence as the direct object.
8. When the reflexive pronoun is the indirect object (= receiver of the direct object) or the beneficiary of the action named by the verb, the ______________________ case is called for.
9. The general word order rule to follow when there is a reflexive pronoun and another object in the sentence is:

   ____

10. When the demonstrative pronoun ______________________ is used with a dative reflexive, the reflexive pronoun comes first, a clear exception to the rule above. The reason for this is that this demonstrative pronoun has the force of a noun.

11. A pronoun that can replace a plural reflexive pronoun is called a ________________ pronoun.
12. In the sentence **Wir wollen uns Briefe schreiben**, the reflexive pronoun **uns** may be replaced by

    ______________________.
13. This reciprocal pronoun may at times be used as the object of a preposition. When so used, is the pronoun joined to the preposition, forming one word, or are they two separate words?

    ____
14. The intensifiers ______________________ and ______________________ may be used interchangeably to intensify the subject or the predicate noun.
15. That means that they are technically in the ______________________ case.
16. They normally ______________________ the noun they intensify and frequently follow a predicate noun or direct object, meaning that they may be separated from the subject by several sentence constituents.
17. When **selbst** precedes the subject, its meaning is ______________________ and it expresses astonishment or sarcasm.

Focus on Form [✓]

2. Supply the correct reflexive pronoun.

A

1. Bedient ____________.
2. Das kann ich ____________ gar nicht vorstellen.
3. Dürfen wir ____________ dem Präsidenten des Vereins vorstellen?
4. Erinnerst du ____________ an den Film?
5. Fürchtet er ____________ nicht?
6. Habt ihr ____________ erkältet?
7. Hat sie ____________ schon geduscht?
8. Ich habe ____________ die Nase gebrochen.
9. Wir haben ____________ gut amüsiert.
10. Man soll ____________ die Zähne putzen, bevor man schlafen geht.

B

1. Ich will ____________ das Haus ansehen.
2. Sie sollen ____________ entschuldigen.
3. Musst du ____________ beeilen?
4. Heidi schämt ____________ nicht.
5. Wir freuen ____________ sehr.

6. Bedienen Sie ____________, bitte.

7. Wir müssen ____________ die Hände waschen, bevor wir essen.

8. Erinnere ____________ daran.

9. Haben sie ____________ erkältet?

10. Ihr sollt ____________ entschließen mit uns zu kommen.

3. To be done orally in class. Substitute the pronouns in parentheses for the original subjects in each sentence. Make any changes necessitated by meaning.

1. Er hat sich das Bein gebrochen. (ich, Karl-Heinz)
2. Er hat sich gestern erkältet. (ich, wir)
3. Detlev hat sich warm angezogen. (ich, wir)
4. Stellen Sie sich vor. (du, ihr)
5. Wir können es uns nicht leisten. (Martina, ich, du)
6. Fürchten Sie sich? (du, er, ihr)
7. Ich muss es mir überlegen. (du, Claudia, die Studenten)
8. Ich habe mich endlich entschlossen. (er, wir, sie [*sg.*])
9. Ich will mir das Gemälde ansehen. (er, wir, sie [*pl.*])
10. Ich will mir das Gesicht waschen. (er, wir, sie [*sg.*])
11. Ich soll mich rasieren. (der Mann, wir)
12. Kannst du es dir vorstellen? (ihr, Sie)
13. Setzen Sie sich. (du, ihr)
14. Sie irren sich. (du, ihr, Friedrich)
15. Wir müssen uns beeilen. (ich, Tina, ihr)
16. Zieht euch schnell an. (du, Sie)
17. Du sollst dich schämen! (wir, ihr, Sie)

Focus on Meaning

4. Fill in the blanks with verbs reviewed in Part Two of this chapter. Various answers are possible for some of these.

A

1. ____________________ dich hin, wenn du so müde bist.

2. ____________________ dir eine wärmere Jacke ____________________, bevor du ausgehst

3. ____________________ Sie sich nicht. Es wird nicht gefährlich sein.

4. Ach, das ist mir viel zu teuer. Ich kann mir das gar nicht ____________________.

5. Bevor ich diese Antiquität kaufe, möchte ich sie mir näher ____________________.

6. Bevor man morgens zur Arbeit geht, duscht man sich, rasiert man sich vielleicht und dann

    ____________________ man sich an.

7. Claudia, ____________________ dir die Zähne, bevor du schlafen gehst.

8. Darf ich Ihnen meinen Mann ____________________? Sie kennen ihn noch nicht.

9. Das Essen ist schon vorbereitet und die Gäste dürfen sich selbst ____________________.

10. Die Kinder haben sich ____________________ und sind ins Bett gegangen.

B

1. Doris hat sich beim Skilaufen das Bein ________________________.
2. Du musst dich jetzt ________________________. Entweder gehst du mit zu Oma oder du bleibst zu Hause.
3. Du sollst dir alles ganz genau ________________________, bevor du dich entscheidest, ihn zu heiraten.
4. Es tut mir leid, aber was Sie sagen ist falsch. Sie haben sich ________________________.
5. Ich habe mich sehr ________________________, dass ich den ersten Preis gewonnen hatte.
6. Ich kann nicht schreiben, denn ich habe mir den Zeigefinger ________________________.
7. Jeden Morgen muss ich mir das Gesicht ________________________.
8. Man soll sich jeden Tag ________________________.
9. Mensch, ich bin so vergesslich! Ich kann mich heute an nichts ________________________.
10. Nehmen Sie täglich Ihre Vitaminpillen und Sie werden sich nicht ________________________.

C

1. Nimm Platz. = ________________________ dich hin.
2. Was hast du ihr gesagt? Du Lump, du sollst dich bei ihr ________________________!
3. Was?! Du hast dich noch nicht bei ihr entschuldigt?! Du sollst dich wirklich ________________________.
4. Ich kann es mir nicht ________________________, dass du so etwas machen würdest!
5. Erinnert euch daran, dass wir uns morgen in der Mensa ________________________.
6. Unsere Tochter hustet und sie hat ein hohes Fieber. Ich glaube, sie hat sich ________________________.
7. Du sollst dich ________________________. Wir haben keine Zeit mehr.
8. Wir sollen einander ________________________, sonst werden wir das Projekt nicht erledigen.
9. Ich weiß es immer noch nicht. Ich muss mir diese Sache noch eine Weile ________________________.
10. Wir haben sehr lange daran gearbeitet. Wir sollen alle nach Hause gehen und uns

    ________________________.

Focus on Meaning and Form

5. Tell me that . . .

1. I have to hurry up. ________________________
2. Even you understand it. ________________________
3. We have to help each other. ________________________

4. You want to think it over. ____________________

5. You brush your teeth every day. ____________________

6. I may look at it (examine it). ____________________

7. You were ashamed. ____________________

8. The teacher was wrong. ____________________

9. The students were afraid. ____________________

10. Everyone caught a cold. ____________________

11. I have to decide. ____________________

12. You broke your foot. ____________________

You Determine the Message and Form

6. Persönliche Fragen. Seien Sie bereit, diese Fragen im Unterricht zu beantworten.

1. Was haben Sie sich neulich gekauft?
2. Wem haben Sie sich in letzter Zeit vorgestellt? Warum?
3. Haben Sie sich oder eine andere Person neulich an etwas erinnert? Wenn ja, was?
4. Haben Sie sich je etwas gebrochen? Wie ist das passiert?
5. Was überlegen Sie sich im Moment?
6. Was können Sie sich im Moment nicht leisten? Wann werden Sie es sich leisten können?
7. Was können Sie sich nicht vorstellen?
8. Wie haben Sie sich in den Winterferien oder Frühlingsferien amüsiert?
9. Haben Sie sich neulich entschuldigen müssen? Warum?
10. Haben Sie sich neulich geirrt? Wie?
11. Was machen Sie zu Hause, um sich zu amüsieren?
12. Was kann man machen, wenn man müde ist und sich ausruhen will?
13. Wann haben Sie sich das letzte Mal erkältet?

7. Indicate what you might say in German in the following situations.

1. You have guests at home for a party. What kinds of things could you say to make them feel comfortable?
2. Mention everything you did today to get ready for work or school and to prepare for your courses.

Phase III

Building on the Fundamentals

Chapter 14 Adverbs

Adverbs are words used to modify verbs. They do so by providing information about *when* an action is performed, *why* it is done, *how* it is performed, and *where* it occurs. The adverbial categories of time, reason, manner, and place will be examined individually.

Adverbs may also modify adjectives and other adverbs. When they do, they are often referred to as *intensifiers.*

Das ist ***sehr* gut**, aber das ist ***viel* besser**.
That's very good, but this is much better.

Helmut fährt **vorsichtig**, aber Ute fährt ***viel* vorsichtiger**.
Helmut drives safely, but Ute drives much more safely.

Noun phrases in the accusative and genitive may also function as adverbs, as can prepositional phrases, which will be examined in the next chapter. This chapter focuses primarily on what might be called "pure adverbs."

Adverbs of Time

Adverbs of time signal *when, how often,* and *for how long* an action occurs, occurred, or will occur.

jetzt *now* · **bald** *soon* · **früh** *early* · **spät** *late* · **später** *later*

selten *seldom* · **oft** *often* · **manchmal** *sometimes* · **immer** *always* · **nie** *never*

vorgestern *the day before yesterday* · **gestern** *yesterday* · **heute** *today* · **morgen** *tomorrow* · **übermorgen** *the day after tomorrow*

tagsüber *during the day* · **täglich** *daily* · **wöchentlich** *weekly* · **monatlich** *monthly* · **jährlich** *yearly* · **lange** *for a long time*

noch *still, yet* · **noch nicht** *not yet* · **immer noch nicht** *still not yet*

Compound Adverbs of Time

The adverbs **vorgestern**, **gestern**, **heute**, **morgen**, and **übermorgen** can be paired with parts of the day (nouns) for an even more specific adverbial time expression:

vorgestern Morgen / gestern Morgen / heute Morgen / morgen früh / übermorgen früh
vorgestern Vormittag / gestern Vormittag / heute Vormittag / morgen Vormittag / übermorgen Vormittag
vorgestern Mittag / gestern Mittag / heute Mittag / morgen Mittag / übermorgen Mittag
vorgestern Nachmittag / gestern Nachmittag / heute Nachmittag / morgen Nachmittag / übermorgen Nachmittag
vorgestern Abend / gestern Abend / heute Abend / morgen Abend / übermorgen Abend
vorgestern Nacht / gestern Nacht / heute Nacht / morgen Nacht / übermorgen Nacht

Adverbs of Time Signaling Regularity

Days of the week and times of the day are frequently used as adverbs of regularity. Note how they are derived from nouns and that they end in -**s**:

Montag → **montags**
Dienstag → **dienstags**
Mittwoch → **mittwochs**
Sonntag → **sonntags**

der Morgen → **morgens**
der Abend → **abends**
der Mittag → **mittags**
die Nacht → **nachts**

Note again that these pure adverbs, like adverbs in general, are not capitalized unless they begin the sentence:

Morgens soll ich zu Hause sein, aber **nachmittags** und **abends** arbeite ich.
I expect to be at home mornings, but afternoons and evenings I work.

Früh and *spät*

The adverbs **früh** and **spät** may be prefixed to other adverbs:

Frühmorgens laufe ich.
I (usually) run early in the morning.

Spätabends lese ich einen Roman.
I (usually) read a novel late in the evening.

Adverbial Suffix -*lich*

The suffix -**lich** is equivalent to the English suffix -*ly* and is used to form adverbs of regularity:

der Tag → **täglich**
die Woche → **wöchentlich**

der Monat → **monatlich**
das Jahr → **jährlich**

Frühestens and *spätestens*

The adverbs **frühestens** (*at the earliest*) and **spätestens** (*at the latest*) are often used with other time expressions to set a time limit:

Sie kommt ***frühestens*** **um sieben**.
She's coming at the earliest at seven.

Ich werde sie ***spätestens*** **nächsten Freitag** treffen.
I will meet her at the latest next Friday.

Note that the general time expressions **frühestens** and **spätestens** are followed by the more specific time expression. This is the normal sequence for ordering two or more time expressions: general → specific, or larger → smaller.

Dann

The adverb **dann** is used to mark the chronology of events. **Dann** frequently is at the beginning of a clause, forcing inversion, that is, forcing the subject to move into third position in the sentence (slot 3):

Morgens stehe ich um acht auf, ***dann*** *dusche ich* mich. Ich ziehe mich an, esse mein Frühstück, und ***dann*** *lese ich* die Zeitung.

Ich komme abends nach Hause, esse mein Abendessen und ***dann*** *mache ich* meine Hausaufgaben. ***Dann*** *lese ich* einen Roman oder eine Zeitschrift oder ich sehe fern. Spätabends ziehe ich mich aus und wasche mich, ***dann*** *gehe ich* ins Bett.

Fast + Adverb

The adverb **fast** (*almost*) is used in conjunction with other adverbs, adjectives, or phrases:

Ich kann das ***fast*** **immer** machen.
Wir sehen Frau Sindermann ***fast*** **jeden Tag.**
Die Arbeit ist ***fast*** **fertig.**
Der Film ist ***fast*** **zu Ende.**

Noun Phrases as Adverbs of Time

Noun phrases, particularly accusative noun phrases denoting specific time and duration of time, as well as genitive phrases denoting vague or indefinite time, may be used as adverbial units.

Sie besuchte uns **letztes Wochenende**. (*specific time—accusative*)
Ich blieb **den ganzen Tag** zu Hause. (*duration of time—accusative*)
Eines Tages ist sie plötzlich verschwunden. (*vague time—genitive*)

Using *jed-* to Express Regularity

All of the adverbial expressions of regularity are equivalents of the accusative specific time expressions involving a form of **jed-**:

Ich kaufe **täglich** eine Zeitung. = Ich kaufe **jeden Tag** eine Zeitung.
Ich gehe **wöchentlich** einkaufen. = Ich gehe **jede Woche** einkaufen.
Samstags besuche ich meine Schwiegereltern. = **Jeden Samstag** besuche ich meine Schwiegereltern.
Morgens trinke ich Orangensaft. = **Jeden Morgen** trinke ich Orangensaft.

Ordering Two Adverbs of Time

As noted previously with **frühestens** and **spätestens**, whenever there are two adverbs of time, the larger or more general one is mentioned first, and the smaller or more specific one second:

Ich mache das **später heute**.
Ich mache das **morgen Nachmittag um fünf Uhr**.

Adverbs of Reason

Adverbs of reason are relatively rare; forming a prepositional phrase with the genitive preposition **wegen** *(because, because of, on account of, due to)* is the most common vehicle:

wegen der Arbeit	Ich bin heute **wegen der Arbeit** ganz erschöpft.
wegen meiner Krankheit	Ich musste wochenlang **wegen meiner Krankheit** im Bett bleiben.
wegen unserer Eltern	Wir dürfen dieses Wochenende **wegen unserer Eltern** nicht ins Kino gehen.

Adverbs of Manner

Adverbs of manner signal *how* or *in what way* an action is performed.

schnell *fast*	**laut** *loudly*	**gut** *well*	**allein** *alone*
langsam *slowly*	**leise** *softly*	**schlecht** *poorly*	**zusammen** *together*

Using Adjectives as Adverbs of Manner

Any adjective can theoretically function as an adverb:

adjectives	*adverbs*
Hans ist **fleißig.**	Er arbeitet **fleißig.**
Deine Antwort ist **falsch.**	Du antwortest **falsch.**
Das ist **gut.**	Das Kind liest **gut.**
Das Auto ist **schnell.**	Das Auto fährt **schnell.**
Die Musik ist **laut.**	Du singst **laut.**

Adverbial Suffix *-weise*

Adverbs can be formed from some adjectives by adding a linking **-er-** plus the suffix **-weise,** which corresponds to the English suffix *-ly:*

normalerweise *normally*	**möglicherweise** *possibly*
dummerweise *stupidly*	**komischerweise** *strangely*

When **-weise** is added to nouns, a linking **-s-** is often added: **ausnahmsweise** (*by way of exception*).

Adverb of Manner *gern*

The adverb **gern** is used to indicate that the subject *likes* doing whatever the verb indicates.

Wir **spielen gern** Fußball. = We *like playing* soccer; We *enjoy playing* soccer; We *like to play* soccer.
Ich **esse gern** italienisch. = I *like eating* Italian [style].

The comparative form of **gern, lieber,** signals a preference:

Ich **trinke gern** englisches Bier, aber ich **trinke lieber** holländisches Bier.
I *like drinking* English beer, but I *prefer drinking* Dutch beer.

The superlative form **am liebsten** indicates one's favorite:

Aber ich **trinke am liebsten** deutsches Bier.
But I *like drinking* German beer *most* [of all].

When used with another adverb of manner, **gern** is normally mentioned first:

Tino, Uwe und Jürgen lernen ***gern*** **zusammen.**

Expressing a Dislike with *nicht gern*

Use the expression **nicht gern** to indicate a dislike for doing something:

Ich **arbeite nicht gern** für diesen Chef.	I *don't like working* for this boss. I *don't enjoy working* for this boss. I *don't like to work* for this boss.

Adverbs of Place

Adverbs of place, including prepositional phrases that function adverbially, can signal location, destination, or point of origin:

location:	**hier / da/dort / da drüben / dort drüben / rechts / links / zu Hause / an der Uni**
destination:	**her / hierher / dahin / dorthin / nach Hause / nach Deutschland / zum Arzt**
point of origin:	**aus Oslo / aus Norwegen / aus Skandinavien / aus Nordeuropa**
direction:	**hin / her / dahin / hierher / nach rechts/links / geradeaus / aus der Schule**

Word Order with Adverbs: Time, Reason, Manner, Place (TRuMP)

Most sentences often contain just one adverb or adverbial phrase:

Wir kommen **heute.**   Wir lernen Deutsch **im Klassenzimmer.**

When there is more than one adverb or adverbial phrase in the sentence, order them according to this sequence: *time . . . reason . . . manner . . . place.* This can easily be remembered by this mnemonic word: TRuMP. Study the following sentences to see how this adverbial "default" word order is expanded from one sentence to the next:

Ich will **nach Hause** fahren.
Ich will **mit dem Bus nach Hause** fahren.
Ich will **wegen des schlechten Wetters mit dem Bus nach Hause** fahren.
Ich will **heute wegen des schlechten Wetters mit dem Bus nach Hause** fahren.

If you violate the time-reason-manner-place sequence (TRuMP), you will certainly still be understood by a native speaker, but because the information flow is out of the expected sequence, your sentence may be viewed as awkward or unnatural. The listener may then be distracted and possibly miss something important.

Negating Adverbs

Nicht is used to negate adverbs. Its position in the sentence will depend in part on the type of adverb it is negating.

Specific Time

Negation of specific time expressions normally requires **nicht** to be placed *after* the time expression.

Ich komme **morgen.** → Ich komme **morgen nicht.**
Wir treffen ihn **heute Nachmittag.** → Wir treffen ihn **heute Nachmittag nicht.**
Inge geht **samstags** schwimmen. → Inge geht **samstags nicht** schwimmen.
Frauke besucht uns **dieses Wochenende.** → Frauke besucht uns **dieses Wochenende nicht.**

Nicht is placed *before* specific time expressions involving **jed-** or **all-,** however. The reason for this is that the adjective **jed-** is the focal point of negation, and **nicht** is placed before adjectives:

Wir machen das **jeden Tag.** → Wir machen das **nicht jeden Tag.** (Wir machen es an anderen Tagen.)
Sie kommt **alle zwei Wochen.** → Sie kommt **nicht alle zwei Wochen.** (Sie kommt einmal im Monat.)

Nicht is also placed before adverbs of regularity that end in **-lich**, especially when used with **aber**:

Du machst das **täglich.** Ich mache das auch, aber **nicht täglich.**
*You do that **every day**. I do that, too, but **not every day**.*

Non-Specific Time

If the adverb to be negated is considered to be rather vague or non-specific, place **nicht** *before* it:

Ich mache das **nicht immer.**	Wir fahren **nicht oft** nach München.
Sie kommen leider **nicht bald.**	Sie bleiben **nicht lange** bei uns.

NOTE: The expression **noch nicht** (*not yet*) is an exception to this general rule: Lene ist **noch nicht** angekommen.

Place **nicht** before a time expression that you wish to negate specifically, provided you follow up immediately with **sondern** and a contrasting adverb:

Ich arbeite **nicht später,** ***sondern*** [ich arbeite] **jetzt.**
I'm not working later, but now.

Sie kommt **nicht heute,** ***sondern*** [sie kommt] **morgen.**
She's not coming today, but [rather] tomorrow.

Manner and Place

Place **nicht** *before* most adverbs of manner and place:

manner:	Wir sprechen **nicht laut.** *(We're not speaking loudly.)* Er schläft **nicht gut.** *(He doesn't sleep well.)* Sie kann das **nicht schnell** tun. *(She can't do that quickly.)*
place:	Ilse ist **nicht da.** *(Ilse isn't there.)* Gehst du **nicht dahin**? *(Aren't you going there?)* Wir kommen **nicht aus Indien.** *(We don't come from India.)*

When there is more than one adverbial expression in a sentence, place **nicht** where it is most logical:

Antworten Sie jetzt **nicht so schnell**! (= Antworten Sie langsamer!)
Wir machen diese Übungen normalerweise **nicht zu Hause.** (= Wir machen sie im Klassenzimmer.)

Keep this portable rule in mind:

In general, **nicht** is placed before most adverbs, but after adverbs of specific time.

Adverbial Intensifiers *recht, sehr, so, zu*

Adverbs may be intensified by using words like **ziemlich** (*pretty*), **recht** (*downright*), **sehr** (*very*), **so** (*so*), **unglaublich** (*unbelievably*), and **zu** (*too*), and weakened by using **nicht** before any of the intensifiers.

Sabine spielt **ziemlich gut** Tennis.
Sabine plays tennis pretty well.

Beate spielet **recht gut** Tennis.
Beate plays tennis really well.

Hanna spielt **unglaublich gut Tennis.**
Hanna plays tennis unbelievably well.

Die Kinder sprechen **nicht zu laut.**
The children are not speaking too loudly.

Bernd liest **sehr schnell.**
Bernd reads very quickly.

Hans liest **nicht sehr schnell.**
Hans does not read very quickly.

Udo liest **nicht so gut.**
Udo does not read so well.

Der Junge ist **nicht ganz allein.**
The boy is not completely alone.

Adverbial Interrogatives

The following are common interrogatives used to elicit adverbial information:

time:	**wann** (*when*)	**Wann** kommst du zurück?
	seit wann (*since when*)	**Seit wann** wohnst du in Bremen?
	wie oft (*how often*)	**Wie oft** fährst du nach Stuttgart?
	wie lange (*how long*)	**Wie lange** willst du dort bleiben?
reason:	**warum** (*why*)	**Warum** hast du das gesagt?
	wieso (*how come*)	**Wieso** ist der Chef in dein Büro gegangen?
	weswegen (*for what reason*)	**Weswegen** würde man so etwas tun?
manner:	**wie** (*how*)	**Wie** macht man das am besten?
place:	**wo** (*where*)	**Wo** sind meine Schlüssel?
	woher (*where from*)	**Woher** kommst du, aus Hamburg?
	wohin (*where to*)	**Wohin** ist Nina gegangen?

Exercises

Theory Review

1. Fill in the blanks with the correct information.

1. Words used to modify verbs are called ____________________.

2. These words describe ____________________, ____________________, ____________________, and ____________________ an action takes place.

3. Stated in another way, adverbs offer information about ____________________, ____________________, ____________________, and ____________________.

4. ____________________ phrases in the accusative or genitive may also function as adverbs. Example: ____________________

5. ____________________ phrases normally function as adverbs, too, and they may be accusative, dative, or genitive.

6. Adverbs of time consisting of two or more components are known as ____________________ adverbs.

7. Whenever two or more time expressions are used together, the ____________________ one is mentioned first and the ____________________ one follows it. Example: ____________________

8. Adverbs of time that signal regularity typically end in __________ or __________. Examples: ____________________

9. Only when adverbs begin a sentence are they ____________________.

10. Adverbs like **täglich** and **jährlich** are equivalent to an adverbial noun phrase using a form of ____________________, and both signal regularity. The equivalents of these two are ____________________ and ____________________.

11. Many ____________________ can serve double duty as adverbs.

12. The adverb **gern** is an adverb of ____________________.

13. What does **gern** signal? ____

14. What does **nicht gern** signal? ____

15. The comparative of **gern** is ______________ and the superlative form is ______________.

16. The adverbial category of place has several dimensions: ____________________, ____________________, and ____________________.

17. Words like **recht**, **sehr**, **so**, and **zu** are used with adverbs as ______________________.
18. The mnemonic device that will help you remember the correct normal ordering of adverbial information is ______________________
19. The normal negator for adverbs is ______________________.
20. This negator is placed ______________________ most adverbs.
    Examples: ______________________ ______________________
21. It comes ______________________ specific time expressions, however.
    Example: ______________________
22. Where is it placed relative to a vague or very general (= non-specific) time expression?
    ____ Example: __________________________
23. Where is **nicht** placed relative to an adverb that has an intensifier? ______________________
    Example: ______________________________________
24. Words like **wann**, **warum**, **wie**, **wo/woher/wohin** are ______________________.
25. They are used to elicit information about ______________________, ______________________, ______________________, and ______________________.

Focus on Form [✓]

2. Fill in the blanks with the German equivalents of the following English expressions.

1. tomorrow ____
2. today ____
3. the day before yesterday ____
4. tomorrow morning ____
5. this morning ____
6. at noon on Tuesday ____
7. this afternoon ____
8. tomorrow evening ____
9. the day after tomorrow ____
10. this evening ____

3. Fill in the blanks with the German equivalents that express these various times.

1. early in the morning ____________________
2. late in the afternoon ____________________
3. in the evening ____________________
4. late at night ____________________
5. at the latest ____________________
6. at the earliest ____________________
7. Thursdays ____________________
8. at the earliest this evening ____________________
9. weekly ____________________
10. yearly ____________________
11. always ____________________
12. almost ____________________
13. almost always ____________________
14. never ____________________
15. almost never ____________________

4. Fill in the blanks with the German equivalent of the noun phrases of regularity.

1. jede Nacht ____________________
2. jeden Abend ____________________
3. jeden Mittag ____________________
4. jeden Freitag ____________________
5. jeden Tag ____________________
6. jeden Sonntag ____________________
7. jeden Monat ____________________
8. jeden Morgen ____________________
9. jeden Nachmittag ____________________
10. jeden Montag ____________________
11. jede Woche ____________________
12. jedes Jahr ____________________

5. Word order. Add the adverbial expression cued in parentheses to each sentence, placing it in its normally expected position.

1. Wir gehen nach Hause. (jetzt) ____________________
2. Sabine arbeitet immer. (zu Hause) ____________________
3. Sie sitzen hier. (lange) ____________________
4. Ingo macht das zu schnell. (immer) ____________________

5. Peter läuft zur Schule. (morgens) ______________________________

6. Ilse fährt immer zur Uni. (mit dem Bus) ______________________________

7. Musst du nach Hause gehen? (schnell) ______________________________

8. Ich studiere in Graz. (bald) ______________________________

9. Sie lernt lieber. (allein) ______________________________

10. Kommt ihr etwas früher? (nach Hause) ______________________________

6. Negate the following adverbs in isolation by placing *nicht* in its normal, expected position.

A

1. bald ____________________
2. jährlich ____________________
3. täglich ____________________
4. morgen ____________________
5. jetzt ____________________
6. selten ____________________
7. immer ____________________
8. wöchentlich ____________________
9. heute ____________________
10. gestern ____________________
11. lange ____________________
12. noch ____________________

B

1. heute Morgen ____________________
2. montags ____________________
3. monatlich ____________________
4. viel ____________________
5. allein ____________________
6. heute Abend ____________________
7. abends ____________________
8. jährlich ____________________
9. schnell ____________________
10. gern ____________________

C

1. hier ____________________
2. nach rechts ____________________
3. zu Hause ____________________
4. sehr gut ____________________
5. normalerweise ____________________
6. dahin ____________________
7. nach Hause ____________________
8. aus Köln ____________________
9. zu schnell ____________________
10. dort ____________________

7. Word order and negation. Place *nicht* properly in the following sentences, focusing on the italicized adverb.

1. Wir wollen jetzt *hier* bleiben. ______________________________
2. Gehen Sie besser *nach rechts*! ______________________________
3. Ich mache das *oft.* ______________________________
4. Kommst du *früher*? ______________________________
5. Jens denkt *so ordentlich.* ______________________________
6. Die Lehrerin spricht *zu schnell.* ______________________________
7. Ich nehme den Bus *bald* zur Uni. ______________________________
8. Verstehen Sie das jetzt *besser*? ______________________________
9. Die Schüler fahren *nach Leipzig.* ______________________________
10. Der Junge schläft *im Klassenzimmer.* ______________________________

8. Word order. Join the two sentences with a comma and *dann* (then) or *danach* (after that) to form a two-dimensional sentence. Remember that since *dann* and *danach* are time expressions and occupy first position in the clause, you'll need inverted word order in the second half of the sentence.

1. Ich bleibe bis vier Uhr an der Uni. Ich gehe einkaufen.

   ____

2. Wir werden Milch, Brot, Fleisch und Gemüse kaufen. Wir fahren nach Hause.

   ____

3. Lisa machte das Abendessen. Ein paar Freunde kamen zu Besuch.

   ____

4. Wir werden alle zusammen essen. Wir werden ins Kino gehen.

   ____

5. Wir werden den neuesten Film sehen. Wir wollen in eine Kneipe gehen.

   ____

6. Ich gehe nach Hause. Ich werde ein bisschen lesen.

   ____

7. Ich werde bestimmt von der Arbeit müde sein. Ich werde bald einschlafen.

   ____

Focus on Meaning

9. Fill in the blanks with logical adverbs or adverbial interrogatives.

1. ______________________ kommst du heute Abend nicht mit? Die Party soll sehr gut sein.
2. ______________________ willst du jetzt gehen? In die Buchhandlung oder ins Fotogeschäft?
3. ______________________ wohnst du in dieser Stadt?
4. Bist du jeden Nachmittag zu Hause? = Bist du ______________________ zu Hause?
5. Blutwurst schmeckt mir gar nicht. Ich esse das gar nicht ______________________.
6. Das ist zu viel Arbeit für heute. Wir werden es ______________________ erledigen müssen.
7. Das sieht relativ kompliziert aus. ______________________ macht man das am besten?
8. Du sprichst ______________________ gut Deutsch. Sprichst du Deutsch zu Hause?
9. Hans isst jeden Dienstag in diesem Restaurant. = Hans isst ______________________ in diesem Restaurant.
10. Ich bekomme diese Zeitschrift jeden Monat. Also bekomme ich sie ______________________.
11. Ich kann das machen, aber nicht ______________________. Vielleicht später.
12. Ich mache das ______________________ jeden Tag, wenn's möglich ist.
13. Ich sehe Martina nicht. ______________________ ist sie?
14. Ihr müsst ______________________ arbeiten, sonst müssen wir ______________________ hier bleiben.
15. Rotwein geht, aber ich würde ______________________ einen Weißwein trinken.
16. Wenn ich um neun Uhr bei der Arbeit sein muss, muss ich ______________________ um acht aufstehen.
17. Wir können das ______________________ in weniger Zeit machen, wenn wir nicht viel Arbeit haben.
18. Wir machen jetzt eine Gruppenarbeit. Also, arbeiten Sie nicht ______________________

    sondern ______________________.
19. Wir tun das ______________________, d.h., nicht sehr oft.
20. Wie ______________________ kannst du unter Wasser bleiben?

You Determine the Form

10. Write sentences in German as directed, employing inverted word order. Situation: You are on the phone talking to your sister.

1. Tell her some friends are coming tonight . . .

____

2. and you will be going to the university early tomorrow morning.

____

3. Tell her we can have lunch together at noon.

____

4. Tell her that you and your friends will probably meet in the **Mensa** at one o'clock.

____

____

5. Let her know that you'll be going out on Friday evening with your boyfriend/girlfriend. Your sister can come along if she wants.

____

____

6. Mention to her that you have to write a term paper and can't go out this weekend.

____

11. Express the following in German. Say that . . .

1. they're not visiting us this year. _______________
2. she doesn't work every day. _______________
3. we're not doing that this weekend. _______________
4. you won't be home this evening. _______________
5. your mother is not working today. _______________
6. you don't need the car tomorrow. _______________
7. you will not be at work this evening. _______________
8. you're not at home afternoons. _______________

12. Answer the following questions negatively, focusing the negation on the italicized word or phrase.

1. Soll ich das *jeden Tag* machen? ______________________________

2. Gehst du *samstags* zur Uni? ______________________________

3. Kannst du *dieses Wochenende* mit uns ausgehen?

____

4. Kannst du mich *heute Abend* treffen?

____

5. Siehst du *täglich* fern? ______________________________

Partnerarbeit

13. Arbeiten Sie mit einem Partner/einer Partnerin und stellen Sie einander diese Fragen.

A

Was machst du gern oder nicht gern in der Freizeit? Warum?
Was machst du bald? Wo wirst du es machen und mit wem?
Was machst du morgens, wenn du nicht zur Uni gehen musst?
Was machst du tagsüber, wenn du zu Hause bleiben kannst?
Was machst du recht gut? Seit wann machst du das?

B

Was machst du leider nicht so gut? Warum nicht?
Was machst du lieber allein? Warum allein und nicht mit anderen?
Was machst du nie allein? Warum?
Was machst du gern zusammen mit Freunden? Wohin gehst du, wenn du das machen willst?
Was machst du wöchentlich oder monatlich?

C

Was machst du morgens, bevor du zur Uni gehst?
Was machst du nachmittags, wenn du von der Uni nach Hause kommst?
Was machst du abends zu Hause, wenn du keine Hausaufgaben hast?
Was machst du gern abends, wenn du ausgehen kannst?
Was machst du manchmal samstags und sonntags, wenn du frei hast?

Review: Getting More Comfortable with Adverbs

Read over the following sentences to gain greater familiarity with adverbs, how they are used, and their normal position in the sentence.

Time:

Ich gehe **heute** zur Uni. • Fritz geht **jetzt** zum Deutschkurs. • Katrin geht **später** zu Biologie.
Ich bin **manchmal** müde. • Wir sind **selten** krank. • Hans ist **oft** traurig. • Sie sind **immer** optimistisch.
Ich mache das **immer**. • Ich mache das **nie**. • Ich mache das **oft**. • Ich mache das **nicht so oft**.
Ich gehe **früh** zur Uni. • Maria kommt **sehr früh** zur Arbeit. • Ich will nicht **zu früh** aufstehen.
Bernd schläft **oft spät**. • Christa geht **viel später** zur Uni. • Ich komme **immer zu spät** zu Deutsch.
Ich gehe **jetzt** nach Hause. • Sie läuft **bald** nach Hause. • Er fährt **später** nach Hause.
Schüler gehen **morgens** zur Schule. • Sie kommen **nachmittags** nach Hause zurück.
Tante Emma kam **gestern** zu Besuch. • Onkel Karl kam **vorgestern Abend** vorbei.
Ich bin **nicht oft** krank. = Ich bin **selten** krank.
Wir müssen **täglich** arbeiten. = Wir müssen **jeden Tag** arbeiten.
Wir können **samstags** zu Hause bleiben. = Wir können **jeden Samstag** zu Hause bleiben.

Reason:

Wir trugen **wegen der Kälte** warme Pullis. • Ich ging heute **wegen des schönen Wetters** zu Fuß zur Arbeit. • Würdest du es **wegen deiner Gesundheit** machen? • Ich habe **wegen meiner Eltern** geschwiegen.

Manner:

Ich arbeite **fleißig**. • Ich arbeite **schnell**. • Ich arbeite **langsam**. • Ich arbeite **gut**. • Ich arbeite **schlecht**.
Karl macht das **gut**. • Tina macht das **sehr gut**. • Inge macht das **so gut**. • Ich mache das **nicht so gut**.
Ich spreche **gut** Spanisch. • Ich spreche **nicht so gut** Deutsch. • Ich spreche **sehr schlecht** Englisch.
Ich lerne **fleißig**. • Ich lerne **allein**. • Ich lerne **dort**. • Ich lerne **tagsüber**.
Die Professorin spricht **schnell**. • Der Lehrer spricht **zu laut**. • Der Assistent spricht nicht **zu leise**.

Place (location, destination, point of origin, direction):

Der Papierkorb ist **dort**. • Gehen Sie **dorthin**! • Die Tür ist **nicht da**. • Gehen Sie **nicht dahin**!
Kommen Sie **her**! • Kommen Sie **hierher**! • Ich bin **hier**. • Bleiben wir **hier**. • Warten wir **hier**.
Die Tür ist **links**. • Gehen Sie **nach links**. • Die Fenster sind **nicht rechts**. • Gehen Sie **nicht nach rechts**.

Chapter 15 Prepositions

Part One

Prepositions are words that:

1. introduce a phrase that normally functions as an adverbial unit;
2. determine the case of the elements in the phrase;
3. have meaning(s) in their own right, which gives them a vocabulary dimension;
4. may sometimes come at the end of the phrase, in which case they are called *post*positions;
5. may be used idiomatically with verbs and adjectives to form special expressions.

There are four sets of prepositions in German: *accusative, dative, dative-accusative,* and *genitive.* Each will be considered separately and with many examples in this chapter.

Adverbial Function of Prepositions

A prepositional phrase—that is, a preposition, its noun or pronoun object, and any articles or adjectives used with the object (for example, **mit meinem Freund; mit ihm; mit dem alten Wagen**)—may function as an adverbial unit. That means the prepositional phrase will modify the verb and provide information about time, reason, manner, or place; the four adverbial categories will normally be ordered according to the TRuMP formula you learned in Chapter 14.

Prepositions and postpositions may be used to form phrases with various meanings:

time:	**nach vier Uhr** *after four o'clock*	**nach dem Mittagessen** *after lunch*
manner:	**den Regeln nach** *according to the rules*	**dem Gesetz nach** *according to the law*
place:	**nach Berlin** *to Berlin*	**nach Irland** *to Ireland*
	nach Afrika *to Africa*	**nach Hause** *[to] home*

Accusative Prepositions

The following prepositions "trigger" or "govern" the accusative case:

Accusative Prepositions

bis • durch • für • gegen • ohne • um // hindurch • pro • entlang

Contractions

Optional accusative contractions, common in spoken German, are:

durch + das → **durchs**	für + das → **fürs**	um + das → **ums**

Bis *to, up to, up till, as far as*

The preposition **bis** is used to signal a limit and is normally is used without an article:

bis August *till August*	**bis nächste Woche** *till next week*	**bis heute Abend** *till this evening*	**bis später** *till later*
bis Deutschland *as far as Germany*	**bis Köln** *as far as Cologne*	**bis dahin** *as far as there*	
bis Seite 147 *up to page 147*	**bis Teil IV** *up to Part IV*	**bis Kapitel 15** *up to chapter 15*	

Bis is frequently used in conjunction with other prepositions—for example, **an**, **zu**, and **nach**—to indicate a limit of travel:

Geh **bis an die Tür** [und nicht weiter].
Go ar far as the door [and no farther].

Wir laufen **bis zur Bibliothek**, dann kommen wir zurück.
We're walking as far as the library, then we're coming back.

Wir sind **bis nach München** gefahren.
We drove/traveled as far as Munich.

NOTE: Whenever two prepositions are paired together, the second or last-mentioned preposition determines the case of the object.

Durch *through, throughout, by (means of)*

The preposition **durch** signals that someone or something is passing through a barrier of some kind or through a passageway:

durchs Fenster *through the window*	**durch die Wand** *through the wall*	**durch die Tür** *through the door*	**durch die Nase** *through the nose*

or passing through a physical or geographical area:

durch Europa *through Europe*	**durch Holland** *through Holland*	**durchs Land** *through the country*	**durch den Wald** *through the forest*

Für *for, in favor of, in support of*

The preposition **für** indicates that something is being done on someone's behalf or for a particular purpose, reason, or time:

für dich/euch/Sie *for you*	**für den Kurs** *for the course*	**für Erwachsene** *for adults*	**für heute/Freitag** *for today/Friday*

In addition, **für** may be used when generalizing about persons and things:

Das ist nicht typisch für Amerikaner oder Europäer.
That's not typical for Americans or Europeans.

Für may also be used to indicate favor or support for a person, cause, or idea:

für diese Idee	**für den Krieg**	**für diese Kandidaten**
for this idea	*in support of the war*	*in favor of these candidates*

and to form time expressions:

für zehn Minuten	**für zwei Semester**	**für ein Jahr**
for ten minutes	*for two semesters*	*for a/one year*

Gegen *against, up against; into [an obstruction]; opposed to; toward/approximately/around*

The preposition **gegen** is used with objects into which one bumps, runs, stumbles, or crashes:

Das Kind lief direkt **gegen einen Baum,** ohne ihn gesehen zu haben.
The child ran directly into a tree without having seen it.

Ich bin **gegen ein Auto/gegen einen Lastwagen/gegen eine Straßenlampe** gefahren.
I crashed into a car/truck/streetlight.

Gegen may be used to indicate an opponent or enemy:

Wir haben **gegen die Münchener Fußballmannschaft** gespielt.
We played against the soccer team from Munich.

Im Zweiten Weltkrieg haben die Vereinigten Staaten **gegen Deutschland** gekämpft.
In Word War II the United States fought against Germany.

or to indicate that something is contrary:

gegen das Gesetz	**gegen die Regeln**	**gegen meine Wünsche**
against the law	*against the rules*	*against my wishes*

In addition, **gegen** may be used to indicate opposition to a person, cause, or idea:

gegen diese Kandidaten	**gegen diese Idee**	**gegen den Krieg**
against these candidates	*against this idea*	*opposed to the war*

Gegen may also indicate an approximate time or amount:

Sollen wir **gegen sieben Uhr** ankommen?
Shall we arrive around seven o'cock?

Die Semesterarbeiten sind **gegen Ende** des Semesters fällig.
The term papers are due around the end of the semester.

Gegen zweitausend Zuschauer waren dabei.
Approximately two thousand spectators were there.

Ohne *without*

The preposition **ohne** signals that something is missing, and very often no article is used with the object:

ohne [einen] Regenschirm	**ohne [eine] Brille**	**ohne [eine] Quittung**
without an umbrella	*without glasses*	*without a receipt*

Um *around, round about; at*

The preposition **um** signals a circular route or space. When used with **herum**, it signals movement around something:

um uns [herum]	**um die Stadt [herum]**	**um den See [herum]**
around us	*around the city*	*around the lake*

The use of **rings** intensifies the meaning to *all around* or *rings around:*

[rings] um uns	**[rings] um die Stadt**	**[rings] um das Schiff**
all around us	*all around the city*	*all around the ship*

The preposition **um** is also used to indicate the time at which something happens:

um ein Uhr	**um halb sieben**	**um Mitternacht**
at one o'clock	*at seven-thirty*	*at midnight*

Less Commonly Used Accusative Prepositions and Postpositions

Pro *per, for each*

The preposition **pro** is normally used without an article:

pro Person	**pro Stück**	**pro Tag**	**pro Stunde**
per person	*per piece*	*per day*	*per hour*

Entlang *along [a pathway or topographical feature of some kind]*

Entlang, when used postpositionally, governs the accusative:

Wir wollen eine Wanderung **den Fluss entlang** machen.
We want to take a hike along the river.

Wir haben einen Spaziergang **die Hauptstraße entlang** gemacht.
We took a walk along Main Street.

Hindurch *throughout, all through*

Hindurch functions as a postposition, normally after a noun phrase:

die ganze Nacht hindurch	**das ganze Jahr hindurch**
all through the night	*throughout the year*

Dative Prepositions

The following prepositions "trigger" or "govern" the dative case:

Dative Prepositions

aus • außer • bei • mit • nach • seit • von • zu // gegenüber

Contractions

Optional dative contractions, common in spoken German, are:

bei + dem → **beim** von + dem → **vom** zu + dem → **zum** zu + der → **zur**

Aus *out of, from*

The preposition **aus** can denote an exit point, a point of origin, or what something is made out of:

exit:	**aus der Schule** *out of the school*	**aus dem Gebäude** *out of the building*	**aus dem Fenster** *out [of] the window*	**aus einer Tasse** *out of/from a cup*
origin:	**aus Bonn** *from Bonn*	**aus Deutschland** *from Germany*	**aus Europa** *from Europe*	**aus dieser Richtung** *from this direction*
substance:	**aus Leder** *[made] of leather*	**aus Plastik** *[made] of plastic*	**aus Stein** *[made] of stone*	**aus Silber und Gold** *[made] of silver and gold*

Note this particularly useful expression: **aus diesem Grund** *for this/that reason.*

Außer *besides, except for, out of*

The preposition **außer** signals an exception of some kind, that one is no longer in a certain state, or that something is not functioning:

außer mir/uns/ihnen *besides me/us/them*	**außer meiner Familie** *besides my family*	**außer meinen Kollegen** *besides my colleagues*
außer sonntags/abends *except for Sundays/evenings*	**außer Betrieb** *out of order*	**außer Atem** *out of breath*
außer Kontrolle *out of control*	**außer Gefahr** *out of danger*	**außer Sicht** *out of sight/view*

Bei *near, by, at*

The preposition **bei** signals that something is situated close to something else. It is also used to denote a person's residence or a professional's office. Since it signals a location, it is not used with any verb that indicates motion from one place to another.

bei München *near Munich*	**bei der Universität** *near the university*	**beim Spiel** *at the game*
bei mir [zu Hause] *at my house*	**bei Kramers** *at the Kramers' house*	**beim Arzt** *at the doctor's office*

It may also used with a noun to denote a weather condition:

bei Regen/Nebel *when there's rain/fog*	**bei dieser Hitze/Kälte** *with this heat/cold*	**bei solchem Wetter** *in/with such weather*

NOTE: In expressions like **bei uns** (*at our house*), **bei meiner Tante** (*at my aunt's [house]*), **bei Maria** *(at Maria's [place])*, the word **Haus** does not come into play.

Note, too, that the weather expressions with **bei** essentially replace a **wenn**-clause:

Wenn es regnet, nehme ich immer einen Schirm mit. = **Bei Regen** nehme ich immer einen Schirm mit.

When **bei** is used with an infinitival noun it means "during" or "while":

Das Kind hat sich **beim Spielen** verletzt.
The child injured him-/herself ***while playing.***

Beim Essen soll man nicht sprechen, wenn der Mund voll ist.
One is not supposed to speak ***while eating*** *when one's mouth is full.*

Mit *with, along with*

The preposition **mit** is used to indicate a union or association with another, foods that accompany each other, and instruments by which actions are accomplished; **mit** is also used to designate a mode of transportation:

mit mir/dir/ihr/ihm/uns/euch/Ihnen/ihnen *with me/you/her/him/us/you/them*	**mit Freunden/Inge** *with friends/Inge*
mit Wein/Bier/Wasser/Tee/Kaffee *with wine/beer/water/tea/coffee*	**mit Sauerkraut/Kartoffeln/Pfeffer/Salz** *with sauerkraut, potatoes, pepper, salt*
mit dem Zug/Bus/Auto/Taxi/Schiff *by train/bus/car/taxi/ship*	**mit der Straßenbahn/S-Bahn/U-Bahn** *by streetcar/commuter train/subway*

Nach *after; to*

The preposition **nach** means *after* when used to form time expressions:

nach zwei Uhr *after two [o'clock]*	**nach dem Frühstück** *after breakfast*	**nach dem Film** *after the movie*

Nach is also used with proper name destinations, like towns, cities, countries, and continents:

nach Edewecht *to Edewecht*	**nach Oldenburg** *to Oldenburg*	**nach Deutschland** *to Germany*	**nach Europa** *to Europe*

The expression **nach Hause** *([to] home)* is idiomatic. The **-e** on the end of **Hause** is an old, vestigial dative **e**-ending that sometimes survives with a few monosyllabic masculine and neuter nouns:

Geh jetzt **nach Hause.** *Go home.*	Gib **dem Manne** etwas. *Give the man something.*

When used as a postposition, **nach** means *according to:*

meiner Meinung nach	**der Bibel nach**	**den Regeln nach**	**dem Gesetz nach**
in my opinion	*according to the Bible*	*according to the rules*	*according to the law*

Seit *since*

The preposition **seit** is used to form a time expression which links the past to the present. This is known as the *continuous present.* A present-tense verb form is used with the **seit**-phrase:

Ich studiere **seit drei Semestern** an dieser Uni.
I've been studying at this university for three semesters.

It may also be used in conjunction with **erst** (*for just*) or **schon** (*already*):

Ich studiere **erst seit einem Semester** an dieser Uni.
I've been studying at this university for just three semesters.

Ich studiere **schon seit drei Semestern** an dieser Uni.
I've already been studying at this university for three semesters.

Consider **erst** and **schon** in the sentences above to be modifiers for **seit.**

Von *from, of*

The preposition **von** signals the beginning of a trip (point of departure), time span, or series:

von Bremen **von der Schule** **von zu Hause**

It is often used with **nach** to signal the start and end of a trip (**von ... nach**):

Wir wollen **von Frankfurt nach London** fliegen.

Von ... nach may be used as well with **über** (*by way of*) to signal a transfer point (**von ... über ... nach**):

Ich bin mit dem Zug **von Bremen über Köln nach Freiburg** gefahren.
I went by train from Bremen to Freiburg by way of/via Cologne.

It may also be used with **bis** to signal the start and end of a series (**von ... bis**):

von diesem Freitag bis Montag *from this Friday to Monday*	**von Mai bis Juli** *from May to July*	
von eins bis zwangig *from one to twenty*	**von zwei [Uhr] bis drei.** *from two o'clock till three*	**von A bis Z** *from A to Z*

Von is often used in spoken German as a substitute for the genitive or a possessive adjective, indicating possession:

Das ist das Auto **von meinem Vater.** = Das ist das Auto **meines Vaters.**
Er ist ein Freund **von mir.** = Er ist **mein** Freund.

Von may also be used to mention a part of a whole (as a replacement for the genitive):

der Anfang **von dem Film** = der Anfang **des Filmes**
das Ende **vom Jahr** = das Ende **des Jahres**
viele **von meinen Freunden** = viele **meiner Freunde**

Zu *to*

The preposition **zu** is used to indicate a destination within a town or city:

zum Bahnhof	**zur Uni**	**zur Bibliothek**	**zur Bank**
to the train station	*to the university*	*to the library*	*to the bank*

Zu may also signal that one is going to a person's home or office:

zu mir/uns/ihnen	**zu Bernd und Katrin**	**zu Schmidts**
to my/our/their house	*to Bernd's and Katrin's house*	*to the Schmidts' house*
zu dieser Familie	**zu meiner Kusine**	**zu meinen Großeltern**
to this family's house	*to my cousin's house*	*to my grandparents' house*
zum Arzt/zur Ärztin	**zum Fleischer/Metzger**	**zum Chef/zur Chefin**
to the doctor's office	*to the butcher('s) shop*	*to the boss's office*

When used with certain adjectives, **zu** often expresses a person's attitude toward someone:

Sie ist immer nett/freundlich/unfreundlich/schrecklich **zu mir**.
She's always nice/friendly/unfriendly/terrible to me.

Zu is also used idiomatically in these common expressions:

zu Fuß	**zu Hause**	**zu Besuch**
by foot	*at home*	*for a visit*

Gegenüber *opposite, across from*

The preposition **gegenüber** is used postpositionally with pronouns:

mir/uns/ihnen gegenüber
opposite/across from me/us/them

and pre- *or* postpositionally with nouns:

gegenüber der Post/der Schule	**dem Laden/dem Rathaus gegenüber**
across from the post office/school	*across from the shop/city hall*

The adverbs **schräg** (*diagonally; at an angle*) and **direkt** (*directly*) are frequently used with **gegenüber** for greater clarity:

Das Rathaus ist **dem Dom direkt gegenüber**.
The city hall is directly across from the cathedral.

Der Laden ist **der Bäckerei schräg gegenüber**.
The shop is diagonally across from the bakery.

Gegenüber von *across from*

The preposition **von** frequently follows **gegenüber**, especially in colloqial speech:

gegenüber von der Uni **gegenüber von dem Laden**

NOTE: Remember, whenever prepositions are used in pairs, as in **gegenüber von**, the *last*-mentioned preposition is always the one that determines the case of the object. This is somewhat analogous to the case of compound nouns, where the last component determines both gender and plural form.

Exercises: Part One

Theory Review

1. Fill in the blanks with the correct information.

1. ______________________ are words that are used to introduce a phrase that contains a noun or pronoun and may contain articles and adjectives as well.
2. This phrase is, therefore, referred to as a ______________________ phrase.
3. These phrases typically function as ______________________.
4. Prepositions determine the ______________________ of the elements in the phrase.
5. The noun or pronoun in it is called the ______________________ of the preposition.
6. Articles and adjectives used with that noun or pronoun will be in the same ________________.
7. A preposition that comes at the end of its phrase rather than at the beginning is called a

   ______________________.
8. Prepositions may be used in combination with other words, such as adjectives and verbs, to form

   special meanings. These special combinations are called ______________________ expressions.
9. Some will be similar to English; some won't. The ones that are different will have to be

   ______________________.
10. There are ______________________ groups or sets of prepositions.
11. These sets are referred to by the ______________________ they "trigger" in the other elements of the prepositional phrase.
12. Specifically, these are: ______________________, ______________________,

    ______________________ - ______________________, and ______________________.
13. __________________ are words that provide information about time, reason, manner, or place.
14. Prepositional phrases may function as ______________________ units because they may provide information about those four categories.
15. The typical sequence, or word order, of adverbs and adverbial units is:

    ____
16. Prepositions may have more than one ______________________, depending on the adverbial category being signaled.
17. The main prepositions that always trigger the accusative case are: ________________,

    ________________, ________________, ________________, ________________,

    and ________________.

18. Common contractions with the definite article are: ______________________________

____

19. The prepositions that always trigger the dative case are: ________________,

________________, ________________, ________________,

________________, ________________, ________________,

________________, and ________________.

20. Common contractions with the definite article are: ______________________________

____

21. ________________ may be used prepositionally or postpositionally.

22. It may be, and in conversation often is, used with the dative preposition ______________.

23. Contractions are optional and common in ________________ German, less common in

________________ German.

Focus on Meaning [✓]

2. Fill in the blanks with correct, logical accusative or dative prepositions. Use contractions when appropriate.

A

1. Am Freitag muss ich ________________ München fahren.
2. ________________ diesen Gründen dürfen wir nicht dahin gehen.
3. ________________ mir ist niemand hier.
4. Bist du ________________ dem Auto hergefahren?
5. Der Laden befindet sich ________________ von der Kirche.
6. Die Familie sitzt ________________ den großen Tisch und isst zusammen Abendessen.
7. Die Jungen haben Steine ________________ die Fenster des alten Gebäudes geworfen.
8. Es regnet wie der Teufel und ich bin ________________ meinen Regenschirm!
9. Hast du Lust ________________ einer Tasse Tee?
10. Ich bin ________________ Montag ________________ Donnerstag in Prag.

B

1. Ich habe zwei Jahre ________________ Schneiders gewohnt, als ich Lehrling war.
2. Ich spiele ________________ drei Jahren Violine.
3. Kannst du blitzschnell ________________ 1 ________________ 20 zählen?

4. Kommst du ____________ Norwegen, Schweden oder Dänemark?
5. Meiner Meinung ____________ ist das eine dumme Idee.
6. Möchtest du einen Spaziergang ____________ den See machen?
7. Gehst du jetzt ____________ Doris?
8. Warum hast du mich ____________ der Faust gehauen?
9. Ich finde Ihre Idee gut. Ich bin also ____________ Ihren Plan.
10. Wir können die Straße ____________ laufen, wenn Sie wollen.

C

1. Würden Sie das ____________ mich machen, bitte? Ich kann es nicht.
2. ____________ diesem Kind sind wir ganz allein.
3. Ja, Käthe ist ____________ uns. Sie ist hier.
4. Warum ist Frau Schröder ____________ meinen Vorschlag? Er is ganz logisch.
5. Mensch, ich habe solch einen großen Hunger und ich bin ____________ Geld!
6. Wie viel Geld hast du ____________ dir?
7. Plötzlich stand sie mir ____________. Ich war überrascht.
8. Der kleine Junge lief ____________ die Tür ins Wohnzimmer.
9. ____________ wann sammelst du Briefmarken? Du hast eine Menge davon.
10. Der Zahn tut mir weh. Ich muss ____________ Zahnarzt gehen.

Focus on Meaning and Form

3. Fill in the blanks with the English equivalent of the cued prepositional phrase.

A

1. Sie wohnt immer noch bei ihren Eltern. *(at her parents' house)*
2. Können Sie nicht bis Montag warten? *(till Monday)*
3. Er ist gerade zum Coiffeur gegangen. *(to the barber's)*
4. Ich habe nichts gegen diese Methode. *(against this method)*
5. Es ist jetzt zwanzig nach acht. *(twenty after eight)*
6. Er kommt aus Bayern. *(from Bavaria)*
7. Geh nicht ohne deine Jacke aus. *(without your jacket)*
8. Ich warte schon seit sechzig Uhr hier. *(since four o'clock)*
9. außer ihm waren alle da. *(aside from him)*
10. Georg hat viel Geld für seinen Mantel ausgegeben. *(for his coat)*

B

1. Er ist ______________ angekommen. *(at eight o'clock)*
2. ______________ ist ein Restaurant. *(across from the train station)*
3. Er fuhr ______________. *(to Berlin)*
4. Das Mädchen ist ______________ gelaufen. *(through the park)*
5. Wir wohnen ______________ in Amerika und werden hier bleiben. *(for two years)*
6. Er ist ______________ gegangen. *(around the corner)*
7. Hast du nicht ______________ gehört? *(from her)*
8. Er ist jetzt ______________. *(at work)*
9. Wollen Sie ______________ fahren? *(by train)*
10. Es soll ______________ fertig sein. *(by next week)*

C

1. Der Zug fährt ______________ nach Stuttgart. *(from Bremen)*
2. Ich lese es ______________. *(for the last time)*
3. Übersetzen Sie nicht ______________ ins Englische. *(word for word)*
4. ______________ sollen wir bald da sein. *(according to the map)*
5. ______________ habe ich das Buch gefunden. *(by chance)*
6. Gehen wir schnell ______________. *(to work)*
7. Kommst du nachher ______________? *(to my house)*
8. ______________ bleiben wir zu Hause. *(when the weather's bad)*
9. Gute Mappen sind ______________. *(made of leather)*
10. Ich habe kein Geld ______________. *(on me)*

D

1. Ich fahre nächste Woche ______________. *(to Australia)*
2. Ich werde ______________ ankommen. *(around six o'clock)*
3. Wir bleiben ______________ hier. *(till July)*
4. Atmen Sie ______________, bitte. *(through your/the nose)*
5. Ist deine Kette ______________? *(made of gold)*
6. Das Auto ist ______________ geraten. *(out of control)*

7. ______________________ ist es gefährlich, Auto zu fahren. *(with this weather)*

8. Ich möchte gern zwei Bratwurst ______________________. *(with potato salad)*

9. Die Geschäftsleute machten dieses Jahr eine Reise ______________________. *(to Asia)*

10. Die Kinder sind gerade ______________________ gekommen. *(home from school)*

E

1. Ich gehe jetzt ______________________. *(to my uncle's house)*
2. Gehst du ______________________ dorthin? *(by foot)*
3. Meine Schwester wird ______________________ in Münster sein. *(from May to October)*
4. Ich habe vor, ______________________ da zu bleiben. *(throughout the whole week)*
5. Trink nicht ______________________. *(from this glass)*
6. Warum bist du so ______________________? *(out of breath)*
7. Lisa ist jetzt ______________________. *(at her girlfriend's house)*
8. Fahren Sie ______________________ nach Berlin oder fliegen Sie lieber dorthin? *(by train)*
9. ______________________ ist das eine schlechte Idee. *(in my opinion)*
10. Hans spielt ______________________ Gitarre. *(for just two months)*

F

1. Herr Busby fährt ______________________. *(from London to Paris)*
2. Bringst du deine Katze ______________________? *(to the veterinarian)*
3. Bist du nächste Woche ______________________ bei den Großeltern? *(on a visit)*
4. Das Ende ______________________ war sehr traurig. *(of the novel)*
5. Sollen wir das ______________________ machen? *(for tomorrow)*
6. Komm bitte ______________________. *(around sevenish)*
7. Kannst du blitzschnell ______________________ zählen? *(from 0 to 10)*
8. Die amerikanische Mannschaft hat ______________________ gespielt. *(against the Russians)*
9. Die Firma liefert alles ______________________. *(except on Sundays)*
10. Wir wollen am Freitag nur ______________________ fahren. *(as far as Vienna)*
11. Diese Maschine ist ______________________. *(out of order)*

G

1. Ach, ich musste ______________________ in der Mensa sitzen. *(across from him)*
2. Der Architekt hat den Plan ______________________ gezeichnet. *(with a pencil)*
3. Die Kinder laufen ______________________. *(out of the playground).*
4. ______________________ ist niemand im Büro. *(besides the boss and the secretary)*
5. Ich habe vor, ______________________ zu übernachten. *(at Friede's)*
6. Ist der Brief ______________________? *(from your mother?)*
7. Möchtest du eines Tages ______________________ reisen? *(to South America)*
8. Petra spielt ______________________ Klarinette. *(for three years)*
9. Willst du jetzt ______________________ gehen? *(to the doctor's)*
10. ______________________ ist das strengstens verboten. *(according to the law)*

Part Two

Dative-Accusative Prepositions

The following prepositions "trigger" or "govern" the dative or accusative case, depending on meaning.

Dative-Accusative Prepositions
an — auf • über — unter • hinter — vor • in • neben • zwischen

Contractions

Optional dative-accusative contractions, frequent in spoken German, are:

an + dem → **am**	hinter + dem → **hinterm**	vor + dem → **vorm**
an + das → **ans**	hinter + das → **hinters**	vor + das → **vors**
über + dem → **überm**	unter + dem → **unterm**	in + dem → **im**
über + das → **übers**	unter + das → **unters**	in + das → **ins**
auf + das → **aufs**		

Of these, **am**, **ans**, **aufs**, **im**, and **ins** are the most common.

Case Selection

Accusative Case for Destinations

Use *accusative* forms after these prepositions to indicate a *destination,* that is, a *change of position* or movement from point A to point B:

Sie ist gerade **ins Zimmer** gekommen. *Sie just came into the room.*	Wir setzten uns **auf das Sofa.** *We sat [ourselves] on[to] the sofa.*

NOTE: When it comes to movement, *either* the subject *or* the object must move or be moved from one place to another, that is, there must be a physical change of position:

subject: *Der Lehrer* ging **vor die Klasse** und las aus dem Buch vor.
The teacher went in front of the class and read aloud from the book.

object: Die Lehrassistentin legte *die Papiere* **auf den Tisch** und schrieb *einen Satz* **an die Tafel.**
The TA laid the papers on[to] the table and wrote a sentence on[to] the blackboard.

Dative Case for Locations and Confined/Local Movement

Use *dative* case forms after these prepositions to indicate *location* or *movement at a location* or *in a confined area.* This means there is *no* motion from point A to point B, *no* change of position or location, and therefore *no* destination:

location: Ich sitze hier **auf dem Sofa/am Tisch/im Sessel.**
I'm sitting here on the sofa/at the table/in the easy chair.

movement at a fixed/confined place:
Udo läuft **im Zimmer/im Garten** herum.
Udo is running around in the room/in the garden.

Der Hubschrauber schwebte **über dem Dorf/dem Wald/dem Unfall.**
The helicopter hovered above the village/forest/accident.

An *at, to, on, onto*

Use **an** when referring to a *vertical surface*—walls, doors, windows, and sides of furniture:

ans/am Fenster *to/at the window*	**an die/der Tür** *to/at the door*	**an die/der Wand** *to/at the wall*
an die/der Tafel *to/at the board*	**an den/dem Tisch** *to/at the table*	**an das/dem Sofa** *to/at the sofa*

Use **an** when referring to *bodies of water*—lakes, streams, rivers, oceans, beaches, coast, etc.:

an den/dem Bach *to/at (on) the stream*	**an den/dem See** *to/at (on) the lake*	**an den/dem Fluss** *to/at (on) the river*
an den/am Strand *to/at (on) the beach*	**an die/der See** *to/at the sea*	**an die /der Küste** *to/at (on) the coast*

Auf *on, onto, to*

Use **auf** when referring to *horizontal surfaces*—floors, tabletops, ceilings, the ground, etc.:

auf den/dem Boden *onto/on the floor*	**auf den/dem Tisch** *onto/on the table*	**auf das/dem Bett** *onto/on the bed*

Use **auf** with destinations/locations that are (or were originally) *wide-open spaces:*

auf den/dem Marktplatz *to/at the market place*	**auf den/dem Sportplatz/Fußballplatz/Spielplatz** *to/at the athletic field/soccer field/playground*
auf den/dem Bahnhof *to/at the train station*	**auf den/dem Flugplatz/Flughafen** *to/at the airport*

Use **auf** with certain other destinations and locations—observe them as they come up in reading:

auf das/dem Amt *to/at the office*	**auf die/der Post** *to/at the post office*	**auf eine/einer Party** *to/at a party*

Hinter *behind, in back of*

The preposition **hinter** is used in a very straightforward manner:

hinter mich/mir *behind/in back of me*	**hinter das/dem Haus** *behind/in back of the house*	**hinter das/dem Auto** *behind/in back of the car*

Vor *in front of, ahead of, before*

Like **hinter**, **vor** is used in a straightforward manner:

vor mich/mir *before/ahead of me*	**vor das/dem Haus** *in front of the house*	**vor das/dem Auto** *in front of the car*

It is also used to express a time before another event:

vor zehn Uhr *before 10 o'clock*	**vor Montag** *before Monday*	**vor dem Semesterbeginn** *before the start of the semester*

When used with a past-tense verb, it means *ago:*

vor einer Stunde *an hour ago*	**vor einigen Minuten** *a few minutes ago*	**vor drei Tagen** *three days ago*	**vor zehn Jahren** *ten years ago*

Über *above, over, across; by way of, via; in excess of; more than*

The preposition **über** can be used variously:

über mich/mir *above me*	**über den/dem Tisch** *above/over the table*	**über die/der Stadt** *above/over the city*

über den/dem Fluss
over/across the river

über die/der Brücke
over/across the bridge

über die/der Straße
across the street

über München
by way of Munich

über die Schweiz
by way of Switzerland

über Japan
by way of Japan

über 200 Euro
over/above/more than 200 euros

über drei Jahre
more than/over three years

Unter *below, under, less than; underneath, beneath; among*

The preposition **unter** can be used in various ways:

unter das/dem Sofa
under(neath) the sofa

unter die/der Brücke
under(neath) the bridge

unter die/der Erde
under/below the earth

unter uns
between us

unter meinen Papieren
among my papers

unter meinen Sachen
among my things

unter meiner Würde
below me/not worthy of me

unter 200 Gäste
below/under/fewer than 200 guests

In *in, into*

The preposition **in** can indicate *entry* (motion into) or *location inside of something:*

in das/dem Haus
into/in the house

in den/dem Wald
into/in the forest

in die/der Bibliothek
into/in the library

NOTE: **In** is used to indicate that one is going to, that is, entering into, a certain street:

Ich gehe jetzt **in die Weichselstraße.**
I'm going to Weichsel Street.

or that one lives on a certain street:

Ich wohne **in der Weichselstraße.**
I live on Weichsel Street.

RATIONALE: A street is an area, that is, a space, that one enters (goes *into*) or *in* which one resides. On the other hand, in the sentence: **Die Kinder spielen auf der Straße, Straße** is referred to here as a road surface (horizontal surface) *on which* the children are playing.

A similar situation is the use of **in** to make reference to the story of a building. While in English one says: *The office is on the third floor,* in German the equivalent is: **Das Büro ist *im* zweiten Stock**. In German, **Stock** (*floor*) refers to an area of space *in* which things are located, not a surface *on* which things are located.

It may also be used to signal a duration of time:

Ich kann das *in zwei Stunden* machen.
I can do it in two hours.

Remember that **in** is used instead of **nach** with countries that are used with definite articles:

masculine: Der Präsident fliegt morgen **in den Iran** für einen offiziellen Staatsbesuch..
feminine: Peter Hess fliegt **in die Schweiz**, um seine Familie zu besuchen.
plural: Hanola und Burkhart reisen bald **in die Vereinigten Staaten/USA**.

Neben *next to, alongside of, beside*

The preposition **neben** signals that something is very close and *to the side* of someone or something:

neben mich/mir	**neben die/der Schule**	**neben das/dem Sofa**
next to me	*next to the school*	*next to the sofa*

Zwischen *between*

The preposition **zwischen** signals a destination or location *between* two objects, both of which are mentioned:

Geh **zwischen die Metzgerei und die Buchhandlung.**
Go between the butcher shop and the bookstore.

Das Fotogeschäft steht **zwischen der Metzgerei und der Buchhandlung.**
The photo shop is between the butcher shop and the bookstore.

Stell es **zwischen das Sofa und den Sessel.**
Put it between the sofa and the easy chair.

Es steht **zwischen dem Sofa und dem Sessel.**
It's between the sofa and the easy chair.

Stell die Vase **zwischen die zwei Bilder.**
Place the vase between the two pictures.

Die Vase steht **zwischen den zwei Bildern.**
The vase is between the two pictures.

Verbs Signaling Activity at a Location

The verbs **halten**, **parken, landen,** and **ankommen** indicate activities that are done *at a location* and therefore require the dative with dative-accusative prepositions:

parken: Man darf nicht **vor der Bibliothek parken.**
One may not park in front of the library.

Man darf aber **im Parkhaus parken.**
One may, however, park in the parking garage.

landen: Wir sind **auf dem Flugplatz/Flughafen** in Berlin **gelandet.**
We landed at the airport in Berlin.

halten: Der Bus **hält vor dem Bahnhof.**
The bus stops in front of the train station.

ankommen: Wir sind gestern **in den USA angekommen.**
We arrived yesterday in the United States.

Wir sind ziemlich spät **bei ihnen angekommen.**
We arrived pretty late at their place.

Genitive Prepositions

The following prepositions, all of which are very straightforward and singular in meaning, "trigger" or "govern" the genitive case:

Genitive Prepositions

statt/anstatt • trotz • während • wegen
innerhalb — außerhalb • diesseits — jenseits

Statt/anstatt *instead of*

anstatt ihres Bruders *instead of her/their brother*	**anstatt seiner Freundin** *instead of his girlfriend*	**anstatt dieser Leute** *instead of these people*
statt des Kindes *instead of the child*	**statt unserer Freunde** *instead of our friends*	**statt meiner Eltern** *instead of my parents*

Statt tends to be more common in spoken German and **anstatt** is more common in written and formal contexts.

Trotz *in spite of*

trotz des Wetters *in spite of the weather*	**trotz der Kälte** *in spite of the cold*	**trotz des Unglücks** *in spite of the accident*

Während *during*

während des Sommers *during the summer*	**während der Woche** *during the week*	**während des Semesters** *during the semester*

Wegen *because of, on account of, due to*

wegen des Unfalls *because of the accident*	**wegen meiner Krankheit** *due to my illness*	**wegen des kalten Wetters** *on account of the cold weather*

Innerhalb *inside, inside of, within*

innerhalb eines Monats *within a month*	**innerhalb der Stadt** *inside the city*	**innerhalb des Hauses** *inside the house*

Außerhalb *outside, ouside of*

außerhalb des Parks *outside the park*	**außerhalb der Stadt** *outside of the city*	**außerhalb des Landes** *outside of the country*

Diesseits *[on] this side of*

diesseits des Flusses *on this side of the river*	**diesseits der Straße** *this side of the street*	**diesseits der Grenze** *this side of the border*

Jenseits *[on] that side of; on the other side of*

jenseits des Sees
on that side of the lake

jenseits der Brücke
on the other side of the bridge

jenseits der Grenze
on the other side of the border

Anomalies

When only a noun follows a genitive preposition, there is no genitive ending on the noun:

Ich würde lieber Fisch **statt Fleisch** essen.
I'd rather eat fish instead of meat.

Ich möchte lieber Gold **statt Silber** haben.
I would rather have gold instead of silver.

In colloquial German the dative is frequently used particularly after **trotz** and **wegen**, for example, **trotz dem Unfall, wegen dem Wetter.** This is not yet a feature of formal German, though it may be sanctioned at some time in the future.

Another feature of spoken German is the frequent use of the preposition **von** in conjunction with some genitive prepositions, in which case **von** determines that the dative case is to be used:

innerhalb von zwei Jahren
within two years

außerhalb von dieser bildschönen Touristenstadt
outside of this postcard-pretty tourist city

diesseits von der engen Straße
on this side of the narrow street

jenseits von der stark bewaffneten Grenze
on the other side of the heavily armed border

-*wegen* Compounds

Since there are no genitive pronouns in modern German, a problem arises when you try to use a pronoun after **wegen**. You can use a dative pronoun (colloquial) or form a "**wegen**-compound" (formal):

meinetwegen = wegen mir
on my account

unseretwegen = wegen uns
on our account

deinetwegen = wegen dir
on your account (sg.)

euretwegen = wegen euch
on your account (pl.)

Ihretwegen = wegen Ihnen
on your account (formal)

seinetwegen = wegen ihm
on his account

ihretwegen = wegen ihr/wegen ihnen
on her/their account

Review of Prepositions Expressing Various Destinations and Locations

1. Use **nach** (*to*) with proper name destinations of villages, towns, cities, states, countries, and continents:

   nach Heidelberg **nach Niedersachsen** **nach Deutschland** **nach Europa**

2. Use **zu** (*to*) for destinations within a town, village, or city. This includes names of shops, stores, residences, and offices:

   zum Rathaus **zur Bäckerei** **zum Kaufhof** **zu Hertie**
   zu Tante Klara **zu uns** **zum Arzt**

3. Use **in** (*in, into*—plus accusative) to express intent to *enter* a destination (instead of **zu**):

in die Innenstadt **ins Konzert** **in die Bibliothek**
ins Kino **in die Bäckerei**

4. Use **auf** (*on[to]*—plus accusative; *on*—plus dative) when referring to horizontal surfaces:

auf den Boden/auf dem Boden **auf diese Seite/auf dieser Seite**
auf den Tisch/auf dem Tisch

and for destinations/locations that are or used to be wide-open spaces (*to*—plus accusative; *at*—plus dative):

auf den Markt/auf dem Markt **auf den Bahnhof/auf dem Bahnhof**
auf den Flughafen/auf dem Flughafen **auf das Land/auf dem Land**

5. Use **an** when referring to vertical surfaces:

an die Wand/an der Wand **an die Tür/an der Tür** **ans Fenster/am Fenster**

and with bodies of water (*to*—plus accusative; *at*—plus dative):

destinations: **an den See/am See** **an die Küste/an der Küste** **an den Strand/am Strand**
locations: **an den Hafen/ am Hafen** **an den Rhein/am/Rhein**

6. Use **zu** or **auf** for these destinations:

zur Bank/auf die Bank **zur Post/auf die Post**
zur Party/zu einer Party **auf die/eine Party**
zum Amt/aufs Amt (for example, **Postamt, Auslandsamt, Arbeitsamt**, etc.)

Exercises: Part Two

Theory Review

1. Fill in the blanks with the correct information.

1. A third set of prepositions may use either the ______________________ or ______________________ case after the prepostion.
2. These are sometimes called "two-way" prepositions, "doubtful" prepositions, or the more straightforward ______________________ prepositions.
3. There are nine of these prepositions. Six of them form contrasting pairs. They are: ____________/____________, ____________/____________, and ____________/____________.
4. The remaining three are "independents." They are: ______________, ______________, and ______________.

5. Contractions of the preposition and the definite article are common in spoken German. Some dative contractions are: ____________________, ____________________, and ____________________.

6. Some accusative contractions are: ____________________, ____________________, and ____________________.

7. The dative case is triggered after these prepositions when a ____________________ is signaled.

8. The dative is also triggered with these when there is what kind of motion?

____

9. The accusative case is required when a ____________________ is signaled. Put another way, a *change* in ____________________ from point A to point B is indicated.

10. Such a change involves ____________________ from one place to another.

11. The person or thing that is moving around or being moved around will be either the ____________________ of the sentence, or the ____________________ ____________________.

12. Indicate the preposition used with the following kinds of prepositional objects, whether dative or accusative:

bodies of water	__________	a party	__________
entry	__________	post office	__________
government offices	__________	vertical surfaces	__________
horizontal surfaces	__________	wide-open spaces	__________

13. Which prepositions mean the following:

above	__________	across	__________
alongside of	__________	among	__________
in front of	__________	ahead of	__________
before	__________	behind	__________
in back of	__________	below	__________
beside	__________	between	__________
into	__________	more than	__________
over	__________	in excess of	__________
next to	__________	on/onto (horiz.)	__________
on/onto (vert.)	__________	to/at (a space)	__________
underneath	__________	to/at (a vertical dimension)	__________

14. Which four verbs are always used with a dative two-way prepositional phrase because they indicate an activity, often involving *motion, at a location*? ____________________, ____________________, ____________________, ____________________

15. Perhaps the most minor, that is, the least frequently used, group of prepositions triggers the

    ____________________ case.

16. The four "major" prepositions in this group are: ____________________,

    ____________________, ____________________, ____________________

17. Four "lesser" prepositions are: ____________________, ____________________,

    ____________________, ____________________

18. Indicate which prepositions mean the following:

because of	____________	due to	____________
during	____________	in spite of	____________
inside of	____________	instead of	____________
on account of	____________	outside of	____________
that side of	____________	this side of	____________
within	____________		

19. As you have learned previously, prepositions may have either a ____________________ or a

    ____________________ as its object.

20. There are no ____________________ pronouns. When you wish to use **wegen** and a pronoun

    (**du**), you may say either ____________________ or ____________________. Since there are

    no genitive pronouns, a ____________________ pronoun may be used instead.

21. In colloquial German, the prepositions ____________________ and ____________________

    are frequently used with a ____________________ object. As you can see, the genitive case is giving way to the dative in some areas. It will continue to do so over time. (Remember, languages are dynamic, not static.)

22. There are several ways to express *to* in German, and the different ways depend on the kind of

    ____________________ that is signaled.

23. Fill in the blank with the preposition meaning *to* that you would immediately associate with these destinations:

a city (Hamburg)	____________	a concert (indoor)	____________
a country (China)	____________	a doctor or lawyer	____________
a friend's house	____________	a lake	____________
a movie	____________	a relative's house	____________
a store (Hertie)	____________	a town (Leer)	____________
a village (Petersfehn)	____________	downtown	____________
the bank	____________	the countryside	____________
the marketplace	____________	the post office	____________

24. Fill in the blank with the preposition meaning *at* or *in* that you would immediately associate with these locations:

a city (Hamburg)	___________	a concert	___________
a country (China)	___________	a doctor's office	___________
a friend's house	___________	a lake	___________
a movie	___________	a relative's house	___________
a store (Hertie)	___________	a town (Leer)	___________
a village (Petersfehn)	___________	downtown	___________
the bank	___________	the countryside	___________
the marketplace	___________	the post office	___________

25. Destinations that are names of towns, cities, countries, and continents require

_________________.

26. Destinations within a city generally require _________________.

27. If you wish to signal *intent to enter*, use _________________ as a general rule.

Focus on Meaning [✓]

2. Fill in the blanks with correct, logical dative-accusative or genitive prepositions. Use contractions when appropriate.

A

1. Der Ball ist _________________ das Bett gerollt.
2. Der Laden befindet sich _________________ der Ecke.
3. Die Freunde sitzen _________________ [de]m Tisch und trinken Kaffee zusammen.
4. Die Kinder sind _________________ [da]s Bett gesprungen und schliefen schnell ein.
5. Wohnen deine Großeltern _________________ der Stadt oder _________________ dem Land?
6. Ich musste _________________ des Gewitters eine Weile im Büro warten.
7. Ich würde lieber Bier _________________ Wein trinken.
8. In diesem Foto steht Tina _________________ Marthe und Luise.
9. Komm bitte _________________ [da]s Zimmer herein.
10. Mein Herr, sind Sie blind? Das Ende der Schlange ist _________________ mir.

B

1. Setz dich _________________ das Sofa.
2. Setz dich _________________ den Sessel.

3. Stell den Stuhl ______________________ den Ecktisch.
4. ______________________ des sonnigen Wetters sind wir den ganzen Tag zu Hause geblieben.
5. Was hängt ______________________ der Wand in der Ecke? Ist das ein Bild oder ein Poster?
6. ______________________ der furchtbaren Hitze spielten wir nicht Fußball.
7. ______________________ der Tür stand ein Fremder.
8. Eine schöne Lampe aus Glas hing ______________________ dem Tisch.
9. Ich wohne nicht direkt in der Stadt sondern ein bisschen ______________________ der Stadt.
10. Unser Haus steht ______________________ des Flusses. Mein Bruder wohnt auf der anderen Seite.

C

1. ______________________ der Pause holte ich mir ein Glas Wein.
2. ______________________ dem Marktplatz kann man viel Fisch, Gemüse und Obst kaufen.
3. Gehen wir ______________________ den See. Ich möchte schwimmen gehen.
4. ______________________ unserem Haus steht ein großer Lindenbaum.
5. Geh ______________________ dein Zimmer und hol dir etwas Wärmeres.
6. Wir möchten diesen Sommer ______________________ die Schweiz fahren.
7. Gehst du ______________________ die Bibliothek?
8. ______________________ des dicken Nebels bin ich mit dem Auto gefahren.
9. ______________________ des dicken Nebels bin ich *nicht* mit dem Auto gefahren.
10. Vielleicht können wir einen Ausflug ______________________ [da]s Land machen.

Focus on Meaning and Form

3. Fill in the blanks with the German equivalent of the cued prepositional phrase.

A

1. Meine Serviette ist ______________________ gefallen. *(under the table)*
2. ______________________ steht ein Nachttisch. *(next to the bed)*
3. Es ist jetzt ______________________. *(twenty after eight)*
4. Komm sofort ______________________. *(into the house)*
5. Er warf seinen Mantel ______________________. *(on[to] the bed)*
6. ______________________ muss er viel reisen. *(because of his work)*
7. Es stehen einige Bäume ______________________. *(between the houses)*
8. Hängen Sie es ______________________. *(on[to] the wall)*
9. ______________________ sehen wir ihn nur selten. *(during the semester)*
10. Er saß den ganzen Tag ______________________. *(at the window)*

B

1. Legen Sie es ________________________. *(on[to] the desk)*
2. Das Mädchen ist ________________________ gelaufen. *(into the hallway)*
3. Er stand gleich ________________________. *(in front of the door)*
4. Die Garage ist gleich ________________________. *(behind the house)*
5. Das Restaurant ist ________________________. *(on the corner)*
6. ________________________ finde ich es schön. *(despite the color)*
7. ________________________ ist er immer pleite. *(because of his low salary)*
8. Bitte machen Sie das nicht ________________________. *(on our account)*
9. Sie setzte sich ________________________. *(at the table)*
10. Der Zug fährt von Bremen ________________________ nach München. *(by way of Cologne)*

C

1. Wir gehen bald ________________________. *(on a trip)*
2. ________________________ kann man die Alpen nicht sehen. *(due to the fog)*
3. Morgen will ich einen Ausflug ________________________ machen. *(to the countryside)*
4. Sie wohnt ________________________. *(on the third floor)*
5. Er ist nur ________________________ gekommen. *(up to the door)*
6. Ich fahre nächste Woche ________________________. *(to Switzerland)*
7. Bei warmem Wetter gehen wir oft ________________________. *(to the lake)*
8. Geh ________________________, nicht ________________________. *(in front of me . . . behind me)*
9. Ich habe letzten Sommer ________________________ verdient. *(more than $3,000)*
10. Die Kinder sind noch ________________________. *(at the playground)*

D

1. ________________________ habe ich Handschuhe getragen. *(due to the cold)*
2. Das Mikrophon muss ________________________ stehen. *(between the two loudspeakers)*
3. Der Hund schläft ________________________ der Tochter. *(under the bed)*
4. Leg deine Kleidung nicht ________________________. *(on the sofa)*

5. Mein Bruder hat Vatis neuen Wagen ________________ gefahren. *(into a car)*

6. Was hast du ________________? *(in your backpack)*

7. ________________ kann ich das für Sie nicht machen. *(for this reason)*

8. ________________ konnte ich meine Eltern mehrmals besuchen. *(during the year)*

9. Das Auto steht ________________. *(in front of the white house)*

10. Das soll nur ________________ bleiben. *(between us)*

E

1. Lies die Warnung ________________. *(on the door)*

2. Zeichne nicht ________________! *(on the wall)*

3. ________________ bin ich zur Arbeit gegangen. *(in spite of a bad cold)*

4. Das Geschäft befindet sich ________________. *(on the other side of the street)*

5. Der Ball rollte ________________. *(behind the big easy chair)*

6. Die Schlüssel liegen ________________. *(on top of the newspaper)*

7. Stell die Blumen ________________. *(in front of the closed window)*

8. Zieh dir einen Mantel ________________ an. *(instead of a jacket)*

9. Die Stadt liegt ________________. *(between the harbor and the airport)*

10. Ich möchte diesen Sommer ________________ fahren. *(to Switzerland)*

F

1. Mach das nicht ________________! *(on my account)*

2. Ich würde gern eines Tages ________________ fahren. *(to Belgium)*

3. Am Freitagabend gehen wir ________________. *(to a concert)*

4. Meine Mutter will ________________ gehen. *(to the fish market)*

5. Unsere Familie geht dieses Wochenende ________________. *(to Aunt Emma's house)*

6. Wir haben es ________________ getan. *(for their sake)*

7. Der Vater brachte den kranken Sohn ________________. *(to the pediatrician)*

8. Willst du morgen einen Ausflug ________________ machen? *(to the country)*

9. Ich muss jetzt ________________ gehen. *(downtown)*

10. ________________ haben wir das Geld gespart. *(for you[r sake])*

Partnerarbeit

4. Arbeiten Sie mit einem Partner/einer Partnerin und besprechen Sie die folgenden Fragen.

1. Identifizieren Sie den Anfang und das Ende einer Reise, die Sie neulich gemacht haben. Mit wem haben Sie die Reise gemacht und was haben Sie während der Reise getan?
2. Nennen Sie zwei Politiker und sagen Sie, was Sie von ihnen halten. Erklären Sie Ihre Meinungen.
3. Seit wann studieren Sie an dieser Universität? Welche Kurse haben Sie dieses Semester? Wie finden Sie sie?
4. Wann beginnt und endet Ihr Deutschkurs? Welche Schwierigkeiten haben Sie damit?
5. Wann machen Sie Ihre Hausaufgaben für diesen Kurs? Beschreiben Sie die Chronologie, der Sie folgen.
6. Seit wann lernen Sie schon Deutsch? Wo haben Sie Deutschkurse gehabt?
7. Wie sind Sie heute zur Uni gekommen?
8. Woher kommen Sie? Seit wann wohnen Sie dort? Gefällt es Ihnen da? Würden Sie lieber woanders wohnen?
9. Wohnen Sie allein oder haben Sie Zimmerkollegen? Welche Probleme oder Schwierigkeiten haben Sie?
10. Wer ist nicht freundlich zu Ihnen? Warum?

5. Stellen Sie einander die folgenden Fragen.

Wohin gehst du, ...

1. wenn es sehr heiß ist?
2. wenn dein Auto kaputt ist?
3. wenn du am Freitagabend ausgehst?
4. wenn du ein Buch oder einen Roman kaufen willst?
5. wenn du einen Freund besuchen willst?
6. wenn du großen Hunger hast?
7. wenn du krank bist?
8. wenn du Lebensmittel brauchst?
9. wenn du mit dem Bus fahren willst?
10. wenn du tanken willst?
11. wenn du Zahnschmerzen hast?
12. wenn es sehr heiß und schwühl ist?
13. wenn du nicht genug Geld hast?
14. wenn du gute Musik hören willst?
15. wenn du Durst hast?

Supplementary Exercises

The following exercises cover all prepositions taught in this chapter. The items are much the same as those you have completed previously, but they have been arranged randomly to minimize case predictability. See if your speed and accuracy has improved since the first round of exercises. Check your answers with the answer key. *Übung macht den Meister!*

Focus on Meaning [✓]

1. Fill in the blanks with the correct prepositions. Use contractions when appropriate.

A

1. ______________ der Pause holte ich mir ein Glas Wein.
2. Am Dienstag muss ich ______________ Bielefeld fahren.
3. Der Ball ist ______________ das Auto gerollt.
4. Ich habe zwei Jahre ______________ Schneiders gewohnt, als ich Lehrling war.
5. Leg dich ______________ das Sofa, wenn du müde bist.
6. Würden Sie das ______________ mich machen, bitte? Ich kann es nicht.
7. Ich habe schlimme Kopfschmerzen. Ich muss wirklich mal ______________ [de]m Arzt gehen.
8. Ich bin ______________ Montag ______________ Freitag in Prag.
9. Mein Herr, das Ende der Schlange ist ______________ mir, nicht vor mir.
10. Unser Haus steht ______________ der Straße. Mein Bruder wohnt auf der anderen Seite.

B

1. Vielleicht können wir einen Ausflug ______________ [da]s Land machen.
2. Wir können den Fluss ______________ laufen, wenn du willst.
3. ______________ diesen Gründen dürfen wir nicht dahin gehen. Es ist zu gefährlich.
4. ______________ dem Marktplatz kann man frischen Fisch, frisches Gemüse und frishes Obst kaufen.
5. Die jungen Leute sind ______________ ihren Freunden ausgegangen.
6. Das Fotogeschäft befindet sich ______________ der Ecke.
7. Ich spiele ______________ einem Jahr Klavier.
8. Setz dich ______________ den Sessel.
9. ______________ mir ist nur der Chef hier.
10. Die Freunde sitzen ______________ [de]m Tisch und reden über vieles.

C

1. Gehen wir heute ____________________ den See. Ich möchte schwimmen gehen.
2. Ja, Käthe ist ____________________ uns. Sie ist hier.
3. Kannst du blitzschnell ____________________ 1 ____________________ 20 zählen?
4. Stell den Stuhl ____________________ den Tisch.
5. ____________________ unserem Haus steht ein großer Lindenbaum.
6. ____________________ des miesen Wetters mussten wir den ganzen Tag zu Hause bleiben.
7. Bist du ____________________ dem Bus hergefahren?
8. Die Kinder sind ____________________ [da]s Bett gesprungen und schliefen schnell ein.
9. Kommst du ____________________ Norwegen, Schweden oder Dänemark?
10. Warum ist Frau Schröder ____________________ meinen Vorschlag? Er is ganz logisch.

D

1. Die Schule ist ____________________ von der Kirche.
2. Geh ____________________ dein Zimmer zurück und hol dir etwas Wärmeres.
3. Ich muss heute ____________________ die Bank gehen. Ich bin knapp an Geld.
4. Meiner Meinung ____________________ ist das eine dumme Idee.
5. Mensch, ich habe solch einen großen Hunger und ich bin ____________________ Geld!
6. Was hängt ____________________ der Wand in der Ecke? Ist das ein Bild oder ein Poster?
7. ____________________ der furchtbaren Hitze spielten wir Fußball.
8. Die Familie sitzt ____________________ [de]m Tisch und isst zusammen Abendessen.
9. Ich musste ____________________ des Gewitters eine Weile im Büro warten.
10. Möchtest du einen Spaziergang ____________________ den See machen?

E

1. Wie viel Geld hast du ____________________ dir?
2. Wir möchten diesen Sommer ____________________ die Schweiz fahren.
3. ____________________ der Tür stand ein Fremder.
4. Die Jungen haben Steine ____________________ die Fenster des alten Gebäudes geworfen.
5. Gehst du ____________________ die Bibliothek?
6. Ich würde lieber Bier ____________________ Wein trinken.

7. Plötzlich stand sie mir ______________________. Ich war überrascht.

8. Warum bist du immer so unfreundlich ______________________ Helmut?

9. ______________________ des dicken Nebels bin ich nicht mit dem Auto hergefahren.

10. Der kleine Junge lief ______________________ die Tür ins Wohnzimmer.

F

1. Eine schöne Lampe aus Glas hing ______________________ dem Tisch.

2. Es regnet wie der Teufel und ich bin ______________________ meinen Regenschirm!

3. In diesem Foto steht Tina ______________________ Marthe und Luise.

4. Warum hast du mich ______________________ der Faust gehauen?

5. ______________________ wann sammelst du Briefmarken? Du hast eine Menge davon.

6. ______________________ meiner schlechten Note bin ich jetzt unter Hausarrest.

7. ______________________ dem Marktplatz kann man immer frisches Gemüse kaufen.

8. Ich finde Ihre Idee recht gut. Ich bin also ______________________ Ihren Vorschlag.

9. Komm bitte ______________________ [da]s Zimmer herein.

10. Ich wohne nicht direkt in der Stadt sondern ein bisschen ______________________ der Stadt.

Focus on Meaning and Form [✓]

2. Fill in the blanks with the English equivalent of the cued prepositional phrase.

A

1. Der Zug fährt ______________________ nach Stuttgart. *(from Bremen)*

2. Er ist ______________________ angekommen. *(at eight o'clock)*

3. Herr Busby fährt ______________________. *(from London to Paris)*

4. Ich fahre nächste Woche ______________________. *(to Australia)*

5. Ich gehe jetzt ______________________. *(to my uncle's house)*

6. Legen Sie es ______________________. *(on[to] the desk)*

7. Meine Serviette ist ______________________ gefallen. *(under the table)*

8. Sie wohnt immer noch ______________________. *(at her parents' house)*

9. Wir gehen bald ______________________. *(to Dieter's place)*

10. Die Kinder sind gerade ______________________ gekommen. *(home from school)*

B

1. Die Kinder sind noch ______________________. *(at the playground)*
2. Der Hund saß den ganzen Tag ______________________ und wartete auf seinen Meister. *(at the window)*
3. Es soll ______________________ fertig sein. *(by next week)*
4. Georg hat viel Geld ______________________ ausgegeben. *(for his coat)*
5. Hans spielt ______________________ Gitarre. *(for just two months)*
6. Ich habe kein Geld ______________________. *(on me/with me)*
7. Ich werde dir ______________________ folgen. *(to the end of the earth)*
8. Der Zug fährt von Bremen ______________________ nach München. *(by way of Cologne)*
9. Diese Maschine ist ______________________. *(out of order)*
10. Mein Bruder hat Vatis neuen Wagen ______________________ gefahren. *(into a wall)*

C

1. ______________________ kann ich das für Sie nicht machen. *(for this reason)*
2. ______________________ steht ein Nachttisch. *(next to the bed)*
3. ______________________ kann man die Alpen nicht sehen. *(due to the fog/ when it's foggy)*
4. ______________________ ist ein Restaurant. *(across from the train station)*
5. Bringst du deine Katze ______________________? *(to the veterinarian's office)*
6. Das Mädchen ist ______________________ gelaufen. *(into the hallway)*
7. Gehst du ______________________ dorthin? *(by foot)*
8. Ich lese es ______________________. *(for the last time)*
9. Ich werde ______________________ ankommen. *(around six o'clock)*
10. Können Sie nicht ______________________ warten? *(till Monday)*

D

1. Er fuhr ______________________. *(to Berlin)*
2. Er ist gerade ______________________ gegangen. *(to the barber's)*
3. Er stand gleich ______________________. *(in front of the door)*
4. Es ist jetzt ______________________. *(twenty after eight)*

5. Kommst du bald ______________________________ bei uns? *(for a visit)*

6. Meine Schwester wird ______________________________ in Münster sein. *(from May to October)*

7. Morgen will ich einen Ausflug ______________________________ machen. *(to the country[side])*

8. Übersetzen Sie das nicht ______________________________ ins Englische. *(word for word)*

9. Wir bleiben ______________________________ hier. *(till July)*

10. ______________________________ sollen wir bald da sein. *(according to the map)*

E

1. Atmen Sie ______________________________, bitte. *(through your/the nose)*

2. Das Ende ______________________________ war sehr traurig. *(of the novel)*

3. Das Mädchen ist ______________________________ gelaufen. *(through the backyard)*

4. Die Garage ist gleich ______________________________. *(behind the house)*

5. Ich habe nichts ______________________________. *(against your method)*

6. Ich habe vor, ______________________________ da zu bleiben. *(throughout the whole week)*

7. Komm sofort ______________________________. *(into the house)*

8. Sie wohnt ______________________________. *(on the third floor)*

9. ______________________________ habe ich das Buch gefunden. *(by chance)*

10. Das Restaurant befindet sich ______________________________. *(on the corner)*

F

1. Er ist nur ______________________________ gekommen. *(up to the door)*

2. Er warf seinen Mantel ______________________________. *(on[to] the bed)*

3. Es ist jetzt ______________________________. *(twenty to eight)*

4. Ist deine Kette ______________________________? *(made of gold)*

5. Sollen wir das ______________________________ machen? *(for tomorrow)*

6. Trink nicht ______________________________. *(from this glass)*

7. Wir wohnen ______________________________ in Amerika und werden hier bleiben. *(for two years)*

8. ______________________________ muss er viel reisen. *(because of his occupation)*

9. ______________________________ finde ich es schön. *(despite the price)*

10. Die Kinder sind ______________________________. *(out of control)*

G

1. Er ist ______________________ gegangen. *(around the corner)*
2. Er kommt ______________________. *(from Bavaria)*
3. Gehen wir schnell ______________________. *(to work)*
4. Ich fahre nächste Woche ______________________. *(to Switzerland)*
5. Komm bitte ______________________. *(around sevenish)*
6. Warum bist du so ______________________? *(out of breath)*
7. ______________________ ist es gefährlich Auto zu fahren. *(with this weather)*
8. ______________________ ist er immer pleite. *(because of his low salary)*
9. Bei warmem Wetter gehen wir oft ______________________. *(to the lake)*
10. Es stehen einige Bäume ______________________. *(between the houses)*

H

1. Geht nicht ______________________ aus. *(without your jackets)*
2. Hast du nicht ______________________ gehört? *(from her)*
3. Kannst du blitzschnell ______________________ zählen? *(from 0–10)*
4. Kommst du nachher ______________________? *(to my house)*
5. Lisa ist jetzt ______________________. *(at her girlfriend's house)*
6. ______________________ machen wir einen Spaziergang. *(when the weather's nice)*
7. Bitte machen Sie das nicht ______________________. *(on our account)*
8. Die amerikanische Mannschaft hat ______________________ gespielt. *(against the Russians)*
9. Er ist jetzt ______________________. *(at work)*
10. Fahren Sie ______________________ nach Berlin oder fliegen Sie lieber dorthin? *(by train)*

I

1. Geh ______________________, nicht ______________________. *(behind me; before me)*
2. Hängen Sie es ______________________. *(on[to] the wall)*
3. Ich möchte gern zweimal Bratwurst ______________________. *(with potato salad)*
4. Ich warte schon ______________________ hier. *(since four o'clock)*

5. ______________________ waren alle da. *(aside from him)*

6. ______________________ sehen wir ihn nur selten. *(during the semester)*

7. ______________________ ist das eine schlechte Idee. *(in my opinion)*

8. Die Firma liefert alles ______________________. *(except on Sundays)*

9. Die Geschäftsleute machten dieses Jahr eine Reise ______________________. *(to Asia)*

10. Gute Mappen sind ______________________. *(made of leather)*

J

1. Meine Serviette ist ______________________ gefallen. *(under the table)*

2. ______________________ steht ein Nachttisch. *(next to the bed)*

3. Es ist jetzt ______________________. *(twenty-five minutes to three)*

4. Komm sofort ______________________. *(into the house)*

5. Er warf seinen Mantel ______________________. *(on[to] the sofa)*

6. ______________________ muss er viel reisen. *(because of his work)*

7. Es stehen einige Bäume ______________________. *(in front of the library)*

8. Hängen Sie es ______________________. *(on[to] the wall)*

9. ______________________ sehen wir ihn oft. *(during the year)*

10. Oma saß den ganzen Nachmittag ______________________. *(at the window)*

K

1. Legen Sie es ______________________. *(on[to] the desk)*

2. Das Mädchen ist ______________________ gelaufen. *(into the hallway)*

3. Er stand gleich ______________________. *(in front of the door)*

4. Die Garage ist gleich ______________________. *(behind the house)*

5. Ich warte auf dich ______________________. *(on the corner)*

6. ______________________ finde ich es schön. *(despite the high price)*

7. ______________________ ist er immer pleite. *(because of his laziness)*

8. Bitte machen Sie das nicht ______________________. *(on my account)*

9. Sie setzte sich ______________________. *(at the table)*

10. Der Zug fährt von Bremen ______________________ nach München. *(by way of Cologne)*

L

1. Wir reisen bald ______________________________. *(to the United States)*

2. ______________________________ kann man die Alpen nicht sehen. *(due to the fog)*

3. Morgen will ich den ganzen Tag ______________________________ verbringen. *(in the country[side])*

4. Sie wohnt ______________________________. *(on the third floor)*

5. Er ist nur ______________________________ gekommen. *(up to the door)*

6. Ich fahre nächste Woche ______________________________. *(to Turkey)*

7. Bei warmem Wetter gehen wir oft ______________________________. *(to the North Sea coast)*

8. Ach, wir haben nichts zu essen ______________________________. *(but calf's liver and blood sausage)*

9. Ich habe letzten Sommer ______________________________ verdient. *(less than $2,000)*

10. Die Kinder sind noch ______________________________. *(at the playground)*

11. Mein Bruder hat Vatis neuen Wagen ______________________________ gefahren. *(into another car)*

12. ______________________________ kann ich das für Sie nicht machen. *(for this reason)*

13. Ich habe letzten Sommer ______________________________ verdient. *(more than $3,000)*

14. Sie saßen ______________________________. *(around the table)*

15. Wollen Sie ______________________________ fahren? *(by boat)*

Chapter 16 Idiomatic Use of Prepositions

Part One

Idioms are combinations of words used to create specialized meanings. Some idioms in German are very similar to English and are therefore easy to learn. (Remember, English is a Germanic language.) Some, however, are more challenging to learn because they do not correspond closely or conveniently with their English equivalents. Your task will essentially be to associate a particular preposition with an adjective, verb, or noun for a specialized meaning.

Idioms can also be challenging to learn because they do not appear with any regularity or frequency in speech or writing. They come into play only when they are needed contextually, and their use is rather spontaneous. Since you won't be exposed to these idioms hundreds of times, as is the case with young native speakers, you will need to use your superior adult learning capacities to make up for this lack of natural exposure. Try repeating the idiomatic expressions over and over until the prepositional associations are automatic, until only that particular preposition "sounds right" with that particular verb, adjective, or noun. Make up vocabulary cards that you can use to test your accuracy and to identify the idioms you have more difficulty remembering, and use them regularly until you are comfortable with the idiomatic pairings. You must take the initiative and be aggressive in learning these expressions, so be prepared to invest several hours learning and reviewing them beyond the completion of this chapter. That's what it takes, otherwise they will not "stick." Short-term memory decays quickly, so review them at regular intervals after completing this chapter to keep them active and "fresh" and to move them gradually into long-term memory, where they need to reside for quick and spontaneous access.

Idiomatic Use of Prepositions with Verbs

Verbs with Dative Prepositions

abhängen von	*to depend on*	Das **hängt von** der Situation **ab**.
einladen zu	*to invite to*	Hast du Monika **zur** Party **eingeladen**?
erzählen von	*to tell a story about*	Vati **erzählt** uns **von** seiner Jugend.
fragen nach	*to ask/inquire about*	Warum hast du **nach** meiner Schwester **gefragt**?
gratulieren zu	*to congratulate on*	Ich **gratuliere** dir **zu** deinem Erfolg!

halten von	*to think of (opinion)*	Was **hältst** du **von** diesem Kandidaten?
handeln von	*to deal with*	Der Film **handelt vom** Krieg.
helfen bei	*to help with*	**Hilf** mir **bei** meinen Hausaufgaben, bitte.
sprechen mit	*to speak with/to*	Ich möchte **mit** dem Chef **sprechen.**
sprechen von	*to speak of*	Wir haben **von** den Frühlingsferien **gesprochen.**
träumen von	*to dream of*	**Träumst** du **von** deiner neuen Liebe?

Verbs with Accusative Prepositions

bitten um	*to ask for, request*	Der Junge hat den Vater **um** den Wagen **gebeten.**
danken für	*to thank for*	Sie hat mir **für** die Blumen **gedankt.**

Verbs with Dative-Accusative Prepositions

As a rule, when verbs link up idiomatically with two-way prepositions, expect the two-way prepositions (dative-accusative) to take the accusative. Make note of the few that take the dative, since they are the exceptions.

antworten auf	*to answer (a thing)*	Der Student hat **auf** die Frage **geantwortet.**
arbeiten an (+ dat.)	*to work on*	Wie lange musst du **an** diesem Projekt **arbeiten**?
aufpassen auf	*to keep an eye on; to pay attention*	Wir sollen **auf** die Kinder **aufpassen.**
denken an	*to think of (briefly)*	Ich **dachte an** meine Reise nach Amerika.
hoffen auf	*to hope for*	Ich **hoffe auf** gutes Wetter für unseren Ausflug.
lachen über	*to laugh about*	Warum **lacht** ihr immer **über** mich?
lesen über	*to read about (in depth)*	Ich **las über** den Unfall in der Zeitung.
[nach]denken über	*to think about (in depth)*	Willi **denkt** immer **über** seine Zukunft **nach.**
reagieren auf	*to react to*	Warum **reagierst** du nicht **auf** meinen Witz?
schreiben über	*to write about (in depth)*	Habt ihr **über** die Sommerferien **geschrieben**?
sprechen über	*to speak/talk about (at length)*	Haben Sie alle **über** die Situation in dem Sudan **gesprochen**?
vorbereiten auf	*to prepare for*	Der Lehrer hat alle Schüler **auf** den Test **vorbereitet.**
warten auf	*to wait for*	Wie lange **wartest** du schon **auf** mich?

Reflexive Verbs Used Idiomatically with Prepositions

Some idiomatic expressions in German require not only the use of a preposition, but also a reflexive pronoun. Their English equivalents, however, often do not employ reflexive pronouns.

sich ärgern über	*to be angry about*	**Ärgern** Sie **sich** nicht **über** die Klausur.
sich erinnern an	*to remind oneself of; to remember*	**Erinnert euch** bitte **an** das Datum.
sich erkundigen nach	*to ask/inquire about*	Hast du **dich nach** dem Grund dafür **erkundigt**?
sich freuen auf	*to look forward to*	Wir **freuen uns auf** unser neues Sommerhaus in den Alpen.
sich freuen über	*to be happy about*	**Freust** du **dich über** das Ergebnis des Fußballspiels?

sich gewöhnen an	*to get used to something; to accustom oneself to something*	Du musst **dich** langsam **an** deine neue Stelle **gewöhnen.**
sich interessieren für	*to be interested in*	Ich **interessiere mich** hauptsächlich **für** Anthropologie.
sich kümmern um	*to concern oneself with; care for*	**Kümmern** Sie **sich um** Ihre Fortschritte in diesem Kurs.
sich sehnen nach	*to long for*	Der Alte **sehnt sich nach** seiner Jugend.
sich sorgen um	*to worry about*	**Sorgen** Sie **sich** nicht **um** mich.
sich streiten über	*to argue [with each other] about*	**Streiten** Sie **sich** nicht **über** solche Sachen.
sich vorbereiten auf	*to prepare oneself for, get ready for*	Wir müssen **uns auf** die Autofahrt nach Italien **vorbereiten.**
sich wundern über	*to be surprised about*	Ich **wundere mich über** meinen unerwarteten Erfolg.

Idiomatic Use of Prepositions with Adjectives

Adjective with Accusative Preposition

verantwortlich für	*responsible for*	Wer ist **verantwortlich für** diese Kinder?

Adjectives with Dative Prepositions

abhängig von	*dependent on*	Bist du noch **von** den Eltern **abhängig**?
unabhängig von	*independent from*	Ist diese Insel jetzt **unabhängig von** Großbritannien?
befreundet mit	*friends with*	Theo und ich sind **mit**einander **gut befreundet.**
begeistert von	*enthusiastic about*	Wir sind sehr **begeistert von** diesem Film.
böse mit	*angry with/at*	Bist du **böse mit** deiner Schwester?
fertig mit	*finished with*	Bist du **fertig mit** der Zeitung?
freundlich zu	*friendly toward*	Diese Frau ist sehr **freundlich zu** Katzen.
geschieden von	*divorced from*	Sind Ihre Eltern [**von**einander] **geschieden**?
getrennt von	*separated from*	Die Soldaten waren **von** ihrer Einheit **getrennt.**
überzeugt von	*convinced by*	Ich bin nicht **überzeugt von** deinem Argument.
verheiratet mit	*married to*	Unsere Tochter ist **mit** ihrem Sohn **verheiratet.**
verlobt mit	*engaged to*	Tina ist **mit** Jürgen **verlobt.**
verrückt nach	*mad/crazy about*	Bist du **verrückt nach** dieser Musikgruppe?
verwandt mit	*related to*	Jetzt sind wir **mit** dem Bürgermeister **verwandt.**
zufrieden mit	*satisfied/pleased with*	Bist du **mit** deinem Computer **zufrieden**?

Adjectives with Dative-Accusative Prepositions

böse auf	*angry at/with*	Warum bist du immer **böse auf** mich?
erstaunt über	*astounded/astonished by*	Wir waren **erstaunt über** diese Erfindung.
froh/glücklich über	*happy about*	Seid ihr **froh/glücklich über** eure Noten?
stolz auf	*proud of*	Du kannst sehr **stolz auf** deine Kinder sein.
traurig über	*sad about*	Bist du **traurig über** den Tod deines Hundes?
verliebt in	*in love with*	**In** wen bist du **verliebt**?
verrückt auf	*mad/crazy about*	Und **auf** wen wirst du morgen **verrückt** sein?

Idiomatic Use of Prepositions with Nouns

Nouns may combine with prepositions for special meanings:

(die) **Angst haben vor** (+ dat.)	*to have fear of; be afraid of*	**Hab** keine **Angst vor** der neuen Chefin.
Freude haben über	*to have joy about; be happy about*	Du **hast** sicher große **Freude über** dieses wunderbare Geschenk.
(der) **Grund für**	*reason for*	Was ist der **Grund für** Ihre Angst vor Insekten?
(die) **Lust haben auf**	*to have desire to; want to*	**Hast** du denn wirklich keine **Lust auf** ein Bier?
(die) **Sehnsucht haben nach**	*to have a longing for*	Die Witwe **hat große Sehnsucht nach** ihrem gestorbenen Mann.
Schwierigkeiten/Probleme haben mit	*to have difficulty/ problems with*	Ich **habe** große **Schwierigkeiten mit** diesem Computerprogramm.
sich **Sorgen machen um**	*to have worries about; be worried about*	Du sollst dir keine großen **Sorgen um** mich **machen.**

Exercises: Part One

Theory Review

1. Fill in the blanks with the correct information.

1. ____________________ are combinations of words used to create special meanings.
2. A noun, adjective, adverb, or verb may team up with a ____________________ for an idiomatic meaning.
3. Compared to other grammatical features of the language, these expressions appear less ____________________ because they are used when a specialized meaning is called for.
4. When these words are used with dative or accusative prepositions, the case of the prepositional object is very ____________________.
5. When these words are used with dative-accusative prepositions, the case of the prepositional object is normally ____________________.
6. Some of these idiomatic expressions require the use of a ____________________ pronoun as well.
7. Name the prepositions that may be used idiomatically with the following nouns, adjectives, adverbs, and verbs:

abhängen	__________	sich freuen	__________	sich sehnen	__________
abhängig	__________	freundlich	__________	Sehnsucht	__________
Angst	__________	froh	__________	sich sorgen	__________

antworten	________	geschieden	________	sprechen	________
arbeiten	________	getrennt	________	stolz	________
sich ärgern	________	glücklich	________	sich streiten	________
aufpassen	________	gratulieren	________	träumen	________
befreundet	________	Grund	________	traurig	________
begeistert	________	halten	________	überzeugt	________
bitten	________	handeln	________	unabhängig	________
böse	________	helfen	________	unfreundlich	________
danken	________	hoffen	________	unzufrieden	________
denken	________	sich interessieren	________	verantwortlich	________
einladen	________	sich kümmern	________	verheiratet	________
sich erinnern	________	lachen	________	verliebt	________
sich erkundigen	________	lesen	________	verlobt	________
erstaunt	________	Lust	________	verrückt	________
erzählen	________	Probleme	________	sich vorbereiten	________
fertig	________	reagieren	________	warten	________
fragen	________	schreiben	________	sich wundern	________
Freude	________	Schwierigkeiten	________	zufrieden	________

Focus on Meaning [✓]

Choosing the correct idiomatic preposition

2. Fill in the blanks with the correct prepositions.

A

1. Antworten Sie bitte ________________ diese Frage.
2. Bist du ________________ dieser Frau verwandt?
3. Die Frau hat ihrem Freund ________________ die Blumen gedankt.
4. Die Mechaniker haben lange ohne Erfolg ________________ dem Motor gearbeitet.
5. Du sollst mehr ________________ deine Eltern denken.
6. Du sollst mehr ________________ deine Zukunft denken.
7. Hast du ________________ deiner alten Freundin gesprochen?
8. Hat der Roman auch ________________ diesem Thema gehandelt?
9. Ich möchte dir ________________ deinem Hochzeitstag gratulieren.
10. Ist Fritz glücklich ________________ seine Zensuren?

B

1. Ist sie verliebt ______________________ dich?
2. Kannst du deine Mutter ______________________ zehn Dollar bitten?
3. Kannst du ein paar Minuten ______________________ mich warten?
4. Meine Eltern sind sehr stolz ______________________ meine Schwester.
5. Meine Schwester ist ______________________ einem Arzt verheiratet.
6. Seid ihr ______________________ eurem neuen Wagen zufrieden?
7. Seit wann bist du ______________________ ihr verlobt?
8. Sind Sie ______________________ diesem Komponisten begeistert?
9. Warum ist Sabine verrückt ______________________ diese Musikgruppe?
10. Warum lachst du immer ______________________ Gisela?

C

1. Wie hast du ______________________ seinen Vorschlag reagiert?
2. Würden Sie lieber ______________________ Herrn Steiner sprechen?
3. ______________________ wem ist sie verheiratet?
4. Antworten Sie ______________________ die Fragen.
5. Bist du böse ______________________ uns?
6. Darf ich dich ______________________ ein Getränk bitten?
7. Denkst du ______________________ deine Famile?
8. Der Film hat ______________________ der französischen Revolution gehandelt.
9. Der Mann hat ______________________ meiner Mutter gefragt.
10. Die Eltern sind sehr stolz ______________________ ihre Tochter.

D

1. Ich bin nicht verwandt ______________________ ihr.
2. Ich bin sehr böse ______________________ dich.
3. Ich möchte dir ______________________ deinem Geburtstag gratulieren.
4. Ich muss noch ______________________ meiner Semesterarbeit arbeiten.
5. Inge ist verlobt ______________________ meinem Freund Jürgen.
6. Ist deine Schwester ______________________ ihrem Mann geschieden?

7. Ist Monika glücklich ______________________ ihre Zensuren?

8. Kannst du mir ______________________ meinen Hausaufgaben helfen?

9. Kannst du zehn Minuten ______________________ mich warten?

10. Sind sie verliebt ______________________ sich?

E

1. Sind Sie zufrieden ______________________ dieser Universität?

2. Warum bist du so unfreundlich ______________________ Kurt?

3. Warum bist du ______________________ dieser Musikgruppe so begeistert?

4. Wie hast du ______________________ seine Antwort reagiert?

5. Willst du ______________________ meinem Vater sprechen?

6. Wir haben ______________________ unsere Lehrerin gelacht.

7. Wir möchten euch ______________________ das Geschenk danken.

8. Wir müssen ein Referat ______________________ diesen Roman schreiben.

9. Wir sind sehr zufrieden ______________________ unserem neuen Haus.

10. Du sollst mehr ______________________ deine beruflichen Angelegenheiten [nach]denken.

3. Fill in the blanks with the verb, adverb, adjective, or noun that matches up contextually with the prepositional phrase.

A

1. ______________________ Sie bitte auf meine Fragen.

2. Bist du mit diesem Mann ______________________?

3. Die Frau hat ihrem Freund für das Geschenk ______________________.

4. Die Forscher haben lange ohne Erfolg an dem Projekt ______________________.

5. Du sollst mehr über deine Verantwortlichkeiten ______________________.

6. Hast du mit deinem Opa über das Problem ______________________?

7. Der Film hat von dem Leben Einsteins ______________________.

8. Ich möchte euch zu eurem Preis ______________________.

9. Ist Fritz ______________________ über seine Note?

10. Das ______________________ völlig von dir ab.

B

1. Ist sie wirklich ______________________ in dich?
2. Kannst du deinen Vater um den Wagen ______________________?
3. Kannst du noch ein paar Minuten auf uns ______________________?
4. Meine Eltern sind sehr ______________________ auf meinen Bruder.
5. Mein Bruder ist seit vier Jahren mit einer Fotografin ______________________. Sie haben zwei Kinder.
6. Bist du mit deinem neuen Computer ______________________?
7. Seit wann bist du mit ihm ______________________? Wann werdet ihr heiraten?
8. Sind Sie wirklich von dieser Oper ______________________? Ich finde sie furchtbar langweilig.
9. Wir ______________________ auf sonniges Wetter für unsere Wanderung.
10. Warum ______________________ ihr immer über mich?

C

1. Wie hast du auf ihre Meinung ______________________? Ich konnte nichts dafür oder dagegen sagen.
2. Ich muss mich noch an meinem neuen Wagen ______________________. Er ist mir immer noch etwas fremd.
3. Mit wem ist sie diesmal ______________________ und wie heißt ihr fünfter Mann?
4. Frau Nodop, Sie sind ______________________ für die Erledigung dieser Aufgabe.
5. Bist du ______________________ mit uns? Du siehst verärgert aus.
6. Darf ich dich um ein Glas Wein ______________________?
7. ______________________ du oft an deine Freundin in Osnabrück? Du musst sie sehr vermissen.
8. Das Buch hat von der Reformation ______________________.
9. Der Mann hat nach meiner Mutter ______________________. Er wollte wissen, wie es ihr geht.
10. Die Eltern sind sehr ______________________ auf ihre Kinder. Sie denken natürlich, sie sind alle Wunderkinder.

D

1. Ich bin nicht ______________________ in sie. Sie ist nur eine alte Freundin von mir.
2. Ich bin ______________________ auf dich, weil du so faul bist.
3. Ich möchte dir zu deinem Geburtstag ______________________.
4. Ich muss noch an diesem Plan ______________________.
5. Inge ist ______________________ in meinen Freund Kevin. Vielleicht werden sie eines Tages heiraten.

6. Sind deine Eltern voneinander ______________________? Ich sehe deinen Vater nicht mehr.
7. Ist Monika ______________________ über ihr neues Auto?
8. Kannst du mir bei meinen Hausaufgaben ______________________?
9. Kannst du eine kurze Weile auf mich ______________________? Es wird nicht lange dauern.
10. Sind die zwei gut ______________________? Sie lächeln immer, wenn sie zusammen sind.

E

1. Sind Sie ______________________ mit der Uni?
2. Warum bist du so ______________________ zu Kurt? Alle finden ihn sympathisch.
3. Hans ist von seinen Computerspielen sehr ________________. Er kann sie stundenlang spielen.
4. Wie hast du auf die Resultate der Wahl ______________________? Hat deine Kandidatin gewonnen?
5. Willst du mit meinen Eltern ______________________?
6. Wir haben über seine komische Kleidung ______________________.
7. Wir möchten euch für das Geld ______________________.
8. Wir müssen einen Bericht über die Katastrophe in Indonesien ______________________.
9. Wir sind sehr ______________________ mit unserer Stereoanlage.
10. Du sollst mehr über deine Finanzen ______________________.

Focus on Meaning and Form

4. Fill in the blanks with the correct idiomatic expression as cued. Various answers are possible for some items.

A

1. ____________________ Sie bitte ____________________________. *(answer their questions)*
2. Der alte Soldat ____________________________________. *(longs for his old comrades)*
3. Die Mädchen waren ____________________________________. *(crazy about the singer)*
4. Habt ihr Sabine ____________________________________? *(invited for dinner)*
5. Hast du immer noch ____________________________________? *(longing for your country)*
6. Ich bin nicht mehr ____________________________________. *(in love with him)*
7. Kannst du nicht ____________________________________? *(get used to your new job)*
8. Sabine muss ____________________________________. *(keep an eye on her children)*
9. Sie hat ____________________________________. *(dreamed of a castle in France)*
10. Sind Sie ____________________________________? *(finished with work)*

B

1. Wie hat man ______________________________? *(reacted to the news)*
2. Alles ______________________________. *(depends on the teacher)*
3. Die Bauer ______________________________. *(are hoping for a lot of rain)*
4. Die Kinder haben nur ______________________________. *(dreamed of their Christmas presents)*
5. Die Schüler sind ______________________________. *(proud of their teacher [f.])*
6. Du könntest mehr ______________________________. *(think about your responsibilities)*
7. Wir sollen mehr ______________________________. *(think about these problems)*
8. Jochen ist ________________ gut ______________________. *(friends with Martin)*
9. Warum ________________ du immer ______________________? *(laugh at her)*
10. Wir sind nicht ______________________________. *(convinced by her reasons)*

C

1. Was ________________ du ______________________? *(think of this university)*
2. Bist du ______________________________? *(engaged to this man)*
3. Seid ihr ______________________________? *(finished with this nonsense)*
4. Hast du mit Toni ______________________________? *(spoken about the course)*
5. Wir sind nicht ______________________________. *(convinced by his explanation)*
6. Ich bin sehr ______________________________. *(angry with/at him)*
7. Katrin muss sich ______________________________. *(prepare for the interview)*
8. Kannst du deine Mutter ______________________________? *(ask for some money)*
9. Vielleicht möchten Sie lieber ______________________________. *(speak with Mr. Kramer)*
10. Warum ________________ du dich nicht ______________________? *(prepare for the party)*

D

1. Warum bist du so ______________________________? *(unfriendly to her)*

2. Wie lange hast du ______________________________? *(worked on your dissertation)*

3. ________________ ist sie im Moment ________________? *(married to whom)*

4. Die Frau hat ihrem Freund ______________________________. *(thanked for the birthday card)*

5. Du solltest ______________________________ sein. *(happy about this opportunity)*

6. Hans ist ________________ sehr ________________. *(enthused about this music group)*

7. Wir ________________ uns sehr ________________. *(looking forward to the winter vacation)*

8. Hast du ______________________________. *(desire for a cup of coffee)*

9. Ich möchte dir ______________________________. *(congratulate on your birthday)*

10. Können wir noch ein paar Minuten ______________________________? *(wait for them)*

E

1. Warum kannst du dich nicht ______________________________? *(remember my phone number)*

2. Wir möchten Ihnen ______________________________! *(congratulate on your graduation)*

3. Ich bin wirklich ______________________________. *(amazed at your success)*

4. Alle Schüler sind ______________________________. *(responsible for the homework)*

5. Die Studenten haben ______________________________. *(worked on their term papers)*

6. Die Vereinigten Staaten wurden 1776 ______________________________. *(independent of Great Britain)*

7. Hubert ist ______________________________. *(related to my brother-in-law)*

8. Ich muss noch ______________________________. *(work on the repair)*

9. Sie können sehr ______________________________ sein. *(proud of your son)*

10. Warum ________________ du dich ________________? *(surprised at these people)*

You Determine the Message and Form

5. Fill in the blanks with a prepositional phrase that logically completes the idiomatic meaning of the sentence.

A

1. ______________________ sind wir wirklich erstaunt.
2. Ab und zu denke ich ______________________.
3. Ach, ich muss ständig ______________________ warten.
4. Wir wundern uns ______________________.
5. Bald sollen wir uns ______________________ vorbereiten.
6. Bist du fertig ______________________?
7. Bitte, antworten Sie ______________________.
8. Das Buch handelt ______________________.
9. Das Kind war traurig ______________________.
10. Der Chef hat sich ______________________ geärgert.

B

1. Der Fremde hat ______________________ gefragt.
2. Der Journalist schrieb ______________________.
3. Der junge Sohn sehnt sich ______________________.
4. Der Lehrer war nicht überzeugt ______________________.
5. Die Kinder sind verrückt ______________________.
6. Die Studentin hat sich ______________________ erkundigt.
7. Hast du ______________________ in der Zeitung gelesen?
8. Habt ihr Angst ______________________?
9. Hat deine Großmutter ______________________ gesprochen?
10. Ich bin nicht sehr begeistert ______________________.

C

1. Ich bin noch abhängig ______________________.
2. Tina hat als Kind immer ______________________ gehofft.
3. Ich habe immer ______________________ geträumt.

4. Hast du noch große Schwierigkeiten ______________________________?
5. Ich habe jetzt Lust ______________________________.
6. Wir können unsere Freunde ______________________________ bitten.
7. Ich möchte Bernd ______________________________ gratulieren.
8. Wir müssen uns ______________________________ erinnern.
9. Ich muss mich ______________________________ gewöhnen.
10. Du sollst dich mehr ______________________________ kümmern.

D

1. Gisela wird bald ______________________________ verlobt sein.
2. Ich will dir ______________________________ danken.
3. Ja, wir sind verantwortlich ______________________________.
4. Ist Klara ______________________________ befreundet?
5. Kannst du mir ______________________________ helfen?
6. Mach dir keine großen Sorgen ______________________________.
7. Mein Bruder ist ______________________________ verheiratet.
8. Unser Freund Thomas ist ______________________________ verliebt.
9. Mein Vater ist sehr stolz ______________________________.
10. Nina ist ______________________________ verwandt.

E

1. Meine Mutter hat Sehnsucht ______________________________.
2. Meine Schwester interessiert sich ______________________________.
3. Mein Bruder ist geschieden ______________________________.
4. Pass ______________________________ auf!
5. Seid ihr zufrieden ______________________________?
6. Sind Sie glücklich ______________________________?
7. Unsere Kinder streiten sich immer ______________________________.
8. Vielleicht kannst du das machen, vielleicht nicht. Das hängt ______________________________.
9. Warum bist du böse ______________________________?
10. Was hältst du ______________________________?

F

1. Was ist der Grund ______________________________?
2. Ich freue mich ______________________________.
3. Wir haben große Freude ______________________________.
4. Karl hat Jürgen nicht ______________________________ einladen.
5. Wir sind alle ______________________________ verantwortlich.
6. Ich muss ______________________________ nicht lachen.
7. Würdest du mir ______________________________ erzählen?
8. Warum bist do so verrückt ______________________________?
9. Ich soll mich ______________________________ gewöhnen.
10. Sorge dich nicht ______________________________.

Part Two

Da-Compounds

Prepositional Phrases and Personal Pronouns

Normally, when we refer to a noun previously mentioned, we employ personal pronouns.

Ich kenne **Karl** und ich kenne **ihn** schon vier Jahre.
I know Karl and I've known him for four years.

Ich habe **einen Volvo** und ich finde **ihn** recht gut.
I have a Volvo and I think it's really good.

When you refer to a previously mentioned noun in a prepositional phrase, and that noun names a person, you use a personal pronoun:

Ist das Geschenk **für deine Mutter**? —Ja, es ist **für sie**.
Ist that present for your mother? —Yes, it's for her.

Gehst du jetzt **mit Paul** aus? —Ja, ich gehe **mit ihm** aus.
Are you going out with Paul? —Yes, I'm going out with him.

Prepositional Phrases and *da*-Compounds

When you wish to refer to a previously mentioned noun in a prepositional phrase, and the noun is a *thing* and not a person, you need to use a **da**-compound (= **da**[**r**] + preposition):

Wie lange wartest du schon **auf den Bus**? —Ich warte schon zehn Minuten ***darauf***.
How long have you been waiting for the bus? —I've been waiting for it for ten minutes.

Sprecht ihr **über die Prüfung**? —Ja, wir sprechen immer noch ***darüber***.
Are you talking about the test? —Yes, we're still talking about it.

Kannst du mir **bei den Hausaufgaben** helfen? —Ja, ich kann dir ***dabei*** helfen.
Can you help me with my homework? —Yes, I can help you with it.

Was hast du **mit meinem neuen Kuli** gemacht? —Ich habe nichts ***damit*** gemacht.
What did you do with my new pen? —I didn't do anything with it.

Common *da*-Compounds

accusative prepositions:	**dadurch, dafür, dagegen, darum**
dative prepositions:	**daraus, dabei, damit, danach, davon, dazu**
two-way prepositions:	**daran, darauf, dahinter, davor, darunter, darüber, darin, daneben, dazwischen**

Spelling and pronunciation note: An **r** is inserted between **da** and the preposition when the preposition begins with a vowel. This facilitates pronunciation. In a **da**-compound, the main stress is normally on the preposition, not **da**. **Da** receives the main stress only when the **da**-compound is emphasized, which usually means it will occupy slot 1 in the sentence:

Ich habe gar nicht **dar*an*** gedacht. BUT: ***Da*ran** habe ich gar nicht gedacht.
I didn't think of it at all.

Some **da**-compounds drop the **a**, especially in conversation: **darauf → drauf**; **darin → drin**; **daran → dran**.

Prepositions That Cannot Form *da*-Compounds

Certain prepositions do not easily form **da**-compounds; with these prepositions personal pronouns *are* used:

- **ohne:** You may use pronouns for things with **ohne**; there is no **da**-compound for **ohne**.
  ohne meine Hilfe → **ohne sie**
  ohne seinen Regenschirm → **ohne ihn**
  ohne mein Portmonee → **ohne es**

- **seit:** The substitute compound is **seitdem** (= *since then*).
  Ich habe Kurt **seitdem** nie wieder gesehen.
  I have never seen Kurt since then.

- **außer:** The substitute compound is **außerdem**, used adverbially (= *moreover, furthermore, additionally, what's more*).
  Ich habe **außerdem** leider nichts für sie machen können.
  Moreover, I was unfortunately not able to do anything for her.

- **wegen:** The substitute compound is **deswegen** or **deshalb** (= *due to that, because of that, as a result*).
  Wir haben uns **deswegen** kein neues Auto leisten können.
  Because of that we have not been able to afford a new car.

- **trotz:** The substitute compound is **trotzdem** (= *in spite of that; nevertheless*).
  Trotzdem liebe ich dich noch.
  In spite of that I still love you.

- **(an)statt:** The substitute compound is **stattdessen** (= *instead of that*).
  Ich würde lieber **stattdessen** an dem anderen Projekt arbeiten.
  I would rather work on the other project instead of that.

Word Order with Prepositional Phrases and *da*-Compounds

Prepositional phrases normally come after nouns with which they are logically associated. This means they are functioning adjectivally:

Welche Diskussion ist langweilig? → *Die Diskussion* ***über dieses Thema*** ist langweilig.
Was soll ich mit dem Deckel machen? → Leg *den Deckel* ***auf den Topf***.

The **da**-compound substitutes occupy the same position as the prepositional phrases they replace:

Die Diskussion über dieses Thema ist langweilig. → *Die Diskussion* ***darüber*** ist langweilig.
Hast du **den Deckel auf den Topf** gelegt? → Hast du *den Deckel* ***drauf*** gelegt?

Interrogative Pronouns and *wo*-Compounds

Prepositions with Forms of *wer*

In Chapter 13 you learned about the pronoun **wer** and its variant forms, **wer**, **wen**, **wem**, and **wessen**. Forms of **wer** may be used with dative, accusative, and dative-accusative prepositions:

Auf wen hast du so lange gewartet?
Whom did you wait for so long?

Für wen hast du das gemacht?
For whom did you do that?

Nach wem hast du gefragt?
Whom did you ask about?

Bei wem warst du das ganze Wochenende?
Whose house were you at the whole weekend?

Mit wem bist du ins Kino gegangen?
With whom did you go to the movies?

Über wen habt ihr geredet?
Whom were you speaking about?

Interrogative Pronoun *was*

The pronoun **was** is used to refer to things and may only be used in the nominative or accusative. There are no genitive or dative forms.

nominative:	**Was** ist das? *What is that?*	**Was** hat den Lärm gemacht? *What made that noise?*
accusative:	**Was** hast du gesagt? *What did you say?*	**Was** soll das bedeuten? *What is that supposed to mean?*

Prepositions and *was* (Colloquial)

In colloquial German, questions about things are often asked using a preposition followed by **was**:

Über was habt ihr gesprochen?
What did you talk about?

Mit was hast du den Wagen repariert?
What did you fix the car with?

Von was hat der Roman gehandelt?
What did the novel deal with?

Auf was hast du das Bild gezeichnet?
What did you draw the picture on?

Wo-Compounds (Formal)

In more formal German, a **wo**-compound (= **wo**[**r**] + preposition) is used instead of a preposition + **was:**

Über was habt ihr gesprochen? → **Worüber** habt ihr gesprochen?
Mit was hast du den Wagen repariert? → **Womit** hast du den Wagen repariert?
Von was hat der Roman gehandelt? → **Wovon** hat der Roman gehandelt?

Exercises: Part Two

Theory Review

1. Fill in the blanks with the correct information.

1. When referring to a previously mentioned noun, one frequently uses a personal ____________________.
2. If you refer to a previously mentioned *person* within a prepositional phrase, the object of the preposition will normally be a ____________________.
3. If you refer to a previously mentioned *thing* within a prepositional phrase, the object of the preposition will normally not be a pronoun. Instead, you use a ____________________.
4. This consists of ____________________ + a preposition.
5. If the preposition begins with a vowel, an ____________________ is inserted between **da** and the preposition to facilitate pronunciation.
6. Write the **da**-compound for these prepositions:

   mit ____________ von ____________ zu ____________ für ____________

   um ____________ durch ____________ auf ____________ über ____________
7. Some prepositions may not form **da**-compounds because they would be too clumsy. Some of these are:

   ____

8. Write the compound used for these prepositions instead of a **da**-compound:

seit ___________ außer ___________ wegen ___________

trotz ___________ statt ___________

9. A ______________ is used instead of a **da**-compound to formulate a question about a *thing.*

10. It consists of ____________________ + a preposition.

11. If the preposition begins with a vowel, an ____________________ is inserted between **wo** and the preposition to facilitate pronunciation.

12. Write the **wo**-compound for these prepositions:

mit ___________ von ___________ zu ___________ für ___________

um ___________ durch ___________ auf ___________ über ___________

13. If a question is formulated about a *person,* a **wo**-compound may not be used. Instead, the preposition is used with a correct form of the interrogative pronoun ____________________.

Focus on Meaning and Form [✓]

2. Fill in the blanks with the appropriate *wo*-compound or preposition + *was* (for things), or preposition + interrogative pronoun (for persons).

1. ____________________ ist der Tisch? (Holz)
2. ____________________ bist du besonders begeistert? (eine neue Musikgruppe)
3. ____________________ ist Maria verlobt? (Hans)
4. ____________________ ist Tobias verheiratet? (Inge)
5. ____________________ ist Frau Steiner verwandt? (meine Schwägerin)
6. ____________________ bist du im Moment sehr zufrieden? (dein Auto)
7. ____________________ ist er böse? (der Lehrer)
8. ____________________ ist der Mann stolz? (seine Tochter)
9. ____________________ bist du verliebt? (Tina)
10. ____________________ wartest du? (der Bus)
11. ____________________ willst du ihm danken? (das Geschenk)
12. ____________________ hast du mit dem Chef gesprochen? (das Problem)

3. Answer the following questions affirmatively and with pronouns and *da*-compounds as needed.

1. Hast du *mit Inge* gesprochen?

____

2. Haben wir schon mit Harald *über diesen Plan* gesprochen?

____

3. Haben Sie *mit Ihren Kollegen* gesprochen?

____

4. Ist dein Vater *mit seinen neuen Werkzeugen* zufrieden?

____

5. Hat der Film *von dem zweiten Weltkrieg* gehandelt?

____

6. Sind Sie auch *von diesem Komponisten* begeistert?

____

7. Bist du *von dieser Musik* begeistert?

____

8. Kannst du deinen Vater *um den Wagen* bitten?

____

9. Hast du Oma *für dein Geburtstagsgeschenk* gedankt?

____

10. Hast du *auf die Einladung* geantwortet?

____

11. Musstest du lange *auf den Bus* warten?

____

12. Sollen wir *auf Sonja* warten?

____

13. Seid ihr stolz *auf euren Bruder*?

____

14. Bist du auch *auf diesen Film* verrückt?

____

15. Sollen wir jetzt *an unserem Projekt* arbeiten?

____

16. Denkst du oft *an dein letztes Jahr an der High School*?

____

17. Wart ihr froh *über den Besuch von euren Freunden*?

____

18. Hast du *über diesen dummen Witz* gelacht?

____

19. Habt ihr *über Herrn Steiner* gelacht?

____

20. Hast du deiner Kusine *zu ihrem Geburtstag* gratuliert?

____

4. Formulate questions to find out from a friend . . .

1. what I'm dissatisfied with ____________________
2. whom I'm dissatisfied with ____________________
3. whom I'm angry at/with ____________________
4. what we were talking about ____________________
5. what the movie deals with ____________________
6. what she's so excited about ____________________
7. what I asked my girlfriend for ____________________
8. whom I'm particularly proud of ____________________
9. what you are expected to thank me for ____________________
10. what I'm working on ____________________
11. what I'm thinking of ____________________
12. what they are laughing about ____________________
13. what he's so happy about ____________________
14. what I'm waiting for ____________________
15. whom I'm waiting for ____________________
16. what I've been doing since then ____________________
17. what I've accomplished in addition to that ____________________
18. what I would rather buy instead of that ____________________
19. what I would change as a result of that ____________________
20. how I can live without it. ____________________

You Determine the Message and Form

5. Fill in the blanks with an appropriate activity.

1. Ich habe nur wenig Geld, deshalb ______________________________
2. Das Wetter soll schlecht sein. Wir werden trotzdem ______________________________
3. Wir wollten einen Film sehen, aber stattdessen ______________________________
4. Wir können zu Hause bleiben, aber meinetwegen ______________________________

Partnerarbeit 

6. Arbeiten Sie mit einem Partner/einer Partnerin und besprechen Sie die folgenden Fragen miteinander.

A

1. Mit wem willst oder müssen du bald sprechen?
2. Auf wen bist du jetzt böse? Warum?
3. Mit was für einer Person möchtest du verheiratet sein?
4. Womit bist du im Moment zufrieden oder unzufrieden?
5. Mit wem bist du zufrieden oder unzufrieden? Warum?
6. Welche Filmstars sind miteinander verwandt?
7. Wozu gratuliert man Freunden einmal im Jahr und am Ende des Studiums?
8. Wovon hast du neulich mit deinen Eltern gesprochen?
9. Wovon hat der letzte Film gehandelt, den du vor kurzem gesehen hast?
10. Wem sollst du jetzt danken und wofür?

B

1. Wie hast du darauf reagiert, als du gelernt hast, dass es keinen Sankt Nikolaus gibt?
2. Auf wen musst du immer warten? Was ist das Problem mit dieser Person?
3. Wer ist böse auf dich? Streitet ihr euch? Sprecht ihr miteinander?
4. Auf welche Person bist du stolz? Was hat diese Person getan?
5. Worauf bist du verrückt? / Wovon bist du begeistert?
6. Woran arbeitest du im Moment?
7. Woran denkst du oft? Worüber denkst du oft? An wen denkst du oft?
8. Über wen oder über was lachst du oft?
9. Worüber bist du jetzt froh/glücklich?
10. In wen ist dein bester Freund/deine beste Freundin verliebt? Wollen sie sich heiraten?

C

1. Worauf hoffst du?
2. Worum hast du deine Eltern oder Freunde gebeten?
3. Wofür sollst du jemandem danken?
4. Worauf freust du dich?
5. Über wen lachst du oft? Warum?
6. Worauf oder auf wen bist du verrückt?
7. Wovon handelt dein Lieblingsfilm oder dein Lieblingsroman?
8. Was haltst du von dem Präsidenten/der Präsidentin?
9. Wovon träumst du? Sind deine Träume realisierbar?
10. Wonach oder nach wem sehnst du dich?

Supplementary Exercises

Focus on Meaning [✓]

1. Fill in the blanks with the correct idiomatic preposition.

A

1. Die Mädchen waren verrückt ______________ den Filmstar.
2. Hast du mit Harald ______________ das Problem gesprochen?
3. Wir möchten Ihnen ______________ Ihrem Geburtstag gratulieren.
4. Was hast ______________ das Theaterstück in der Zeitung gelesen?
5. Der Film handelt ______________ der Liebe zwei junger Leute.
6. ______________ wem willst du sprechen?
7. Habt ihr euch ______________ die Prüfung vorbereitet?
8. Kannst du deine Mutter ______________ etwas zu essen bitten?
9. Was? Du hast Opa noch nicht ______________ sein Geschenk gedankt?
10. Würden Sie bitte direkt ______________ diese Frage antworten?

B

1. Käthe ist sehr begeistert ______________ diesem Konzert.
2. Warum bist du immer so böse ______________ deine Schwester?
3. Du solltest froh ______________ diese Gelegenheit sein.
4. Sie können sehr stolz ______________ Ihre Tochter sein.
5. Ist Karola ______________ Stefan oder mit Heiko verheiratet?
6. Warum bist du so verrückt ______________ dieser Musikgruppe?
7. Bist du zufrieden ______________ deiner neuen Kamera?
8. Seid ihr verwandt ______________ Schmidts?
9. Schreibst du ein Referat ______________ die Armut in der Dritten Welt?
10. Du könntest ein bisschen mehr ______________ deine Pläne für die Zukunft [nach]denken. Sei nicht so faul!

C

1. Wir wundern uns ______________ ihren neuen Luxuswagen.
2. ______________ welchem Thema handelt der Roman?

3. Was hältst du ______________________ diesem Plan? Du darfst nicht neutral sein.
4. Bist du fertig ______________________ deiner Arbeit?
5. Bist du verwandt ______________________ dieser Person?
6. Das hängt ______________________ der Krankheit ab.
7. Kümmere dich ______________________ deinen Job.
8. Ärgern Sie sich nicht ______________________ seine politische Philosophie.
9. Seid ihr auch begeistert ______________________ dieser Autorin?
10. Hast du Angst ______________________ großen Hunden?

D

1. Hast du Lola ______________________ deiner Party eingeladen?
2. Alle Lehrer müssen ______________________ die Schulkinder während der Pause aufpassen.
3. Ach, ich kann mich nicht ______________________ ihren Geburtstag erinnern.
4. Warum bist du böse ______________________ sie?
5. Was sind die Gründe ______________________ deine negative Reaktion?
6. Kannst du uns ______________________ deiner Aufenthalt in Südamerika erzählen?
7. Ich muss ein Buch ______________________ den Krieg in Vietnam lesen.
8. Wir freuen uns ______________________ die kommenden Ferien.
9. Bist du fertig ______________________ diesen neuen Werkzeugen?
10. Hast du Lust ______________________ eine Tasse Kaffee?

E

1. Die junge Frau träumt ______________________ einem neuen Haus in Monaco.
2. Ich soll eine Semesterarbeit ______________________ die französische Revolution schreiben.
3. Ich freue mich sehr ______________________ deinen neuesten Erfolg.
4. Warum bist du so verrückt ______________________ dieser Musik? Ich finde sie einfach schrecklich!
5. Habt ihr große Schwierigkeiten ______________________ eurem Chef?
6. Wir müssen uns ______________________ das Examen vorbereiten.
7. Hast du dich ______________________ diesen Film interessiert? Ich fand ihn spannend.
8. Klara musste sich ______________________ ihre kranke Großmutter kümmern.
9. Sind Sie zufrieden ______________________ Ihrem neuen Volvo?
10. Der alte Ausländer sehnt sich immer noch ______________________ seiner Heimat.

F

1. Wie lange hast du ______________________ deiner Magisterarbeit gearbeitet?
2. Habt ihr schon ______________________ eure zukünftige Reise nach Brasilien gedacht?
3. Harald ist so doof. Wir lachen immer ______________________ ihn.
4. Warum hast du nicht ______________________ seine Antwort reagiert?
5. Bist du ______________________ Ingo Maier befreundet?

2. Fill in the blanks with the correct idiomatic verbs, adjectives, or nouns.

A

1. Die Mädchen waren ______________________ auf den Filmstar.
2. Hast du mit Harald über das Problem ______________________?
3. Wir möchten Ihnen zur neuen Arbeitsstelle ______________________. Prima!
4. Was ______________________ er von dem Film von George Lucas? Findet er ihn gut?
5. Der Film ______________________ vom Kalten Krieg.
6. Mit wem möchten Sie ______________________?
7. Habt ihr euch für Schach oder Karten ______________________?
8. Kannst du deine Schwester um Hilfe ______________________? Ich bin im Moment beschäftigt.
9. Was? Du hast Vati noch nicht für deinen neuen Wagen ______________________?
10. Würden Sie bitte auf alle Fragen ______________________?

B

1. Anke ist sehr ______________________ von diesem Roman.
2. Warum ______________________ du dich immer über deine Schwester? Du bist ihr gegenüber zu negativ.
3. Du solltest ______________________ über diese Angelegenheit sein.
4. Sie können sehr ______________________ auf Ihren Sohn sein.
5. Ist Karola mit Bernd ______________________?
6. Warum bist du so ______________________ nach dieser Sängerin?
7. Bist du ______________________ mit deiner neuen Kamera?
8. Seid ihr ______________________ mit Schneiders? Ihr seht einander ähnlich aus.
9. ______________________ du ein Referat über die Situation in dem Sudan?
10. Du könntest mehr über deine Verantwortlichkeiten ______________________ und nicht immer faulenzen.

C

1. Von welchem Thema ______________________ der Roman?
2. Bist du ______________________ mit dem Unsinn? Ich will nichts mehr von dir darüber hören.
3. Wir sind ______________________ über seine schnellen Fortschritte in Deutsch.
4. Die Vereinigten Staaten wurden 1776 von England ______________________.
5. Die Kinder waren sehr ______________________ über die Scheidung ihrer Eltern.
6. ______________________ Sie sich mehr um Ihre Familie.
7. Er hat über meine Dummheiten ______________________.
8. Bist du ______________________ von diesem Film?
9. Hast du ______________________ vor großen Hunden?
10. Die Urlauber ______________________ auf sonniges Wetter.

D

1. Habt ihr Dieter zu deiner Party ______________________?
2. Wir sollen auf die Kinder im Park ______________________.
3. Warum kannst du dich nicht an meine Telefonnummer ______________________?
4. Warum ______________________ du dich mit deiner Mutter über deinen Freund? Was hat sie gegen ihn?
5. Was ist der ______________________ für dein schlechtes Benehmen?
6. Würdest du uns etwas von deiner Jugendzeit in Japan ______________________?
7. Ich muss ein Buch über Goethe und Shakespeare ______________________.
8. Wir ______________________ uns auf einen Urlaub in den Alpen.
9. Bist du ______________________ mit der Arbeit oder brauchst du mehr Zeit?
10. Hast du ______________________ auf ein gutes Essen in einem italienischen Restaurant?

E

1. Die Kinder ______________________ von Weihnachtsgeschenken.
2. Ich muss mich auf die Grammatikübungen in der nächsten Unterrichtsstunde ______________________.
3. Ich ______________________ mich sehr auf die kommenden Frühlingsferien. Ich mache dann Urlaub.
4. Warum bist du so ______________________ nach diesem Jungen? Ist er unglaublich schön, oder was?

5. Hast du große ______________________ mit dem neuen Job?

6. Wir wollen uns nach einer Reise nach Indien ______________________. Wir wissen wenig über dieses Land.

7. Hast du dich für dieses Mädchen immer ______________________, oder ist deine Liebe für sie etwas Neues?

8. Ich muss mich um meine Familie ______________________.

9. Sind Sie noch ______________________ über den Tod Ihres Großvaters?

10. Bist du mit Ingo Maier nicht mehr ______________________? Ich sehe euch fast nie miteinander reden.

F

1. Der Musiker ______________________ sich nach seiner alten Violine. Seine neue klingt wie eine sterbende Katze.

2. Wie lange hast du an deiner Doktorarbeit ______________________?

3. Wir ______________________ uns über deinen neuesten Erfolg. Wir haben das eigentlich nicht erwartet.

4. Hubert ist so komisch. Wir ______________________ immer über ihn.

5. Ich bin von deinen schwachen Argumenten nicht ______________________. Ich kann sie nicht akzeptieren.

Focus on Meaning and Form [✓]

3. Fill in the blanks with the correct idiomatic expression as cued.

A

1. Warum bist du so ____________________________________? Ist er unglaublich schön, oder was? *(crazy about this guy)*

2. Was ______________________ du ____________________________? *(think of our president)*

3. Wie hast du ____________________________________? *(reacted to the candidate's speech)*

4. Wir sind sind ____________________________________. *(very proud of our daughter)*

5. Bist du ____________________________________? *(angry with/at us)*

6. Der Film ____________________________________. *(deals with a young girl in India)*

7. Die Kinder waren sehr ____________________________________. *(sad about their lost dog)*

8. Du sollst mehr ________________________________. *(think about your profession)*

9. Habt ihr große ________________________________? *(difficulties with your new job)*

10. Ich bin nicht ________________________________. *(convinced by her speech)*

B

1. Ist Ute ________________________________? *(related to Raimund)*

2. Ich bin seit vier Jahren ________________________________. *(married to a girl from Ulm)*

3. Mein Vater ist immer noch tief ________________________________. *(in love with my mother)*

4. Was ist der ________________________________? *(reason for your bad behavior)*

5. Willst du ________________________________? *(chat with her)*

6. ____________________ Sie sich mehr ____________________. *(care for your family)*

7. Bist du ________________________________? *(satisfied with your new stereo system)*

8. Darf ich dich ________________________________? *(ask for a piece of cheese)*

9. Hast du ____________________ über sein beschädigtes Auto ____________________? *(spoken with your father)*

10. Ist deine Schwester ________________________________? *(separated from her husband)*

C

1. Mit wem möchten Sie ________________________________? *(speak about the exam)*

2. Warum bist du so ________________________________? *(crazy about this person)*

3. Ich habe ________________________________. *(laughed at his dumb joke)*

4. Wir wollen uns ________________________________. *(inquire about this company)*

5. Würdest du uns etwas ________________________________? *(tell about your youth)*

6. ____________________ du dich schon lange ____________________? *(be interested in this author)*

7. ____________________ ihr oft ____________________? *(think of your relatives in Switzerland)*

8. ____________________ er sich ____________________? *(interested in soccer)*

9. Bist du ________________________________? *(sad about the death of your grandmother)*

10. Der Roman hat ________________________________. *(dealt with the life of the Kaiser)*

D

1. Er hat sich ______________________ gut ______________________. *(prepared for the test)*
2. Ich muss ein Buch ______________________. *(read about Franz Kafka)*
3. Ist Monika ______________________? *(happy about her new job)*
4. Mein Sohn möchte dir ______________________. *(thank for his birthday gift)*
5. Seit wann bist du ______________________? *(engaged to her)*
6. Seid ihr ______________________? *(independent of your parents)*
7. Das Theaterstück hat ______________________. *(dealt with the revolution in Argentina)*
8. Ich habe mich nicht ______________________. *(remembered the appointment)*
9. Wir möchten Ihnen ______________________. *(congratulate on your success)*
10. Sie soll sich mehr ______________________. *(be concerned about this course)*

E

1. Ich wollte dir etwas ______________________. *(say about the war in Iraq)*
2. Kann sie ihren Bruder ______________________? *(ask for help)*
3. Kannst du mir ______________________? *(help with the housework)*
4. Sind Sie wirklich ______________________? *(enthusiastic about this concert)*
5. Wir ______________________ uns ______________________ in den Alpen. *(looking forward to our vacation)*
6. ______________________ du ein Referat ______________________ in Südamerika? *(writing about the current situation)*
7. Sind Sie ______________________ oder brauchen Sie mehr Zeit? *(finished with the magazine)*
8. Der Polizist hat ______________________. *(asked about you)*
9. Hast du ______________________? *(fear of spiders, rats, or snakes)*
10. Ist Fritz ______________________? *(happy about his grade)*

F

1. Paul hat uns ______________________. *(told about his year in Spain)*
2. Sind Sie noch ______________________? *(sad about the end of the film)*
3. Du sollst noch ein bisschen länger ______________________. *(wait for the children)*
4. Wir ______________________. *(hoping for a victory)*
5. Die Arbeiter sind sehr ______________________. *(dissatisfied with their new boss)*

Chapter 17 Numerals and Time Expressions

Cardinal Numbers

Cardinal numbers are counting numbers.

1	eins	11	elf	21	einundzwanzig	40	vierzig
2	zwei	12	zwölf	22	zweiundzwanzig	50	fünfzig
3	drei	13	dreizehn	23	dreiundzwanzig	60	sechzig
4	vier	14	vierzehn	24	vierundzwanzig	70	siebzig
5	fünf	15	fünfzehn	25	fünfundzwanzig	80	achtzig
6	sechs	16	sechzehn	26	sechsundzwanzig	90	neunzig
7	sieben	17	siebzehn	27	siebenundzwanzig	100	(ein)hundert
8	acht	18	achtzehn	28	achtundzwanzig	200	zweihundert
9	neun	19	neunzehn	29	neunundzwanzig	1 000	(ein)tausend
10	zehn	20	zwanzig	30	dreißig	2 000	zweitausend

Be mindful of the spelling of:

16: **sechzehn** (*not* sechszehn)
17: **siebzehn** (*not* siebenzehn)
21: **einundzwanzig** (*not* einsundzwanzig)
30: **dreißig** (*not* dreizig)
60: **sechzig** (*not* sechszig)
70: **siebzig** (*not* siebenzig)

1 000 000 = **eine Million**
1 000 000 000 = **eine Milliarde** (*not* eine Billion)
1 000 000 000 000 = **eine Billion** (*not* eine Trillion)

Note the use of a space instead of a comma for numbers one thousand and above. Sometimes a period is used instead of a space.

The following adverbs are often used in conjunction with numbers:

etwa, rund, ungefähr = *about, roughly, approximately:* ***Rund 200 Zuschauer*** **sind anwesend.**
über = *more than, over:* **Die Universität hat** ***über 50 000 Studenten.***
unter = *below, less than:* **Die Zahl der Kranken liegt** ***unter 5 Prozent.***

Commas and Math Signs

Use a comma in German where we would use a decimal point: English 3.7 = German **3,7.** This is read as **drei Komma sieben.**

Remember to use commas instead of decimal points with prices: **Das kostet 10,75 Euro.**

math signs:	+ **plus** *or* **und**	− **minus** *or* **weniger**	
	× **mal**	: **geteilt durch**	= **ist/sind/macht**

Fractions

1/100	**ein Hundertstel**	1/20	**ein Zwanzigstel**
1/10	**ein Zehntel**	1/8	**ein Achtel**
1/6	**ein Sechstel**	1/5	**ein Fünftel**
1/4	**ein Viertel**	1/3	**ein Drittel**
1/2	**die Hälfte; eine Halbe,** *or* **ein- halb-: eine halbe Stunde; ein halbes Pfund; ein halber Tag**		

NOTE: 1,5 = **anderthalb; eineinhalb** (OR: **eins Komma fünf**)
4,5 = **viereinhalb** (OR: **vier Komma fünf**)

Ordinal Numbers

Ordinal numbers are *adjectival numbers* used to show the position or rank order of something in a series, for example, *first, second, third.* Numbers 1–19 have a **t**-sound before the adjective ending; numbers 20 and above have an **st**-sound before the adjective ending. Ordinal numbers are used most frequently to express dates:

Heute ist ***der*** ers**te** Juni / vier**te** Juni / zehn**te** Juni / zwanzig**ste** Juni / siebenundzwanzig**ste** Juni / dreißig**ste** Juni.
Heute haben wir ***den*** ers**ten** Juni / vier**ten** Juni / zehn**ten** Juni / zwanzig**sten** Juni / siebenundzwanzig**sten** Juni / dreißig**sten** Juni.

Since some of the numbers are long and clumsy-looking in print, often a decimal point is used after a number to signal that the number is an ordinal number. You must remember to sound the case ending correctly:

Heute ist *der* 1. Juni / 4. Juni / 10. Juni / 20. Juni / 27. Juni / 30. Juni.
Heute haben wir *den* 1. Juni / 4. Juni / 10. Juni / 20. Juni / 27. Juni / 30. Juni

Be mindful of the spelling of these: 1st = **erst-** 3rd = **dritt-** 7th = **siebt-** 8th = **acht-**

When listing points in an argument or presentation, use:

erstens *firstly* **zweitens** *secondly* **drittens** *thirdly*

Names and Titles

When using ordinal numbers as titles with a person's name, place the ordinal number in the same case as the name:

Das ist ein Bild **von König Harald dem Ersten.** = Das ist ein Bild **des Königs Harald des Ersten.**
That's a picture of King Harald I.

Elements of Time

Die Zeit, das Mal, and *-mal*

die Zeit = *time* and refers to the notion of time in a general sense: **Wir haben noch viel Zeit**
das Mal = *time* in the sense of *occurrence:* **das erste Mal, das zweite Mal, das letzte Mal**

Use **zu + Mal** to indicate *for the nth time:* **zum ersten Mal, zum zweiten Mal, zum letzten Mal**

-mal is used as an adverbial suffix:

einmal *once* | **dreimal** *three times*
zweimal *twice* | **zehnmal** *ten times*
hundertmal *a hundred times* | **tausendmal** *a thousand times*

noch einmal = **noch 'mal** = *once more; one more time; once again:* **Mach das noch einmal, bitte.**

Noun Genders

Days of the week, months, and seasons are masculine. (BUT: *week* = **die Woche**)

Parts of days are masculine except for **die Nacht** and **die Mitternacht.**

Note these neuters: **das Jahr, das Jahrzehnt, das Jahrhundert; das Wochenende, das Semester**

Im and *am*

The definite article is normally used with months:

der Juni = *June* **im Juni** = *in June*
im (**in** + **dem**) is used with months and seasons: **im Januar; im Winter**
am (**an** + **dem**) is used with days and parts of days: **am Freitag, am Freitagabend, am Wochenende, am Abend** (BUT: **in der Nacht** and **um Mitternacht**)

Adverbial Forms Ending in *-s*

Adverbs ending in *-s* signal a regular or repeated occurrence:

montags = jeden Montag
donnerstagnachmittags = jeden Donnerstagnachmittag
morgens = jeden Morgen
nachts = jede Nacht

Adverbial Phrases with *gestern, heute,* and *morgen*

Use **gestern, heute,** and **morgen** with parts of the days (nouns) as in these examples:

gestern Morgen	heute Morgen	**morgen** ***früh***
gestern Vormittag	heute Vormittag	morgen Vormittag
gestern Mittag	heute Mittag	morgen Mittag
gestern Nachmittag	heute Nachmittag	morgen Nachmittag
gestern Abend	heute Abend	morgen Abend
gestern Nacht (letzte Nacht)	heute Nacht	morgen Nacht

Noun Phrases as Adverbs of Time

Specific Time

Noun phrases denoting specific time employ the accusative case:

diesen Mittwoch *this Wednesday*

letzte Woche = **vorige Woche** = **vergangene Woche**
last week = *the previous week* = *the past week*

nächsten Monat = kommenden Monat *next month = this coming month*	**nächstes Wochenende = kommendes Wochenende** *next weekend = this coming weekend*
jeden Freitagabend = freitagabends *every Friday evening = Friday evenings*	**jeden Winter** *each/every winter*
letztes Wochenende *last weekend*	**dieses Wochenende** *this weekend*

Duration of Time

Noun phrases denoting a span or duration of time employ the accusative:

den ganzen Tag *all day*	**den ganzen Abend** *all evening*	**die ganze Woche** *all week*
den ganzen Monat *all month*	**das ganze Jahr** *all year*	**die ganze Zeit** *all the time*

Indefinite Time

The genitive case is used with noun phrases to designate indefinite or vague time references. The most common of these phrases is **eines Tages** *(one day; someday).*
The following phrases are also used but not quite as common:

eines Morgens *one/some morning*	**eines Abends** *one/some evening*	**eines Nachts** *one/some night*	**eines Jahres** *one/some year*

Note the form of **eines Nachts**. **Nacht** is a feminine noun, and the **-s** ending is a masculine or neuter genitive ending. It is employed here, somewhat counterintuitively, for reasons of symmetry, that is, to keep it similar to the other expressions.

Prepositions and Time Expressions

Most of the prepositional phrases that denote a point in time are dative prepositions. When two-way prepositions are employed, the dative case normally prevails.

in einer Woche *in a week*	**vor einem Jahr** *a year ago*	**nach einem Monat** *after a month*
heute in acht Tagen *a week from today*	**heute in einem Monat** *a month from today*	**heute in einem Jahr** *a year from today*
heute vor einer Woche *a week ago from today*	**heute vor einem Monat** *a month ago from today*	**heute vor einem Jahr** *a year ago from today*

einmal am Tag = einmal täglich = einmal pro Tag
---------- *once a day* ----------

einmal in der Woche = einmal wöchentlich = einmal die Woche = einmal pro Woche
---------- *once a week* ----------

Dates

Dates can be expressed a number of ways:

1. To ask the date:

   Der Wievielte *ist* heute? OR: **Den Wievielten** *haben* wir heute?

2. To give the date:

   Heute *ist* **der siebte Juni.** OR: Heute *haben* wir **den siebten Juni.**

3. To ask the date of an event:

   Wann geschiet das? OR: **Am Wievielten** geschiet das?
   Wann findet es statt? OR: **Am Wievielten** findet es statt?

4. To give the date of an event:

   Das Konzert findet **am** siebt**en** Juni statt.

When writing the date of a letter, mention the city and then the date in the accusative: München, **den 7. April** 2010

When writing the date numerically, mention day—month—year in that order, and use periods instead of dashes or slashes: **7.4.2010** = **den 7. April 2010**

Years as Dates

Years may be indicated as dates in only two ways: Use the year alone, or precede it with **im Jahr(e):**

Ich bin **1986** geboren. = Ich bin **im Jahre 1986** geboren.
------------------------------ *I was born in 1986.* ------------------------------

Clock Time

All elements of clock time are feminine (see below). Basic time elements of time may be combined with the prepositions **vor** (*ago*), **in** (*in*), and **nach** (*after*):

die Sekunde, -n	vor/in/nach zehn Sekunden
die Minute, -n	vor/in/nach zehn Minuten
die Stunde, -n	vor/in/nach einer Stunde
eine Viertelstunde	vor/in/nach einer Viertelstunde
eine halbe Stunde	vor/in/nach einer halben Stunde

Note how clock time would be stated in five-minute intervals from noon to one o'clock:

12-hour clock (conversational)	*24-hour clock (official)*
Es ist zwölf (Uhr).	Es ist [genau] 12 Uhr.
Es ist fünf (Minuten) nach zwölf (Uhr).	Es ist zwölf Uhr fünf.
Es ist zehn nach zwölf.	Es ist zwölf Uhr zehn.
Es ist Viertel nach zwölf.	Es ist zwölf Uhr fünfzehn.
Es ist zwanzig nach zwölf.	Es ist zwölf Uhr zwanzig.
Es ist fünf vor halb eins.	Es ist zwölf Uhr fünfundzwanzig.
Es ist halb eins.	Es ist zwölf Uhr dreißig.

Es ist fünf nach halb eins.	Es ist zwölf Uhr fünfunddreißig.
Es ist zwanzig vor eins.	Es ist zwölf Uhr vierzig.
Es ist Viertel vor eins.	Es ist zwölf Uhr fünfundvierzig.
Es ist zehn vor eins.	Es ist zwölf Uhr fünfzig.
Es ist fünf vor eins.	Es ist zwölf Uhr fünfundfünfzig.
Es ist eins/ein Uhr.	Es ist dreizehn Uhr.

null Uhr = Mitternacht: Der Zug kommt um null Uhr dreizehn an.
The train arrives at 12:13 a.m.

When mentioning the time *at which* something happens, use the preposition **um**:

***at** one o'clock* = **um** eins = **um** ein Uhr
***at** eight in the evening* = **um** acht Uhr abends

To mention an approximate time, use the preposition **gegen** (*around, toward, -ish*):

toward one o'clock = **gegen** eins = **gegen** ein Uhr
around eight in the evening = **gegen** acht Uhr abends
sevenish in the morning = **gegen** sieben Uhr morgens

Exercises

Theory Review

1. Fill in the blanks with the correct information.

1. ____________________ are numbers used in counting.
2. Numerical modifiers that signal an *approximate* number of items are: ____________________, ____________________, and ____________________.
3. The preposition ____________________ signals an amount *over and above* the number of items mentioned.
4. The preposition ____________________ signals an amount *below* the number of items mentioned.
5. In German a ____________________ is used where in English one uses a decimal point.
6. ____________________ numbers are adjectival and indicate the rank order of an item in a series.
7. Because they are adjectival, they display case ____________________ according to the rules you have learned for adjectives.
8. These numbers are used most frequently to express dates. *June 7th* would be ____________________.
9. The noun ____________________ refers to *time* in a general sense: seconds, minutes, hours, days, weeks, months, years, etc.
10. The noun ____________________ refers to *time* in the sense of an *occurrence*.

11. To ask the date one may say: ______________________________

    or ______________________________

12. To express today's date one may say: ______________________________

    or ______________________________

13. To express the day on which an event occurs or occurred, use the preposition __________,

    contracted with the definite article to __________. Example: ______________________

14. All of the clock time elements are ____________________ (gender).

15. There are several ways to ask someone for the time: ______________________

    or ______________________________

16. The __________-hour clock is generally used for most conversational purposes.

17. The __________-hour clock is used for timetables, schedules, and official record keeping.

18. Express the current time using both clock systems: ______________________

    or ______________________________

19. To indicate an approximate time, use the preposition ____________________. Example:

    ____

20. Noun phrases of specific time or duration of time are in the ____________________ case.

21. Noun phrases of vague or indefinite time are in the ____________________ case.

Focus on Meaning [✓]

2. Fill in the blanks with the German equivalents.

A

1. this evening/tonight ______________________________
2. next summer ______________________________
3. last Sunday ______________________________
4. this Sunday afternoon ______________________________
5. this morning ______________________________
6. next year ______________________________
7. last semester ______________________________
8. next month ______________________________
9. this year ______________________________
10. every Tuesday ______________________________

B

1. all day ______
2. in an hour ______
3. two days ago ______
4. after a while ______
5. one day ______
6. a month from today ______
7. twice a year ______
8. once a day ______
9. three days from now ______
10. two years ago ______

C

1. in ten minutes ______
2. all year ______
3. someday ______
4. tomorrow morning ______
5. this morning (11:00) ______
6. every three days ______
7. at midnight ______
8. during the day ______
9. one evening ______
10. all the time ______

D

1. every month ______
2. for a year ______
3. for (since) a year ______
4. in a few days ______
5. an hour ago ______
6. all evening ______
7. afternoons ______
8. in the afternoon ______
9. in the spring ______
10. this coming Friday ______

Focus on Meaning and Form

3. Time expressions. Fill in the blanks with the German equivalents of the cued time expressions.

A

1. ______________________ regnet es immer. *(Sundays)*
2. ______________________ war es sehr heiß. *(in 2003)*
3. ______________________ ist es schön. *(during the summer)*
4. ______________________ bleibst du zu Hause. *(next time)*
5. ______________________ bleibt er immer zu Hause. *(evenings)*
6. ______________________ kommt er nach Paderborn. *(next week)*
7. ______________________ war er im Büro. *(all morning)*
8. ______________________ war er noch am Leben. *(a year ago)*
9. ______________________ war sie nicht mehr da. *(one day)*
10. ______________________ bin ich wieder zu Hause. *(a week from today)*

B

1. ______________________ fahren wir ab. *(tomorrow morning)*
2. Arbeitet sie ______________________? *(nights)*
3. Das geschiet ______________________. *(every year)*
4. Der Zug ist ______________________ abgefahren. *(ten minutes ago)*
5. Er arbeitet ______________________. *(Mondays)*
6. Er wohnt ______________________ hier. *(for many years)*
7. Er ist ______________________ abgefahren. *(a month ago)*
8. Er kommt ______________________. *(tomorrow morning)*
9. Es ist ______________________. *(five after five)*
10. Es ist genau ______________________. *(twenty-five to ten)*

C

1. Frau Jürjens ist ______________________ in Aurich geblieben. *(over a year)*
2. Friede kommt ______________________. *(at nine o'clock)*
3. Heute haben wir ______________________. *(the 20th of October)*
4. Hier ist es ______________________ noch sehr kalt. *(in March)*
5. Ich bin ______________________ zurück. *(at 1:15)*
6. Ich bin ______________________ da geblieben. *(less than six months)*
7. Ich bin nur ______________________ da gewesen. *(once)*
8. Ich fahre ______________________ ab. *(on Tuesday)*
9. Ich habe diesen Film ______________________ gesehen. *(three times)*
10. Ich lese diese Novelle ______________________. *(for the first time)*

D

1. Ich sehe ihn ______________________________. *(on the 27th)*

2. Ich wohne ______________________________ hier. *(for a month)*

3. Ilse kommt ______________________________. *(around 7:30)*

4. Liest du das ______________________________? *(for the first time)*

5. Warst du ______________________________ zu Hause? *(yesterday evening)*

6. Wir fahren ______________________________ nach Deutschland. *(for a year)*

4. Zählen Sie schnell ...

von 0 bis 10   von 10 bis 0   von 0 bis 20   von 20 bis 0   von 50 bis 60 ...

in Einheiten von zwei, von drei, von vier, von fünf, von zehn, von elf ...

Partnerarbeit 

5. Arbeiten Sie mit einem Partner/einer Partnerin und stellen Sie einander die folgenden Fragen.

A

1. Der Wievielte ist heute/morgen/übermorgen?
2. Den Wievielten haben wir heute?
3. Der Wievielte war gestern/vorgestern/vorvorgestern?
4. Den Wievielten hatten wir gestern?
5. Wann bist du geboren?
6. Wann hast du Geburtstag? Deine Eltern? Deine Geschwister? Dein bester Freund/deine beste Freundin?
7. Wann feiert man das Neue Jahr? Fasching oder Karneval? Ostern? Sankt Valentinstag? Ostern? Muttertag? Vatertag? Den amerikanischen Freiheitstag? Kolumbustag? Thanksgiving (das Erntedankfest)? Weihnachten? Chanukka?
8. Wie oft wäschst du dein Auto? Deine Kleidung?
9. Wie oft besuchst du deine Eltern? Deine Großeltern?
10. Wann kamen deine Eltern das letzte Mal zu Besuch?

B

1. Wie oft gehst du in ein Restaurant? Ins Kino? In ein Konzert? In die Oper?
2. Wann hast du das letzte Mal einen Film gesehen? Lebensmittel gekauft? Deinen Wagen getankt? Sport getrieben? Einen Roman gelesen?
3. Wann gehst du normalerweise aus? Ski fahren? Angeln? Schwimmen? Auf die Jagd?
4. Wann findet die nächste Prüfung in diesem Kurs statt?
5. Wann endet das jetzige Semester? Wann beginnt das nächste Semester?
6. Wann fährst du das nächste Mal nach Hause?
7. Wann wirst du das nächste Mal die Nachrichten im Fernsehen sehen?
8. Wann muss man seine Steuererklärung abschicken?
9. Wann ist das Wetter an der Küste Kaliforniens schön?
10. Wann wirst du das nächste Mal aufstehen?

C

1. Wann beginnt und endet diese Unterrichtsstunde?
2. Wie spät ist es jetzt? Wie lange hast du schon Unterricht? Wann hat er begonnen?
3. Wann endet der Tag?
4. Wann bist du gewöhnlich an der Uni?
5. Wann wirst du deine nächste Prüfung haben?
6. Ich möchte dich später anrufen. Wann wirst du zu Hause sein?
7. Wann wird das Gras grün?
8. Wann fallen die Blätter von den Bäumen ab?
9. Wann kannst du vielleicht einen Ausflug aufs Land machen?
10. Wann wirst du das nächste Mal Ferien haben? Wie lange werden sie dauern?

D

1. Wie spät ist es jetzt? Wann wird dieser Unterricht enden?
2. Wann wirst du fertig mit deinem Studium sein?
3. Wann hast du das letzte Mal einen Deutschkurs gehabt?
4. Wie oft isst du etwas im Laufe des Tages? Um wieviel Uhr isst du dein Abendessen?
5. Wann wirst du einkaufen gehen müssen?
6. Um wieviel Uhr wirst du heute nach Hause gehen?
7. Wann (zu welcher Tageszeit) denkst und arbeitest du am besten?
8. Wann gehst du normalerweise ins Bett und wann stehst du auf?

Review of Time Expressions

Read over these time expressions repeatedly to gain greater familiarization with them. Circle the ones you know you are likely to forget and review them several times.

um acht Uhr • um Viertel nach sieben • um halb drei • um Viertel vor neun
in zehn Minuten • in einer Stunde • in zwei Stunden
heute Morgen • heute Nachmittag • heute Abend • heute Nacht
morgen früh • morgen Vormittag • morgen Mittag • morgen Abend

heute um zwei • morgen um fünf
heute Morgen um sieben • heute Nachmittag um zwei • heute Abend um acht • heute Abend gegen acht
um sechs Uhr morgens • um sechs Uhr abends • um drei nachmittags • gegen drei nachmittags

jede Minute • alle fünf Minuten • in zehn Minuten
jede Stunde • alle vier Stunden • in zwölf Stunden
jeden Tag • alle zwei Tage • in drei Tagen • in acht Tagen

diese Woche • nächste Woche • kommende Woche • letzte Woche
[heute] in acht Tagen • in zwei Wochen • vor einer Woche

am Dienstag • diesen Dienstag • kommenden Dienstag • nächsten Dienstag

am Morgen • am Nachmittag • am Abend • in der Nacht
jeden Morgen • jeden Nachmittag • jeden Abend • jede Nacht

am Freitagabend • freitagabends • am Dienstagmorgen • dienstagmorgens am Wochenende • dieses Wochenende • nächstes Wochenende

dieses Jahr • nächstes Jahr • letztes Jahr • in zehn Jahren

im Sommer • im Winter • diesen Frühling • kommenden Herbst

im April • diesen März • kommenden Dezember
im Juni • nächsten Mai • letzten Dezember

die ganze Stunde • den ganzen Tag • den ganzen Abend • die ganze Woche
den ganzen Monat • den ganzen Sommer • das ganze Jahr • die ganze Zeit

gestern • vorgestern • letzte Woche • dieses Mal
gestern Nachmittag • vorgestern Morgen • letzten Freitag • jedes Mal
gestern Abend • vorgestern Abend • letzten Monat • nächstes Mal
vorige Woche • letzten Sommer • letztes Mal
früher—später • vergangenes Jahr • letztes Jahr • das letzte Mal
vorher—nachher • vorletztes Jahr • letztes Semester • das nächste Mal

Chapter 18 Conjunctions and Clauses

Conjunctions are words that are used to join words, phrases, and clauses. Note the examples using the conjunction **und**:

words:	du **und** ich	dies **und** das	Freund **und** Feind	Männer **und** Frauen
phrases:	mein Freund **und** mein Bruder		aus dem Haus **und** ins Auto	
clauses:	Dieter will heute Abend ausgehen **und** Bettina will zu Hause bleiben.			

There are two groups or types of conjunctions: coordinating and subordinating conjunctions.

Coordinating Conjunctions

Coordinating conjunctions can join words, phrases, and clauses *without affecting word order.* The clauses they join are independent clauses, meaning that each clause can stand alone as a sentence and be fully understood.

Coordinating Conjunctions

und • aber • oder • denn • sondern

Und *and*

words:	Vati **und** Mutti	Land **und** Leute	klipp **und** klar
phrases:	mit meiner Schwester **und** ihren Freundinnen		
clauses:	Kannst du mit uns ins Restaurant gehen **und** [kannst du] später ins Kino [gehen]?		

Aber *but*

words:	gut **aber** teuer	schnell **aber** sicher	intelligent **aber** faul
phrases:	viel Sonne **aber** kalte Luft		
clauses:	Ich wache um sieben Uhr auf, **aber** ich stehe nicht immer sofort auf.		

Oder *or*

words:	Freund **oder** Feind	gut **oder** schlecht
phrases:	mit Liebe **oder** mit Hass	ins Kino **oder** in den Park
clauses:	Wir können Schach spielen **oder** wir können einkaufen gehen.	

Denn *because*

clauses: Ich muss zu Hause bleiben, **denn** ich habe zu viel zu Hause zu tun.

Nicht ..., sondern *not . . ., but*

words:	**nicht** schön, **sondern** hässlich	**nicht** blau, **sondern** schwarz
phrases:	**nicht** zur Bibliothek, **sondern** in die Kirche	
clauses:	Ich gehe **nicht** aus, **sondern** ich bleibe zu Hause.	

Nicht nur ..., sondern auch *not only . . ., but also*

words:	**nicht nur** schick, **sondern auch** preisgünstig
phrases:	**nicht nur** mein Vater, **sondern auch** mein Großvater
clauses:	Ich bin **nicht nur** nach Nigerien geflogen, **sondern** [ich bin] **auch** nach Südafrika gereist.

Punctuation

Commas are not required when using **und** and **oder** to join clauses, but they may be used to clarify the meaning of a sentence. Under the new spelling guidelines they are still prescribed for the other coordinating conjunctions when joining clauses, however.
Examples:

1. No commas with **und** and **oder**:

   Ich bleibe hier **und** du bleibst da.
   Wir kommen heute Abend zu dir **oder** ihr kommt morgen zu uns.

2. A comma is required before **aber**, **denn**, and **sondern**:

   Ich bleibe hier**,** **aber** du bleibst da.
   Ich will nach Hause gehen**,** **denn** ich bin müde.
   Hans ist **nicht** zu Hause**,** **sondern** [er ist] bei der Arbeit.

Ellipsis

When joining two clauses with normal word order with **und**, **oder**, and **sondern**, elements in the second clause that are common to the first (usually the subject and sometimes also the verb) may be omitted (= *ellipsis*).

Ich bleibe zu Hause **und** [ich] sehe fern.
I'm staying at home and [I'm] watching TV.

Wir kommen heute Abend **oder** [wir kommen] morgen Abend.
We'll come this evening or [we'll come] tomorrow evening.

Karl ist nicht bei mir, **sondern** [er ist] bei seiner Freundin.
Karl's not at my place but rather [he's] at his girlfriend's [place].

Subordinating Conjunctions

Subordinating conjunctions are used to join a main clause (also called an *independent* clause) with a subordinate clause (also called a *dependent* clause). The dependent clause makes no sense until it is joined to a main clause:

makes no sense by itself:	Wenn ich Zeit habe
makes sense with a main clause:	Ich werde dich besuchen, wenn ich Zeit habe.

Subordinate Word Order

Because the subordinate clause is dependent on the main clause, it exhibits a type of word order known as *subordinate* word order. This word order is triggered by a *subordinating* conjunction. The prominent feature of this word order is:

1. that the subject must follow the conjunction, and
2. the verb that agrees with the subject moves to the end of the sentence.

Note the examples:

Ich werde kommen, ***wenn ich*** *später etwas Zeit* ***habe.***
Es ist mir noch nicht klar, ***ob ich*** *heute oder morgen Abend zu dir kommen* ***soll.***
Der Lehrer sagt, ***dass er*** *die Prüfung auf nächsten Dienstag verschieben* ***wird.***

Subordinating Conjunctions

als • bevor • bis • da • damit • dass • ehe • indem • nachdem • ob • obgleich • obwohl • seit/seitdem • sobald • solange • sooft • während • weil • wenn

Wenn *when, whenever, if*

Wenn **wir unsere Hausaufgaben machen**, werden wir gut Noten verdienen.
If we do our homework, we'll earn good grades.

Wenn **ich krank bin**, nehme ich immer zwei Aspirintabletten.
Whenever I'm sick I take two aspirin tablets.

Wenn **ich Zeit habe**, werde ich vorbeikommen.
When I have time I'll come on by.

Auch wenn *even if*

Ich würde dich nicht heiraten, ***auch wenn*** **du die letzte Person auf der Welt wärest.**
I would not marry you, even if you were the last person on earth.

Ob *if* (but only in the sense of *whether*)

Sabine weiß nicht, ***ob* sie mit uns ins Kino kommen darf.**
Sabine doesn't know if/whether she can (that is, may) come with us to the movies.

Als *when* (past time reference, so it is always used with a past-tense verb)

***Als* ich jünger war,** spielte ich viel Fußball.
When I was younger I played a lot of soccer.

Wann *when* (when the time is not known)

Ich weiß nicht, ***wann* ich das erledigen kann**.
I don't know when I can finish that.

Nachdem *after*

***Nachdem* ich meine Hausaufgaben fertig gemacht habe,** werde ich mit Freunden ausgehen.
After I've finished my homework, I'll go out with friends.

Wir sind nach Hause gegangen, ***nachdem* wir Tennis gespielt hatten.**
We went home after we [had] played tennis.

Bevor/ehe *before*

Ich muss zuerst diese Arbeit erledigen, ***bevor* ich mit euch ausgehen kann.**
First I have to finish this work before I can go out with you.

***Ehe* Dieter ein neues Auto kaufen kann,** muss er viel Geld sparen.
Before Dieter can buy a new car he'll have to save lot of money.

Bevor **wir ausgehen durften**, hatten wir unsere Zimmer aufräumen müssen.
Before we were allowed to go out, we had to have straightened up our rooms.

Weil *because* (causal, and the cause is strong or deliberate: cause → effect)

A **weil**-clause normally follows the main clause.

Ich kann das nicht kaufen, ***weil* ich kein Geld habe.**
I can't buy that because I don't have enough money.

Moni wird die Prüfung nicht bestehen, ***weil* sie nicht fleißig genug dafür gelernt hat.**
Moni won't pass the test because she hasn't studied hard enough for it.

Da *since, because* (causal, and the cause is more accidental or coincidental)

Da is used primarily in formal writing and is not common in spoken German. Often a word like **zufällig** (*by chance*) or **sowieso** (*anyway*) will appear in the **da**-clause. The **da**-clause typically is mentioned before the main clause, that is, it begins the sentence.

***Da* der Kanzler [zufällig/sowieso] in Heidelberg sein wird,** wird er das alte Schloss besichtigen.
Since the chancellor will be in Heidelberg [anyway], he'll take a look at the old castle.

***Da* die Krise noch ernster wird,** werden sich die Minister in Berlin treffen.
Since the crisis has become more serious, the ministers will meet in Berlin.

Seitdem *since, ever since* (referring to time)

***Seitdem* ich in Berlin wohne,** höre ich viel Live-Musik.
Since I've been living in Berlin I've been listening to lots of live music.

***Seitdem* ich nicht mehr so spät arbeiten muss**, habe ich abends frei.
Ever since I haven't had to work so late, I've had evenings free.

Solange *as long as*

Es ist mir egal, was wir jetzt machen, ***solange* ich pünktlich nach Hause komme.**
I don't care what we do as long as I get home on time.

Sobald *as soon as*

Ich komme zu dir, ***sobald* ich [zu dir kommen] kann.**
I'll come to your place as soon as I can [come to your place].

Sooft *as often as, every time [that]*

Meine Frau weint, ***sooft* sie das Lied von dem Film *Romeo und Julia* hört.**
My wife cries whenever she hears the song from the film Romeo and Juliet.

Dass *that*

Ich habe nicht gesagt, ***dass* ich gestern Abend in der Kneipe war.**
I didn't say that I was in the pub last night.

Bis *until*

Du musst hier warten, ***bis* ich vom Einkaufen zurückgekommen bin.**
You have to wait here until I've returned from shopping.

Damit/Sodass/So Dass *so that*

Ich wiederhole es dir, ***damit/sodass/so dass* du das bestimmt richtig verstehst.**
I'll repeat it to you so [that] you'll definitely understand it.

Obwohl/Obgleich *although, even though*

Ich werde keinen Porsche kaufen, ***obwohl* ich mir einen [Porsche] leisten kann.**
I won't be buying a Porsche even though I can afford one.

Während *while*

***Während* ich in Wien studierte,** ging ich in viele Konzerte.
While I studied in Vienna I went to many concerts.

Indem *by, by means of, insofar as* (indicates a *means* by which something is done or accomplished)

Ich habe eine ganz gute Note verdient, ***indem* ich lange und fleißig gelernt habe.**
I earned a good grade by [means of] studying long and hard.
I earned good grades insofar as I studied long and hard.

W-Fragewörter Used as Subordinating Conjunctions

Interrogative pronouns and adverbs may be used as subordinating conjunctions:

wer: Weißt du, ***wer* das ist?**
Do you know who that is?

Kannst du mir sagen, ***wen* du getroffen hast?**
Can you tell me whom you met?

Sag mir, bitte, ***wem* du das gesagt hast.**
Tell me please whom you told that to.

Würden Sie mir bitte sagen, ***wessen* Kreditkarte das ist?**
Would you please tell me whose credit card this is?

wie: Können Sie mir sagen, ***wie* man zum Bahnhof kommt?**
Can you tell me how to get to the train station?

Der Koch wollte uns nicht sagen, ***wie* er das Gericht gekocht hatte.**
The chef did not want to tell us how he cooked the meal.

wie weit: Können Sie mir sagen, ***wie weit* es zum Bahnhof ist?**
Can you tell me how far it is to the train station?

wie schnell: Es ist nicht zu glauben, ***wie schnell* Franz' Auto fährt!**
It's unbelievable how fast Franz's car drives.

warum: Ich möchte wissen, ***warum* es geschehen ist.**
I'd like to know why it happened.

Wirst du mir denn nicht mitteilen, ***warum* du das gemacht hast?**
Won't you tell me, then, how you did that?

wo: Weißt du, ***wo* Theo wohnt?**
Do you know where Theo lives?

woher: Ich habe keine Ahnung, ***woher* sie kommt.**
I have no idea where she comes from.

wohin: Wir wussten nicht, ***wohin* Hans verschwunden war.**
We don't know where Hans had disappeared to.

Double Infinitives in Subordinate Clauses

As you have learned in Chapter 8, whenever a modal verb is used with a helping verb and a dependent infinitive, a double-infinitive construction results. The double infinitive *must* be the *last item* in a clause, coordinate or subordinate. No sentence element may follow it. In a subordinate clause the helping verb goes as far back in the clause as it can—to the double infinitive, but no farther. Study the examples:

Thomas behauptet immer noch, *dass er so was nicht* ***hat*** **machen müssen.**
Thomas still claims that he did not have to do anything like that.

Ich verstehe nicht, *warum wir das* ***haben*** **machen sollen.**
I don't understand why we were obligated to do that.

Der Mechaniker sagt, *dass er den Wagen nicht* ***wird*** **reparieren können.**
The mechanic says he won't be able to fix the car.

The ability to use double-infinitive constructions in subordinate clauses is very challenging for native speakers of English to learn to do. In time and with sufficient exposure and practice, this will become easier. You will be able to do this more successfully when writing, since you have time to edit your output. It's more difficult to do when conversing because of the speed required. Until you can use this construction comfortably, be patient with yourself. Expect to make mistakes and engage in self-correction. It's a normal part of the learning process.

Exercises

Theory Review

1. Fill in the blanks with the correct information.

1. Conjunctions are words used to ______________________ various sentence elements.
2. Specifically, conjunctions may be used with words, phrases, and ______________________.
3. A ______________________ always consists of at least a subject and a verb.
4. One that can stand alone as a full sentence is known as a(n) ______________________ clause.
5. A clause that makes little or no sense by itself is known as a ______________________ clause.
6. It must be attached to a(n) ______________________ clause to make logical sense.
7. ______________________ conjunctions are used to join two independent clauses.
8. Do they affect word order when the clauses are joined? ____________
9. Commas are required when joining independent clauses, but not when the conjunctions are ______________________ or ______________________.
10. Leaving out elements in the second clause that are common to the first is known as ______________________.
11. ______________________ conjunctions are used to join a subordinate/dependent clause to a main/independent clause.
12. Do they affect word order when the clauses are joined? ____________
13. Which clause is affected? The ______________________ clause.

14. What moves out of its normal position in a subordinate clause? The ____________________.

15. If there are more than two verb forms in this clause, which one moves?

    ____

16. To where does it move?

    ____

17. Where is the subject of a subordinate clause located?

    ____

18. There are three subordinating conjunctions that may mean *when:* ____________________, ____________________, and ____________________.

19. The correct conjunction to use when the time is not known is ____________________.

20. The correct conjunction to use when a single, completed past event is mentioned is ____________________.

21. The correct conjunction to use when speaking about generalities is ____________________.

22. There are two ways to express *if:* ____________________ and ____________________.

23. To state a simple condition (for example, *if I have time, . . .*), use ____________________.

24. If *whether* may be substituted for *if,* then ____________________ is the correct conjunction, not **wenn**.

25. When **weil** is used, a strong, deliberate ____________________ responsible for a result or effect is mentioned.

26. A **weil**-clause typically comes ____________________ the main clause.

27. By contrast, **da** is used instead of **weil** when the cause is relatively ____________________ (for example, convenience or luck).

28. A **da**-clause typically is mentioned ____________________ the main clause.

29. A **weil**-clause is common in ____________________ German; a **da**-clause is generally relegated to ____________________ German.

30. The conjunction ____________________ is used to explain the process by which something is done.

31. As stated previously, the last word in a subordinate clause is ____________________.

32. The lone exception to this expectation is when there is a ____________________ in the subordinate clause.

33. In this case, the helping verb does not move to the end of the clause, as expected, but rather . . .

    ____________________.

34. This means that the last thing heard in a clause with a double infinitive is ____________________.

Focus on Meaning [✓]

2. Fill in the blanks with logical coordinating or subordinating conjunctions. Observe the word order used before determining the proper conjunction.

A

1. ______________________ ich jung war, wohnte ich in Leipzig.
2. Ich spare viel Geld, ______________________ ich rauche nicht mehr.
3. ______________________ ich ihre Stimme hörte, erkannte ich sie gleich.
4. Jedesmal, ______________________ er das Büro verlässt, macht er immer die Fenster zu.
5. ______________________ es schon Winter geworden ist, kann man erwarten, dass es nötig sein wird, einen Eisbrecher im Hafen zu stationieren.
6. Ich konnte den Film gut verstehen, ______________________ ich ihn mehrmals gesehen hatte.
7. ______________________ er siebzig Jahre alt ist, geht er täglich ins Büro.
8. Der Mantel ist hübsch, ______________________ ich finde ihn zu teuer.
9. Thomes hat mein Auto repariert, ______________________ er den Ventilator ersetzt hat.
10. Er geht nicht gern ins Kino, ______________________ er besucht lieber seine Freunde.

B

1. Er grüßte mich nicht, ______________________ [er] ging stumm weiter.
2. Wir haben uns warm angezogen, ______________________ es ist kalt geworden.
3. Du rauchst viel, ______________________ du einfach nervös bist.
4. Er sieht besser aus, ______________________ er weniger arbeitet.
5. Es ist möglich, ______________________ die Chefin wieder im Büro ist.
6. Hier ist die Bibliothek ______________________ dort ist das Verwaltungsgebäude.
7. Hören Sie mit dem Lärm auf, ______________________ es sehr spät ist und die Nachbarn schlafen.
8. Ich bin nicht ganz sicher, ______________________ ich glaube, es ist wahr.
9. Wir haben euch zugewinkt, ______________________ ihr habt uns anscheinend nicht gesehen.
10. Ich lernte sie kennen, ______________________ wir beide in München an der Uni studierten.

C

1. Ihr müsst euch beeilen, ______________________ unsere Gäste bald kommen.
2. Ich sage es dir noch einmal, ______________________ du besser darauf vorbereitet bist.
3. Ich trank eine Tasse Tee, ____________________ ich auf sie wartete. Sie kam in einigen Minuten.
4. Ich weiß nicht, ______________ wir ihn nicht sehen können. Vielleicht is er noch zu weit weg.
5. Ich weiß nicht, _______________ Inge heute Abend zu Hause sein wird. Vielleicht um sieben?
6. Ich weiß nicht, wo Manfred ist, ______________________ ich werde ihn suchen.
7. Ich werde warten, ______________________ Doris zurückkommt.
8. Ich wusste nicht, ______________________ Peter so gern liest. Liest er Literatur oder Krimis?
9. Ruf mich an, ______________________ er ankommt. Ich muss dringend mit ihm sprechen.
10. Sie können mit ihr sprechen, ______________________ ich mit ihr gesprochen habe.

D

1. Sie stand um fünf Uhr auf, ______________________ sie nicht schlafen konnte.
2. Soll ich die Weinflasche öffnen ______________________ willst du das tun?
3. Sprechen Sie lauter, ______________________ ich Sie besser verstehen kann.
4. ______________________ ich ins Bett gehe, putze ich mir immer die Zähne.
5. Wissen Sie, ______________________ er den Schlüssel gefunden hat?
6. Ich fühle mich hier fremd, ______________________ wir umgezogen sind.
7. Wir sind an den Strand gegangen, ______________________ das Wetter nicht so schön war.
8. Sie will nicht zu Hause bleiben, ______________________ sie möchte lieber tanzen gehen.
9. ___________________ du das richtig machen willst, musst du dich sehr gut darauf vorbereiten.
10. Karola sagte, ______________________ sie das nie wieder machen würde.

Focus on Form [✓]

3. Join each pair of sentences logically and naturally with the cued conjunction. Make all necessary word order changes.

A

1. Ich bleibe hier. Du gehst dahin. (und)

   ____

2. Wir haben Briefmarken gesammelt. Wir waren Jungen. (als)

   ____

3. Die Jacke ist schön. Die Farbe gefällt mir nicht. (aber)

   ____

4. Ihr werdet das Examen bestehen können. Ihr habt genug dafür gelernt. (wenn)

   ____

5. Man kann Gitarre schneller lernen. Man übt täglich. (indem)

____

6. Es ist mir immer noch nicht klar. Hast du die Theorie verstanden? (ob)

____

7. Willst du ins Kino gehen? Willst du ins Konzert gehen? (oder)

____

8. Wir mussten zwei Tage länger an dem Projekt arbeiten. Wir haben nicht gut zusammenarbeiten können. (weil)

____

9. Lisa hat [es] mir schon gesagt. Sie kommt am Wochenende mit. (dass)

____

10. Peter hat Steak bestellt. Er hat Fisch bestellt. (nicht ... , sondern)

____

B

1. Ich werde Sie darum bitten. Ich brauche Hilfe. (wenn)

____

2. Du hast es nicht tun können? Ich habe es dir hundertmal erklären müssen! (obwohl)

____

3. Wir sind schon mehrmals ins Museum gegangen. Wir wohnen hier. (seitdem)

____

4. Anna konnte die Aufgabe nicht erledigen. Sie hatte nicht genug Zeit dafür. (denn)

____

5. Hans musste mit dem Bus fahren. Er hat seine Autoschlüssel nicht finden können. (weil)

____

6. Der Mechaniker bestellt die richtigen Ersatzteile. Er wird meinen Wagen reparieren können. (damit)

____

____

7. Ich gehe einkaufen. Ich rufe meine Mutter an. (bevor)

____

8. Warte auf mich, bitte. Ich schreibe diesen Zettel fertig. (bis)

____

9. Ich bin immer schläfrig. Ich wache vor sechs Uhr morgens auf. (wenn)

____

10. Ute hat diese Hose gekauft. Sie hat diesen Gürtel gekauft. (nicht nur ... , sondern auch ...)

____

Focus on Meaning and Form

4. Join the sentences together with any conjunctions that makes good, logical sense. Be sensitive to word order requirements based on your choices.

A

1. Es ist mir nicht klar. Sie ist zu Hause.

   ____

2. Ich hatte den Wecker gestellt. Ich ging ins Bett.

   ____

3. Sollen wir hier bleiben? Sollen wir nach Hause gehen?

   ____

4. Willi will nach draußen gehen und Fußball spielen. Er muss zuerst sein Zimmer aufräumen.

   ____

5. Wir wollen nicht ins Kino gehen. Wir wollen lieber an den See gehen.

   ____

6. Schließ die Fenster. Es regnet.

   ____

7. Ich spielte viel Schach mit meinen Freunden. Ich war jünger.

   ____

8. Geht das? Wir kommen um acht an.

   ____

9. Könnt ihr auf mich warten? Ich habe meine Arbeit erledigt.

   ____

10. Bernd konnte kein Essen bestellen. Er hatte nicht genug Geld dafür.

    ____

B

1. Haben Sie eine Ahnung? Wann beginnt der Film?

   ____

2. Er war sowieso in der Nähe. Er ist plötzlich vorbeigekommen.

   ____

3. Du kannst einkaufen gehen. Ich kann (zur gleichen Zeit) mein Auto polieren.

4. Ich will mit dir sprechen. Ich kann deine Argumente dafür oder dagegen besser verstehen.

5. Willi hat den Ventilator geölt. Er funktionert viel besser und auch leiser.

6. Weißt du? Kommt Käthe heute zur Arbeit?

7. Die Lehrerin korrigierte Hausaufgaben. Die Schüler machten eine Prüfung.

8. Wir haben wesentlich mehr Freunde. Wir gehen zu einer neuen Schule.

9. Ich habe die Prüfung nicht bestanden. Ich habe fleißig dafür gelernt.

10. Hans besucht seine Verwandten. Er kommt nach Hamburg.

You Determine the Message and Form

5. Write sentences using each conjunction to join clauses. Be sure their meanings are logical.

und

aber

oder

denn

nicht ... , sondern ... (Note punctuation!)

nicht nur ... , sondern auch ... (Note punctuation!)

als

wenn

ob

weil

dass

obwohl

seitdem

nachdem

sobald

bevor

bis

da

damit

während

indem

Chapter 19 Relative Clauses and Infinitive Phrases and Constructions

Part One

Relative Pronouns and Relative Clauses

Relative pronouns introduce a relative clause—a type of subordinate clause—and *relate* to a noun antecedent/referent in terms of gender and number. *The case of the relative pronoun is the operative variable and depends solely on its function in the relative clause.* That means that relative pronouns may function in the relative clause as subjects, objects, indirect objects, possessors, and objects of prepositions, and they may, and often do, differ in case from their antecedents.

Relative Pronouns in English

In English, the relative pronoun *who/whom/whose* is generally used when referring to persons. The pronoun *that* is generally used to refer to things. The pronoun *which* often refers to an idea expressed as a whole clause. The direct-object relative pronoun is sometimes not mentioned explicitly in English.

The woman *who* came yesterday is my mother-in-law.
The student [*whom*] we met yesterday in the coffee shop is brilliant.
The man *with whom* I spoke is my boss. (Colloquial: The man [whom] I spoke to is my boss.)
The child *whose* name I've forgotten is about six years old.
The car [*that*] I bought is in pretty good shape.
The book [*that*] I've been reading is very good.
That's something [*that*] I'll never forget.
Joel finally found a good job, *which* is very fortunate.

Relative Pronoun *der/die/das*

The forms of the relative pronoun **der/die/das** are identical to the forms of the demonstrative pronoun. While all forms of the relative pronoun supply the primary case sound, the dative plural and all genitives (in italics) supply both the primary and secondary case sounds.

Forms of the Relative Pronoun

	masculine	*feminine*	*neuter*	*plural*
nominative:	**der**	**die**	**das**	**die**
accusative:	**den**	**die**	**das**	**die**
dative:	**dem**	**der**	**dem**	***denen***
genitive:	***dessen***	***deren***	***dessen***	***deren***

In German, the relative pronoun may *never* be omitted. A comma must be used to separate the relative clause from the main clause. Note the variations possible with the first example sentence. (Masculine forms are used for the examples here since they show the most variance.)

Ist das *der Junge,* **der** gestern hier war? *(who was here yesterday)*
den wir gestern Abend kennen gelernt haben? *(whom we got to know last evening)*
dem du den Brief geschickt hast? *(to whom you sent the letter)*
dessen Familie in Stuttgart wohnt? *(whose family lives in Stuttgart)*
bei dem du übernachtet hast? *(at whose house you stayed)*
über den wir vieles gehört haben? *(about whom we've heard much)*
mit dem du gesprochen hast? *(with whom you spoke)*
auf den du gewartet hast? *(for whom you waited)*
in den du verliebt bist? *(with whom you are in love)*
ohne den du nicht leben kannst? *(without whom you can't live)*

Relative Pronoun *welch-*

A form of **welch-** can also serve as a relative pronoun, but this construction is not used frequently and is therefore not recommended to you. You will be able to comprehend it easily, should you encounter it.

Wer ist der Mann, **mit welchem** du gesprochen hast?
Who is the man, with whom you spoke?

Wo-Compounds

When **was** is the intended object of a preposition, a **wo**-compound is sometimes used instead.

Das ist *etwas,* **worauf** ich lange gewartet habe.
That's something for which I have waited a long time.
That's something [that] I've waited a long time for.

Relative Pronouns *wer* and *was*

The pronouns **wer** (*whoever, anyone who*) and **was** (*whatever, anything that*) are used to introduce a relative clause for which there is no antecedent/referent. In this case, the relative clause starts off the sentence. Using **immer** or **auch** after **wer** or **was** intensifies the degree of vagueness.

Wer das [immer] glaubt, muss ein Idiot sein!
Whoever believes that must be an idiot!

Wer [auch immer] fit werden will, muss jeden Tag eine halbe Stunde lang aktiv sein!
Whoever wants to get fit needs to be active every day for half an hour.

Was [immer] du machst, geht mich nichts an.
Whatever you do is none of my business.
Whatever you do doesn't affect me.

Was er [auch immer] redet, ist reiner Quatsch.
Whatever he says is pure baloney.

The relative pronoun **was** is used when the antecedent/referent is a vague or non-specific pronoun or abstract superlative adjectival noun:

vague pronoun antecedents:

Das ist **etwas, *was*** ich nicht begreifen kann.
That's something [that] I can't grasp.

Hast du **alles, *was*** du brauchst?
Do you have everything [that] you need?

abstract superlative adjectival nouns:

Das ist **das Schlimmste, *was*** passieren kann.
That's the worst that can happen.

Ist das **das Beste, *was*** du dir vorstellen kannst?
Is that the best [that] you can imagine?

It is also used when the antecedent is an entire clause/idea:

Annette hat das Examen bestanden, *was* mich wirklich erstaunt.
Annette passed the exam, which really amazes me.

Herr Friedrichs behauptet, **dass er nie vorher verheiratet war, *was*** eine nackte Lüge ist, denn ich kenne seine ehemalige Frau.
Herr Friedrichs claims [that] he was never married before, which is a naked lie, because I know his ex-wife.

Exercises: Part One

Theory Review

1. Fill in the blanks with the correct information.

1. ____________________ pronouns introduce relative clauses.
2. A relative clause is a type of ____________________ clause.
3. This means that the conjugated verb is at the ____________________ of the sentence.
4. The relative pronoun relates to a noun ____________________.
5. It must agree with the antecedent in terms of ____________________ and ____________________.

6. Its ______________________, however, is determined by its role in the relative clause.

7. The forms of the relative pronoun are identical to the forms of the ______________________.

8. These forms are similar to those of the definite article except for all of the ______________________ and for the ______________________ plural.

9. Instead of the genitive **des** and **der** we have ______________________ and ______________________.

10. Instead of the dative plural **den** we have ______________________.

11. In German the relative pronoun is ______________________ omitted. In English it sometimes is, especially for objects.

12. A relative clause is separated from the main clause by a ______________________.

13. The relative pronoun **was** is used rather than **das** when the antecedent is a[n] ______________________ pronoun or abstract superlative adjectival noun.

14. **Was** is also used when the antecedent is an entire ______________________, that is, an entire idea.

15. If a relative pronoun is needed, and there is no antecedent, then an indefinite relative pronoun is called for. Variant forms of ______________________ (for persons) and ______________________ (for things) are used.

Focus on Meaning and Form [✓]

2. Fill in the blanks with the correct relative pronoun.

A

1. Da kommt der Freund, in ______________________ Schwester du verliebt bist.
2. Das Buch, ______________________ ich kaufen wollte, war zu teuer.
3. Das ist der Mann, ______________________ du danken sollst.
4. Das ist der Mann, mit ______________________ ich sprechen möchte.
5. Das ist die Frau, für ______________________ Mann ich arbeite.
6. Das ist die Sekretärin, ______________________ ich es gesagt habe.
7. Das ist ein Haus, mein Lieber, in ______________________ ich gern wohnen würde.
8. Das ist ein Land, ______________________ Innenpolitik mich nicht interessiert.
9. Das ist eine Suppe, ______________________ ich immer gern bestelle.
10. Der Kunde, ______________________ Einkäufe hier liegen, kommt gleich zurück.

B

1. Die Gemälde, ______________________ ich kaufen wollte, sind nicht mehr zu haben.
2. Die Bluse, ______________________ Farbe mir gefällt, ist sehr preisgünstig.
3. Die Famile, ______________________ Wagen vor unserem Haus steht, ist sehr freundlich zu uns.
4. Die Familie, bei ______________________ ich wohnte, sprach kein Englisch.
5. Die Frau, ______________________ Handschuhe da liegen, wird zurückkommen.
6. Die Käsesorten, ______________________ mir am besten gefallen, kommen aus Frankreich.
7. Die Leute, ______________________ Wohnung wir jetzt mieten, sind im Urlaub.
8. Die Wohnung, in ______________________ ich jetzt wohne, ist mir zu klein.
9. Hier ist ein Roman, ______________________ mich interessiert.
10. Hier ist ein Wagen, ______________________ Preis mir gefällt.

C

1. Hier sind die Papiere, auf ______________________ Sie warten.
2. Ich zeige dir den Zettel, ______________________ sie uns geschrieben hat.
3. Ist das das Glas, aus ______________________ du getrunken hast?
4. Ist das der Mantel, ______________________ du neulich gekauft hast?
5. Ist das die Frau, ______________________ du so uninteressant findest?
6. Schleiermacher ist ein Philosoph, ______________________ Ideen noch heute interessant sind.
7. Siehst du das Kind, ______________________ an der Ecke vor der Schule steht?
8. Siehst du die Lehrerin, ______________________ gerade aus der Schule kommt?
9. Siehst du die zwei Mädchen, ______________________ vor dem Geschäft stehen?
10. Sind das die Jungen, mit ______________________ du gestern gespielt hast?

D

1. Sind das die Leute, ______________________ Sie meinen?
2. Vielen Dank für das Hemd, ______________________ du mir geschenkt hast.
3. Was ist die Sache, nach ______________________ du dich erkundigt hast?
4. Was kosten die Flugkarten, ______________________ Sie bestellt haben?
5. Was war der Gefallen, um ______________________ du deine Eltern gebeten hast?
6. Wer war der Mann, nach ______________________ du gefragt hast?
7. Wer sind die Leute, mit ______________________ du geredet hast?
8. Wie heißt der Politiker, über ______________________ du gesprochen hast?
9. Wir warten immer noch auf das Paket, ______________________ sie uns geschickt haben.
10. Wo ist der Bericht, auf ______________________ ich warte?

3. Fill in the blanks with whatever is needed to make good sense, for example, relative pronouns, prepositions, *wo*-compounds, etc. Various answers are possible for some.

A

1. ______________________ du sagst, ist eine nackte Lüge.
2. ______________________ freut er sich?
3. Das ist das Beste, ______________________ du je gemalt hast.
4. Das war das Wichtigste, ______________________ er zu sagen hatte.
5. Hast du gelesen, ______________________ er geschrieben hat? Was war das Thema davon?
6. Ich bin nicht sicher, ______________________ ich es liefern soll. Der Sekretärin oder dem Chef?
7. Ich habe keine Ahnung, ______________________ er so lange nachgedacht hat.
8. Ich habe nicht gehört, ______________________ er gesagt hat.
9. Ich habe nicht gemerkt, ______________________ er getan hat.
10. Ich kann vieles, ______________________ er sagte, einfach nicht verstehen.

B

1. Ich möchte wissen, ______________________ Buch das ist. Gehört es dir?
2. Ich weiß nicht, ______________________ heute Abend zu Besuch kommt. Ist es Petra?
3. Ich weiß nicht, ______________________ Auto das ist. Gehört es Peters?
4. Sag mir alles, ______________________ du weißt.
5. Der Laden hat nichts zu verkaufen, ______________________ uns interessiert.
6. Sie sagte uns nicht, mit ______________________ sie ins Kino gegangen ist.
7. Weißt du, ______________________ du machen willst?
8. Weißt du, ______________________ er meinte?
9. Wissen Sie, ______________________ er die E-Mail geschickt hat? Einem Bekannten?
10. Wissen Sie, auf ______________________ sie wartet? Auf Bernd?

Focus on Meaning and Form

4. Express the following in German using relative clauses. The English sentences are colloquial in tone, not formal. If you don't "see" the relative clause right away, try paraphrasing the sentence into more formal English first before attempting to express the idea in German (see A.1 below). Remember, relative pronouns (for direct objects) may be omitted in English, but never in German.

A

1. That's the boy I want to talk to. (Paraphrase: That's the boy to whom I want to talk.)

____

2. That's something that doesn't interest me.

____

3. That's the woman whose husband I assisted.

____

4. I heard that it is supposed to rain again today, which doesn't surprise me.

____

5. She's not the first person you should thank.

____

6. Do you see the two old ladies standing on the corner?

____

7. The man whose coat is lying here on the sofa is coming back soon.

____

8. Here's a blouse whose color is nice.

____

9. Many thanks for the check you sent us.

____

10. Is that the novel you find so dull?

____

B

1. The family whose boat we are sailing is currently on vacation in Germany.

____

2. Is that the bottle you were drinking from?

____

3. I'll show you the photos he sent us.

____

4. The car I'm driving is much too big for me.

____

5. Do you see the girl who is just now coming out of [the] school?

____

6. Those are the children we gave cookies to.

___

7. Is that the man you were chatting with yesterday afternoon?

___

8. What do you think of the presents I gave my wife?

___

9. I am always having to repeat things to you, which is getting very frustrating.

___

10. Those are the same things I used to have.

___

C

1. That's not a car I'd like to buy.

___

2. The girl he's going out with only speaks French.

___

3. The beer I like best comes from Germany.

___

4. Is that the package you've been waiting for?

___

5. Do you remember the family we visited last year in Switzerland?

___

6. Is that the family at whose house you spent the night last weekend?

___

7. Where are the tools you repaired the broken window with?

___

8. Is that the plan you spoke against?

___

9. Which university was it that you were talking about?

___

10. The building she went into is where my father works.

___

Part Two

Infinitive Phrases and Constructions

As you know, phrases do not have subjects and verbs, but clauses do. Infinitive phrases utilize an infinitive (without a subject) plus **zu**:

Ich hatte vor **zu kommen.**
I intended/planned to come.

Ich hatte Lust **zu gehen.**
I wanted to go.

Das ist schwer **zu glauben.**
That's hard to believe.

When the infinitive has its own complement, a comma is employed:

Ich hatte Lust**, ins Kino zu gehen.**
I wanted to go to the movies.

Ich hatte vor**, etwas früher zu kommen.**
I intended to arrive a bit earlier.

The infinitive phrase often has its own direct object. The direct object, as well as other complements such as adverbs, prepositional phrases, or indirect objects, will precede **zu** + the infinitive.

Es würde mir nicht gefallen, ***diesen Hosenanzug*** **zu tragen.**
I wouldn't like wearing this pants suit.

Ich hatte die Absicht, ***diese Aufgabe sofort*** **zu erledigen.**
I had the intention of finishing this assignment immediately.

The infinitive phrase may have several complements:

Ich habe versucht, ***heute Nachmittag mit meiner Mutter privat*** **zu sprechen.**
I tried to speak privately with my mother this afternoon.

Punctuation with Infinitive Phrases

Note the use of a comma to separate the infinitive phrase from the main clause when the infinitive phrase contains a complement. As a result of the new spelling reforms of 2005, the use of the comma for infinitive phrases is now optional. This is a contested change, largely due to the fact that the infinitive phrase has long been viewed as something akin to a subordinate clause, and many Germans, German scholars, German authors, and German newspapers continue to employ the comma because it contributes to more precise communication. Since that is, in fact, the general practice, it is followed here.

Functions of Infinitive Phrases

Generally, we think of persons, places, and things as typical subjects and objects in a sentence.

Marlies hat **den Plan** für die Firma entwickelt.
Marlies developed the plan for the company.

Infinitive phrases, on the other hand, name an action/activity or state. They most often serve functionally as the direct object of the entire sentence.

Was hast du versucht? (We're eliciting a direct object.)
What did you try [to do]?

Ich habe versucht ***zu schlafen.*** (Note that there is no comma because the infinitive has no complement.)
I tried to sleep.

Ich habe versucht, **meine Finanzen wieder in Ordnung zu bringen.**
I tried to bring my finances in order again.

They may also serve as the subject, but this is not quite as common. When they do, no comma is used.

Was gefällt dir? (We're eliciting a subject.)
What is pleasing to you? = What pleases you? = What do you like?

Dir zu helfen gefällt mir.
To help you pleases me. = Helping you pleases me. = I like to help you. = It pleases me to help you.

Einen interessanten Roman zu lesen gefällt mir. OR: Es gefällt mir, **einen interessanten Roman zu lesen.**
Reading a good novel pleases me. = I like to read a good novel. = I like reading a good novel.

NOTE: When the infinitive phrase functions as the subject of the sentence *and* occupies "slot 1," a comma is not employed.

What does all of this mean for you in practical terms? It means that you need to expand your definition of subjects and direct objects to include *an entire activity* expressed by an infinitive phrase.

Infinitive Phrases with Separable-Prefix Verbs

If the verb in the infinitive phrase has a separable prefix, **zu** is inserted between the prefix and the verb stem:

Wir haben gewollt, *etwas früher* ***anzukommen.***
We wanted to arrive a bit earlier.

Ich habe versucht, *dieses große Paket* ***aufzuheben.***
I tried to lift this heavy package.

Doris hat lange daran gearbeitet, *ihr Zimmer* ***aufzuräumen.***
Doris worked for a long time on straightening up her room.

Verbs with inseparable prefixes, however, are preceded by **zu**:

Ich habe lange daran gearbeitet, meine Semesterarbeit **zu verbessern.**
I worked a long time on improving my term paper.

Special Infinitive Phrase Constructions

There are several special infinitive constructions, set off from the main clause by a comma, that are introduced by **um**, **ohne**, and **statt/anstatt**:

Um ... zu + Infinitive *in order to*

Ich habe mein Geld gespart, ***um*** *mir ein neues Auto* ***zu kaufen.***
I saved my money [in order] to buy myself a new car.

Um *eine gute Note* ***zu bekommen,*** muss man fleißig lernen.
In order to/To receive a good grade one must study hard.

Ohne ... zu + Infinitive *without*

Maria ist zu uns zu Besuch gekommen, ***ohne*** *ihre Kinder* **mitzubringen.**
Maria came to us for a visit without bringing her children along.

Ohne *darüber* **nachzudenken,** habe ich die Frage beantwortet.
Without thinking about it I answered the question.

Statt/anstatt ... zu + Infinitive *instead of*

Ich bin zu Hause geblieben, ***statt*** *zur Arbeit* ***zu gehen.***
I stayed home instead of going to work.

Anstatt *mit einer Kreditkarte dafür* ***zu zahlen,*** habe ich einen Scheck geschrieben.
Instead of paying for it with a credit card I wrote a check.

When Infinitive Phrases May Not Be Used in German

There are times when infinitive phrases in English may not be rendered as infinitive phrases in German, and these need to be explored in order to avoid Anglicisms.

Dass-Clauses after *wollen* and *möchten*

The modal verbs **wollen** and **möchten** employ **dass**-clauses instead of infinitive phrases to signal that the subject wants, expects, believes, thinks, etc., that *someone else* will do something:

Meine Eltern **wollen, dass** ***ich*** gute Zensuren bekomme.
My parents want me to get good grades.

Karola **möchte, dass** ***du*** sie bald anrufst.
Karola wants you to call her up.

If you live in a neighborhood where people speak German or Yiddish, a Germanic language, or if you've heard Jewish comedians on TV, you've probably heard similar Germanicized sentences in English:

I want *that you [should] eat* more. = I want you to eat more.
Ich **will, dass** ***du*** mehr isst/essen solltest.

You would like *that I [should] do* that now? = You would like me to do that now?
Du **möchtest, dass** ***ich*** das jetzt mache/machen sollte?

We want *that our son should study* medicine. = We want our son to study medicine.
Wir **wollen, dass** ***unser Sohn*** Medizin studiert/ studieren sollte.

When Two Different Subjects Are Mentioned Explicitly

As you have seen, infinitive phrases have no subject, so the verb must take on a neutral verb form (an infinitive) + **zu**:

Wir haben versucht, einige Äpfel **zu kaufen.**
We tried to buy some apples.

Note that the subject of **versuchen** is **wir**, and that the understood subject of **kaufen** is also **wir**, though it is not stated explicitly. (*We tried. We wanted to buy some apples.*) Since a second subject is not mentioned explicitly, the second verb has nothing with which to agree, so an infinitive is used.

When two subjects are mentioned explicitly, an infinitive phrase is not possible in German. Two "doers," or subjects, require two verbs, and each verb must agree with its subject. The first subject will usually be in a main clause, and the subject of the second verb will be in a subordinate clause.

Zeigen *Sie* mir, wie *man* das besser macht.
Show me how to do that better. = Show me how one does that better.

Zeigen *Sie* mir, wie *ich* das besser machen kann.
Show me how to do that better. = Show me how I can do that better.

This is also true if the subjects in both clauses are one and the same:

Zeigen *Sie* mir, wie *Sie* das besser machen.
Show me how to do that better. = Show me how you do that better.

In virtually all cases an interrogative word is employed as the subordinating conjunction:

Show me *how to build* a house. = **Zeigen Sie mir, *wie* man ein Haus baut.**
Tell them *what to do.* = **Sagen Sie ihnen, *was* sie machen sollen.**
Show me *where to find* it. = **Zeigen Sie uns, *wo* wir es finden können.**
Tell me *whom to speak to.* = **Sagen Sie mir, *mit wem* ich sprechen soll.**

Modal verbs may also be part of the subordinate clause when logical meaning dictates their use.

Exercises: Part Two

Theory Review

1. Fill in the blanks with the correct information.

1. By definition, a ______________ consists of at least a subject and a verb.
2. An infinitive phrase does contain a verb form, an infinitive, but the infinitive has no ______________.
3. The infinitive is always preceded by ______________.
4. There may be other ______________ within the infinitival phrase: objects, adverbs, prepositional phrases.
5. Infinitive phrases name an ______________ or ______________.
6. Infinitive phrases may function as the ______________ or ______________ of the sentence.
7. In the sentence **Ich versuche, mein Fahrrad zu reparieren**, the infinitive phrase functions as the ______________.

8. In the sentence **Einen guten Film zu sehen gefällt mir immer**, the infinitive phrase functions as the ______________________ of the sentence.
9. If the verb in the infinitive phrase has a separable prefix, where is **zu** located?

____

10. There are several special infinitive phrase constructions that are introduced by ______________________ (*in order to*), ______________________ (*without*), and ______________________ (*instead of*).
11. Is a comma required to separate the infinitive phrase from the rest of the sentence? __________
12. **Wollen** and **möchten** are often followed by a ______________________ -clause to indicate that the subject wants someone else to do something. (This contrasts with English, which uses infinitive constructions instead.)

Focus on Form [✓]

2. Create sentences from the fragments.

A

1. Anstatt / essen / zu Hause, ... gehen wir lieber in ein Restaurant

____

2. Anstatt / fliegen / nach Wien, ... blieben wir eine Weile länger in München

____

3. Barbara ging weg, ... ohne / geben / mir / ihre Adresse und Telefonnummer

____

4. Bergmanns Filme / sein / schwer / verstehen

____

5. Darf ich Sie darum bitten, ... nehmen / Platz?

____

6. Das / ist / schwer / sagen

____

7. Das / sein / glauben / kaum

____

8. Dieser Wein / sein / kaum / trinken

____

9. Er bat mich, ... helfen / ihm

____

10. Er findet es schwer, ... verstehen / Film

____

B

1. Sie will nicht, ... ich / helfen / ihr

___

2. Er zeigte uns, ... wo / wir / sollen / parken / Wagen

___

3. Erich sagte uns, ... wir / sollen / bleiben / hier

___

4. Es hörte auf ... regnen

___

5. Es ist fast unmöglich, ... bekommen / Karten / jetzt

___

6. Es ist immer nett, ... lesen / Briefe von dir

___

7. Es ist Zeit, ... gehen / nach Hause

___

8. Es ist zu spät, ... gehen / heute Abend / Kino

___

9. Ich ging in die Stadt, ... um / kaufen / schicke Kleider

___

10. Ich habe keine Lust, ... werden / Arzt

___

C

1. Ich werde dir sagen, ... wen / du / sollen / anrufen

___

2. Ich sagte dir, ... du / sollen / warten / auf uns

___

3. Ich will, ... Anna / auch / mitkommen

___

4. Ich wusste nicht, ... was / ich / sollen / sagen

___

5. Kannst du mir sagen, ... wie / man / machen / das?

___

6. Karl arbeitet nachts, ... um / verdienen / mehr Geld

___

7. Oft nimmt er den Wagen, ... ohne / bitten / Vater / darum

____

8. So etwas / sein / eigentlich / erwarten

____

9. Volkswagen / sein / leicht / fahren

____

10. Willst du nicht, ... ich / einladen / Sabine?

____

11. Wir haben vor, ... nach Wien / fahren / nächstes Jahr

____

12. Wir wissen nicht, ... mit wem / wir / sollen / sprechen

____

13. Wissen Sie, ... wohin / sie / müssen / gehen?

____

Focus on Meaning and Form [✓]

3. Knowing when a subordinate clause must be used in German instead of an infinitive phrase. The following sentences contain infinitive phrases in English that may not be rendered as such in German. They will require a subordinate clause instead. Since this will not be obvious from the form of the English sentence, paraphrase the English sentence first, adding modal verbs, if needed, to make the paraphrase work. Some paraphrases will work better with *man* as the subject. Meaning will dictate this.

The common denominator is the fact that the paraphrase will require you to mention the doer of the second-mentioned verb explicitly. Infinitive phrases have no subject, no "doer." That's why a subordinate clause is required instead—subordinate clauses always have an explicit subject.

Examples: Tell me what to write to her.
Paraphrase: *Tell me what I am supposed to write to her.*
→ *Sag mir, was ich ihr schreiben soll.*

Show us how to play the piano.
Paraphrase 1: *Show us how we can play the piano.*
→ *Zeig uns, wie wir Klavier spielen können.* OR:
Paraphrase 2: *Show us how one plays the piano.*
→ *Zeig uns, wie man Klavier spielt.*

1. Can you show us how to make lasagna?

Paraphrase: ____________________________________

____

2. Please explain to them how to fix this engine.

Paraphrase: ____

3. Show me how to correct this mistake.

Paraphrase: ____

4. Show us what to do.

Paraphrase: ____

5. Tell me when to begin.

Paraphrase: ____

6. Tell them where to look for it.

Paraphrase: ____

7. Tell him whom to speak to.

Paraphrase: ____

8. Tell us what to say.

Paraphrase: ____

9. Ask her to come earlier.

Paraphrase: ____

10. I would like them to work a bit harder on it.

Paraphrase: ____

11. She doesn't want you to go out with him.

Paraphrase: ____

12. Toni wants Dieter to buy her a red sweater for her birthday.

Paraphrase: ____________________

____

13. We want you to invite our friends to the party.

Paraphrase: ____________________

____

4. Express the following sentences in German. These will employ infinitive phrases, subordinate clauses, and *dass*-clauses as required. Use informal forms when possible.

A

1. Can you show me how to play the piano?

____

2. He explained to me how to help them.

____

3. He doesn't want me to ask him.

____

4. He often takes the car without asking his father for it.

____

5. He showed us how to do it correctly.

____

6. I didn't know what to say.

____

7. I have no desire to become a politician.

____

8. I told you to disappear.

____

9. I want grandma to visit us soon.

____

10. I want to go out this weekend.

____

B

1. I want you to go out with me this weekend.

2. I went downtown to buy some books.

3. I would like him to order us a bottle of wine.

4. I would like to order a glass of wine.

5. I'll tell you when to begin it.

6. It stopped snowing.

7. It's almost impossible to book (**buchen**) a flight now.

8. It's always nice to hear from you.

9. It's time to go home.

10. It's too late to go shopping.

C

1. Kafka's novellas are hard to understand.

2. Let's go swimming instead of going to the zoo.

3. Lisa doesn't want me to invite Rüdiger.

4. May I ask you not to smoke?

5. Some men find it hard to understand women. And vice-versa!

____

6. Mother told us to stay here.

____

7. She left without giving him back the ring.

____

8. That's hard to believe.

____

9. We didn't know whom to speak to.

____

10. We intend to go to Europe next summer.

____

You Determine the Message and Form

5. Complete the following sentences with an infinitive phrase. Include a complement or two in each phrase.

1. Es ist nicht so schwer, _______________
2. Es ist nicht gesund, _______________
3. Es ist äußerst wichtig, _______________
4. Versuchen Sie das nächste Mal, _______________
5. Es ist leicht, _______________
6. Vergiss nicht, _______________
7. Ich fand es schwer, _______________
8. Ich habe keine Zeit, _______________
9. Es ist nicht sehr nett von dir, _______________
10. Es ist jetzt Zeit, _______________
11. Hast du vor, _______________?
12. Es macht mir keinen Spaß, _______________
13. Es hat plötzlich begonnen, _______________
14. Wir sind bereit, _______________
15. Hast du Lust, _______________?

6. Complete the following with infinitive constructions: *um ... zu, ohne ... zu, (an)statt ... zu* + infinitive.

1. Ich musste lange sparen, ______________________________
2. Sie hat das Zimmer verlassen, ______________________________
3. Ich wollte ins Konzert gehen, ______________________________
4. Der Berater hat mit mir gesprochen, ______________________________
5. Der Chef ist böse. Er ist zur Arbeit gekommen, ______________________________
6. Karl hat uns sein Auto geliehen, ______________________________
7. Er hat seiner Frau eine Kette geschenkt, ______________________________
8. Ich habe versucht, das noch einmal zu machen, ______________________________
9. Wir haben Karten gespielt, ______________________________
10. Er hat mich angerufen, ______________________________

Partnerarbeit

In the following three exercises you will be using relative clauses, infinitive phrases and constructions, and *dass*-clauses to answer questions. Remember that all of these involve an activity, so they will be "verb-focused." Think beyond the usual person-or-thing answer. This is challenging!

7. Answer the following questions and use a relative clause in each answer.

1. Mit welchem Studenten oder welcher Studentin hast du heute geredet?
2. Welche Person hast du neulich kennen gelernt?
3. Wem hast du neulich etwas geliehen?
4. Von wem hast du in letzter Zeit gehört?
5. Wem hast du etwas gekauft, geschenkt oder geschickt?
6. Wer oder was interessiert dich?
7. Worauf hast du dich vorbereitet?
8. Was gefällt dir?
9. Wer ist nicht freundlich zu dir?
10. Auf wen oder was musstest du warten?
11. Womit bist du zufrieden oder unzufrieden?
12. Vor wem oder was hast du Angst?

8. Use infinitive phrases or constructions when answering these questions.

1. Was hast du heute Abend vor?
2. Hast du Lust auf etwas?
3. Was würde dir gefallen oder nicht gefallen?
4. Was hast du neulich versucht?
5. Was hast du neulich vorgehabt?
6. Woran hast du mit Freunden oder Familienmitgliedern gearbeitet?
7. Warum lernst du so fleißig?

8. Warum sparst du dein Geld?
9. Was hast du in letzter Zeit vergessen?
10. Du hast etwas gemacht, aber du hättest etwas anderes tun sollen. Erklär das.

9. Answer these questions with a *dass*-clause.

1. Was wollen deine Eltern von dir?
2. Was willst du von ihnen?
3. Was willst oder möchtest du von deinen Freunden?
4. Was willst oder möchtest du von deinem besten Freund oder deiner besten Freundin?
5. Was willst oder möchtest du von deinen Lehrern?

Chapter 20 Clarifying *da*-Compounds; Extended Adjective Modifiers

Part One

Using Subordinate Clauses and Infinitive Phrases to Clarify a *da*-Compound

Da-compounds normally are used to refer to a noun that has already been mentioned. In some cases, however, especially with idiomatic expressions, they will be used without any reference to an antecedent noun. This is particularly true in formal, written German. In such cases a subordinate clause, an infinitive phrase, or an infinitive phrase construction will follow the **da**-compound and clarify its meaning. In effect, the following clause, phrase, or construction explains what the **da**-compound means. This is closely approximated in English by a "that is" clarification:

Wir müssen uns **darauf** vorbereiten, ***die Prüfung zu machen.***
literal: *We have to prepare ourselves for it, that is, to take the test.*
natural: *We have to prepare [ourselves] to take the test.*

Ich habe lange **darüber** nachgedacht, ***was wir machen sollten.***
literal: *I have thought about it for a long time, that is, what we are supposed to do.*
natural: *I have thought for a long time about what we are supposed to do.*

Luise hat lange **daran** gearbeitet, ***wie man das Problem löst.***
literal: *Louise has worked on it for a long time, that is, how one solves the problem.*
natural: *Louise has worked a long time on solving the problem.*

Ich bin böse **darauf**, ***dass wir am Samstag zur Arbeit gehen müssen.***
literal: *I am angry about it, that is, that we have to go to work on Saturday.*
natural: *I am angry about our having to go to work on Saturday.*

Hans denkt **daran**, ***dass er nächste Woche seine Verwandten in Dresden besucht.***
literal: *Hans is thinking of it, that is, that he will visit his relatives in Dresden next week.*
natural: *Hans is thinking of his visit to his relatives in Dresden next week.*

Wir freuen uns **darüber**, ***nächsten Monat nach Italien reisen zu können***.
literal: *We are happy about it, that is, that we can travel to Italy next month.*
natural: *We're happy about being able to travel to Italy next month.*

Since this construction is absent in English, first try to understand the German sentence on its own literal terms, then find a good way to render it in English more naturally. Often, there are several possible renderings:

Wir müssen uns **darauf** vorbereiten, *die Prüfung zu bestehen.*
We have to prepare [ourselves] to pass the test.
We have to get [ourselves] ready to pass the test.
We have to be preparing [ourselves] for passing the test.

NOTE: In informal, spoken German the **da**-compound is sometimes omitted.

Using an Infinitive Phrase vs. a Subordinate Clause after a *da*-Compound

If the subject of the main clause is considered to be the one acting in the **da**-compound clarification, then an infinitive phrase may be used:

Ich habe mich **darauf** vorbereitet, ***alle Fragen richtig zu beantworten***.
I prepared [myself] to answer all of the questions correctly.

Wir freuen uns **darauf**, ***dich diesen Sommer zu besuchen***.
We're looking forward to visiting you this summer.

Peter hat lange **daran** gearbeitet, ***den Plan für das nächste Semester zu entwickeln***.
Peter worked a long time on developing a plan for the next semester.

If you wish to state the "doer" in the clarification clause explicitly, then an infinitive phrase may no longer be used. Instead a subordinate clause, most often a **dass**-clause, will be required.

Wir freuen uns **darauf**, *dass* ***wir*** *dich diesen Sommer besuchen werden.*
We're looking forward to visiting you this summer.

Ich habe mich **darauf** vorbereitet, *damit* ***ich*** *alle Fragen richtig beantworten könnte.*
I prepared [myself] so [that] I could answer all of the questions correctly.

If the subject of the main clause is not the actor in the **da**-compound clarification, however, that is, if another person is the actor, then the "doer" must be mentioned and a subordinate clause will be required:

Wir freuen uns **darauf**, *dass* ***du*** *uns diesen Sommer besuchst.*
We're looking forward to your visiting us this summer.

Ich bestehe **darauf**, *dass* ***man*** *uns sofort die Rechnung bringt.*
I insist that one bring us the bill immediately.

PUNCTUATION NOTE: Since the infinitive phrase or subordinate clause used to clarify a **da**-compound is considered to lie outside the domain of the main clause, it is set off from the main clause by a comma. The comma is required.

Exercises: Part One

Theory Review

1. Fill in the blanks with the correct information.

1. ______________________________ and ______________________________ are frequently used to clarify or explain the meaning of a **da**-compound mentioned earlier in the sentence.

2. In such cases the **da**-compound is typically part of an ______________________ expression.

Focus on Meaning [✓]

2. Fill in the blanks with the correct *da*-compound.

1. Wir haben mit ihr ______________________ gesprochen, dass sie ihr Geld sparen sollte.

2. Vati ist böse ______________________, dass er sein Scheckbuch nicht finden kann.

3. Mutti ist unzufrieden ______________________, dass ich das Geschirr nicht gespült habe.

4. Wir möchten euch ______________________ gratulieren, dass ihr ganz gute Noten bekommen habt.

5. Der Film hat ______________________ gehandelt, dass Colonel Mustard Miss Scarlet mit einem Messer im Weinkeller ermordet hat.

6. Warum bist du so begeistert ______________________, dass wir morgen eine Prüfung haben? Bist du verrückt?

7. Ich möchte meine Eltern ______________________ bitten, dass sie mir etwas Geld schicken.

8. Wir sollten euch ______________________ danken, dass ihr so viel Zeit für uns hatten.

9. Wir haben lange ______________________ gewartet, eine Erklärung der Sache zu bekommen.

10. Wir sind besonders stolz ______________________, dass du mit deiner neuen Karriere angefangen hast.

11. Mein Bruder ist verrückt ______________________, dass der Weihnachtsmann bald kommt.

12. Wir müssen noch weiter ______________________ arbeiten, um unser Ziel rechtzeitig zu erreichen.

13. Wir waren ______________________ sehr begeistert, dass du uns in Europa besuchen wolltest.

14. Wir haben uns ______________________ kaputt gelacht, als du aus dem Ruderboot hinausgefallen bist.

15. Ich werde glücklich ______________________ sein, wenn das Semester zu Ende ist.

You Determine the Form

3. Express the following sentences in German, using a logical subordinate clause or infinitive phrase that clarifies the meaning of the *da*-compound.

1. I talked with my parents about studying in Germany or Austria.

____

2. I talked with my parents about your spending the night here.

____

3. She's angry about having to do her homework.

____

4. She's angry about her Dad not giving her the car.

____

5. Mother is happy about having a new car.

____

6. Mother is happy about my buying her a new car.

____

7. They're not too excited about working this summer.

____

8. They're not too excited about your working this summer with them.

____

9. We have to wait to go outside and play soccer.

____

10. We had to wait for Hans to bring the soccer ball.

____

You Determine the Message and Form

4. Fill in the blanks with a logical clarification.

A

1. Ich habe mit meinen Freunden *davon* gesprochen,
____
2. Ich bin ganz böse *darauf,*
____
3. Mein Vater ist sehr unzufrieden *damit,*
____
4. Ich möchte Ihnen *dazu* gratulieren,
____
5. Dieser Roman handelt *davon,*
____
6. Ich bin nicht so begeistert *davon,*
____
7. Ich möchte meine Eltern *darum* bitten,
____
8. Ich muss meine Eltern *dafür* danken,
____
9. Ich habe *darauf* geantwortet,
____
10. Ich musste *darauf* warten,
____

B

1. Ich bin besonders stolz *darauf,*
____
2. Meine Freunde sind verrückt *darauf,*
____
3. Ich muss noch weiter *daran* arbeiten,
____
4. Ich habe oft *daran* gedacht,
____
5. Ich musste immer *darüber* lachen,
____
6. Mein Freund/Meine Freundin interessiert sich *dafür,*
____
7. Ich soll froh/glücklich *darüber* sein,
____

Part Two

Extended Adjective Modifiers: A Stylistic Alternative to Relative Clauses

In English we sometimes encounter extended adjective modifiers: present or past participles with their own adverbial modifiers that together modify a noun. This results in a literary/historical tone that only rarely occurs in conversational English:

The quick-moving and onward-rushing mob attacked the city gates.
The already severely mauled infantry unit continued to fight doggedly.

German makes more frequent use of extended adjective modifiers, especially in news accounts, both written and spoken. Extended adjective modifiers in German are adjectival constructions that "spread out" according to the number of pieces of information they contain, and they often contain more bits of information than in English. They will be easier to understand and become comfortable with if you consider them to be a journalistic alternative, that is, a stylistic alternative, to a relative clause.

Key Elements of Extended Adjective Modifiers

In most cases the basic ingredients of the extended adjective modifier are 1) an article, 2) a participial adjective, and 3) a noun. Anything in addition to these elements serves as an "extender."

The Participle

The participle is the main adjectival part of the construction and will require a primary or secondary case ending depending on the article used with it. Depending on meaning you wish to convey, you may need a present or past participle. Past participles are more commonly encountered.

past participle:	Ich habe die **zerbrochenen** Gläser ersetzt. *I replaced the broken glasses.*
present participle:	Es war der Geruch eines **verfaulenden** Tieres. *It was the odor of a rotting animal.*

Adverbial Extenders

The participial adjective is "extended" by adding adverbs (remember, adverbs modify adjectives!) and/or prepositional phrases (remember, prepositional phrases generally function adverbially). These "extenders" are positioned between the article and the participle.

To make this more concrete, consider the article and noun to be like the pieces of bread of a gourmet sandwich. The participle and any other extenders are analogous to the ingredients found between the pieces of bread. One can add many ingredients to enhance the flavor of the sandwich.

past participle: Ich habe **die *bei der wilden Party* zerbrochenen Gläser** ersetzt.
I replaced [the] glasses broken at the wild party.

present participle: Es war der Geruch **eines *in der heißen Sonne* verfaulenden Tieres.**
It was the odor of an animal rotting in the hot sun.

The Transformation of a Relative Clause Modifier into an Extended Adjective Modifier

Since extended adjective modifiers are usually substitutes for relative clauses, let's start with a basic sentence and then modify a noun phrase with a relative clause:

Die Forscher werden bald eine Lösung finden.
The researchers will find a solution soon.

Die Forscher, **die schon jahrelang an diesem Projekt arbeiten**, werden bald eine Lösung finden.
The researchers who have been working on this project for many years will find a solution soon.

Now let's take the information contained in the relative clause in the example sentence above and, through the magic of transformational grammar, turn it into an extended adjective modifier construction.

Die *schon jahrelang an diesem Projekt arbeitenden* Forscher werden bald eine Lösung finden.

If you didn't follow the sleight of hand here, let's do a couple of instant replays in slow motion:

Die *arbeitenden* Forscher werden bald eine Lösung finden.
Die *an diesem Projekt arbeitenden* Forscher werden bald eine Lösung finden.
Die *schon jahrelang an diesem Projekt arbeitenden* Forscher werden bald eine Lösung finden.

Let's try another sentence:

Die Studenten werden die Klausur bestehen.
The students will pass the test.

Let's modify the noun phrase with a relative clause:

Die Studenten, **die sich täglich auf den Unterricht gut vorbereiten**, werden die Klausur bestehen.
The students who prepare [themselves] well every day for the lesson will pass the test.

Now let's say the same thing with an extended adjective modifier:

Die *sich täglich auf den Unterricht gut vorbereitenden* Studenten werden die Klausur bestehen.

Now let's deconstruct it and then gradually reconstruct it:

Die *sich vorbereitenden* Studenten werden die Klausur bestehen.
Die *sich gut vorbereitenden* Studenten werden die Klausur bestehen.
Die *sich auf den Unterricht gut vorbereitenden* Studenten werden die Klausur bestehen.
Die *sich täglich auf den Unterricht gut vorbereitenden* Studenten werden die Klausur bestehen.

A practical goal is to be able to comprehend this construction when you encounter it, namely, in a newspaper or magazine article, during a television news broadcast, or in a formal speech or presentation. You may also discover it in German poetry or descriptive writing. It is encountered very infrequently in everyday conversation, however.

Exercises: Part Two

Theory Review

1. Fill in the blanks with the correct information.

1. ______________________ modifiers are frequently used in formal German instead of a relative clause.
2. Such a modifier is used with a noun and involves at least an ______________________ (or **der-** or **ein**-word) and a ______________________.
3. Since this last element functions adjectivally, it will display a(n) ______________________.
4. The participle may be a ______________________ or ______________________ participle, depending on meaning.
5. The participle (a verbal adjective) may be modified by ______________________ or ______________________ phrases, thus "extending" the length of the overall phrase. There may be more than one adverbial modifier/extender.
6. Extended adjective modifiers are rather rare in conversation but are common in formal German. You would expect to see them in ______________________ or hear them during a ______________________.
7. Put another way, your main goal is to be able to ________________ them.

Focus on Meaning

2. Express the following in good English.

1. Wir wollen *ein* von diesem Architekten *restauriertes Haus* kaufen.

   ____

2. Hast du *das* von einem blinden Mädchen *gezeichnete Bild* gesehen?

   ____

3. *Die* letzte Woche von Florida *abgeschossene Rakete* ist heute auf dem Mond gelandet.

   ____

4. *Die* von dieser Firma in China *hergestellten Waren* sind ziemlich billig aber von guter Qualität.

   ____

5. Die englischen Matrosen *des* von einem U-Boot *versenkten Öltankers* sind sicher in Halifax angekommen.

   ____

Focus on Meaning and Form

3. Paraphrasing. Paraphrase the following sentences with extended adjective modifiers that replace the italicized relative clauses. If you can construct these accurately, you certainly will have no difficulties comprehending them when you read or hear them.

1. Der Manager, *der immer fleißig arbeitet,* wird eines Tages Chef sein.

   ____

2. Die Studenten, *die ständig fleißig lernen,* verdienen meistens die besten Noten.

   ____

3. Das Auto, *das mit dickem Eis und Schnee bedeckt war,* wollte nicht leicht anspringen.

   ____

4. Die Häuser, *die man nicht nur mit Holz, sondern auch mit Stein gebaut haben,* sind teurer.

   ____

5. Die Personen, *die wegen der großen Explosion verwundet sind,* bleiben bis jetzt unbekannt.

   ____

6. Die Polizei hat das Auto in Bielefeld gefunden, *das drei junge Männer gestern gestohlen hatten.*

   ____

Partnerarbeit

4. When answering the following questions, be sure to include a *da*-compound and an explanatory *dass*-clause.

1. Worüber hast du mit deinen Eltern gesprochen?
2. Worauf bist du böse?
3. Womit bist du zufrieden oder unzufrieden?
4. Wozu sollst du jemandem gratulieren?
5. Wovon handelt dein Lieblingsfilm oder Lieblingsroman?
6. Wovon bist du im Moment begeistert?
7. Worum willst du deine Eltern oder Freunde bitten?
8. Wofür sollst du jemandem danken?
9. Worauf bist du stolz?
10. Woran sollst du jetzt oder bald arbeiten?
11. Worüber hast du gelacht?
12. Worüber bist du glücklich?

Phase IV Advanced Work with Verbs

Chapter 21 Present Subjunctive II

Part One

The Subjunctive Mood/Mode

The subjunctive is a *mood*, a term that is sometimes problematic for some students. It has nothing to do with a state of mind or emotional feelings. The word *mood* is derived from the Latin **modus**, meaning *way*, *manner*, or *mode*. It has to do with the way in which one is communicating. For the sake of greater clarity, *mode* will be used instead of *mood*.

There are three modes in German: the *indicative*, the *subjunctive*, and the *imperative*. The imperative mode is the mode used when giving commands, which you have reviewed previously. The indicative mode is used to talk about actions and states that are real, that is, that are not in doubt. The vast majority of sentences and verb forms reviewed thus far have been in the indicative mode. The subjunctive mode, on the other hand, is used to talk about actions and states that are not real. For purposes of contrasting modes, we will focus only on the indicative and subjunctive modes to see how they differ in form and usage.

Indicative Mode

Indicative verb forms are used to discuss *reality*, that is, *factual* occurrences, occurrences the speaker believes to be true, real, likely, or possible. There are six tenses, all of which you have reviewed thus far: present, simple past, present perfect, past perfect, future, and future perfect. Review Chapters 2–4 if needed.

Subjunctive Mode

Subjunctive verb forms are used to discuss *non-reality*, that is, events that are:

1. contrary-to-fact (= not real)
2. unlikely or doubtful
3. purely speculative, theoretical, hypothetical, or conjectural (= not yet real)
4. wishful (one wishes for things that are not real or not yet realized)

Two Tenses of the Subjunctive

There are only *two* subjunctive *tenses:* present and past. In English, the present subjunctive forms look exactly like the simple past indicative, and the past subjunctive looks just like the past perfect indicative. This is, as you might expect and may have noticed, a cause of great confusion to many native speakers of English who quite often use indicative forms instead of subjunctive ones and also present subjunctive forms when past subjunctive forms are called for. The sentences below will illustrate this.

Here are some poor present- and past-tense subjunctive sentences and their corrections:

present:	poor:	If that *was* true, I'd know about it.
	good:	If that **were** true, I'd know about it.
past:	poor:	If he *stopped* at the stop sign, he wouldn't have hit the other car.
	good:	If he **had stopped** at the stop sign, he wouldn't have hit the other car.

Since learning the present subjunctive in German will be futile if accurate use of the present subjunctive in English is absent or not understood, we will first take a side trip to some exercises to review the present subjunctive in English.

Exercises: Part One

Theory Review

1. Fill in the blanks with the correct information.

1. The subjunctive, like the indicative and imperative, is a ____________.
2. A more "user-friendly" synonym for this is ____________.
3. The indicative (mood/mode) is used to refer to actions and states that are ____________.
4. The subjunctive (mood/mode) is used to refer to actions and states that are ____________.
5. The indicative has ____________ tenses.
6. The subjunctive has only ____________ tenses.
7. These subjunctive tenses are the ____________ and ____________.
8. In English, present subjunctive verb forms are identical to the ____________ indicative and the past subjunctive forms are identical to the ____________ ____________ indicative. This is perhaps the chief reason why there is confusion about the forms of the subjunctive.

Focus on Meaning [✓]

2. Present subjunctive in English. Change the following statements about reality in the present indicative to conjectural ones by converting the verb forms to the present subjunctive.

1. If I have time, I'll go with you.

   ____

2. If you spend all your money, you'll have nothing left.

   ____

3. If you have nothing left, you can't go to the movies with us.

   ____

4. If you can't go to the movies with us, you will miss seeing the film.

   ____

5. If you miss the film, I won't tell you anything about it.

   ____

6. If I buy that, my wife will be very angry with me.

   ____

7. If you lose your credit cards, you'll have big problems.

   ____

8. If I don't know the answer, I will not be able to do it.

   ____

9. If I find what I'm looking for, I'll be happy.

   ____

10. If I am depressed, I tend to sleep a lot.

   ____

Part Two

The Subjunctive in German

In German, things are a bit less confusing because the subjunctive forms are more distinctive than in English, that is, more unlike the indicative forms. There's less chance of using the indicative when you should use the subjunctive, and there's less chance of using the wrong subjunctive tense. However, if your control of the subjunctive in English is inconsistent, your German may tend to be inaccurate unless you really work at monitoring your own language output.

General and Special Subjunctives

In German, there are two sets of subjunctive forms: the *general subjunctive,* known as subjunctive II, and the *special subjunctive,* known as subjunctive I. They are used for different purposes. In this chapter we will focus exclusively on the more common general subjunctive (subjunctive II) and its main applications. The special subjunctive (subjunctive I) will be treated in Chapter 23.

Demystifying the Terms "Subjunctive II" and "Subjunctive I"

Many students are befuddled by the terms *subjunctive I* and *subjunctive II* and are equally confused about why subjunctive II is usually learned before subjunctive I, and perhaps about why the two subjunctives are reviewed in that sequence in this book as well. The explanation is tied to the principal parts of verbs. As you know, there are three principal parts: the infinitive, the simple past form, and the past participle:

sagen, sagte, gesagt	mitkommen, kam ... mit, *ist* mitgekommen
arbeiten, arbeitete, gearbeitet	haben, hatte, gehabt
gehen, ging, *ist* gegangen	sein, war, *ist* gewesen

To form the general subjunctive, or subjunctive II, one goes to the *second* principal part of the verb to generate the subjunctive forms. To form the special subjunctive, or subjunctive I, one goes to the *first* principal part of the verb, the infinitive, to generate forms. The general subjunctive is used much more frequently than the special subjunctive, so it is normally taught (and reviewed) first. Mystery solved.

The standard verb endings below are used for both subjunctive I and II in German:

Present Subjunctive Endings

ich:	**-e**	wir:	**-en**		
du:	**-est**	ihr:	**-et**	Sie:	**-en**
er/sie/es:	**-e**	sie:	**-en**		

General Subjunctive/Subjunctive II

The general subjunctive is used primarily to discuss unreal, doubtful, unlikely, hypothetical, and speculative conditions *and* their not-real results. We lump all of this into the category "contrary-to-fact." Most contrary-to-fact sentences will fall into the **wenn-dann** type with which you are already quite familiar: **Wenn ich Zeit hätte, würde ich mitkommen.**

There are two ways to form the present subjunctive in German, and two ways to form the past subjunctive. We'll call these two sets "pure forms" and "alternate forms."

Present Subjunctive II of Regular Verbs: "Pure" Forms

The pure form of the present subjunctive depends on whether the verb is regular or irregular. If the verb is regular, the present subjunctive forms are *identical to the simple past forms.* This is just like English. This means that **sagte** could be simple past indicative *or* present subjunctive, depending on how it is used in a sentence.

indicative (reality):

Ich **fragte** Irene, was sie gemacht hatte.
*I **asked** Irene what she had done.* (That I asked her is *factual,* hence, *indicative.*)

subjunctive (speculative):

Wenn ich Irene **fragte**, [dann] würde sie mir die Wahrheit sagen.
*If I **asked** Irene, [then] she would tell me the truth.* (I didn't ask her = not real.)

Present Subjunctive II Forms of a Regular Verb

sagen, *sagte,* gesagt

ich **sagte**	wir **sagten**	
du **sagtest**	ihr **sagtet**	Sie **sagten**
er/sie/es **sagte**	sie **sagten**	

Present Subjunctive II of Irregular Verbs: "Pure" Forms

If the verb is irregular, the subjunctive form is arrived at differently:

1. Start with the second principal part of the verb.
2. Add an umlaut, if possible, to the stem vowel.
3. Add the appropriate subjunctive ending. Voilà!

Examples:

	step 1	*step 2*	*step 3*
gehen:	ging	ging	**ginge**
rufen:	rief	rief	**riefe**
kommen:	kam	käm	**käme**
sprechen:	sprach	spräch	**spräche**
tun:	tat	tät	**täte**
fliegen:	flog	flög	**flöge**
haben:	hatte	hätte	**hätte**
sein:	war	wär	**wäre**
werden:	wurde	würde	**würde**

You can see that these subjunctive forms (step 3 above) look and sound different from simple past forms (step 1), so there should never be any confusion.

Present Subjunctive II Forms of Typical Irregular Verbs

gehen, *ging*, ist gegangen

ich **ginge**	wir **gingen**	
du **gingest**	ihr **ginget**	Sie **gingen**
er/sie/es **ginge**	sie **gingen**	

bleiben, *blieb*, ist geblieben

ich **bliebe**	wir **blieben**	
du **bliebest**	ihr **bliebet**	Sie **blieben**
er/sie/es **bliebe**	sie **blieben**	

kommen, *kam*, ist gekommen

ich **käme**	wir **kämen**	
du **kämest**	ihr **kämet**	Sie **kämen**
er/sie/es **käme**	sie **kämen**	

sprechen, *sprach*, gesprochen

ich **spräche**	wir **sprächen**	
du **sprächest**	ihr **sprächet**	Sie **sprächen**
er/sie/es **spräche**	sie **sprächen**	

nehmen, *nahm*, genommen

ich **nähme**	wir **nähmen**	
du **nähmest**	ihr **nähmet**	Sie **nähmen**
er/sie/es **nähme**	sie **nähmen**	

ziehen, *zog*, gezogen

ich **zöge**	wir **zögen**	
du **zögest**	ihr **zöget**	Sie **zögen**
er/sie/es **zöge**	sie **zögen**	

fahren, *fuhr*, ist gefahren

ich **führe**	wir **führen**	
du **führest**	ihr **führet**	Sie **führen**
er/sie/es **führe**	sie **führen**	

Alternate Form of the Present Subjunctive II: *würde* + Infinitive

You may use a form of **würde** and an infinitive as a replacement for a pure form, but this is extremely common in spoken German, less so in formal, written German.

"pure" forms (formal)		*alternate forms (colloquial)*
Wenn ich dich **fragte**, ...	=	Wenn ich dich **fragen würde**, ...
Wenn du es mir **sagtest**, ...	=	Wenn du es mir **sagen würdest**, ...
Wenn er dich **anriefe**, ...	=	Wenn er dich **anrufen würde**, ...
Wenn wir nach Rom **führen**, ...	=	Wenn wir nach Rom **fahren würden**, ...
Wenn ihr nicht **mitkämet**, ...	=	Wenn ihr nicht **mitkommen würdet**, ...
Wenn sie nicht hier **wären**, ...	=	Wenn sie nicht hier **sein würden**, ...
Wenn ich mehr Geld **hätte**, ...	=	Wenn ich mehr Geld **haben würde**, ...
Wenn ich krank **würde**, ...	=	Wenn ich krank **werden würde**, ...

NOTE: English has an additional alternate form: *If I were to do (= did) that, you would know.* German does not employ a parallel construction.

The *würde*-Construction with *haben, sein,* and *werden*

Generally, the **würde**-construction is frowned upon when used with **haben**, **sein**, or **werden**, especially in formal German. It definitely is used in colloquial German with these verbs, however.

colloquial:	Wenn ich mehr Geld **haben würde**, könnte ich das kaufen.
more formal:	Wenn ich mehr Geld **hätte**, könnte ich das kaufen.
	If I ***had*** *more money, I could buy that.*
colloquial:	Wenn du nicht so isoliert **sein würdest**, **würdest** du mehr Freunde **haben.**
more formal:	Wenn du nicht so isoliert **wärest**, **hättest** du mehr Freunde.
	If you ***weren't*** *so isolated, you* ***would have*** *more friends.*
colloquial:	Es könnte vielleicht schneien, wenn es kälter **werden würde**.
more formal:	Es könnte vielleicht schneien, wenn es kälter **würde**.
	It could perhaps snow, if it ***got*** *colder.*

The *würde*-Construction in *wenn*- and *dann*-Clauses

In the colloquial sentence below, you see back-to-back **würde**-constructions. This sounds rather repetitive and is viewed as stylistically inferior, so in formal German the **würde**-construction is usually avoided in a **wenn**-clause. As you might expect, in colloquial German this is less of an issue.

colloquial:	Wenn ich den Brief heute schreiben **würde**, **würdest** du ihn in drei Tagen bekommen.
formal:	Wenn ich den Brief heute **schriebe**, **würdest** du ihn in drei Tagen **bekommen**.
	If I ***would write/wrote*** *the letter today,* ***you would*** *receive it in three days.*

In English we also tend to avoid the *would*-construction in an *if*-clause in formal writing:

colloquial:	If I **would write** the letter today, you would receive it in three days.
formal:	If I **wrote** the letter today, you would receive it in three days.

The alternate form (**würde**-construction) is normal and usually expected in the **dann**-clause:

Wenn ich den Brief schriebe, [dann] **würdest** du ihn in drei Tagen **bekommen**.
If I wrote the letter, [then] you ***would receive*** *it in three days.*

Wenn ich mehr Geld hätte, [dann] **würde** ich mit dir ins Kino **gehen**.
If I had more money, [then] I ***would go*** *with you to the movies.*

Mixed Verbs in the Present Subjunctive

The present subjunctive for mixed verbs is a bit different. Some of these forms are common, others are not.

common:	*uncommon, occur rarely:*
denken → **dächte**	brennen → **brennte** → **brennen würde**
bringen → **brächte**	kennen → **kennte** → **kennen würde**
wissen → **wüsste**	nennen → **nennte** → **nennen würde**
	rennen → **rennte** → **rennen würde**

For the uncommon forms, use the alternate forms (**würde** + infinitive) instead in spoken German.

Modal Verbs in the Present Subjunctive

The **würde**-construction is not used with modal verbs. Always use the pure subjunctive form of a modal verb. Note these pure present subjunctive forms:

können → **könnte** dürfen → **dürfte** wollen → **wollte**
müssen → **müsste** mögen → **möchte** sollen → **sollte**

Note how the German subjunctive may be rendered in English:

Ich könnte das richtig reparieren.
I could fix that properly.
I would be able to fix that right.
I would have the ability to fix that right.
I would know how to fix that right.

Wir müssten das zuerst erledigen.
We would have to finish that first.
We would need to finish that first.

Du dürftest nicht mit uns ausgehen.
You would not be permitted/allowed to go out with us.
You might not be permitted/allowed to go out with us.

Ich möchte ein Glas Wein bestellen.
I would like to order a glass of wine.

Wenn ich das wollte, ...
If I wanted to do that, . . .
If I wished to do that, . . .
If I had the desire to do that, . . .

Wenn ich das machen sollte, ...
If I were supposed to do that, . . .
If I were obliged/obligated to do that, . . .
If I should do that, . . .

NOTE: The English *should* is a subjunctive form and is properly represented in German by the subjunctive form **sollte**, not the indicative form **soll** (= *is* supposed to [factual]).

In the subjunctive as well as the indicative, an infinitive of the main verb is located at the end of the clause:

Könntest du das für mich jetzt **machen**, bitte?
Could *you* ***do*** *that for me now, please?*

Sollten wir das für morgen **erledigen**?
Should *we* ***finish*** *that for tomorrow?*

Subjunctive Forms That Are Generally Avoided

A number of verbs form their subjunctives in somewhat unexpected ways, that is, with an unexpected vowel shift.

Use the **würde**-construction for these verbs instead, since their **ö** and **ü** vowels sound stilted to some native speakers.

These are a few examples:

helfen → **hülfe** (instead of the logical **hälfe**)
sterben → **stürbe** (instead of the logical **stärbe**)
verlieren → **verlöre**
fliegen → **flöge**

Exercises: Part Two

Theory Review

1. Fill in the blanks with the correct information.

1. The general subjunctive, the focus of this chapter, is also known as subjunctive ____________.
2. This is because the forms of this subjunctive are derived from the ______________________ principal part of the verb.
3. The general subjunctive is used to discuss unreal actions or states: non-reality, doubtful conditions, unlikely events, and speculative or hypothetical situations. These are lumped together under the broad term " ______________________-to- ______________________."
4. There are two forms of the present subjunctive. The "pure" form of the present subjunctive consists of ______________________ verb form. The alternate form consists of ______________________.
5. If the verb is a regular verb (has a stable stem), the present subjunctive verb form will be ______________________ to the second principal part.
6. If the verb is an irregular verb (has stem changes), the present subjunctive verb form will be a modification of the ______________________ principal part.
7. This modification is normally the addition of an ______________________, if possible, followed by the correct subjunctive ending.
8. The "pure" form has an alternate form consisting of a form of ______________________ + an infinitive.
9. This corresponds to the ______________________ construction in English.
10. This alternate form is a rather common substitute in ______________________ German for the "pure" subjunctive forms.
11. It would generally be avoided in ______________________ German, however.
12. In more formal German, the **würde**-construction would be avoided with these verbs: ______________________, ______________________, and ______________________.
13. The **würde**-construction is also not used with ______________________ verbs.
14. For stylistic reasons, the alternate form is frowned upon in formal German, as well as in English, in ______________________/ ______________________ clauses.
15. The **würde**-construction is preferred, however, when the "pure" form of the subjunctive is especially ______________________ (= unusual and awkward-sounding).

Focus on Form [✓]

2. For each of the following verbs, provide the second principal part of the verb (the simple past indicative form) and then the "pure," one-word present subjunctive form. Remember: They are distinctive for irregular verbs.

	simple past	*present subjunctive*
1. sprechen	*sprach*	*spräche*
2. schreiben		
3. gehen		
4. sagen		
5. fahren		
6. geben		
7. warten		
8. finden		
9. kommen		
10. laufen		
11. tun		
12. denken		
13. ziehen		
14. arbeiten		
15. sein		
16. haben		
17. werden		
18. fragen		
19. können		
20. müssen		
21. dürfen		
22. sollen		
23. mögen		

3. Write the present-tense subjunctive II (general subjunctive) forms that are the equivalent of the following.

1. würde sprechen = ____________________
2. würde schreiben = ____________________
3. würde gehen = ____________________
4. würde fahren = ____________________
5. würde geben = ____________________
6. würde warten = ____________________
7. würde kommen = ____________________
8. würde tun = ____________________
9. würde denken = ____________________
10. würde ziehen = ____________________
11. würde machen = ____________________
12. würde lesen = ____________________
13. würde sein = ____________________
14. würde haben = ____________________
15. würde werden = ____________________
16. würde können (*not used*) = ____________________
17. würde müssen (*not used*) = ____________________
18. würde dürfen (*not used*) = ____________________
19. würde sollen (*not used*) = ____________________
20. würde mögen (*not used*) = ____________________

Focus on Form (for in-class review)

4. Change the following sentences from a colloquial tone to a more formal one by replacing the *würde*-construction in the *wenn*-clause with a pure form (simple form).

1. Wenn er *kommen würde,* würden wir ihn herzlich begrüßen.

   ____

2. Wenn Ingrid einfacher *leben würde,* wäre sie reich.

   ____

3. Wenn es nicht *regnen würde,* könnten wir spazieren gehen.

____

4. Wenn du mich um Hilfe *bitten würdest,* würde ich dir helfen.

____

5. Wenn er mich *einladen würde,* würde ich auf die Party gehen.

____

6. Wenn sie weniger Fehler *machen würden,* würden sie gute Noten bekommen.

____

7. Wenn ich Inge den Brief heute *schreiben würde,* würde sie ihn in zwei Tagen bekommen.

____

8. Wenn du das so *tun würdest,* hättest du bestimmt große Schwierigkeiten.

____

9. Wenn wir länger *schlafen würden,* würden wir den Zug verpassen.

____

10. Wenn wir unser Geld *sparen würden,* hätten wir vielleicht genug für ein neues Auto.

____

Focus on Meaning

5. Fill in the blanks with a logical indicative or subjunctive present-tense verb form.

1. Wenn ich mehr Zeit ____________, würde ich mit dir einkaufen gehen.
2. ____________ wir mehr Geld, so könnten wir uns einen neuen Fernseher leisten.
3. Wenn ich noch zwei Seiten ____________, habe ich genug für das Referat.
4. Vorsicht! Wenn du das Maria ____________, müsstest du dich bei ihr entschuldigen.
5. Wenn ich an deiner Stelle ____________, würde ich das nicht tun.
6. Wenn du das nicht machen ____________, könntest du mit uns ins Konzert gehen.
7. Wenn es nicht bald ____________, werden alle Planzen und Blumen sterben.
8. Wenn er mich ____________, würde ich ihm nicht antworten.
9. Wenn Petra das ____________, könnte ich ihr nicht vergeben.
10. Wenn wir noch länger auf Dietrich warten ____________, werden wir den Zug verpassen.
11. Wenn ich das ____________, würde ich niemandem etwas davon sagen.
12. Wenn du das ____________, hättest du Unrecht.
13. Wenn ich schneller ____________, wäre ich schon fertig mit diesem Roman.
14. Ich könnte den Lehrer besser verstehen, wenn er nicht so schnell ____________.
15. Wenn meine Mutter mich ____________, würde ich ihr alles davon erzählen.

Part Three

Conditional Sentences: Real and Contrary-to-Fact

Wenn ..., dann ... Sentences

Conditional sentences consist of a condition—expressed by a **wenn**-clause—and a result, expressed by a **dann**-clause. The condition gives rise, logically, to the result. Real conditions lead to real results; hypothetical conditions can lead only to hypothetical results.

real:	Wenn ich zehn Dollar **habe**, [dann/so] **werde** ich mit dir ins Kino **gehen**. *If I **have** ten dollars, [then] I **will go** with you to the movies.*
hypothetical:	Wenn ich zehn Dollar **hätte**, [dann/so] **würde** ich mit dir ins Kino **gehen**. *If I **had** ten dollars, [then] I **would go** with you to the movies.*

Stylistic Concerns with *Wenn ..., dann ...* Sentences

Normally, conditional sentences begin with the **wenn**-clause:

Wenn ich zehn Dollar hätte, [dann/so] könnte ich mit dir ins Kino gehen.
If I had ten dollars, [then] I could go with you to the movies.

You may omit the conjunction **wenn**, but note the stylistic result: The verb must then begin the clause, and **dann** or **so** must be used:

Hätte ich zehn Dollar, dann/so könnte ich mit dir ins Kino gehen.
Had I ten dollars, [then] I could go with you to the movies.

In English the *would*-construction is frowned upon in an *if*-clause. Similarly, the **würde**-construction is frowned upon stylistically in **wenn**-clauses in formal German. The reason for this is that back-to-back **würde** forms are not desirable. Nonetheless, they are fairly common in colloquial German:

colloquial:	Wenn ich mein Geld jetzt **sparen würde, würde** ich genug Geld für ein neues Auto **haben**.
formal:	Wenn ich mein Geld jetzt **sparte, würde** ich bald genug Geld für ein neues Auto **haben**. *If I **saved** my money now, I **would have** enough for a new car soon.*

You may begin with the **dann**-clause, in which case **dann** or **so** are not used:

Ich könnte mit dir ins Kino gehen, wenn ich zehn Dollar hätte.
***I could go with you to the movies**, if I had ten dollars.*

Hypothetical Questions with *wenn*-Clauses

Questions may be formed in conjunction with **wenn**-clauses:

Was würdest du machen, wenn du im Lotto gewinnen würdest?
***What would you do** if you won the lottery?*

Dann-Clauses without *wenn*-Clauses

A result clause can stand alone, simply because it is a main clause. A **wenn**-clause is often understood, though not stated explicitly:

Ich würde nichts sagen [wenn ich an deiner Stelle wäre].
I wouldn't say a thing [if I were you].

Exercises: Part Three

Theory Review

1. Fill in the blanks with the correct information.

1. Conditional sentences consist of two parts, the ______________________ and the ______________________ arising from it.
2. In English, the condition clause normally begins with ______________________, and the result clause often begins with ______________________.
3. In German, the condition clause normally begins with ______________________, and the result clause often begins with ______________________.
4. Real conditions yield ______________________ results.
5. When discussing real conditions and results, the ______________________ mood/mode is used.
6. Unreal conditions yield ______________________ results.
7. When discussing unreal conditions and results, the ______________________ mood/mode is used instead.

Focus on Form [✓]

2. Change each of the following factual scenarios into one that is contrary-to-fact by using the subjunctive in *wenn ... , dann ...* sentences, as demonstrated in sentence 1.

1. Ich kann das nicht machen, also werde ich es nicht versuchen.

   Wenn ich das machen könnte, würde ich es versuchen.
2. Ich darf nicht ausgehen, also muss ich zu Hause bleiben.

   ____
3. Ich soll meine Hausaufgaben machen, also darf ich nicht ins Kino gehen.

   ____
4. Ich muss meinem Vater helfen, also kann ich dir nicht helfen.

   ____
5. Ich will das nicht machen, also werde ich es nicht machen.

   ____

6. Ich kann es nicht machen und werde es nicht machen.

___

7. Ich muss alles aufräumen. Ich muss [sonst] den ganzen Tag zu Hause bleiben.

___

8. Ich soll zu Hause bleiben. Ich darf nicht mit euch ins Museum gehen.

___

Focus on Meaning and Form

3. Generate logical result clauses for the real and hypothetical conditions given.

1. Wenn ich mehr Zeit habe, ___

   Wenn ich mehr Zeit hätte, ___

2. Wenn du dein Geld ausgibst, ___

   Wenn du dein Geld ausgäbest, ___

3. Wenn deine Hausaufgaben nicht fertig sind, ___

   Wenn deine Hausaufgaben fertig wären, ___

4. Wenn du nicht schlafen gehst, ___

   Wenn du länger schliefest, ___

5. Wenn ich das nicht kaufe, ___

   Wenn ich das nicht kaufte, ___

6. Wenn ich später nicht zu Hause bin, ___

   Wenn ich später nicht zu Hause wäre, ___

7. Wenn ich es finde, ___

   Wenn ich es fände, ___

8. Wenn ich erfolgreich bin, ___

   Wenn ich erfolgreich wäre, ___

4. Generate conditions (*wenn*-clauses) that are logical for the following pairs of results.

1. Ich gehe mit dir, ______________________________

   Ich würde mit dir gehen, ______________________________

2. Wir werden Monika die Wahrheit sagen, ______________________________

   Wir würden Monika die Wahrheit sagen, ______________________________

3. Ich kaufe dir dein Mittagessen, ______________________________

   Ich würde dir dein Mittagessen kaufen, ______________________________

4. Du kannst mich in der Bibliothek finden, ______________________________

   Du könntest mich in der Bibliothek finden, ______________________________

5. Ich werde glücklich sein, ______________________________

   Ich wäre glücklich, ______________________________

6. Ich soll dir nichts davon sagen, ______________________________

   Ich sollte dir nichts davon sagen, ______________________________

7. Ich gehe gern mit dir aus, ______________________________

   Ich ginge gern mit dir aus, ______________________________

8. Du wirst nichts haben, ______________________________

   Du würdest nichts haben, ______________________________

5. Generate logical conditions for these results.

1. Ich würde das nicht tun, ______________________________
2. Ich hätte mehr Geld, ______________________________
3. Ich bin glücklich, ______________________________
4. Ich wäre noch glücklicher, ______________________________
5. Ich würde weniger Fehler machen, ______________________________
6. Wir hätten mehr Zeit, ______________________________
7. Du wärest energischer, ______________________________
8. Karl hätte mehr Freunde, ______________________________
9. Wir werden Tina zur Party einladen, ______________________________
10. Ich würde das machen, ______________________________
11. Wir werden das nicht machen, ______________________________
12. Die Studenten hätten bessere Noten, ______________________________

13. Meine Eltern würden mich besser verstehen, ______________________________

14. Du hättest genug Geld, ______________________________

15. Ich würde das nicht sagen, ______________________________

16. Maria wird dich heiraten, ______________________________

17. Ich würde das nicht machen, ______________________________

6. Complete the following sentences with a logical *wenn-* or *dann*-clause.

1. Ich könnte das erledigen, ______________________________

2. Wenn sie ihn heiratete, ______________________________

3. Wir würden dir helfen, ______________________________

4. Wenn du dein Zimmer nicht aufräumst, ______________________________

5. Du kämest pünktlich zur Arbeit an, ______________________________

6. Wenn Marc das noch einmal versuchte, ______________________________

7. Wenn du nicht langsamer fährst, ______________________________

8. Wenn ich das nicht täte, ______________________________

9. ______________________________, bliebe ich länger im Bett.

10. Du hättest mehr Freunde, ______________________________

Part Four

Additional Uses of the Subjunctive

Wishes: *Ich wünschte/wollte, ...*

When one wishes for something, one wishes for something that does not yet exist, for something that is not real, for example, *I wish I* ***were*** *an Oscar Mayer Wiener . . .* As a result, subjunctive verb forms are required. You may introduce a wish with either **ich wünschte, ...** or **ich wollte, ...** followed by a statement in the subjunctive:

Ich wünschte, ich **hätte** mehr Zeit für die Prüfung.
I wish *I* ***had*** *more time for the test.*

Ich wollte, du **würdest** etwas früher **ankommen**.
I wish *you* ***would come/arrive*** *a bit earlier.*

Wishes with *wenn*-Clauses + *nur*

To make a wish (again, for something not real), use a **wenn**-clause + **nur** (*only*) + a subjunctive verb and an exclamation point:

Wenn ich **nur** mehr Zeit für diesen Kurs **hätte!**
If only I ***had*** *more time for this course!*

Wenn es **nur** nicht so oft **regnen würde!**
If only *it* ***would*** *not* ***rain*** *so often!*

Wenn unsere Prüfungen **nur** nicht so schwer zu bestehen **wären!**
If only *our tests* ***were*** *not so hard to pass!*

Illusions: *als, als ob, als wenn*

Als, **als ob**, and **als wenn** (*as if, as though*) all signal that what follows is contrary to fact, that it is illusory, and that it is therefore not real. For this reason, the subjunctive must be used:

Du siehst aus, **als ob** du krank **wärest**. (Du bist aber nicht krank.)
You look ***as if*** *you* ***were*** *sick. (But you're not sick.)*

Herr Braun sieht aus, **als ob** er eine Million Dollar **hätte**. (Er ist aber nicht reich.)
Mr. Braun looks ***as if*** *he* ***had*** *a million dollars. (But he's not rich.)*

Der Mann tut, **als arbeitete** er wirklich. (Er faulenzt.)
The man acts ***as if*** *he* ***were*** *really* ***working****. (But he's goofing off.)*

Die Frau spricht, **als wenn** sie viel Erdnussbutter im Mund **hätte**. (Ihr Mund ist aber leer.)
The woman speaks ***as if*** *she* ***had*** *a mouth full of peanut butter. (But her mouth is empty.)*

Tactful Suggestions or Admonishments

Use subjunctive forms instead of indicative ones when you want or need to be tactful, sensitive, or non-prescriptive, or when being direct with someone might be risky or hurtful:

direct, indicative:	Ich hoffe, Sie machen diesen Fehler nie wieder. *I hope you do not make this mistake again.*
tactful, subjunctive:	Ich **würde hoffen**, Sie **würden** diesen Fehler nie wieder **machen**. *I* ***would hope*** *you* ***wouldn't make*** *this mistake again.*

Polite Requests

Use the subjunctive rather than the indicative to make very polite requests, that is, to sugarcoat them. Using the subjunctive makes it harder for your request to be turned down!

direct:	Können Sie mir sagen, wo der Bahnhof ist? *Can you tell me where the train station is?*
polite:	**Könnten** Sie mir **sagen**, wo der Bahnhof ist? ***Could*** *you* ***tell*** *me where the train station is?*

direct: Haben Sie jetzt etwas Zeit für mich?
Do you have some time for me now?
polite: **Hätten** Sie jetzt etwas Zeit für mich?
***Would** you **have** some time for me now?*

direct: Soll ich das jetzt machen?
Shall I do that now?
polite: **Sollte** ich das jetzt **machen**?
***Should** I **do** that now?*

direct: Darf ich Sie einladen, uns irgendwann zu besuchen?
May I invite you to visit us sometime?
polite: **Dürfte** ich Sie **einladen**, uns irgendwann zu besuchen?
***Might** I **invite** you to visit us sometime?*

Exercises: Part Four

Theory Review

1. Fill in the blanks with the correct information.

1. When one wishes for something, one is wishing for something that is not (yet) ____________________.
2. As a result, ____________________ verb forms are used when making wishes.
3. Wishes may be formulated two ways. One may simply use a ____________________-clause, using the adverb ____________________, ending with a ____________________ mark when written.
4. Another way to formulate a wish is to begin with the introductory ____________________ or ____________________, followed by the wish in the subjunctive.
5. Illusions are not ____________________ because they are contrary-to-fact. ____________________ verb forms will therefore be required when discussing illusions.
6. "Triggering devices" for an illusion are the subordinating conjunctions ____________________, ____________________, or ____________________.
7. When one needs to be tactful or sensitive to another person, one often uses ____________________ verb forms to "soften" the message.
8. The subjunctive is often used instead of the indicative to make a request more ____________________.

Focus on Form [✓]

2. Use the subjunctive to make the following requests extremely polite.

1. Können Sie mir bitte helfen?

____

2. Darf man hier fotografieren?

____

3. Holen Sie mir bitte ein Glas Rotwein. (*use **würde**-construction*)

____

4. Sollen wir das für morgen machen?

____

5. Machen Sie das für mich, bitte. (*use **würde**-construction*)

____

6. Muss ich das eigentlich tun?

____

7. Sprechen Sie lauter.

____

8. Ich rate dir, das niemandem zu sagen.

____

You Determine the Message and Form

3. Wishes. Construct *wenn*-clauses to wish for a solution to the following problems.

1. Sie haben kein Geld. ______________________________
2. Sie haben nie genug Zeit. ______________________________
3. Sie sind immer müde. ______________________________
4. Sie machen alles falsch. ______________________________
5. Niemand liebt Sie. ______________________________

4. Make wishes using the *ich wollte* or *ich wünschte* introduction for the following scenarios.

1. Sie brauchen ein neues Auto.

____

2. Sie haben eine schlechte Note im Examen.

____

3. Eine Freundin geht weg – auf immer.

____

4. Das Wetter ist heute zu kalt.

____

5. Sie gewinnen nie im Lotto.

____

6. Der Deutschlehrer ist beim Korrigieren der Prüfungen absolut brutal.

____

5. Use the *wenn*-clause or the *Ich wollte/wünschte,* ... construction to wish that . . .

1. you were rich

____

2. you had better grades

____

3. you spoke better German

____

4. you could buy a new car

____

5. you might be permitted to go out with your friends

____

6. you were more tolerant

____

7. you had more courage

____

8. we could do more

____

6. Make three wishes of your own.

____

____

____

7. **Formulate five requests you might make to get someone to do a favor of some kind for you.**

___

___

___

___

___

Partnerarbeit

8. **Arbeiten Sie mit einem Partner/einer Partnerin und beantworten Sie die folgenden Fragen.**

Was würdest du machen, wenn ...

du viel Zeit hättest?
du viel Geld hättest?
du morgen eine Prüfung hättest?
du jetzt sehr großen Hunger hättest?
es unheimlich warm wäre?
du deine Autotür nicht öffnen könntest?
du dein Deutschbuch verlörest?
du plötzlich krank würdest?
es stark regnete?
du Urlaub machen könntest?

9. **Arbeiten Sie mit einem Partner/einer Partnerin und beantworten Sie die folgenden Fragen mit *wenn-dann*-Sätzen.**

Beispiel: Wann würdest du folgendes machen?
ein großes Bier trinken
→ *Ich würde ein großes Bier trinken, wenn ich in einer deutschen Kneipe wäre.*

Wann würdest du folgendes machen?

ein großes Bier trinken
mit deinem Chef/deiner Chefin privat sprechen
zum Arzt gehen
einen neuen Anzug oder ein neues Kleid kaufen
mit deinen Freunden ausgehen
mit einer Kreditkarte zahlen?
nicht ins Bett gehen/nicht schlafen gehen
den ganzen Tag zu Hause bleiben
weniger essen
deinen Eltern nichts davon erzählen

Chapter 22 Past Subjunctive II

Part One

Past Subjunctive: *hätte/wäre* + Past Participle

When speculating about the past, past subjunctive verb forms must be used. Just as for the present subjunctive, there is a "pure" form and an alternate form. The pure form consists of **hätte** (with **haben**-verbs) or **wäre** (with **sein**-verbs) + a past participle. You are advised to use the pure form exclusively. Study these examples and notice that the English past subjunctive looks exactly like the past perfect indicative with *had* + a past participle. The alternate *would have* construction is used frequently in the result clause:

Wenn wir mehr Geld **gespart hätten, wären** wir nach Mexiko **gefahren.**
*If we **had saved** more money, we **would have traveled** to Mexico.*

Wenn ich mehr Zeit **gehabt hätte, wäre** ich mit dir ins Kino **gegangen.**
*If I **had had** more time, I **would have gone** with you to the movies.*

Wenn er da **gewesen wäre, hättest** du ihn bestimmt **gesehen.**
*If he **had been** there, you **would** definitely **have seen** him.*

Wenn wir nach Deutschland **geflogen wären, hätten** wir unsere Verwandten in Osnabrück **besucht.**
*If we **had flown** to Germany, we **would have visited** our relatives in Osnabrück.*

Double-Infinitive Construction with Modal Verbs

Modal verbs are all **haben**-verbs, so **hätte** will always be used in the past subjunctive with them. Remember that when you use a modal verb with a helping verb and an infinitive, you must employ the double-infinitive construction:

Wenn ich mehr Zeit gehabt hätte, **hätte** ich mit dir ins Kino **gehen können.**
*If I had had more time, I **would have been able to go/could have gone** with you to the movies.*

Wenn er da gewesen wäre, **hättest** du ihn bestimmt **sehen müssen.**
*If he had been there, you **would have had/would have needed** to see him.*

Wenn du dich nicht schneller vorbereitet hättest, **hättest** du nicht **mitkommen dürfen.**
*If you hadn't prepared faster, you **wouldn't have been allowed/permitted** to come along.*

The Double Infinitive in *wenn*-Clauses

As noted previously, if the double infinitive is employed in a subordinate clause, like a **wenn**-clause, the double infinitive must be the last element, not the helping verb:

Wenn ich mehr Geld **hätte sparen können**, hätte ich einen neuen Fernseher kaufen können.
*If I **had been able to save** more money, I could have bought a new television.*

Wenn du früher **hättest kommen können**, hättest du meine Eltern kennen lernen können.
*If you **could have come** earlier, you could have met my parents.*

As you have learned before, when modals are not used with a dependent verb, past participles take the form of a regular verb: **ge** + stem + **t**:

Ich **hätte** das nicht **gesollt**. (= nicht machen sollen)
*I **shouldn't have** (done it).*

Wir **hätten** das nicht **gemusst**. (= nicht machen müssen)
*We **wouldn't have had to** (do it).*

The Alternate Form of the Past Subjunctive

The alternate form of the past subjunctive consists of a form of **würde** + a *past* infinitive:

Ich **würde** das nicht **gesagt haben**. = Ich hätte das nicht gesagt.
------------------------------ *I **would** not **have said** that.* ------------------------------

Wir **würden** nach Schottland **gereist sein**. = Wir wären nach Schottland gereist.
------------------------------ *We **would have traveled** to Scotland.* ------------------------------

The alternate form of the past subjunctive (actually a subjunctivization of the future perfect) is not nearly as frequently employed as the participles with **hätte** or **wäre**. The "pure" form is simpler and more economical to use.

Mixing Tenses Logically in *Wenn ..., dann ...* Sentences

Usually, the tenses in the **wenn**- and **dann**-clauses are the same:

Wenn ich zehn Dollar **hätte**, [dann/so] **würde** ich mit dir ins Kino **gehen**.
Wenn ich zehn Dollar **gehabt hätte**, [dann/so] **wäre** ich mit dir ins Kino **gegangen**.

When logic dictates, the tenses can (and must) be different. Since the condition gives rise to the result, the condition, expressed by the **wenn**-clause, must exist first. That means the **wenn**-clause is in the past subjunctive, and the **dann**-clause is in the present:

Wenn ich nicht so viel auf der Party **getrunken hätte**, [dann/so] **wäre** ich *heute* nicht so krank.
*If I **had** not **drunk** so much at the party, [then] I **would** not **be** so sick <u>today</u>.*

Wenn ich für die Prüfung fleißiger **gelernt hätte**, [dann/so] **würde** ich *jetzt* eine bessere Note verdienen.
*If I **had studied** harder for the test, [then] I **would earn** a better grade <u>now</u>.*

Using time expressions like **jetzt** or **heute** greatly assist in making the time difference even clearer.

NOTE: There is a somewhat rare exception to the above. When the condition is constant, for example, as in the case of a chronic illness, the condition will be stated in the present because it is an ongoing, persistent condition. The result clause may be either in the present or past, depending on the impact of that constant condition:

Wenn ich nicht immer so krank und schwach wäre, könnte ich mehr tun.
If I weren't always so sick and weak, I could do more.

Wenn du einfach mehr von dir erwartetest, hättest du bis jetzt mehr schaffen können.
If you simply expected more of yourself, you could have accomplished more by now.

Exercises: Part One

Theory Review

1. Fill in the blanks with the correct information.

1. When speculating about the past, the ______________________ ______________________ must be used.
2. In English this tense looks exactly like the ______________________ ______________________ indicative. The helping verb used with a past participle will either be *had* or *would have.*
3. There are two forms of this tense in German as well, the "______________________" form and an alternate **würde**-form.
4. The ______________________ form is much more common.
5. To form the past subjunctive one simply uses the correct subjunctive form of ______________________ or ______________________ plus a past participle.
6. So, for the verb **essen**, the past subjunctive would be ______________________ ______________________.
7. For the verb **gehen**, the past subjunctive would be ______________________ ______________________.
8. Remember this old rule: If you have a helping verb, a modal verb, and a main verb, you must form a ______________________ - ______________________ construction.
9. That will hold true in the past subjunctive as well. The helping verb will always be a form of ______________________, since all modal verbs use this as their helping verb in compound past constructions.
10. Remember also that when a double infinitive is in a subordinate clause (in this case, a **wenn**-clause), the last thing in that clause must be the ______________________. Nothing may follow behind it in the clause.
11. A past condition normally yields a ______________________ result.

12. When logic dictates, however, a past condition may produce a ______________________ result.

13. In such instances the **wenn**-clause is in the ______________________ tense and the **dann**-clause is in the ______________________ tense.

14. Express such a sentence in German: *If I had eaten that last night, I would be sick today.*

____

Focus on Form [✓]

2. Past subjunctive in English. The following sentences, though grammatically false, are commonly heard in colloquial speech. Correct them to the formal standard. Remember, the past subjunctive in English looks just like the past perfect indicative.

1. If he caught an earlier flight, he would have arrived on time.

____

2. If you started work earlier, you would have finished by now.

____

3. If we studied harder, we would have gotten better grades.

____

4. If I knew the answer, I'd have gotten a higher score.

____

5. If I didn't spend all my money, I would have had enough for it.

____

6. If you listened to me, you wouldn't have gotten into trouble.

____

7. If she came earlier, she would have seen us.

____

8. If the mechanic fixed the car, it would work right now.

____

9. If you were here, you would have met my roommate.

____

10. If I ran just a bit faster, I would have won the race.

____

3. Past subjunctive in German. Change each of the following factual sentences about the past to speculative ones by using past subjunctive forms instead. When making the transformations, replace *als* with *wenn*.

1. Als ich meine Familie besuchte, sprach ich mit Opa.

____

2. Als ich in Berlin wohnte, besuchte ich oft das Museum.

____

3. Als ich bei Siemens arbeitete, habe ich zwei Millionen Euro verdient.

____

4. Als ich mit Kolumbus segelte, entdeckten wir die Neue Welt.

____

5. Als ich ihr den Brief schrieb, habe ich ihr die Sache nicht erwähnt.

____

6. Als er das hörte, lachte er sich kaputt.

____

7. Als sie auf Hans wartete, wurde sie ungeduldig.

____

8. Als wir diese Erklärung lasen, verstanden wir alles viel besser.

____

9. Als ich die Rechnung bekam, bezahlte ich sie gleich.

____

10. Als ich das Scheckheft fand, wurde ich ganz glücklich.

____

4. Mixing tenses. Logic determines when tenses can be mixed. Normally, the *wenn*-clause contains the past subjunctive, and the *dann*-clause contains the present subjunctive. The reason for this is that the condition that gives rise to an event obviously exists before the event and is therefore older (more past) than the event itself. Express the following in German:

1. If I had known that last night, I wouldn't be here now.

____

2. I would take the test today if I hadn't broken my arm [yesterday].

____

3. I would have enough money for a new car now if I had saved my money.

____

4. We would still be friends now if we had stayed in contact with each other.

____

5. You wouldn't have any problems today if you had worked harder [before].

____

You Determine the Message and Form

5. Mixing tenses. Complete the sentences with a logical present-tense *dann*-clause. Use *jetzt* in your answer to accentuate the time difference causing the tense mixing.

1. Wenn ich das früher gewusst hätte, _______________________
2. Wenn du das hättest machen können, _______________________
3. Wenn er nicht so spät gekommen wäre, _______________________

6. Modal verbs. Change each of the following factual scenarios into a hypothetical one by using the subjunctive in *wenn ... , dann ...* sentences.

1. Ich kann das nicht machen, also werde ich es nicht versuchen.

____

2. Ich darf nicht ausgehen, also muss ich zu Hause bleiben.

____

3. Ich soll meine Hausaufgaben machen, also darf ich nicht ins Kino gehen.

____

4. Ich muss meinem Vater helfen, also kann ich dir nicht helfen.

____

5. Ich will das nicht machen, also werde ich es nicht machen.

____

6. Ich wollte es nicht machen und habe es nicht gemacht.

____

7. Ich musste diese Sachen erledigen. Ich konnte nicht Fußball spielen.

____

8. Ich sollte zu Hause bleiben. Ich durfte nicht mit euch ins Museum gehen.

____

7. Complete the following with an appropriate and logical *wenn*-clause in the past subjunctive.

A

1. Ich würde weniger Fehler machen, ______
2. Wir hätten mehr Zeit, ______
3. Du wärest energischer, ______
4. Karl hätte mehr Freunde, ______
5. Wir würden Tina zur Party einladen, ______
6. Ich würde das machen, ______
7. Wir würden das nicht machen, ______
8. Die Studenten hätten bessere Noten, ______
9. Meine Eltern würden mich besser verstehen, ______
10. Du hättest genug Geld, ______

B

1. Ich würde das nicht sagen, ______
2. Bettina hätte das nicht gesagt, ______
3. Wir wären mit dir ins Kino gegangen, ______
4. Du hättest auch mitspielen können, ______
5. Maria würde dich heiraten, ______
6. Der Besuch zu Hause wäre besser gewesen, ______
7. Ich wäre früher nach Hause gekommen, ______
8. Wir hätten einen neuen Fernseher kaufen müssen, ______
9. Du hättest das Spiel nicht verloren, ______
10. Ihr hättet länger schlafen können, ______

8. Complete these sentences with logical result clauses.

A

1. Wenn ich an deiner Stelle gewesen wäre, ______
2. Wenn ich das gemacht hätte, ______
3. Wenn ich nicht krank wäre, ______
4. Wenn Tina uns eingeladen hätte, ______

5. Hätten wir mehr Geld gespart, ______________________________

6. Wärest du gestern Abend zu Hause gewesen, ______________________________

7. Wenn ich das gewusst hätte, ______________________________

8. Wenn wir das hätten machen sollen, ______________________________

9. Wenn ich zu Hause geblieben wäre, ______________________________

10. Wenn du es mir früher gesagt hättest, ______________________________

B

1. Wenn ich den Mut gehabt hätte, ______________________________

2. Wenn du nicht so arrogant gewesen wärest, ______________________________

3. Wenn Heinrich nicht so faul gewesen wäre, ______________________________

4. Wenn wir mehr gearbeitet hätten, ______________________________

5. Wenn ich nicht so schüchtern gewesen wäre, ______________________________

6. Wenn es nicht geschneit hätte, ______________________________

7. Wenn du mich in Ruhe gelassen hättest, ______________________________

8. Wenn Ute netter gewesen wäre, ______________________________

9. Wenn das Konzert früher stattgefunden hätte, ______________________________

10. Wenn die Politikerin die Wahrheit gesagt hätte, ______________________________

11. Wenn du nicht so lange geschlafen hättest, ______________________________

Part Two

Expressing Regret about the Past

You learned in Chapter 21 that you can express a wish directly by using a **wenn**-clause + **nur** with the subjunctive. Making a wish for something in the past is actually expressing a regret of some kind because whatever is wished for never happened. To express a regret, use the past subjunctive with **nur** in a **wenn**-clause ending with an exclamation point.

Wenn ich **nur** noch mehr Zeit **gehabt hätte**!
*If I only **had had** more time.*

Wenn ich **nur** nicht so spät **angekommen wäre**!
*If only I **hadn't arrived** so late.*

You may also state a regret by beginning with **Ich wollte, ...** or the more common **Ich wünschte, ...** followed by a past subjunctive:

Ich **wünschte**, ich **hätte** noch mehr Geld **gehabt**.
*I wish I **had had** more money.*

Er **wollte**, er **hätte** das nie **gesagt.**
He wishes he ***had*** *never* ***said*** *that.*

NOTE: In this format, you do not use **wenn**, **nur**, or an exclamation point.

Expressing Illusions with *als, als ob, als wenn*

Als, als ob, and **als wenn** (*as if, as though*) all signal that the statement is contrary-to-fact, that is, illusory, not real. For this reason the subjunctive is used, and if the illusion happened in the past, the past subjunctive is required. Note the word order following **als** when it is used instead of **als ob** or **als wenn.** (Recommendation: Use **als ob.** It is more common than the other two.)

Du sahst aus, **als ob** du krank **gewesen wärest.** (Du warst aber nicht krank gewesen.)
You looked ***as if*** *you* ***had been*** *sick. (But you hadn't been sick.)*

Du sahst aus, **als ob** du außer Atem **geworden wärest.** (Du warst aber nicht außer Atem gewesen.)
You looked ***as if*** *you* ***had gotten*** *out of breath. (But you had not gotten out of breath.)*

Der Mann tat, **als wäre** er halb im Schlaf **gewesen.** (Er war aber nicht halb im Schlaf gewesen.)
The man acted ***as if*** *he* ***had been*** *half asleep. (But he hadn't.)*

Die Frau sprach, **als wenn** sie zu viel Wein **getrunken hätte.** (Sie hatte aber nicht zu viel Wein getrunken.)
The woman spoke ***as if*** *she* ***had drunk*** *too much wine. (But she hadn't drunk too much wine.)*

Du lächeltest, **als hättest** du gerade einen Kanarienvogel **geschluckt.** (Aber du hattest keinen geschluckt.)
You smiled slyly, ***as if*** *you* ***had*** *just* ***swallowed*** *a canary. (But you didn't swallow one.)*

Du hast dich so benommen, **als hättest** du das schon tausendmal **gemacht.** (Aber du hattest es nicht tausendmal gemacht.)
You behaved ***as if*** *you* ***had*** *already* ***done*** *that a thousand times. (But you hadn't done it a thousand times before.)*

Almost, but Not Quite: *beinah*[*e*] and *fast* + Subjunctive

In English we use the word *almost* with an indicative past tense form to indicate that something almost happened:

I almost passed the test (but didn't). We almost died (but didn't).

In German, **beinah**[**e**] and **fast** may be used interchangeably to mean *almost.* These two adverbs signal that something was *almost* done but not quite pulled off = lack of reality. The past subjunctive is therefore required in German:

Ich **hätte** das ***fast*** **verstanden.** (Ich habe es aber nicht verstanden.)
I ***almost understood*** *that.*

Wir **hätten** es ***beinahe*** **erledigen können.** (Aber wir haben es nicht erledigen können.)
We ***could almost finish*** *it.*

Since using the past subjunctive with **beinah**[**e**] and **fast** is dissimilar to English and its use of the indicative, more practice will probably be required to gain familiarity.

Exercises: Part Two

Theory Review

1. Fill in the blanks with the correct information.

1. When one makes a wish, one is wishing for something unreal or not yet real, so the ______________________ mode is employed in German.
2. When making a wish about the past, one wishes for something that (unfortunately) did not happen. This means that a wish about the past is normally expressed as a ______________________.
3. Wishes may be formed by using a ______________________ -clause with **nur**, or a statement introduced by ____________________ or ____________________, followed by the wish itself.
4. A wish for or regret about anything in the past requires the ____________________ subjunctive.
5. Illusions are not ______________________, so they will be expressed in the ______________________ mode.
6. The subordinating conjunctions ______________________, ______________________, and ______________________ signal that the subordinate clause deals with an illusion.
7. Something that *almost* happened but did not is unreal, so describing such an event in German will require that a past tense verb in the ______________________ mode be used.
8. The two "trigger words" that mean *almost* are ______________________ and ______________________. They may be used interchangeably.
9. Does English employ the subjunctive when expressing that something *almost* happened? ____________

Focus on Meaning and Form [✓]

2. Regrets. Construct *wenn*-clauses with *nur* to express regret about the following scenarios. *Sie* refers to you.

1. Sie haben kein Geld gehabt. ______________________________________
2. Sie haben nie genug Zeit gehabt. ______________________________________
3. Sie sind sehr müde geworden. ______________________________________
4. Sie haben viele Fehler gemacht. ______________________________________
5. Niemand hat Sie als Kind geliebt. ______________________________________

3. Express regret about the following, using *ich wollte* or *ich wünschte.*

1. Ihr Auto ist plötzlich kaputt gegangen.

____

2. Sie haben eine schlechte Note in der Prüfung verdient.

____

3. Ihre Freundin von zwei Jahren hat Sie verlassen.

____

4. Das Wetter war heute zu kalt.

____

5. Sie haben im Lotto nichts gewonnen.

____

6. Der Deutschlehrer hat die Prüfungen zu streng korrigiert.

____

7. Sie haben das Examen nicht bestanden.

____

4. Use the *wenn*-clause or *Ich wollte/wünschte, ...* construction to wish that . . .

1. you had been healthy

____

2. you had had better grades

____

3. you had spoken better German

____

4. you had been able to buy a new car

____

5. you might have been permitted to go out with your friends

____

6. you had been more tolerant

____

7. you had had more time

____

8. we could have done more

____

5. Illusions. Use the subjunctive to indicate the following:

1. You looked like (as if) you had just woken up.

   ____

2. It looked as if it had snowed.

   ____

3. He looked as though he had been working a long time.

   ____

4. It sounded as if something had exploded.

   ____

5. He looked as if he had been drunk.

   ____

6. It sounded like she had known what she was talking about.

   ____

6. Use the subjunctive with *beinahe* or *fast* to indicate that something *almost* happened.

1. It almost rained. ______________________________
2. You almost came too late. ______________________________
3. Thomas almost passed the test. ______________________________
4. Sabine almost had a car accident. ______________________________
5. Now mention something you almost did or that almost happened.

   ____

You Determine the Message and Form

7. Express three regrets that you have.

____

____

____

Partnerarbeit

8. Arbeiten Sie mit einem Partner/einer Partnerin, und beantworten Sie die folgenden Fragen.

1. Was hättest du kaufen können, wenn du zweitausend Dollar gehabt hättest?
2. Was hättest du heute gemacht, wenn du ein bisschen mehr Zeit gehabt hättest?
3. Was hättest du wahrscheinlich gemacht, wenn du bei der Party bei [Melanie] gewesen wärest?
4. Was hättest du vielleicht getan, wenn du letzten Sommer nach Deutschland gereist wärest?
5. Was hättest du letztes Wochenende machen sollen, wenn du diese Woche mehrere Prüfungen gehabt hättest?
6. Wie fühltest du dich jetzt, wenn du gestern Abend nicht so viel Wein getrunken hättest?
7. Was hättest du gemacht, wenn du dein Auto nicht hättest reparieren können?
8. Was hättest du wahrscheinlich gemacht, wenn du letztes Wochenende nach Hause gefahren wärest?
9. Was wäre passiert, wenn wir gestern ein heftiges Gewitter gehabt hätten?
10. Was hättest du gemacht, wenn du gestern Abend spät nach Hause gekommen wärest und du deinen Hausschlüssel nicht hättest finden können?
11. Was würdest du jetzt machen, wenn du dich auf eine große Prüfung nicht genügend vorbereitet hättest?
12. Was würdest du jetzt machen, wenn du im Lotto viel Geld gewonnen hättest?

Chapter 23 Direct and Indirect Discourse

Part One

Direct Discourse

Direct discourse takes place when one relates what someone else has stated, asked, or commanded, using the speaker's exact words:

Er sagt: „Ich kann das nicht machen."
He says, "I can't do that."

Sie fragte mich: „Warum hast du uns nicht besuchen können?"
She asked me, "Why haven't you been able to visit us?"

Er sagte: „Frag mich nicht wieder!"
He said, "Don't ask me again!"

Note the use of the colon and the different quotation marks in the German examples above.

Indirect Discourse in English

Indirect discourse involves relating the *gist* or *sense* of what someone else says, asks, or commands. This means we are saying what that person means without using his or her exact words. That in turn means we are usually reporting from the perspective of the third person—*he, she,* or *they.* In many cases, subordinating conjunctions like *that, if/whether,* and *w*-question words may be used.

direct quite:	She said, "I am coming later."
indirect quote:	She said that that *she* was coming later. OR: She said *she* was coming later.
direct quote:	She said, "I can come later."
indirect quote:	She said that *she* could come later. OR: She said *she* could come later.
direct quote:	She asked, "Have you traveled to Europe often?"
indirect quote:	She asked if/whether *I* had traveled to Europe often."
direct quote:	He asked her, "Were you there?"
indirect quote:	He asked her if *she* had been there.

Conversational Indirect Discourse in German

Expressing Faith in the Quote → Indicative

Use indicative forms in the indirect quote when you wish to signal that you believe you are relating factual or accurate information:

direct quote:	Sie sagte: „Ich komme später."
indirect quote:	Sie sagte, *sie* kommt später. OR:
	Sie sagte, dass *sie* später kommt.
direct quote:	Sie sagte: „Ich kann später kommen."
indirect quote:	Sie sagte, *sie* kann später kommen. OR:
	Sie sagte, dass *sie* später kommen kann.

Observe the following sentences featuring indirect discourse in various tenses. Note that in German the tense of the direct quote determines the tense of the indirect quote; they are the same.

direct quote → indirect quote

present: Er sagt, „Ich **mache** das nie." → Er sagt, dass er das nie **macht**.
Sie fragt: „**Kommt** Karola **mit**?" → Sie fragt, ob Karola **mitkommt**.

past: Er sagte: „Maria **hat** mich nicht **gefragt**." → Er sagte, Maria **hat** ihn nicht **gefragt**.
Er sagte: „Bernd **ist** spät **angekommen**." → Er teilte uns mit, dass Bernd spät **angekommen ist**.

future: Sie sagen, „Wir **werden** die Arbeit **erledigen**." → Sie sagen, sie **werden** die Arbeit **erledigen**.
Sie sagen: „Wir **werden** Ihnen **helfen**." → Sie sagen, dass sie uns **helfen werden**.

modal: Er sagte: „Ich **kann** es nicht **machen**." → Er sagte, er **kann** es nicht **machen**.
Elene sagte: „Ich **wollte** Hans **besuchen**." → Elene sagte, dass sie Hans **besuchen wollte**.

Note also that the clause containing the indirect quote may use normal word order or subordinate word order after **dass**. The choice is yours, though the general tendency is to not use **dass**.

Expressing Reservation or Doubt → Subjunctive II

In English, if the speaker has any reservation, doubt, or skepticism about the accuracy or truthfulness of the indirect quote, he or she may signal that with the introductory verb:

no skepticism or doubt:	He says he's coming.
skepticism, reservation, doubt:	He *claims/maintains/suggests* he's coming.

Or the speaker may add a following comment to signal skepticism or doubt:

He said he's coming, but I don't see him. He should be here by now. (reservation.)
He said he's coming, but I have a feeling he won't. (doubt)
He said he's coming, but he didn't sound convincing. (skepticism)

Or the speaker may use the subjunctive to express some reservation or doubt:

He said [that] he would come. (But where is he?)
They said [that] they would bring some food for the party. (But they're here, and I see no food.)

Things are a bit different in German. German uses subjunctive forms in the indirect quote to signal that the speaker is not sure about the truthfulness or reliability of the indirect quote or that there is some doubt or skepticism as to its veracity. By using the subjunctive the speaker distances him- or herself from the quote. There is no overt need to elaborate on the reason for the distancing.

Er sagt: „Ich weiß es nicht." → Er sagt, er wüsste das nicht.

Tenses Used with Indirect Quotes in the Subjunctive

The overarching rule is that the indirect quote in German is in the same tense as the original quote. If the original quote is in the present tense and the speaker has reservations about it, use the present subjunctive in the indirect quote:

Er sagte: „Ich **kann** das nicht **machen.**" → Er sagte, er **könnte** das nicht **machen**.
Er sagt: „Ich mache das nie." → Er sagt, dass er das nie **machte.**
Sie sagt: „Ich komme mit." → Sie sagt, dass sie **mitkäme.**

If the tense of the original quote is *any* past indicative tense, state the indirect quote in the past subjunctive:

Er sagte: „Ich **kannte** die Frau nicht." → Er sagte, dass er die Frau nicht **gekannt hätte**.
Er sagte: „Maria **fragte** mich nicht." → Er sagte, dass Maria ihn nicht **gefragt hätte**.

Sie fragte: „Warum **bist** du nicht **gekommen**?" → Sie fragte, warum er nicht **gekommen wäre**.
Er sagte: „Bernd **ist** spät **angekommen.**" → Er teilte uns mit, dass Bernd spät **angekommen wäre**.

If the original quote is in the future, use the conditional **würde**-construction, a subjunctivization of the future indicative, in the indirect quote:

Er sagte: „Ich **werde** nicht **mitkommen.**" → Er sagte, er **würde** nicht **mitkommen**.
Sie sagen: „Wir **werden** Ihnen **helfen**." → Sie sagen, dass sie uns **helfen würden**.

When a modal verb is in the direct quote, it will be the target of subjunctivization, not the dependent infinitive:

Er sagt: „Ich **kann** das nicht **machen.**" → Er sagt, er **könnte** das nicht **machen**.
Sie sagten: „Wir **wollten** ihn nicht **fragen.**" → Sie sagten, sie **hätten** ihn nicht **fragen wollen**.

Remember that in a subordinate clause the helping verb is placed before a double infinitive construction:

Elene sagte, dass sie Bernd nicht **hätte besuchen wollen**.
Sabine teilte mir mit, dass sie nicht nach Hause **hätte gehen sollen**.

When the Original Quote Is in the Subjunctive

When the original quote is already in the subjunctive, simply pass it on as an indirect quote in the subjunctive:

Frau Möhring sagte: „Ich **würde** das nicht **tun.**" → Frau Möhring meinte, sie **würde** das nicht **tun**.
Inge sagt: „Ich **hätte** nichts dagegn." → Inge meint, sie **hätte** nichts dagegen.
Helmut sagt: „Das **könnte** wahr **sein**." → Helmut glaubt, das **könnte** wahr **sein**.

Note the use of various "reporting verbs" like **meinen** and **glauben** to introduce the indirect quote.

Indirect Commands and *sollten*

When you quote a command indirectly, use a form of **sollten** (*should*, a subjunctive II form of **sollen**):

Sie haben uns gesagt: „Kommt nie wieder!“ → Sie haben uns gesagt, dass wir nie wieder **kommen sollten.**
*They told us, "Never come again!" → They told us that we **should** never **come** again.*

Der Chef sagte: „Arbeite schneller!“ → Der Chef sagte, dass ich schneller **arbeiten sollte.**
*The boss said, "Work harder!" → The boss said that I **should work** harder.*

Exercises: Part One

Theory Review

1. Fill in the blanks with the correct information.

1. ________________________ discourse occurs when one quotes another with his or her exact words.
2. ________________________ discourse occurs when one quotes another but NOT with his or her exact words.
3. In many instances, such discourse is often a part of a ________________________ of some kind, oral or written.
4. When quoting someone indirectly, especially in conversation, the verb in the quote is cast in the ________________________ to show that the veracity of the indirect quote is high, that is, that the speaker believes the information in the indirect quote is true, or likely to be true. Credibility is high.
5. In German, the tense of the indirect quote will be the ________________________ as the tense in the direct quote.
6. When quoting someone indirectly, the verb in the quote will be cast in the ____________________ to signal that the veracity of the information in the indirect quote is very low or non-existent, that is, there is some doubt or skepticism or even disbelief about its truthfulness.
7. When quoting indirectly with subjunctive II, if the tense of the original quote is in the present indicative, the tense of the indirect quote will be in the ________________________ subjunctive.
8. When quoting indirectly with subjunctive II, if the tense of the original quote is in any past indicative tense, the tense of the indirect quote will be in the ____________________ subjunctive.

9. When quoting indirectly with subjunctive II, if the tense of the original quote is in the future, the ______________________ -construction will be used. This construction is a subjunctivization of the future.
10. When quoting indirectly with subjunctive II, if the original quote is already in the subjunctive, the indirect quote will be in the ______________________ as well, in the same tense.
11. When quoting indirectly with subjunctive II, if the original quote is a command, a subjunctive II form of ______________________ will be a part of the indirect quote.

Focus on Meaning and Form

2. In reporting these sentences indirectly, perform the operation two ways to simulate these conditions and vary the reporting verbs as desired:

a. You strongly believe the original message to be true—use indicative.
b. You are skeptical or have some reservation about the accuracy of the message—use subjunctive II.

1. Klaus: „Ich hole Tina um acht Uhr ab."

   true: ______________________

   reservation: ______________________

2. Elke: „Ich habe Franks Telefonnummer vergessen. Ich brauche sie heute."

   true: ______________________

   reservation: ______________________

3. Frau Berger: „Ich bin nur drei Tage in Hamburg geblieben. Meine Verwandten wohnen da."

   true: ______________________

   reservation: ______________________

4. Ankes Mutter: „Alles hat geklappt. Ich bin in München gut angekommen."

   true: ______________________

   reservation: ______________________

5. Martin: „Kannst du heute Abend mitkommen?"

   true: ______________________

   reservation: ______________________

6. Karen: „Wo hast du Peter kennen gelernt?"

   true: ______________________

   reservation: ______________________

7. Monika: „Ich halte nicht viel von ihr."

   true: ______________________________

   reservation: ______________________________

8. Trudi: „Unsere Freundin Ulrike lügt immer."

   true: ______________________________

   reservation: ______________________________

9. Hans: „Du sollst das nicht sagen. Du hast sie missverstanden."

   true: ______________________________

   reservation: ______________________________

Part Two

Neutral, Unbiased Reporting → Special Subjunctive/ Subjunctive I

The *special subjunctive,* also called *subjunctive I,* is based on the *first* principal part of the verb, the infinitive. Simply isolate the infinitive stem and add the standard subjunctive endings. The special subjunctive forms are used in formal German (for example, speeches, reports, essays, newspaper and magazine articles) for indirect quoting that is neutral, unbiased, and non-prejudicial. For all practical purposes, you will most likely read something written in subjunctive I or hear news reports couched in subjunctive I. It is rather unlikely that you will use it in everyday speech, but you may wish to use it when writing an academic essay.

Formation of Present Subjunctive I

To generate the subjunctive I present-tense form, do the following to *any and all verbs:*

1. Isolate the stem of the infinitive:

sprechen → sprech-	**sehen → seh-**	**lernen → lern-**
haben → hab-	**sein → sei-**	**werden → werd-**
können → könn-	**müssen → müss-**	**wollen → woll-**

2. Add the standard subjunctive endings to the stem to agree with the subject. Study the example verbs in the chart below: representative regular, irregular, auxiliary, and modal verbs.

Present Subjunctive I Forms

lernen

ich **lerne**	wir **lernen**	
du **lernest**	ihr **lernet**	Sie **lernen**
er/sie/es **lerne**	sie **lernen**	

sprechen

ich **spreche**	wir **sprechen**	
du **sprechest**	ihr **sprechet**	Sie **sprechen**
er/sie/es **spreche**	sie **sprechen**	

sehen

ich **sehe**	wir **sehen**	
du **sehest**	ihr **sehet**	Sie **sehen**
er/sie/es **sehe**	sie **sehen**	

haben

ich **habe**	wir **haben**	
du **habest**	ihr **habet**	Sie **haben**
er/sie/es **habe**	sie **haben**	

sein (especially irregular)

ich **sei**	wir **seien**	
du **sei(e)st**	ihr **seiet**	Sie **seien**
er/sie/es **sei**	sie **seien**	

werden

ich **werde**	wir **werden**	
du **werdest**	ihr **werdet**	Sie **werdet**
er/sie/es **werde**	sie **werden**	

können

ich **könne**	wir **können**	
du **könnest**	ihr **könnet**	Sie **können**
er/sie/es **könne**	sie **können**	

müssen

ich **müsse**	wir **müssen**	
du **müssest**	ihr **müsset**	Sie **müssen**
er/sie/es **müsse**	sie **müssen**	

wollen

ich **wolle**	wir **wollen**	
du **wollest**	ihr **wollet**	Sie **wollen**
er/sie/es **wolle**	sie **wollen**	

Study the example sentences in the present, future, and past: a credible indirect quote in the indicative is given as a neutral indirect quote in subjunctive I. Note that it is the tense of the direct quote that determines the tense of the indirect quote, not the introductory verb:

„Ich komme nicht.“ → Sie sagte, dass sie nicht **komme**.
„Ich habe das nicht.“ → Sie sagte, sie **habe** das nicht.
„Ich kann es nicht machen.“ → Er sagte, dass er es nicht **machen könne**.
„Frag mich nicht wieder.“ → Er sagte, dass ich ihn nicht wieder **fragen solle**.
„Ich werde nicht mitkommen.“ → Er sagte, er **werde** nicht **mitkommen**.
„Ich habe die Frau nicht gekannt.“ → Er sagte, er **habe** die Frau nicht **gekannt**.
„Warum willst du nicht dahin gehen?“ → Sie fragte, warum ich nicht dahin **gehen wolle**.
„Er ist nicht gekommen.“ → Sie fragte, warum er nicht **gekommen sei**.

When Subjunctive I Forms Are Identical to Indicative → Subjunctive II

Switch to general subjunctive *whenever* subjunctive I and indicative forms are identical. Third-person singular special subjunctive forms (with **er/sie/es**, or a singular noun) are always distinctive. Plural forms (with **wir**, **sie**, or plural nouns) are NOT. When special subjunctive forms look exactly like present indicative forms, use general subjunctive forms (subjunctive II) instead to avoid ambiguity and make the “subjunctiveness” obvious.

The following sentences are similar to the ones that appeared in the previous section, only this time they are presented in the plural. Note that the plural subjunctive I forms are identical to the indicative, triggering a switch to subjunctive II to make the “subjunctiveness” of the verb crystal clear.

„Die Studenten **kommen** nicht.“
Sie sagte, die Studenten **kommen** nicht. → Sie sagte, dass die Studenten nicht **kämen**.

„Meine Freunde **machen** das nicht.“
Sie sagte, dass ihre Freunde das nicht **machen**. → Sie sagte, dass ihre Freunde das nicht **machten**.

„Wir **können** das nicht **erledigen**.“
Er sagte, sie **können** das nicht **erledigen**. → Er sagte, sie **könnten** das nicht **erledigen**.

„Die Kinder **sollen** hier **bleiben**. “
Sie sagten, die Kinder **sollen** hier **bleiben**. → Sie sagten, die Kinder **sollten** hier **bleiben**.

„Wir **werden** nicht **warten**.“
Sie sagten, dass sie nicht **warten werden**. → Sie sagten, dass sie nicht **warten würden**.

„Wir **haben** die Frau nicht **gekannt**.“
Sie sagten, dass sie die Frau nicht **gekannt haben**. → Sie sagten, dass sie die Frau nicht **gekannt hätten**.

„Wir **sind** um zwei nach Hause **gefahren**.“
Sie sagten, sie **sind** nach Hause **gefahren**. → Sie sagten, sie **seien** nicht **gekommen**.

(Because **seien** is clearly distinct from the indicative **sind**, there is no need to switch to subjunctive II.)

When the Original Quote Is in the Subjunctive

When the original quote is in the subjunctive, usually subjunctive II, use subjunctive II in the indirect quote instead of subjunctive I. Again, note the use of various reporting verbs used to introduce the indirect quote.

Herr Steiner sagt: „Ich **könnte** diesen Tisch wahrscheinlich nicht **reparieren.**"
Herr Steiner glaubt, er **könnte** diesen Tisch wahrscheinlich nicht **reparieren.**

Frau Meyer sagte mir: „Es **würde** mir nichts **ausmachen.**"
Frau Meyer meinte, es **würde** ihr nichts **ausmachen.**

Unser Sohn Völker schrieb uns: „Ich **wäre** in Bremen gut **angekommen**, aber das Wetter war mies."
Unser Sohn Völker schrieb uns, er **wäre** in Bremen gut **angekommen**, aber das Wetter war mies.

Susanne sagte: „Mein Kurs letztes Semester **hätte** nicht so viele Studenten **haben sollen.**"
Susanne meinte, ihr Kurs letztes Semester **hätte** nicht so viele Studenten **haben sollen.**

Exercises: Part Two

Theory Review

1. Fill in the blanks with the correct information.

1. When quoting someone indirectly, putting the verb in ______________________ signals that the reporter is striving for neutrality, in other words is not indicating any bias or personal belief about the veracity or accuracy of the indirect quote.
2. Subjunctive I is also referred to as the "______________________" subjunctive.
3. It is called subjunctive I because its forms are derived from the ______________________ principal part of the verb, which is the ______________________.
4. To come up with the correct subjunctive I form of any verb, including helping verbs and modal verbs, take the ______________________ of the first principal part and add the standard subjunctive endings to it.
5. Whenever a subjunctive I form is identical to an indicative form, to avoid any possible confusion a subjunctive ______________________ form is to be substituted for it.
6. If the original quote is in the subjunctive II, do you use subjunctive I forms in the indirect quote?

   ____

Focus on Meaning and Form

2. In reporting these sentences indirectly, perform the operation to simulate this condition: You want to signal that you are *neutral* and *unbiased* toward the message.

1. Klaus: „Ich hole Tina um acht Uhr ab."

   neutral ________________________________

2. Elke: „Ich habe Franks Telefonnummer vergessen. Ich brauche sie heute."

   neutral ________________________________

3. Frau Berger: „Ich bin nur drei Tage in Hamburg geblieben. Meine Verwandten wohnen da."

   neutral ________________________________

4. Ankes Mutter: „Alles hat geklappt. Ich bin in München gut angekommen."

   neutral ________________________________

5. Martin: „Kannst du heute Abend mitkommen?"

   neutral ________________________________

6. Karen: „Wo hast du Peter kennen gelernt?"

   neutral ________________________________

7. Monika: „Ich halte nicht viel von deinem Freund."

   neutral ________________________________

8. Trudi: „Unsere Freundin Ulrike lügt immer."

   neutral ________________________________

9. Hans: „Du sollst das nicht sagen. Du hast sie missverstanden."

   neutral ________________________________

10. Ephraim: „Ich würde das nicht machen, wenn ich an deiner Stelle wäre."

    neutral ________________________________

Chapter 24 The Passive Voice

Part One

Voice = Perception of the Subject

The term *voice,* like the term *mood,* can sometimes be problematic for students. The term *voice* has nothing to do with vocal qualities. It has to do, rather, with how one perceives the subject of the sentence: whether the subject is seen as the actor or as the person or thing being acted upon will determine the verb forms that agree with it.

There are two voices: active and passive.

active voice:	The subject of the sentence *acts.* The subject is an *actor.* Therefore the subject is *active.*
passive voice:	The subject *does not act.* Rather, the subject is *acted upon* by someone/something else.

The subject is therefore *passive.*

The Passive Voice in English: *to be* + Past Participle

English passive constructions usually use the helping verb *to be* + a past participle. The tense of the helping verb determines the tense of the sentence.

present:	The book *is [being] read* by the students.
past:	The book *was [being] read* by the students.
pres. perf.:	The book *has been read* by the students.
past perf.:	The book *had been read* by the students.
future:	The book *will be read* by the students.

Designating the Agent in Passive Sentences: *by, with, through*

The agent, or "doer," is usually indicated by a prepositional phrase with *by* if the agent is a person. The agent may be left out if it is not needed or not important enough to mention explicitly.

The work . . . *is being done*
was being done
has been done
had been done
will be done . . . by a qualified mechanic.

The preposition *with* is sometimes used instead of *by:* The work was finished *with [the help of] an assistant. With* is used to identify an instrumental agent: This letter was written *with a pen. Through* is sometimes used with abstract agents: The task was accomplished *through hard work.*

Avoiding the Passive in English

Students are often advised by English teachers to avoid using, or certainly overusing, the passive when writing. While there are times when the use of the passive is stylistically justified and natural and sometimes unavoidable, as in scientific and technical writing, the advice is still sound. The reason has to do with the fact that the verb *to be* has a statal, non-dynamic ring to it that is hard to escape. The passive voice in English is, simply put, wimpy, lifeless.

The "Forgotten" Form of the Passive in English: *to get* + Past Participle

English is a Germanic language, and as you have seen, there are many obvious German characteristics in English. One of them is the use of *to get* instead of *to be* with a past participle to form the passive. This is actually quite common, especially in colloquial English, though not so much in formal, written English. Because *to get* signals a *change,* and therefore *action,* it is inherently dynamic:

present:	The campers *are getting rescued* right now.
past:	The campers *got rescued* just in time.
pres. perf.:	Campers *have gotten rescued* from this ravine before.
past perf.:	The campers *had* already *gotten rescued* by the time the news helicopters arrived.
future:	The rangers tell us the campers *will get rescued* by this evening.

NOTE: When *get* is used to form the passive, no agent needs to be mentioned explicitly. Why? Because the combination of *get* + a past participle is, by itself, clearly dynamic; the activity is being named is the focus of attention. The person(s) performing the action are often relatively unimportant. When that is the case, no agent or actor is explicitly necessary.

Recognizing *get* + a past participle as an alternate form of the passive in English will help you better understand and appreciate the German passive and allow you to get more comfortable with it.

Statal vs. Passive

Some students are easily confused about the difference between statal and passive sentences, since both make use of the verb *to be*, for example, *The book is read.* This sentence could be ambiguous. Are we talking about a book lying on a table after someone has finished reading it, or are we talking about a book that many people read? The key ingredient to look for is the presence (or absence) of an agent. Passive sentences describe an activity performed by someone or something, and an agent will usually be expressed to highlight that fact. A statal sentence can have no agent, or "doer," because there is no action.

passive: The book is read *by students.*
statal: The book is read. (The reading is over and done with = no action = a state is described.)

The Passive Voice in German: *werden* + Past Participle

In German the helping verb for the passive is **werden** (*to get; to become*), not **sein**. It is used with a past participle. The passive in German is indeed vibrant and dynamic and may be used without any stylistic qualms. Its overuse should be avoided, however.

The tense of the helping verb **werden** signals the tense of the sentence, just as in English. The main verb morphs into a past participle and migrates to the end of the sentence, to where neutral verb forms always go.

Present and Simple Past Passive

The present passive is formed with present-tense forms of **werden** + a past participle.

Das Buch **wird** von den Studenten **gelesen.**
The book is being read by the students.

Die Arbeit **wird** von uns bald **erledigt.**
The work will be completed by us soon.

Ich **werde** heute vom Arzt **untersucht.**
I'm being examined today by the doctor.

Die Kinder **werden** von Oma **verwöhnt.**
The children are being spoiled by grandma.

The simple past forms are constructed by using a past-tense form of **werden**, that is, **wurden**, with a past participle:

Das Buch **wurde** von den Studenten **gelesen.**
The book was [being] read by the students.

Die Arbeit **wurde** von uns bald danach **erledigt.**
The work was soon completed by us.

Ich **wurde** heute vom Arzt **untersucht.**
I was examined by the doctor today.

Die Kinder **wurden** von Oma **verwöhnt.**
The kids were spoiled by grandma.

Present Perfect and Past Perfect Passive

The present perfect passive is formed by injecting another helping verb into the sentence. This helping verb assists **werden**, which becomes neutralized and migrates to the end of the sentence where the past participle of the main verb already is located. The helping verb **sein** is brought in to help **werden** because **werden** is a **sein**-verb. Present forms of **sein** are used for the present perfect, and past forms of **sein** (**waren**) are used for the past perfect. All very logical.

At the end of the sentence now is not just a past participle, but a *passive* past participle. Study the following sentence for a moment and observe how things have moved and morphed:

Das Kunstwerk **ist** von diesem reichen Mann **gekauft worden.**

As you can see in the sentence above, **ist**, the helping verb for **werden**, is in second, or normal, position, as expected, and **werden** has moved to the very end of the sentence behind the past participle, again, as expected. Notice its form, however. Instead of the expected

***ge*worden**, we merely find **worden**; the past participle combines with **werden** (that is, **worden**) to form a unit—the *passive past participle.* Since the past participle of the main verb normally presents the participial **ge**-prefix, it is not repeated with **werden**. Hence, the expected ***ge*worden** is reduced to **worden**. Remember to view **gekauft worden** as a unit, not as two independent words.

pres. perf.:	Das Buch **ist** von den Studenten **gelesen worden**.
	Die Arbeit **ist** von uns bald danach **erledigt worden**.
	Ich **bin** heute vom Arzt **untersucht worden**.
	Die Kinder **sind** von Oma **verwöhnt worden**.
past perf.:	Das Buch **war** von den Studenten **gelesen worden**.
	Die Arbeit **war** von uns bald **erledigt worden**.
	Ich **war** heute vom Arzt **untersucht worden.**
	Die Kinder **waren** von Oma **verwöhnt worden**.

Future = *werden* + Passive Infinitive

As you have learned previously, the future tense in German is formed by using **werden** as a helping verb with an infinitive that is located at the end of the sentence. To form the future passive, we use **werden** as the future helping verb, which agrees with the subject. **Werden** also comes in as the helping verb for the passive. That means we are using **werden** *twice* (!) in the same sentence, once as a helping verb for the future, and once as a helping verb for the passive.

Die Arbeit **wird** von den Studenten **erledigt werden**.

In the previous sentence, **wird** is the helping verb for the future, and it agrees with the subject, **die Arbeit**. The passive helping verb, **werden**, is in the infinitive and moves to the very end of the sentence, just as expected for the future (helping verb **werden** + infinitive). The past participle **erledigt** is already at the rear of the sentence. The participle **erledigt** and the infinitive **werden** join forces to form a unit—the *passive infinitive.*

future:	Das Buch **wird** von den Studenten **gelesen werden**.
	Die Arbeit **wird** von uns bald **erledigt werden**.
	Ich **werde** heute vom Arzt **untersucht werden**.
	Die Kinder **werden** von Oma **verwöhnt werden**.

Designating Agents with *von, mit,* and *durch*

Agents may be left out of the sentence if they are unimportant enough to mention. When mentioning the agent is desirable, it is expressed with a prepositional phrase, and selecting the correct preposition becomes important.

Personal Agents with *von*

An agent or "doer" that is a person, a group or organization of persons, or a living being (animal, insect, fish, bird) is indicated by a prepositional phrase with **von** (*by*) followed by a dative object:

Die Prüfungen wurden **von dem Lehrer** korrigiert.
Die Patientin wurde **von der Frauenärztin** geheilt°. *healed*

Das neue Lied wird morgen **von dieser Musikgruppe** gesungen werden.
Der Hund ist **von einer Schlange** gebissen worden.
Ich war schon einmal **von einer Biene** gestochen worden.

Instrumental Agents with *mit*

Use **mit** (*with*) with instrumental agents, followed by a dative.

Der Brief wurde **mit einem Kuli** geschrieben.
Der Bolzen° ist **mit einer Zange°** losgelöst worden. *bolt / pliers*
Ein Autofenster war **mit einem Hammer** zerbrochen worden.

Impersonal Agents → *durch*

With impersonal or natural force agents, use **durch** followed by an accusative.

Das Kind ist **durch Nachlässigkeit°** verletzt worden. *negligence*
Das Haus war **durch Wind und Feuer** zerstört worden.

Exercises: Part One

Theory Review

1. Fill in the blanks with the correct information.

1. The term *voice* refers to the ______________________ one has about the subject of the sentence.
2. There are two voices: ______________________ and ______________________.
3. In the ______________________ voice the subject *acts*.
4. In the ______________________ voice the subject does not act, but rather, is *acted upon* by someone or something else.
5. We call that *someone* or *something* else the ______________________.
6. In both German and English this is expressed as a ______________________ phrase.
7. In English the passive consists of a form of the verb ______________________ plus a past participle.
8. Because the verb *to be* comes off as static or lifeless, the passive is generally ______________________ in English, especially in writing. The sentence *The workers are being paid by the boss* is rather dull and listless.
9. A much more dynamic verb sometimes used especially in colloquial English instead of *to be* is ______________________. The sentence "The workers *got paid* by the boss" is more dynamic because it places more emphasis on the action.
10. In German the passive is formed by using ______________________ plus a past participle. This is the same as using ______________________ plus a past participle in English.

11. To signal the tense in a passive sentence, simply come up with the correct form of

 ____________________.

12. The past participle remains ____________________.

13. When **werden** is used in the present and past perfect tenses, it needs its own helping verb, which will be a form of ____________________.

14. The passive **werden** then moves to the end of the sentence and morphs into

 ____________________. This is a truncated form of ____________________. The reason for the disappearance of **ge-** is that it is used in combination with another past participle, which normally supplies the **ge**-prefix, to form the passive past participle.

15. To form the future passive, one uses the helping verb ____________________ plus a

 ____________________ ____________________.

16. This is a compound construction consisting of a ____________________ ____________________ and the infinitive ____________________.

17. In German, if the agent is a person or a machine operated by a person (for example, a car), the preposition ____________________ is used.

18. If the agent is an instrument (usually handheld) by which the action is carried out, then

 ____________________ is used.

19. If the agent is an impersonal force (wind, fire, storm, flood), then ____________________ is used.

20. Is the passive frowned upon in German, as it is in English? ______________ Why or why not?

 ____

Focus on Form [✓]

2. Fill in the correct form of *werden* to indicate tense.

A. Present

1. ____________________ du von Doktor Schneider behandelt?
2. Die Läden ____________________ um neun Uhr morgens geöffnet.
3. Ich ____________________ vom Chef oft schlecht behandelt.
4. Die Hausarbeit ____________________ nie richtig erledigt.
5. Fußball ____________________ überall gespielt.
6. Unser Wagen ____________________ heute repariert.
7. Wein ____________________ gewöhnlich aus einem Glas getrunken.

B. Simple past

1. Amerika ________________ 1492 von Kolumbus entdeckt.
2. Das ________________ letzte Woche erledigt.
3. Der Tisch ________________ ans Fenster geschoben.
4. Wir ________________ von der Polizei erwischt.
5. Die Tür ________________ langsam von einem Fremden geöffnet.
6. Diese Werke ________________ in fünf Sprachen übersetzt.
7. Eine neue Pädagogik ________________ dieses Jahr eingeführt.

C. Present perfect

1. Das Essen ________________ uns vom Kellner schnell serviert ________________.
2. Die Briefmarken ________________ schon gekauft ________________.
3. Die Ehe ________________ in der Kirche geschlossen ________________.
4. Die Rechnungen ________________ am Anfang des Monats bezahlt ________________.
5. Ich ________________ beim Unfall verletzt ________________.

D. Past perfect

1. ________________ der Brief schon abgeschickt ________________?
2. Viele Probleme ________________ von den Ministern besprochen ________________.
3. Mahlers Fünfte Sinfonie ________________ damals zum ersten Mal vom Orchester gespielt ________________.

E. Future

1. Die Romane ________________ von allen Studenten gelesen ________________.
2. Die Möbel ________________ am Montag geliefert ________________.
3. Die Referate ________________ nächste Woche eingehändigt ________________.

3. Put each of the sentences into the passive, then move the sentences through the various tenses: present, past, present perfect, past perfect, future. Mention the agent or doer when necessary or desirable—a judgment call in some cases. When in doubt, include it.

1. Alle suchen das verlorene zweijährige Kind.

   present ________________________________

   past ________________________________

   pres. perf. ________________________________

   past perf. ________________________________

   future ________________________________

2. Ich verkaufe das alte Auto.

present ______________________________

past ______________________________

pres. perf. ______________________________

past perf. ______________________________

future ______________________________

3. Frau Dorner verkauft in diesem Laden Antiquitäten.

present ______________________________

past ______________________________

pres. perf. ______________________________

past perf. ______________________________

future ______________________________

4. Die Stadt baut hier billige Wohnungen.

present ______________________________

past ______________________________

pres. perf. ______________________________

past perf. ______________________________

future ______________________________

5. Der Professor berät Studenten fürs nächste Semester.

present ______________________________

past ______________________________

pres. perf. ______________________________

past perf. ______________________________

future ______________________________

6. Der Arzt untersucht die Patientin.

present ______________________________

past ______________________________

pres. perf. ______________________________

past perf. ______________________________

future ______________________________

Focus on Meaning

4. Fill in the blanks with a past participle that makes good contextual sense.

1. Alles ist gut ____________________ worden. Jetzt kann das Fest beginnen.
2. Der Audi wird in Deutschland ____________________.
3. Der Schlüssel wurde nicht ____________________.
4. Der Tisch war in die Ecke ____________________ worden.
5. Der Wagen wird morgen ____________________ werden.
6. Die Frau wurde von ihrem Frauenarzt ____________________.
7. Die Rolle wurde von einem Tenor ____________________.
8. Die Sache wird gleich ____________________ werden.
9. Die Zeitung ist schon ____________________ worden.
10. Eine neue Methode wurde dieses Jahr ____________________.
11. Herr Steiner wird heute im Friedhof ____________________. Er war neunzig Jahre alt.
12. Hier werden keine alkoholischen Getränke ____________________.
13. Ihr Auto wurde gestern ____________________.
14. In dieser Stadt werden die Läden um sechs Uhr abends ____________________.
15. Sind die Referate schon ____________________ worden?
16. Sind Sie nicht zur Party ____________________ worden?

Focus on Meaning and Form

5. Express the following sentences in the passive. Maintain the same tense. Remember that the direct object of the active sentence will be the subject of the passive equivalent sentence.

1. Die beiden besprachen das Problem ohne Ärger.

   ____

2. Das Ehepaar hat die Gäste im Garten empfangen.

   ____

3. Kolumbus hat Amerika 1492 entdeckt.

   ____

4. Wir erledigten die Aufgabe gestern Abend.

   ____

5. Unsere Mannschaft wird dieses Spiel bestimmt verlieren.

____

6. Ich habe die zwei Autos miteinander verglichen.

____

7. Der Klempner repariert die Heizung jetzt.

____

8. Die Kinder räumen das Zimmer auf.

____

9. Paul wird zwanzig Freunde zur Party einladen.

____

10. Hans und Anja hatten alles schnell vorbereitet.

____

Part Two

Modal Verbs and Passive Infinitives

As you know, modal verbs are used with infinitives. To use a modal verb in a passive sentence, one must employ a passive infinitive with it. You have already learned in this chapter that the passive infinitive consists of a past participle of the main verb + **werden:**

zerstört werden = *to be/get/become destroyed*
vergessen werden = *to be/get/become forgotten*

Present and Simple Past

The modal verb will signal not only the subject's attitude toward the action (infinitive) but also the tense.

present: Dieser Film **muss** unbedingt **gesehen werden.**
Die Übungen **können** für morgen leicht **erledigt werden.**
Das Referat **soll** nächsten Mittwoch **eingereicht werden.**
Solche Details **dürfen** nicht **übersehen werden.**

past: Ich **wollte** von der Polizei über den Unfall **informiert werden.**
Wir **konnten** zu der Zeit nicht **erreicht werden.**
Die Eltern **sollten** von den Lehrern **benachrichtigt werden.**
Die Semesterarbeit **musste** schon letzte Woche **eingereicht werden.**

Present Perfect, Past Perfect, and Future → Passive Double Infinitives

You have learned in Chapter 8 that whenever a modal verb is used with a dependent infinitive in the present perfect, past perfect, or future, the helping verb **haben** or **werden** is used with a double infinitive:

pres. perf.:	Ich **habe** das Projekt nicht **beenden können.**
past perf.:	Ich **hatte** das Projekt nicht **beenden können.**
future:	Ich **werde** das Projekt nicht **beenden können.**

Note how the same sentences are expressed in the passive:

pres. perf.:	Das Projekt **hat** nicht **beendet werden können.**
past perf.:	Das Projekt **hatte** nicht **beendet werden können.**
future:	Das Projekt **wird** nicht **beendet werden können.**

Other than the different subjects in the two sets of sentences, the helping verbs remain the same, and there is a double infinitive construction as well. The difference in the second set is due to the coupling of a *passive* infinitive with a modal infinitive: **beendet werden + können.** The result is a *passive* double infinitive.

The present and past passives are very commonly used in most conversational exchanges, the compound tenses requiring passive double infinitives considerably less so. Be able to produce the present and past with ease, and gain enough familiarity with the compound tenses in the passive to recognize them when heard or read and use them when the need arises.

Introductory *es* in Passive Sentences

The pronoun **es** is sometimes used to hold down slot 1 in a passive sentence. It is essentially a stylistic ploy, and **es** is not rendered in English. The form of **werden** agrees with the subject, which follows it. Merely learn to recognize it when you read it or hear it.

Zwanzig Passagiere wurden verletzt. = **Es** wurden zwanzig Passagiere verletzt.

Dative Objects in Passive Sentences

The direct object in an active sentence is the person or thing acted upon by the subject:

Ich mache **meine Hausaufgaben.** Toni hat **den Roman** gelesen.

The subject in a passive sentence is the person or thing acted upon by some agent, named or unnamed:

Meine Hausaufgaben werden gemacht. **Der Roman** wird [von Toni] gelesen.

As you can see, the accusative object of an active sentence is the same as the subject in its corresponding passive sentence, meaning that any active sentence can theoretically be rendered in the passive, and vice versa. But what happens when the verb takes a dative object rather than an accusative one? Does it also morph into a nominative subject when the same sentence is rendered in the passive? NO. The dative object remains dative. We may begin the sentence with the dative object, thus filling slot 1, but we will not add a subject. If we keep the dative object behind the verb, we will have to come up with a "dummy subject" to occupy slot one in a statement. That dummy subject will be **es**, and the verb must agree with it. Study the equivalent sentences:

Jemand hat **mir** geholfen. = **Mir** ist geholfen. = *Es* ist **mir** geholfen.
Niemand glaubte **ihm**. = **Ihm** wurde nicht geglaubt. = *Es* wurde **ihm** nicht geglaubt.

Man hat **uns** gesagt, dass der Präsident unsere Stadt bald besucht. =
Uns wurde gesagt, dass der Präsident unsere Stadt bald besucht. =
Es wurde **uns** gesagt, dass der Präsident unsere Stadt bald besucht.

Passive Idioms to Designate an Event

The passive is used to indicate an activity or event in which there seems to be no agent and nothing acted upon; just an activity is named. Often the dummy subject **es** is used to fill slot 1 in the sentence. If the sentence begins with another complement, however, **es** may not be used, since slot 1 is filled:

Es wird samstags geschlossen. = Samstags wird geschlossen.
Es wird am Samstag nur geliefert. = Am Samstag wird nur geliefert.
Es wurde bei der Party viel getanzt. = Bei der Party wurde viel getanzt.
Es wurde in der High School nicht viel gelernt. = In der High School wurde nicht viel gelernt.

"Statal/False Passive": *sein* + Past Participle

The statal passive is an unfortunate misnomer. By definition, a passive sentence names an activity; a statal sentence does not. There can be nothing passive about a statal sentence because no action is being described whatsoever, only a state. Therefore, using the term *passive* is erroneous and misleading. All that is involved here is the use of a past participle with **sein** to indicate a factual *state* or the *condition* of something. What we have is a simple *statal* sentence. You will note the complete absence of an agent in so-called "statal passive" sentences. Another name for the *statal passive* is *false passive*. It is just as erroneous and misleading, and for the same reason.

*state = **no** action*		*true passive = action*
Der Laden **ist geschlossen.**	vs.	Der Laden **wird** [vom Besitzer] **geschlossen.**
Der Roman **ist geschrieben.**	vs.	Der Roman **wird** [von der Frau] **geschrieben.**
Das Auto **war repariert.**	vs.	Das Auto **wurde** [vom Mechaniker] **repariert.**

Alternatives to the Passive

Although the German passive is dynamic and its use is not frowned upon, there are a number of constructions that may be employed as alternatives to the passive.

The Use of *man*

Man may be used with an active verb to express any passive equivalent that does not contain an agent.

Das Lied wurde gesungen. → **Man sang** das Lied.
Der Fehler ist übersehen worden. → **Man hat** den Fehler **übersehen**.

Sein + *zu* + Infinitive

Sein + **zu** + an infinitive is used to create a statal sentence that is sometimes expressed in the passive in English.

Solche Dinge **sind** leicht **zu übersehen.**
Such things are easy to overlook.

Hunde **sind** an der Leine **zu führen.**
Dogs are to be kept (lead) on a leash.

Die Chefin **ist** im Moment nicht **zu erreichen.**
The boss is not to be reached at the moment.

Reflexive Constructions

Reflexive pronouns used with 1) verbs and 2) with **lassen** + an infinitive may frequently serve as a substitute for the passive.

Das **versteht sich** leicht. = Das wird leicht verstanden.
Der Roman **liest sich** leicht. = Der Roman wird leicht gelesen.

Das **lässt sich** leicht **verstehen.** = Das wird leicht verstanden.
Der Roman **ließ sich** leicht **lesen.** = Der Roman wurde leicht gelesen.

Exercises: Part Two

Theory Review

1. Fill in the blanks with the correct information.

1. As you learned in a previous chapter, modal verbs are used with an ____________________ found at the ____________________ of the sentence or clause.
2. The same holds true in the passive except that the infinitive must be a ____________________ infinitive.
3. To form one, first mention the ____________________ ____________________ followed immediately by ____________________.
4. Provide an example: ____
5. To form a passive with a modal verb in a compound past tense (present and past perfect), the modal verb will need a helping verb, which will be a form of ____________________.
6. The modal verb moves to the end of the sentence where there already is a ____________________ infinitive.

7. The modal verb morphs into an ______________________, thus forming a double infinitive, a *passive* double infinitive.

8. Anytime there is a need to "invent" a subject to hold down slot 1 in a statement, the pronoun ______________________ is used.

9. If a verb that takes a dative object is used in a passive sentence, does the dative object morph into a nominative the same way an accusative object would? ____________

10. Explain what happens to the dative object: ______________________________________

____

11. In the sentence: **Das Buch *wird* gelesen**, is an action taking place? ____________

12. In the sentence **Das Buch *ist* gelesen**, is an action taking place? ____________

13. This latter sentence is neither active nor passive. It is a ______________________ sentence because no action takes place.

14. There are a number of ways that a passive sentence may be expressed by an alternative active construction. Express this sentence several different ways: **Der Wagen wird sofort ohne Schwierigkeiten repariert**.

____

____

____

____

Focus on Form [✓]

2. Modal verbs. Express these sentences in the passive. Maintain the same tense.

1. Ich muss mein Zimmer aufräumen.

____

2. Wir sollten unsere Hausaufgaben machen.

____

3. Man darf dieses neue Auto nicht fahren.

____

4. Man soll diese Tür reparieren.

____

5. Wir müssen noch zwei Konzertkarten kaufen.

____

6. Wir sollten alles verbessern.

7. Man hat es endlich tun dürfen.

8. Man muss das Badezimmer putzen.

9. Man musste den Klempner und den Elektriker anrufen.

10. Ich werde etwas Geld sparen können.

11. Ich muss mein Büro renovieren.

12. Steffi und Sonja sollen eine Party planen.

13. Wie soll man Ihren Namen schreiben?

Focus on Form and Meaning

3. Alternatives to the passive. Paraphrase the following sentences three different ways.

1. Die Reparatur wird leicht gemacht.

2. Die Aufgabe wurde schnell erledigt.

4. Paraphrase the following in the passive. Maintain the same tense.

1. Die Studenten haben das Theaterstück gelesen.

2. Man hatte den Wagen gegen einen Baum gefahren.

3. Der Zerstörer hat das U-Boot versenkt.

____

4. Man liefert das Sofa am Dienstag.

____

5. Ich muss die Arbeit für morgen erledigen.

____

6. Man soll die Kinder von der Schule abholen.

____

7. Die Mannschaft wird das Spiel verlieren.

____

5. Express the following sentences in German, using active or passive voice.

A

1. The watch has to be repaired.

____

2. That will have to be done in the office.

____

3. The furniture is supposed to be delivered (**liefern**) today.

____

4. I'd like to be invited.

____

5. That has to be taken care of.

____

6. This picture must not be sold.

____

7. It had to be repeated three times.

____

8. She wasn't helped at all.

____

9. Are we really believed?

____

10. Is there a dance tonight?

____

B

1. The professor was never contradicted.

____

2. They were threatened.

____

3. You were thanked for your help.

____

4. Is there a lot of drinking at the university?

____

5. No smoking in restaurants!

____

6. The house is being sold.

____

7. The doors are closed.

____

8. The bills are paid.

____

9. That's taken care of (finished).

____

10. The war is lost.

____

C

1. Are the students well prepared?

____

2. Is gasoline sold here?

____

3. The car is repaired.

____

4. The hotel was destroyed by fire.

____

5. Everything is thoroughly prepared.

____

Appendix

1. Present Tense [Ch. 1]

Standard Present-Tense Endings

singular	*plural*	*formal/polite*
ich: stem + **-e**	**wir**: stem + **-en**	
du: stem + **-st**	**ihr**: stem + **-t**	**Sie**: stem + **-en**
er/sie/es: stem + **-t**	**sie**: stem + **-en**	

	Regular Verb	*Regular Verbs with **d**- and **t**-Stems*	
	machen	**warten**	**finden**
ich	mache	warte	finde
du	machst	wart**est**	find**est**
er/sie/es	macht	wart**et**	find**et**
wir	machen	warten	finden
ihr	macht	wart**et**	find**et**
sie	machen	warten	findet
Sie	machen	warten	finden

Present Tense of *haben, sein,* and *werden*

	haben	**sein***	**werden**
ich	habe	**bin**	werde
du	**hast**	**bist**	**wirst**
er/sie/es	**hat**	**ist**	**wird**
wir	haben	**sind**	werden
ihr	habt	**seid**	werdet
sie	haben	**sind**	werdet
Sie	haben	**sind**	werden

*Remember that the final **-d** in **sind** and **seid** is devoiced, meaning the **-d** sounds like a **-t**.

2. Simple Past [Ch. 3]

	Regular Verb	*Irregular Verb*	*Mixed Verb*
	machen	**sprechen**	**bringen**
ich	mach**te**	**sprach**	brach**te**
du	mach**test**	sprachst	brach**test**
er/sie/es	mach**te**	**sprach**	brach**te**
wir	mach**ten**	sprachen	brach**ten**
ihr	mach**tet**	spracht	brach**tet**
sie	mach**ten**	sprachen	brach**ten**
Sie	mach**ten**	sprachen	brach**ten**

Simple Past of *haben, sein,* and *werden*

	haben	**sein**	**werden**
ich	**hatte**	**war**	**wurde**
du	**hattest**	**warst**	**wurdest**
er/sie/es	**hatte**	**war**	**wurde**
wir	**hatten**	**waren**	**wurden**
ihr	**hattet**	**wart**	**wurdet**
sie	**hatten**	**waren**	**wurden**
Sie	**hatten**	**waren**	**wurden**

3. Principal Parts of Verbs: Irregular and Mixed Verbs [Ch. 3]

Principal Parts of Irregular (Strong) and Mixed Verbs

infinitive	*present*	*past*	*past participle*	*English meaning*
backen	bäckt	buk	gebacken	*to bake*
beißen	beißt	biss	gebissen	*to bite*
biegen	biegt	bog	gebogen	*to bend*
bieten	bietet	bot	geboten	*to offer*
binden	bindet	band	gebunden	*to bind/tie*
bitten	bittet	bat	gebeten	*to ask/request*
bleiben	bleibt	blieb	*ist* geblieben	*to stay/remain*
brechen	bricht	brach	gebrochen	*to break*
brennen	brennt	brannte	gebrannt	*to burn*
bringen	bringt	brachte	gebracht	*to bring*
denken	denkt	dachte	gedacht	*to think*

infinitive	*present*	*past*	*past participle*	*English meaning*
essen	isst	aß	gegessen	*to eat*
fahren	fährt	fuhr	*ist/hat* gefahren	*to travel/drive a vehicle*
fallen	fällt	fiel	*ist* gefallen	*to fall*
fangen	fängt	fing	gefangen	*to catch*
finden	findet	fand	gefunden	*to find*
fliegen	fliegt	flog	*ist/hat* geflogen	*to fly*
fliehen	flieht	floh	*ist* geflohen	*to flee*
fressen	frisst	fraß	gefressen	*to eat (by an animal)*
frieren	friert	fror	*ist/hat* gefroren	*to freeze*
geben	gibt	gab	gegeben	*to give*
gehen	geht	ging	*ist* gegangen	*to go*
gießen	gießt	goss	gegossen	*to pour*
greifen	greift	griff	gegriffen	*to grasp/grab/seize*
haben	hat	hatte	gehabt	*to have*
halten	hält	hielt	gehalten	*to hold*
hängen	hängt	hing	gehangen	*to hang (intransitive)*
heben	hebt	hob	gehoben	*to lift/heft*
heißen	heißt	hieß	geheißen	*to be called (by name)*
helfen	hilft	half	geholfen	*to help*
kennen	kennt	kannte	gekannt	*to know/be familiar with*
klingen	klingt	klang	geklungen	*to sound*
kommen	kommt	kam	*ist* gekommen	*to come*
laden	lädt	lud	geladen	*to load*
lassen	lässt	ließ	gelassen	*to allow/let; to have done*
laufen	läuft	lief	*ist* gelaufen	*to run*
leiden	leidet	litt	gelitten	*to suffer*
leihen	leiht	lieh	geliehen	*to lend*
lesen	liest	las	gelesen	*to read*
liegen	liegt	lag	gelegen	*to lie/recline*
lügen	lügt	log	gelogen	*to lie/tell a lie*
messen	misst	maß	gemessen	*to measure*
nehmen	nimmt	nahm	genommen	*to take*
nennen	nennt	nannte	genannt	*to name*
reiten	reitet	ritt	*ist/hat* geritten	*to ride*
rennen	rennt	rannte	*ist* gerannt	*to race/run*
riechen	riecht	roch	gerochen	*to smell*
rufen	ruft	rief	gerufen	*to call*
saufen	säuft	soff	gesoffen	*to drink to excess or like an animal*
schaffen	schafft	schuf	geschaffen	*to create*

Principal Parts of Irregular (Strong) and Mixed Verbs—*Continued*

infinitive	*present*	*past*	*past participle*	*English meaning*
scheiden	scheidet	schied	geschieden	*to separate*
scheinen	scheint	schien	geschienen	*to seem/appear; to shine*
schieben	schiebt	schob	geschoben	*to shove*
schießen	schießt	schoss	geschossen	*to shoot*
schlafen	schläft	schlief	geschlafen	*to sleep*
schlagen	schlägt	schlug	geschlagen	*to strike/hit*
schließen	schließt	schloss	geschlossen	*to close*
schmeißen	schmeißt	schmiss	geschmissen	*to throw/fling*
schmelzen	schmilzt	schmolz	*ist/hat* geschmolzen	*to melt*
schneiden	schneidet	schnitt	geschnitten	*to cut*
schreiben	schreibt	schrieb	geschrieben	*to write*
schreien	schreit	schrie	geschrien	*to scream/cry*
schreiten	schreitet	schritt	*ist* geschritten	*to stride*
schweigen	schweigt	schwieg	geschwiegen	*to be silent*
schwimmen	schwimmt	schwamm	*ist* geschwommen	*to swim*
sehen	sieht	sah	gesehen	*to see*
sein	ist	war	*ist* gewesen	*to be*
senden	sendet	sandte	gesandt	*to send*
singen	singt	sang	gesungen	*to sing*
sinken	sinkt	sank	*ist* gesunken	*to sink*
sitzen	sitzt	saß	gesessen	*to sit (state of sitting)*
sprechen	spricht	sprach	gesprochen	*to speak*
stehen	steht	stand	gestanden	*to stand*
stehlen	stiehlt	stahl	gestohlen	*to steal*
steigen	steigt	stieg	*ist* gestiegen	*to climb*
sterben	stirbt	starb	*ist* gestorben	*to die*
stinken	stinkt	stank	gestunken	*to stink*
stoßen	stößt	stieß	gestoßen	*to push*
streichen	streicht	strich	gestrichen	*to stroke/pet; to spread*
streiten	streitet	stritt	gestritten	*to argue*
tragen	trägt	trug	getragen	*to carry*
treffen	trifft	traf	getroffen	*to meet; to hit*
treiben	treibt	trieb	getrieben	*to drive; to propel*
treten	tritt	trat	*ist/hat* getreten	*to step/kick*
trinken	trinkt	trank	getrunken	*to drink*
tun	tut	tat	getan	*to do*
wachsen	wächst	wuchs	*ist* gewachsen	*to grow*
waschen	wäscht	wusch	gewaschen	*to wash*
wenden	wendet	wandte	gewandt	*to turn*
werden	wird	wurde	*ist* geworden	*to become*

infinitive	*present*	*past*	*past participle*	*English meaning*
werfen	wirft	warf	geworfen	*to throw*
wissen	weiß	wusste	gewusst	*to know (factually)*
ziehen	zieht	zog	*ist/hat* gezogen	*to move/pull*
zwingen	zwingt	zwang	gezwungen	*to force*

4. Future [Ch. 4]

Helping Verb *Werden*

singular	*plural*	*formal/polite*
ich **werde**	wir **werden**	
du **wirst**	ihr **werdet**	Sie **werden**
er/sie/es **wird**	sie **werden**	

future = *werden* + infinitive

Ich **werde** für den Test **lernen**.
Er **wird** es **verstehen**.
Wird Sabine das **wissen**?
Wirst du auch **kommen**?
Werdet ihr das **kaufen**?
Werden Sie das für uns **machen**?

5. Common Verbs with Inseparable Prefixes [Ch. 6]

- **Be-** makes the verb automatically transitive and may affect the meaning of the core verb.
  beantworten *to answer*
  befehlen *to order, command*
  beginnen *to begin*
  begreifen *to comprehend, grasp*
  begrüßen *to greet*
  bekommen *to receive*
  beruhigen *to calm [down]*
  besprechen *to discuss*
  besuchen *to visit*
  beweisen *to prove*

- **Emp-** colors the meaning of the core verb variously.
  empfangen *to receive, welcome*
  empfehlen *to recommend*
  empfinden *to feel*

- **Ent-** signals a removal, detachment, or separation of some kind.
  entdecken *to discover, find*
  sich **entfalten** *to unfold*
  entkommen *to escape*
  entwickeln *to develop*

- **Er-** signals *to make.*
  erfinden *to invent*
  erledigen *to complete, finish*
  erleichtern *to ease, make easy*
  ermöglichen *to make possible*
  ersetzen *to replace*
  erzählen *to tell a story*

- **Ge**- colors the meaning of the core verb variously.
  gefallen *to please*
  gehören *to belong to*
  gelingen *to succeed*
  genießen *to enjoy*
  geschehen *to happen*
  gewinnen *to win*

- **Hinter**- signals *behind* and sometimes a deception.
  hinterlassen *to leave behind*

- **Miss**- signals that something is amiss, false, or incorrect.
  missdeuten *to misinterpret*
  misshandeln *to mistreat, abuse*
  misstrauen *to mistrust*
  missverstehen *to misunderstand*

- **Ver**- can signal that an error has been made, that something is being consumed, that something is being pushed away, or, like **er**-, that something is being made or altered in some way.
  sich **verändern** *to change (appearance)*
  verbergen *to hide, conceal*
  verbessern *to improve*
  verbrauchen *to consume, use up*
  verbrennen *to burn up*
  verbringen *to spend time*
  sich **verfahren** *to get lost driving*
  verfaulen *to spoil, rot, decompose*
  vergessen *to forget*
  vergleichen *to compare*
  verzeihen *to forgive, pardon*
  sich **verlaufen** *to get lost walking*
  verlieren *to lose*
  verlegen *to misplace*
  vermeiden *to avoid*
  vernichten *to annihilate*
  verschwinden *to disappear*
  versprechen *to promise*
  vertreiben *to drive off, repel*
  verursachen *to cause*
  verwöhnen *to spoil (children)*

- **Zer**- signals *to pieces, to shreds* and denotes the end or destruction of something.
  zerbrechen *to break into pieces*
  zerfallen *to fall to pieces*
  zerreißen *to tear to pieces*
  zerschneiden *to cut to pieces*
  zerstören *to destroy*

6. Common Verbs with Separable Prefixes [Ch. 7]

- **Ab**- *off, away, down*
  abfahren *to drive off*
  abholen *to pick up*
  abnehmen *to take off weight*
  abschließen *to lock, complete*
  abschneiden *to cut off*
  abschreiben *to copy*

- **An**- *on, at, to*
  anfangen *to begin*
  anhören *to listen to*
  ankommen *to arrive*
  anmachen *to turn on*
  anrufen *to call up* (phone)
  ansehen *to look at, watch*

- **Auf**- *up, open, on*
  aufheben *to lift up*
  aufhören *to stop, cease*
  aufmachen *to open [up]*
  aufpassen *to pay attention*
  aufräumen *to straighten up*
  aufstehen *to stand/get up*
  aufwachen *to wake up*

- **Aus**- *out, off*
  ausbrechen *to break out*
  ausgeben *to spend*
  ausgehen *to go out*
  auslachen *to mock, make fun of*
  ausmachen *to turn out, turn off*
  aussehen *to look, appear*
  austauschen *to exchange*
  ausziehen *to pull off, undress*

- **Ein-** *in, into*
  einführen *to introduce*
  einkaufen *to shop*
  einladen *to invite*
  eintreten *to enter, step into*

- **Fern-** *distant, far off*
  fernsehen *to watch TV*

- **Fort-** *away, forth*
  fortfahren *to depart* (by vehicle)
  fortgehen *to depart* (on foot)
  fortsetzen *to continue, set forth*

- **Los-** *loose* (a detachment of some kind is indicated)
  loslassen *to let go, let loose*
  loslösen *to detach*
  losschneiden *to cut loose*
  loswerden *to get rid of*

- **Mit-** *with, along [with]*
  mitbringen *to bring along*
  mitgehen *to go along*
  mitkommen *to come along*
  mitmachen *to participate*
  mitspielen *to play with*
  mitteilen *to inform, tell*

- **Nach-** *after, behind*
  nacherzählen *to retell*
  nachgeben *to give in*
  nachschlagen *to look up*

- **Um-** *around, over, about*
  umdrehen *to turn around*
  umkippen *to tip over*
  umsteigen *to transfer* (train, bus)
  umziehen *to move* (one's residence)

- **Vor-** *before, ahead of time (pre-)*
  vorbereiten *to prepare*
  vorgehen *to run fast* (clock)
  vorhaben *to intend*
  vorlesen *to lecture, read aloud*
  vorschlagen *to suggest*
  vorstellen *to introduce*

- **Vorbei-** *by, past*
  vorbeifahren *to drive by*
  vorbeikommen *to come by*
  vorbeilaufen *to run by*

- **Weg-** *away*
  wegfahren *to drive away*
  weggehen *to go away*
  weglaufen *to run away*
  wegstellen *to put away*
  wegwerfen *to throw away*

- **Weiter-** *further, farther, additionally, continually*
  weiterfahren *to travel farther*
  weitergehen *to go farther*
  weiterlesen *to read further*
  weitermachen *to carry on*

- **Zu-** *to, toward, closed, shut off*
  zuhören *to listen to*
  zumachen *to close*
  zunehmen *to gain/put on weight*
  zuwinken *to waveto/at*

- **Zurück-** *back*
  zurückbleiben *to stay behind*
  zurückbringen *to bring back*
  zurückgehen *to go back*
  zurückkommen *to come back*
  zurückwerfen *to throw back*

- **Zusammen-** *together*
  zusammenarbeiten *to work together, collaborate*
  zusammenbinden *to tie/bind together*
  zusammenbrechen *to collapse*
  zusammenbringen *to bring together, join*
  zusammenkommen *to come together, assemble*
  zusammenstellen *to put/place together*

7. Modal Verbs [Ch. 8]

Present Tense of Modal Verbs

	dürfen	können	mögen	müssen	sollen	wollen
ich	darf	kann	mag	muss	soll	will
du	darfst	kannst	magst	musst	sollst	willst
er/sie/es	darf	kann	mag	muss	soll	will
wir	dürfen	können	mögen	müssen	sollen	wollen
ihr	dürft	könnt	mögt	müsst	sollt	wollt
sie	dürfen	können	mögen	müssen	sollen	wollen
Sie	dürfen	können	mögen	müssen	sollen	wollen

The *möchte*-Forms

ich **möchte**	wir **möchten**	
du **möchtest**	ihr **möchtet**	Sie **möchten**
er/sie/es **möchte**	sie **möchten**	

Simple Past Tense of Modal Verbs

	dürfen	können	mögen	müssen	sollen	wollen
ich	durfte	konnte	mochte	musste	sollte	wollte
du	durftest	konntest	mochtest	musstest	solltest	wolltest
er/sie/es	durfte	konnte	mochte	musste	sollte	wollte
wir	durften	konnten	mochten	mussten	sollten	wollten
ihr	durftet	konntet	mochtet	musstet	solltet	wolltet
sie	durfen	konnten	mochten	mussten	sollten	wollten
Sie	durften	konnten	mochten	mussten	sollten	wollten

8. Noun Genders [Ch. 9]

Masculine Nouns

- male persons
- male animals
- occupations
- nationalities
- makes of cars
- days of the week
- parts of days
- months
- seasons
- weather terms
- directions
- nouns ending in **-en**
- most nouns ending in **-er**
- nouns ending in **-ich** or **-ig**
- nouns ending in **-ang**
- Rhine river and tributaries

Masculine Weak/N-Nouns

Junge, Knabe, Kollege, Kunde, Name, Neffe, Zimmerkollege, Franzose, Russe; Agent, Patient, Präsident, Student; Kamerad, Soldat; Journalist, Polizist

Feminine Nouns

- female persons
- female animals
- occupations
- nationalities
- German rivers

- nouns ending in these common endings and suffixes:

-e	**-ik**	**-tät**
-ei	**-ion**	**-ung**
-enz	**-heit**	**-ur**
-ie	**-keit**	
-in	**-schaft**	

Neuter Nouns

- small, immature persons and animals
- many nouns with the prefix **Ge-**
- most metals
- most countries
- gerunds
- letters of the alphabet
- fractions

- nouns ending in these common suffixes:

-chen	**-lein**	**-el** or **-l**

9. Case Affiliations [Ch. 9]

Nominative Case

- the subject of the sentence
- the predicate noun
- the predicate adjective
- direct address

Accusative Case

- the direct object
- prepositions **bis, durch für, gegen, ohne, um**
- noun phrases denoting specific time, duration of time, and specific measure

Dative Case

- the indirect object
- the beneficiary
- verbs with dative objects: **ähneln, antworten, danken, folgen, gefallen, gehören, geschehen, glauben, helfen, trauen**
- prepositions **aus, außer, bei, mit, nach, seit, von, zu, gegenüber**

Dative-Accusative Cases

- prepositions **an, auf, hinter, vor, über, unter, in, neben, zwischen**

Genitive Case

- the possessor or owner
- a part of a whole
- prepositions **(an)statt, trotz, während, wegen, diesseits, jenseits, innerhalb, außerhalb**
- noun phrases indicating indefinite or vague time

10. Definite Article and *der*-Words [Ch. 10]

Definite Article, *der*-Words, and Their Primary Case Sounds

	masculine	*feminine*	*neuter*	*plural*
nominative:	**der** dieser **r**	**die** diese **e**	**das** dieses **s**	**die** diese **e**
accusative:	**den** diesen **n**	**die** diese **e**	**das** dieses **s**	**die** diese **e**
dative:	**dem** diesem **m**	**der** dieser **r**	**dem** diesem **m**	**den** diesen **n**
genitive:	**des** dieses **s**	**der** dieser **r**	**des** dieses **s**	**der** dieser **r**

The **der**-words are **dieser, jeder, jener, welcher, mancher, solcher,** and **beide** *(pl.)*.

11. Indefinite Article, *ein*-Words, and Primary Case Sounds [Ch. 10]

Indefinite Article, *ein*-Words, and Their Primary Case Sounds

	masculine	*feminine*	*neuter*	*plural*
nominative:	**ein** mein **—**	**eine** meine **e**	**ein** mein **—**	**keine** meine **e**
accusative:	**einen** meinen **n**	**eine** meine **e**	**ein** mein **—**	**keine** meine **e**
dative:	**einem** meinem **m**	**einer** meiner **r**	**einem** meinem **m**	**keinen** meinen **n**
genitive:	**eines** meines **s**	**einer** meiner **r**	**eines** meines **s**	**keiner** meiner **r**

The **ein**-words are **kein** and the possessive adjectives (**mein, dein, sein, ihr, euer, Ihr**).

12. Primary Sound Paradigm of *der*-Words and *ein*-Words [Ch. 10]

Summary of Primary Case Sounds:
***der*-Words or *ein*-Words + Noun Endings**

	masculine	*feminine*	*neuter*	*plural*
nominative:	**r** *or* —	**e**	**s** *or* —	**e**
accusative:	**n**	**e**	**s** *or* —	**e**
dative:	**m**	**r**	**m**	**n + n**
genitive:	**s + s**	**r**	**s + s**	**r**

13. *Der*-Words and Following Adjectives [Ch. 11]

Primary and Secondary Case Sounds:
***der*-Words and Following Adjectives**

	masculine	*feminine*	*neuter*	*plural*
nominative:	der alte Mann $\mathbf{r}^{\mathbf{e}}$	die kleine Frau $\mathbf{e}^{\mathbf{e}}$	das schöne Mädchen $\mathbf{s}^{\mathbf{e}}$	die jungen Leute $\mathbf{e}^{\mathbf{n}}$
accusative:	den alten Mann $\mathbf{n}^{\mathbf{n}}$	die kleine Frau $\mathbf{e}^{\mathbf{e}}$	das schöne Mädchen $\mathbf{s}^{\mathbf{e}}$	die jungen Leute $\mathbf{e}^{\mathbf{n}}$
dative:	dem alten Mann $\mathbf{m}^{\mathbf{n}}$	der kleinen Frau $\mathbf{r}^{\mathbf{n}}$	dem schönen Mädchen $\mathbf{m}^{\mathbf{n}}$	den jungen Leuten $\mathbf{n}^{\mathbf{n}} + \mathbf{n}$
genitive:	des alten Mannes $\mathbf{s}^{\mathbf{n}} + \mathbf{s}$	der kleinen Frau $\mathbf{r}^{\mathbf{n}}$	des schönen Mädchens $\mathbf{s}^{\mathbf{n}} + \mathbf{s}$	der jungen Leute $\mathbf{r}^{\mathbf{n}}$

14. *Ein*-Words and Following Adjectives [Ch. 11]

Primary and Secondary Case Sounds:
***ein*-Words and Following Adjectives**

	masculine	*feminine*	*neuter*	*plural*
nominative:	ein alter Mann $\_\_^{r}$	eine kleine Frau e^{e}	ein schönes Mädchen $\_\_^{s}$	keine jungen Leute e^{n}
accusative:	einen alten Mann n^{n}	eine kleine Frau e^{e}	ein schönes Mädchen $\_\_^{s}$	keine jungen Leute e^{n}
dative:	einem alten Mann m^{n}	einer kleinen Frau r^{n}	einem schönen Mädchen m^{n}	keinen jungen Leuten $n^{n} + n$
genitive:	eines alten Mannes $s^{n} + s$	einer kleinen Frau r^{n}	eines schönen Mädchens $s^{n} + s$	keiner jungen Leute r^{n}

15. Unpreceded Adjectives [Ch. 11]

Primary Sounds: Unpreceded Adjectives

	masculine	*feminine*	*neuter*	*plural*
nominative:	schwarzer Kaffee r	kalte Milch e	deutsches Bier s	junge Leute e
accusative:	schwarzen Kaffee n	kalte Milch e	deutsches Bier s	junge Leute e
dative:	schwarzem Kaffee m	kalter Milch r	deutschem Bier m	jungen Leuten n + n
genitive:	schwarzen Kaffees $^{n} + s$	kalter Milch r	deutschen Bieres $^{n} + s$	junger Leute r

16. Complete Paradigm of Primary and Secondary Case Sounds [Ch. 11]

Synthesis of Primary and Secondary Case Sounds:
***der*-words, *ein*-words, Following Adjectives + Noun Endings**

	masculine	*feminine*	*neuter*	*plural*
nominative:	r^{e} *or* $\_\_^{r}$	e^{e}	s^{e} *or* $\_\_^{s}$	e^{n}
accusative:	n^{n}	e^{e}	s^{e} *or* $\_\_^{s}$	e^{n}
dative:	m^{n}	r^{n}	m^{n}	$n^{n} + n$
genitive:	$s^{n} + s$	r^{n}	$s^{n} + s$	r^{n}

17. Pronouns [Ch. 13]

Personal Pronouns

	singular					*plural*			*formal*
nominative:	ich	du	er	sie	es	wir	ihr	sie	Sie
accusative:	mich	dich	ihn	sie	es	uns	euch	sie	Sie
dative:	mir	dir	ihm	ihr	ihm	uns	euch	ihnen	Ihnen

Demonstrative Pronouns

	masculine	*feminine*	*neuter*	*plural*
nominative:	der	die	das	die
accusative:	den	die	das	die
dative:	dem	der	dem	**denen**
genitive:	**dessen**	**deren**	**dessen**	**deren**

Forms of the Reflexive Pronoun

	singular					*plural*			*formal*
nominative:	ich	du	er	sie	es	wir	ihr	sie	Sie
accusative:	mich	dich	**sich**	**sich**	**sich**	uns	euch	**sich**	**sich**
dative:	mir	dir	**sich**	**sich**	**sich**	uns	euch	**sich**	**sich**

18. Prepositions [Ch. 16]

Accusative Prepositions	**Dative Prepositions**	**Dative-Accusative Prepositions**	**Genitive Prepositions**
bis	aus	an — auf	statt/anstatt
durch	außer	über — unter	trotz
für	bei	hinter — vor	während
gegen	mit	in	wegen
ohne	nach	neben	innerhalb — außerhalb
um	seit	zwischen	diesseits — jenseits
	von		
hindurch	zu		
pro			
entlang	gegenüber		

19. Idioms [Ch. 16]

Verbs with Dative Prepositions

abhängen von *to depend on*
einladen zu *to invite to*
erzählen von *to tell a story about*
fragen nach *to ask/inquire about*
gratulieren zu *to congratulate on*
halten von *to think of (opinion)*
handeln von *to deal with*
helfen bei *to help with*
sprechen mit *to speak with/to*
sprechen von *to speak of*
träumen von *to dream of*

Verbs with Accusative Prepositions

bitten um *to ask for, request*
danken für *to thank for*

Verbs with Dative-Accusative Prepositions

antworten auf *to answer (a thing)*
arbeiten an (+ dat.) *to work on*
aufpassen auf *to keep an eye on; to pay attention*
denken an *to think of (briefly)*
hoffen auf *to hope for*
lachen über *to laugh about*
lesen über *to read about (in depth)*
[nach]denken über *to think about (in depth)*
reagieren auf *to react to*
schreiben über *to write about (in depth)*
sprechen über *to speak/talk about (at length)*
vorbereiten auf *to prepare for*
warten auf *to wait for*

Reflexive Verbs with Prepositions

sich ärgern über *to be angry about*
sich erinnern an *to remind oneself of; to remember*
sich erkundigen nach (+ dat.) *to ask/inquire about*
sich freuen auf *to look forward to*
sich freuen über *to be happy about*
sich gewöhnen an *to get used to something; to accustom oneself to something*
sich interessieren für *to be interested in*
sich kümmern um *to concern oneself with; care for*
sich sehnen nach *to long for*
sich sorgen um *to worry about*
sich streiten über *to argue [with each other] about*
sich vorbereiten auf *to prepare oneself for, get ready for*
sich wundern über *to be surprised about*

Adjective with Accusative Preposition

verantwortlich für *responsible for*

Adjectives with Dative Prepositions

abhängig von *dependent on*
unabhängig von *independent from*
befreundet mit *friends with*
begeistert von *enthusiastic about*
böse mit *angry with/at*
fertig mit *finished with*
freundlich zu *friendly toward*
geschieden von *divorced from*
getrennt von *separated from*
überzeugt von *convinced by*
verheiratet mit *married to*
verlobt mit *engaged to*
verrückt nach *mad/crazy about*
verwandt mit *related to*
zufrieden mit *satisfied/pleased with*

Adjectives with Dative-Accusative Prepositions

böse auf *angry at/with*
erstaunt über *astounded/astonished by*
froh/glücklich über *happy about*
stolz auf *proud of*
traurig über *sad about*
verliebt in *in love with*
verrückt auf *mad/crazy about*

Nouns Used Idiomatically with Prepositions

(die) **Angst haben vor** (+ dat.) *to have fear of; be afraid of*
Freude haben über *to have joy about; be happy about*
(der) **Grund für** *reason for*
(die) **Lust haben auf** *to have desire to; want to*
(die) **Sehnsucht haben nach** *to have a longing for*
Schwierigkeiten/Probleme haben mit (+ dat.) *to have difficulty/problems with*
sich **Sorgen machen um** *to have worries about; be worried about*

20. Cardinal Numbers [Ch. 17]

1	eins	11	elf	21	einundzwanzig	40	vierzig
2	zwei	12	zwölf	22	zweiundzwanzig	50	fünfzig
3	drei	13	dreizehn	23	dreiundzwanzig	60	sechzig
4	vier	14	vierzehn	24	vierundzwanzig	70	siebzig
5	fünf	15	fünfzehn	25	fünfundzwanzig	80	achtzig
6	sechs	16	sechzehn	26	sechsundzwanzig	90	neunzig
7	sieben	17	siebzehn	27	siebenundzwanzig	100	(ein)hundert
8	acht	18	achtzehn	28	achtundzwanzig	200	zweihundert
9	neun	19	neunzehn	29	neunundzwanzig	1 000	(ein)tausend
10	zehn	20	zwanzig	30	dreißig	2 000	zweitausend

21. Clock Time [Ch. 17]

Elements of Clock Time

die Sekunde, -n	vor/in/nach zehn Sekunden
die Minute, -n	vor/in/nach zehn Minuten
die Stunde, -n	vor/in/nach einer Stunde
eine Viertelstunde	vor/in/nach einer Viertelstunde
eine halbe Stunde	vor/in/nach einer halben Stunde

12-hour clock (conversational)	*24-hour clock (official)*
Es ist zwölf (Uhr).	Es ist [genau] 12 Uhr.
Es ist fünf (Minuten) nach zwölf (Uhr).	Es ist zwölf Uhr fünf.
Es ist zehn nach zwölf.	Es ist zwölf Uhr zehn.
Es ist Viertel nach zwölf.	Es ist zwölf Uhr fünfzehn.
Es ist zwanzig nach zwölf.	Es ist zwölf Uhr zwanzig.
Es ist fünf vor halb eins.	Es ist zwölf Uhr fünfundzwanzig.
Es ist halb eins.	Es ist zwölf Uhr dreißig.

12-hour clock (conversational)	*24-hour clock (official)*
Es ist fünf nach halb eins.	Es ist zwölf Uhr fünfunddreißig.
Es ist zwanzig vor eins.	Es ist zwölf Uhr vierzig.
Es ist Viertel vor eins.	Es ist zwölf Uhr fünfundvierzig.
Es ist zehn vor eins.	Es ist zwölf Uhr fünfzig.
Es ist fünf vor eins.	Es ist zwölf Uhr fünfundfünfzig.
Es ist eins/ein Uhr.	Es ist dreizehn Uhr.
null Uhr = Mitternacht ...	Der Zug kommt um null Uhr dreizehn an.

22. Conjunctions [Ch. 18]

Coordinating Conjunctions

und • aber • oder • denn • sondern

Subordinating Conjunctions

als • bevor • bis • da • damit • dass • ehe • indem • nachdem • ob • obgleich • obwohl • seit/seitdem • sobald • solange • sooft • während • weil • wenn

***W-Fragewörter* Used as Subordinating Conjunctions**

wer • wen • wem • wessen • wann • warum • wie • wie schnell • wie weit • wo • woher • wohin

23. Relative Pronouns [Ch. 19]

Forms of the Relative Pronoun

	masculine	*feminine*	*neuter*	*plural*
nominative:	**der**	**die**	**das**	**die**
accusative:	**den**	**die**	**das**	**die**
dative:	**dem**	**der**	**dem**	***denen***
genitive:	***dessen***	***deren***	***dessen***	***deren***

24. Present Subjunctive II [Ch. 21]

Standard Subjunctive Endings

ich:	**-e**	wir:	**-en**		
du:	**-est**	ihr:	**-et**	Sie:	**-en**
er/sie/es:	**-e**	sie:	**-en**		

Present Subjunctive II Forms

	Regular Verb	*Irregular Verbs*	
	sagen, *sagte,* gesagt	**gehen, *ging,* gegangen**	**sprechen, *sprach,* gesprochen**
ich	**sagte**	**ginge**	**spräche**
du	**sagtest**	**gingest**	**sprächest**
er/sie/es	**sagte**	**ginge**	**spräche**
wir	**sagten**	**gingen**	**sprächen**
ihr	**sagtet**	**ginget**	**sprächet**
sie	**sagten**	**gingen**	**sprächen**
Sie	**sagten**	**gingen**	**sprächen**

Present Subjunctive II of Modal Verbs

können → **könnte**	dürfen → **dürfte**	wollen → **wollte**
müssen → **müsste**	mögen → **möchte**	sollen → **sollte**

25. Past Subjunctive II [Ch. 21]

past subjunctive II = *hätte/wäre* + past participle

Wir **hätten** das gar nicht **getan**, wenn wir das **gewusst hätten.**
Ich **wäre** nicht dahin **gegangen**, wenn ich vorsichtiger **gewesen wäre**.

26. Present Subjunctive I [Ch. 23]

Present Subjunctive I Forms

	Regular Verb	*Irregular Verbs*	
	lernen	**gehen**	**sein** (especially irregular)
ich	**lerne**	**gehe**	**sei**
du	**lernest**	**gehest**	**sei(e)st**
er/sie/es	**lerne**	**gehe**	**sei**
wir	**lernen**	**gehen**	**seien**
ihr	**lernet**	**gehet**	**seiet**
sie	**lernen**	**gehen**	**seien**
Sie	**lernen**	**gehen**	**seien**

German-English Dictionary

The following conventions are employed in this dictionary:

- Noun gender is indicated by the definite article. Noun plural endings are given. Where umlauts are added to form the plural, the complete form is shown.
- Regular verbs are given in infinitive form only. Irregular and mixed verbs show all principal parts, including any irregular present-tense forms.
- The case governed by prepositions is indicated, including prepositions used idiomatically.

der **Abend, -e** evening
das **Abendessen** evening meal, supper
aber but
abfahren (fährt ... ab), fuhr ... ab, ***ist*** **abgefahren** to drive off
abhängen, hing ... ab, abgehangen (von + *dat.*) to depend (on)
  abhängig von (+ *dat.*) dependent on
abholen to pick up
abnehmen (nimmt ... ab), nahm ... ab, abgenommen to take off weight
abonnieren to subscribe
abschießen, schoss ... ab, abgeschossen to shoot off
abschließen, schloss ... ab, abgeschlossen to lock, complete
abschneiden, schnitt ... ab, abgeschnitten to cut off
abschreiben, schrieb ... ab, abgeschrieben to copy
die **Absicht, -en** intention
absichtlich intentional(ly)
abstrakt abstract
ab und zu now and then
Afrika Africa
der **Agent, -en, -en** agent
ähneln (+ *dat.*) to resemble
ähnlich similar
die **Ahnung, -en** idea, clue, notion
akademisch academic
die **Aktivität, -en** activity
all- all
allerbest- the very best
allerlei all kinds of
allerschönst- the most beautiful
alles everything
  alles klar all clear; understood
die **Alpen** (*pl.*) Alps
als as; when (*sub. conj. with past tense*)
alt old
altmodisch old-fashioned, out of fashion
das **Aluminium** aluminum
amerikanisch American
das **Amt, Ämte** offical office
sich **amüsieren** to have fun
an (+ *acc./dat.*) at, to, on, onto
ander other
anfangen (fängt ... an), fing ... an, angefangen to begin
die **Angelegenheit, -en** opportunity
angeln to fish
der **Angler, -**/die **Anglerin, -nen** fisherman, angler
die **Angst** anxiety, fear
  Angst haben vor (+ *dat.*) to have fear of; to be afraid of
anhören to listen to
ankommen, kam ... an, ***ist*** **angekommen** to arrive
anmachen to turn on
der **Anruf, -e** telephone call
anrufen, rief ... an, angerufen to call up (by phone)
anschauen to look at, watch
anscheinend apparently
ansehen (sieht ... an), sah ... an, angesehen to look at, watch
anstatt/statt (+ *gen.*) instead of
die **Anthropologie** anthropology
die **Antiquität, -en** antique
antworten (+ *dat.*) to answer (a person)
  antworten auf (+ *acc.*) to answer (a thing)
der **Anwalt, Anwälte**/die **Anwältin, -nen** lawyer, attorney
anziehen, zog ... an, angezogen to dress, put on
  sich **anziehen** to get dressed
der **Anzug, Anzüge** suit of clothes
die **Arbeit, -en** work
arbeiten to work
  arbeiten an (+ *dat.*) to work on
der **Arbeiter, -**/die **Arbeiterin, -nen** worker
die **Arbeitsstelle, -n** job, position
(das) **Argentinien** Argentina

ärgern to annoy
sich **ärgern über** (+ *acc.*) to make oneself angry about; be angry about
argumentieren to argue
arm poor
der **Arm, -e** arm
die Armbanduhr, -en wristwatch
die **Armee, -n** army
der **Arzt, Ärzte** doctor, physician
(das) **Asien** Asia
die **Aspirintablette, -n** aspirin tablet
der **Atem** breath
atmen to breathe
auf (+ *acc./dat.*) on, onto, to
der **Aufenthalt, Aufenthälte** stay, sojourn
aufheben, hob ... auf, aufgeboben to lift up
aufhören to stop, cease
aufmachen to open (up)
aufpassen to pay attention
aufpassen auf (+ *acc.*) to pay attention to
aufräumen to straighten up
der **Aufsatz, Aufsätze** composition
aufstehen, stand ... auf, *ist* aufgestanden to stand up
aufwachen to wake up
das **Auge, -n** eye
aus (+ *dat.*) out of; from
ausbrechen (bricht ... aus), brach ... aus, *ist* ausgebrochen to break out, happen suddenly
der **Ausflug, Ausflüge** day trip, day out
ausgeben (gibt ... aus), gab ... aus, ausgegeben to spend (money)
ausgehen, ging ... aus, *ist* ausgegangen to go out
auslachen to mock, laugh at, make fun of
der **Ausländer, -**/die **Ausländerin, -nen** foreigner, alien
ausländisch foreign
ausmachen to turn off/out
(sich) **ausruhen** to rest up, rest completely
die **Aussage, -n** statement
das **Aussehen** appearance
aussehen (sieht ... aus), sah ... aus, ausgesehen to look, appear
außer (+ *dat.*) beside; except; aside from
außergewöhnlich extraordinary, unusual
außerhalb (+ *gen.*) outside, outside of
äußerst extremely, highly
austauschen to exchane
(das) **Australien** Australia
der **Ausweis, -e** identification papers
auswendig by heart (memorize)
ausziehen, zog ... aus, ausgezogen to pull off, take off, undress
sich **ausziehen** to get undressed

das **Baby, -s** baby
backen (bäckt), buk, gebacken to bake
die **Bäckerei, -en** bakery
baden to bathe
das **Badezimmer, -**bathroom
die **Bahn, -en** (die **Eisenbahn**) train
bald soon
der **Ball, Bälle** ball
die **Banane, -n** banana
die **Bank, -en** bank; bench
basteln to make (crafts)
die **Batterie, -n** battery
bauen to build
der **Baum, Bäume** tree
bayrisch Bavarian
bevor before (*sub. conj.*)
beantworten to answer
bedienen to serve (persons)
sich **beeilen** to hurry
beenden to end (something)
befehlen (befiehlt), befahl, befohlen to command, order
befinden, befand, befunden to be found at, located at, situated at
befreundet befriended
befreundet mit (+ *dat.*) friends with
begeistert enthusiastic
begeistert von (+ *dat.*) enthusiastic about
beginnen, begann, begonnen to begin, commence
begreifen, begriff, begriffen to grasp, comprehend
begrüßen to greet
behaupten to claim
bei (+ *dat.*) by; near; at
das **Bein, -e** leg
beißen, biss, gebissen to bite
bekannt acquainted, known
bekommen, bekam, bekommen to receive, get
(das) **Belgien** Belgium
sich **benehmen (benimmt), benahm, benommen** to behave
das **Benehmen** behavior
das **Benzin** gasoline, petrol
bequem comfortable
beraten (berät), beriet, beraten to advise
der **Bericht, -e** report
(sich) **beruhigen** to calm down, quiet down
berühmt famous
beschäftigt busy, occupied
besoffen drunk, besotted
besonder- special
besprechen (bespricht), besprach, besprochen to discuss
best- best
bestehen, bestand, bestanden auf (+ *acc.*) to insist on
bestellen order
bestimmt definitely
besuchen to visit
der **Betrieb, -e** operation
das **Bett, -en** bed
beweisen, bewies, bewiesen to prove
die **Bibel, -n** Bible
die **Bibliothek, -en** library
biegen, bog, gebogen to bend
das **Bier, -e** beer
bieten, bot, geboten to offer
das **Bild, -er** picture
die **Bildung, -en** education, formation
billig cheap
binden, band, gebunden to bind, tie
die **Biologie** biology
bis (+ *acc.*) until, till; to; until (*sub. conj.*)
bisschen bit
ein bisschen a little bit
bitten, bat, gebeten to ask (for something), request
bitten um (+ *acc.*) to ask for, request
blasen (bläst), blies, geblasen to blow
das **Blatt, Blätter** leaf
blau blue; (*coll.*) drunk
das **Blech** tin
das **Blei** lead
bleiben, blieb, *ist* geblieben to stay, remain
blind blind
blitzen to flash (lightning)
blitzschnell lightning-fast

blöd stupid, dumb, foolish
der **Blödsinn** nonsense, foolishness
blond blond
die **Blume, -n** flower
die **Bluse, -n** blouse
blutrot bloodred
der **Boden, Böden** floor
der **Bolzen, -** bolt; pin
das **Boot, -e** boat
böse angry; evil
  böse auf (+ *acc.*) angry at
  böse mit (+ *dat.*) angry with/at
brasilianisch Brazilian
(das) **Brasilien** Brazil
brauchen to need
braun brown
brechen (bricht), brach, gebrochen to break
brennen, brannte, gebrannt to burn
der **Brief, -e** letter
die **Briefmarke, -n** stamp
der **Briefträger, -**/die **Briefträgerin, -nen** mail carrier
die **Brille, -n** pair of eyeglasses, glasses
bringen, brachte, gebracht to bring
das **Brot, -e** bread
das **Brötchen, -** roll
die **Brücke, -n** bridge
der **Bruder, Brüder** brother
die **Brüderschaft, -en** brotherhood
brutal brutal
die **Brutalität** brutality
das **Buch, Bücher** book
die **Bücherei, -en** library
das **Büchlein, -** little book, booklet
(das) **Bulgarien** Bulgaria
der **Bürgermeister, -**/die **Bürgermeisterin, -nen** mayor
das **Büro, -s** office
der **Bursche, -n** lad, boy, guy
bürsten brush
die **Bushaltestelle, -n** bus stop

die **Chance, -n** chance
der **Chef, -s**/die **Chefin, -nen** boss; chef
die **Chemie** chemistry
(das) **China** China
die **Chronologie, -n** chronology

da there; because (*sub. conj.*)
  da drüben over there
dafür for it
dahin [to] there
die **Dame, -n** lady
damit with it; so that (*sub. conj.*)
danach after that, afterward
Dänemark Denmark
danken (+ *dat.*) to thank
  danken für (+ *acc.*) to thank for
dann then
das this, that
dass that (*sub. conj.*)
dazu along with that
die **Decke, -n** ceiling; covering
decken to cover
dein your
die **Demokratie, -n** democracy
demonstrieren to demonstrate
denken, dachte, gedacht to think
  denken an (+ *acc.*) to think of (briefly)
  denken über (+ *acc.*) to think about (in depth)
denn then; because (*sub. conj.*)
deutsch- German
(das) **Deutsch** German language
der/die **Deutsche, -n** German (person)
(das) **Deutschland** Germany
die **Deutschprüfung, -en** German test
der **Dienstag** Tuesday
dies- this, that
diesseits (+ *gen.*) (on) this side of
das **Dilemma, -en** dilemma
direkt direct(ly)
diskutieren to discuss
doch certainly, by all means
die **Doktorarbeit, -en** doctoral dissertation
das **Dokument, -e** document
der **Dom, -e** cathedral
die **Donau** the Danube river
donnern to thunder
der **Donnerstag** Thursday
doof stupid
das **Dorf, Dörfer** village
dort there
  dort drüben over there
dringend urgently
das **Drittel** one-third
drittens third
die **Dummheit, -en** stupidity
dunkel dark
die **Dunkelheit** darkness
durch (+ *acc.*) through
dürfen (darf), durfte, gedurft to be allowed to, permitted to
durstig thirsty
duschen to shower
echt genuinely
die **Ecke, -n** corner
der **Ecktisch, -e** corner table
ehe before (*sub. conj.*)
ehemalig former, onetime
das **Ei, -er** egg
eigentlich actually
ein a, one
  ein bisschen a little
  ein paar a few
  ein wenig a little
einander one another
einfach simple, simply
einführen to introduce
einhändigen to hand in, turn in
die **Einheit, -en** unity; unit
einige some
einkaufen to shop
einladen (lädt ... ein), lud ... ein, eingeladen to invite
  einladen zu (+ *dat.*) to invite to
die **Einladung, -en** invitation
einmal once
eintreten (tritt ... ein), trat ... ein, *ist* eingetreten to enter
einzig single
der **Eisbrecher, -** icebreaker
das **Eisen** iron
eiskalt ice cold
die **Elbe** Elbe river
elegant elegant
die **Eltern** (*pl.*) parents
der **Empfang, Empfänge** formal reception
empfangen (empfängt), empfing, empfangen to receive (e.g., guests)
empfehlen (empfiehlt), empfahl, empfohlen to recommend
empfinden, empfand, empfunden to feel, perceive
das **Ende** end
endlich finally
(das) **England** England
der **Engländer, -**/die **Engländerin, -nen** Englishman, British person
das **Enkelkind, -er** grandchild
entdecken to discover
die **Entdeckung, -en** discovery, finding
entfalten to unfold
entkommen, entkam, *ist* entkommen to escape
entlang (*postposition* + *acc.*) along (a pathway or topographical feature)

sich **entscheiden, entschied, entschieden** to decide
sich **entschließen, entschloss, entschlossen** to decide
sich **entschuldigen** to excuse oneself
entweder ... oder either . . . or
entwickeln to develop
die **Erbsen** (*pl.*) peas
die **Erdbeertorte, -n** strawberry torte (Jell-O cake)
erfinden, erfand, erfunden to invent
die **Erfindung, -en** discovery, invention
der **Erfolg, -e** success
erfolgreich successful
erinnern to remind
sich **erinnern an** (+ *acc.*) to remind oneself of; to remember
sich **erkälten** to catch [a] cold
die **Erklärung, -en** explanation
sich **erkundigen nach** (+ *dat.*) to ask/inquire about
erledigen to complete, finish
erleichtern to ease, make easy
ermöglichen to make possible
ersetzen to replace
erst first, just
erst seit for just, just since
erstaunt astounded, astonished, amazed
erstaunt über (+ *acc.*) astounded/astonished by, amazed at/by
erstens first of all, firstly
erzählen to tell a story
erzählen von (+ *dat.*) to tell a story about
es gibt there is/there are (with imprecise quantities)
es ist/sind there is, there are (with precise quantities)
das **Essen** food
essen (isst), aß, gegessen to eat
der **Essig** vinegar
etwas something; some (sing.); somewhat
etwas anderes something else
(das) **Europa** Europe
das **Examen,** -examination
die **Existenz** existence
explodieren to explode
die **Explosion, -en** explosion

die **Fabrik, -en** factory
das **Fach, Fächer** subject area; box, cubbyhole
die **Fähigkeit, -en** skill
fahren (fährt), fuhr, *ist/hat* gefahren to travel/drive a vehicle
das **Fahrrad, Fahrräder** bicycle, bike
fallen (fällt), fiel, *ist* gefallen to fall
falsch false, wrong, erroneous
die **Familie, -n** family
das **Familienmitglied, -er** family member
fangen (fängt), fing, gefangen to catch
die **Fantasie, -n** fantasy
fantastisch fantastic
die **Farbe, -n** color
die **Faulheit** laziness
die **Faust, Fäuste** fist
feiern to celebrate
der **Feind, -e** enemy
die **Feindlichkeit** animosity, hostility
die **Feindschaft, -en** hostility
das **Fenster, -** window
die **Ferien** (*pl.*) days off from work/school/university; vacation
das **Fernsehen** television (medium)
fernsehen (sieht ... fern), sah ... fern, ferngesehen to watch TV
der **Fernseher, -** TV set
die **Fernsehsendung, -en** TV program
fertig finished, ready, prepared
fertig machen to finish up
fertig mit (+ *dat.*) finished with
die **Festung, -en** fortress
das **Feuer** fire
der **Fieber** fever
die **Figur, -en** figure
der **Film, -e** film, movie
filmen to film, make a film
der **Filmstar, -s** film star
finanzieren to finance
finden, fand, gefunden to find
die **Firma, Firmen** company
der **Fisch, -e** fish
fischen to fish
das **Fischlein, -** little fish, fry
fit fit, in shape
die **Flasche, -n** bottle
das **Fleisch** meat
die **Fleischerei, -en** butcher shop
fleißig hard, industriously
fliegen, flog, *ist/hat* geflogen to fly
fliehen, floh, *ist* geflohen to flee
das **Flugzeug, -e** airplane
der **Fluss, Flüsse** river
folgen (+ *dat.*) to follow
folgend- following
formell formal
fortfahren (fährt ... fort), fuhr ... fort, *ist* fortgefahren to depart (by vehicle)
fortgehen, ging ... fort, *ist* fortgegangen to depart (on foot)
der **Fortschritt, -e** progress
fortsetzen to continue, set forth
fotografieren to photograph, take a picture
die **Frage, -n** question
fragen to ask (for information)
fragen nach (+ *dat.*) to ask/inquire aabout
die **Fraktur** Fraktur (old Gothic style of print)
(das) **Frankreich** France
der **Franzose, -n, -n**/die **Französin, -nen** French person
französisch French
(das) **Französisch** French language
die **Frau, -en** woman; Mrs. (form of address)
der **Frauenarzt, Frauenärzte/** die **Frauenärztin, -nen** gynecologist
das **Fräulein, -** young woman
die **Freiheit, -en** freedom
der **Freitag** Friday
die **Freizeit, -en** free time
fremd strange, foreign
fressen (frisst), fraß, gefressen to eat (like an animal); to eat to excess
die **Freude, -n** joy
Freude haben über (+ *acc.*) to have joy about; to be happy about
freuen to please
sich **freuen auf** (+ *acc.*) to look forward to
sich **freuen über** (+ *acc.*) to be happy about
der **Freund, -e** friend; boyfriend
die **Freundin, -nen** girlfriend, female friend
freundlich friendly
freundlich zu (+ *dat.*) friendly toward
die **Freundlichkeit** friendliness
die **Freundschaft, -en** friendship
frieren, fror, *ist/hat* gefroren to freeze
frisch fresh

froh happy
froh über (+ *acc.*) happy about
früh early
früher earlier, previously, formerly
frühestens at the earliest
der **Frühling** spring
die **Frühlingsferien** (*pl.*) spring vacation, spring break
das **Frühstück** breakfast
fühlen to feel
führen to lead
der **Führerschein, -e** auto license
das **Fünftel** one-fifth
für (+ *acc.*) for
die **Furcht** fear
furchtbar dreadful(ly), terrible/terribly
sich **fürchten** to fear
der **Fußball, Fußbälle** soccer, soccer ball
die **Fußballmannschaft, -en** soccer team
der **Fußballplatz, Fußballplätze** soccer field
das **Futur** future tense (grammatical term)

ganz whole, entire[ly], complete[ly], all
gar at all (*as in* **gar nicht; gar kein**)
die **Garage, -n** garage
der **Garten, Gärten** garden
der **Gast, Gäste** guest
der **Gastarbeiter, -** guest worker
die **Gaststätte, -n** inn
gebacken baked
das **Gebäude, -** building
geben (gibt), gab, gegeben to give
gebraten fried, roasted
gebraucht used
gebrochen broken
die **Geburt, -en** birth
der **Geburtstag, -e** birthday
die **Geburtstagskarte, -n** birthday card
das **Gedicht, -e** poem
das **Gefahr, -en** danger
gefährlich dangerous
gefallen (gefällt), gefiel, gefallen (+ *dat.*) to please
das **Gefängnis, -se** prison
das **Gefecht, -e** fight, skirmish
gegen (+ *acc.*) against; opposed to; toward (time)
gegenüber (+ *dat.*) opposite, across from
das **Gehalt, Gehälter** salary
geheim secret(ly)
gehen, ging, *ist* gegangen to go
das **Gehirn, -e** brain
gehören (+ *dat.*) to belong to
gekocht- boiled
das **Geld, -er** money
gelingen, gelang, *ist* gelungen to succeed
das **Gemüse** vegetables
genau exactly, precisely
genauso just as
genießen, genoss, genossen to enjoy
genug enough, sufficient
genügend sufficiently
die **Geographie** geography
das **Gepäck** baggage, luggage
das **Gerät, -e** device, gadget
die **Germanistik** Germanic Studies
gern gladly, with pleasure, willingly
gern haben to like
das **Gerücht, -e** rumor
das **Geschäft, -e** place of business, shop
die **Geschäftsleute** (*pl.*) business-people
geschehen (geschieht), geschah, *ist* geschehen (+ *dat.*) to happen
das **Geschenk, -e** present, gift
die **Geschichte, -n** story; history
geschieden von (+ *dat.*) divorced from
die **Gesellschaft, -en** company (social)
das **Gesetz, -e** law
das **Gesicht, -er** face
das **Gespräch, -e** conversation, talk
gestern yesterday
gestohlen stolen
gestorben dead
gesund healthy
das **Getränk, -e** drink, beverage
getrennt separated
getrennt von (+ *dat.*) separated from
gewinnen, gewann, gewonnen to win
das **Gewitter, -** thunderstorm
gewöhnen to accustom
sich **gewöhnen an** (+ *acc.*) to get used to something; to accustom oneself to something
gewöhnlich usually, customarily
gießen, goss, gegossen to pour
glänzend shining, dazzling
das **Glas, Gläser** glass
glauben (+ *dat.*) to believe
gleich just
die **Gleichheit** equality, evenness
das **Glück** luck
glücklich über (+ *acc.*) happy about
das **Gold** gold
golden golden
die **Grammatik** grammar
gratulieren to congratulate
gratulieren zu (+ *dat.*) to congratulate on
grau gray
greifen, griff, gegriffen to grasp, grab, seize
die **Grippe, -n** flu
groß big, large, tall
die **Großeltern** (*pl.*) grandparents
die **Großmutter, Großmütter** grandmother
der **Großvater, Großväter** grandfather
grün green
der **Grund, Gründe** reason
Grund für (+ *acc.*) reason for
grüßen to greet
gut good; well
das **Gymnasium, Gymnasien** gymnasium (school)

das **Haar, -e** hair
haben (hat), hatte, gehabt to have
der **Hafen, Häfen** harbor
der **Hagel** hail
hageln to hail
halb- half
die **Hälfte, -n** half
halten (hält), hielt, gehalten to hold
halten von (+ *dat.*) to think of, hold an opinion about
die **Haltung, -en** bearing
der **Hammer, -** hammer
die **Hand, Hände** hand
handeln to treat, deal with
handeln von (+ *dat.*) to deal with
die **Handlung, -en** action, deed; performance
die **Handschrift, -en** handwriting
das **Handtuch, Handtücher** hand towel
hängen, hängte, gehängt to hang (*transitive*)
hängen, hing, gehangen to hang (*intransitive*)
hassen to hate
hässlich ugly, hateful
hauen to hit, punch
hauptsächlich mainly, chiefly
die **Hauptstraße, -n** main street

das **Haus, Häuser** house
die **Hausaufgaben** (*pl.*) homework (assignments)
heben, hob, gehoben to lift, heft
die **Heiligkeit** holiness
die **Heimat, -en** homeland, native country
heiraten marry
der **Heiratstag, -e** wedding day
heiß hot
heißen, hieß, geheißen to be called (by name)
helfen (hilft), half, geholfen (+ *dat.*) to help
helfen bei (+ *dat.*) to help with
hell bright, light
das **Hemd, -en** shirt
der **Herbst** fall, autumn
der **Herr, -n, -en** gentleman; Mr. (form of address)
herstellen to produce, manufacture
herum around
das **Herz, -ens, -en** heart
hetzen to pursue, run after
heute today
hier here (location)
hierher [to] here (destination)
die **Hilfe** help, assistance
der **Himmel** sky; heaven
hindurch (+ *acc.*) through, all through
hinter (+ *acc./dat.*) behind, in back of
hinterlassen (hinterlässt), hinterließ, hinterlassen to leave behind
der **Historiker, -** historian
die **Hitze** heat
hoch high, tall
höchst highly
höchstens at the highest; at the most
hoffen to hope
hoffen auf (+ *acc.*) to hope for
hoffentlich hopefully, hoffentlich
holen to get, fetch
(das) **Holland** Holland
holländisch Dutch
das **Holz, Hölzer** wood
der **Honig** honey
hören to hear
das **Hörsaal, Hörsäle** lecture hall
die **Hose, -n** pair of pants
der **Hosenanzug, Hosenanzüge** pantsuit
hübsch pretty, attractive
der **Hubschrauber, -** helicopter
der **Hund, -e**/die **Hündin, -nen** dog
das **Hündchen, -** puppy
das **Hundertsel** one-hundredth
der **Hunger** hunger
hungrig hungry
husten to cough
die **Hymne, -n** hymn

die **Idee, -n** idea
immer always
in (+ *acc./dat.*) in, into
in Ordnung in order, OK
indem by, by means of, insofar as (*sub. conj.*)
(das) **Indonesien** Indonesia
die **Innenstadt** downtown
innerhalb (+ *gen.*) inside, inside of, within
das **Institut, -e** institute
die **Intelligenz** intelligence
interessant interesting
interessieren to interest
sich **interessieren für** (+ *acc.*) to interest oneself in; to be interested in
die **Interpretation, -en** interpretation
iregendwo somewhere (vague)
irgend- *signals vagueness*
irgendein some (vague)
irgendetwas something (vague)
irgendwann sometime or other
irgendwelche some (vague)
irgendwer somebody (vague)
irgendwie somehow (vague)
irgendwo somewhere or other
irgendwoher from somewhere (vague)
irgendwohin to somewhere or other
irgendwohin [to] somewhere (vague)
(das) **Irland** Ireland
sich **irren** to err, be wrong
(das) **Italien** Italy
italienisch Italian

das **Jägerschnitzel, -** hunter's schnitzel (cutlet with mushrooms and gravy)
das **Jahr, -e** year
das **Jahrhundert, -e** century
das **Jahrzehnt, -e** decade
je[mals] ever
jed- each, every
jemand someone
jemand anders someone else
jenseits (+ *gen.*) (on) that side of; on the other side of
jetzt now
der **Journalist, -en, -en** journalist
jüdisch Jewish
die **Jugend[zeit]** youth
der **Junge, -n, -n** boy

der **Kaffee** coffee
kalt cold
die **Kälte** cold
der **Kamerad, -en, -en** colleague, comrade, buddy
der **Kamin, -e** fireplace
kämmen comb
(das) **Kanada** Canada
der **Kanadier, -**/die **Kanadierin, -nen** Canadian
der **Kanarienvogel, Kanarienvögel** canary
der **Kandidat, -en, -en**/die **Kandidatin, -nen** candidate
der **Kanzler, -**/die **Kanzlerin, -nen** chancellor
der **Kapitän, Kapitäne** captain of a ship, navy captain (rank)
das **Kapitel, -** chapter
kaputt broken, nonfunctioning
kariert checkered, checked, plaid
die **Karte, -n** ticket; card
der **Kartoffel, -n** potato
der **Käse** cheese
die **Katastrophe, -n** catastrophe
der **Kater, -** cat, tomcat
katholisch Catholic
das **Kätzchen, -** kitten
die **Katze, -n** cat (female)
kaufen to buy
der **Kaufhof, Kaufhöfe** department store
kaum scarcely, hardly
die **Kaution, -en** security deposit
kein no, none, not any
der **Keks, -e** cookie
der **Kellner, -**/die **Kellnerin, -nen** waiter/waitress
kennen, kannte, gekannt to know, be familiar with
kennen lernen to get to know, become acquainted with
die **Kette, -n** chain; necklace
das **Kilo, -s** kilo(gram)
das **Kind, -er** child
das **Kindchen, -** little child
das **Kindlein, -** little child
das **Kino, -s** movies/movie theater
die **Kirche, -n** church
die **Klamotten** (*pl.*) clothes (*colloquial*)
klären to clarify, make clear

klassisch classical
die **Klausur, -en** test
die **Kleidung** clothing
der **Klempner, -** plumber
klein small, little
das **Klima** climate
klingen, klang, geklungen to sound
die **Kneipe, -n** pub
kochen to cook, boil
der **Kollege, -n, -n**/die **Kollegin, -nen** colleague
komisch odd
kommen, kam, *ist* gekommen to come
kommend- this coming
die **Kompetenz** competence
der **Komponist, -en, -en**/die **Komponistin, -nen** composer
die **Konditorei, -en** pastry shop
der **König, -e** king
können (kann), konnte, gekonnt to be able to; can; to know how to
die **Kontrolle, -n** control, check
die **Konversation, -en** conversation
das **Konzert, -e** concert
der **Kopfhörer, -** headphones
korrigieren to correct
kosten to cost
das **Kostüm, -e** outfit
krank sick
das **Krankenhaus, Krankenhäuser** hospital
der **Krankenpfleger, -**/die **Krankenschwester, -n** nurse
die **Krankheit, -en** sickness, illness
die **Kreide** chalk
der **Krieg, -e** war
die **Kriegsgeschichte, -n** war stories
der **Krimi, -s** detective story
der **Kugelschreiber, -** pen
die **Kuh, Kühe** cow
der **Kuli, -s** pen
die **Kultur, -en** culture
kümmern to concern
sich **kümmern um** (+ *acc.*) to concern oneself with; to care for
der **Kunde, -n, -n**/die **Kundin, -nen** customer
das **Kupfer** copper
der **Kurs, -e** course (academic)
kurz short(ly), brief(ly)
die **Kusine, -n** female cousin
die **Küste, -n** coast

lachen to laugh
lachen über (+ *acc.*) to laugh about
laden (lädt), lud, geladen to load
der **Laden, Läden** shop, small store
die **Lampe, -n** lamp, light fixture
das **Land, Länder** country
die **Landkarte, -n** map
die **Landung, -en** landing
lang long (length)
lange for a long time
langsam slow(ly)
langweilig boring, tiring
der **Lärm, -e** noise
lassen (lässt), ließ, gelassen to allow; to let; to have done
der **Lastwagen, -** truck
laufen (läuft), lief, *ist* gelaufen to run
laut loud
leben to live
das **Leben, -** life
das **Lebensmittel, -** food
lebhaft lively
das **Leder** leather
legen to lay
der **Lehrer, -**/die **Lehrerin, -nen** teacher, instructor
der **Lehrling, -e** apprentice, trainee
leiden, litt, gelitten to suffer
leider unfortunately
leihen, lieh, geliehen to lend
leise quiet(ly)
sich (*dat.*) **etwas leisten** to afford something
die **Leseaufgabe, -n** reading assignment
lesen (liest), las, gelesen to read
lesen über (+ *acc.*) to read about (in depth)
letzt- last
die **Leute** (*pl.*) people
das **Licht, -er** light
lieb dear
die **Liebe, -n** love
lieber preferably
der **Lieblingsautor, -en**/die **Lieblingsautorin, -nen** favorite author
der **Lieblingsschauspieler, -**/die **Lieblingsschauspielerin, -nen** favorite actor
liefern to deliver
liegen, lag, gelegen to lie, recline
logisch logical(ly)
der **Lohn, Löhne** wage(s), pay
löschen, extinguish, put out
lösen to solve
loslassen (lässt ... los), ließ ... los, losgelassen to let go, let loose
loslösen to detach
losschneiden, schnitt ... los, losgeschnitten to cut loose
die **Lösung, -en** solution
loswerden (wird ... los), wurde ... los, *ist* losgeworden to get rid of
der **Löwe, -n** lion
lernen to learn, study
die **Luft** air
lügen, log, gelogen to lie, to tell a lie
der **Lump** scoundrel
die **Lust** desire
Lust haben auf (+ *acc.*)/**zu** (+ *dat.*) to have desire to/for; to want to
lutherisch Lutheran
der **Luxuswagen, -** luxury car

machen to do
das **Mädchen, -** girl, maiden
der **Main** Main river
mal (*signals some impatience*)
das **Mal** time, occurrence
malen to paint (artistically)
manchmal sometimes
der **Mann, Männer** man
das **Männchen, -** little man
männlich male
der **Mantel, Mäntel** coat
das **Manuskript, -en** manuscript
die **Mappe, -n** folder
das **Märchen, -** tale, story
der **Marktplatz, Marktplätze** marketplace, market square
die **Maschine, -n** machnine
der **Mast, -en** mast
die **Mathematik** mathematics
der **Matrose, -n, -n** sailor
die **Maus, Mäuse** mouse
das **Mäuschen, -** little mouse
der **Mechaniker, -**/die **Mechanikerin, -nen** mechanic
mehr more
mehrere several
mehrmals several times
mein my
meistens most of the time, mostly, usually
die **Menge, -n** bunch, a lot
die **Mensa, Mensen** student cafeteria
merken to notice
messen (misst), maß, gemessen to measure
das **Messer, -** knife

das **Meter, -** meter
die **Methode, -n** method
mieten to rent
die **Milch** milk
mindestens at the least
der **Minister, -**/die **Ministerin, -nen** minister
die **Minute, -n** minute
miserabel miserable
missdeuten to misinterpret
misshandeln to mistreat, abuse
misstrauen (+ *dat.*) to mistrust
missverstehen, missverstand, missverstanden to misunderstand
mit (+ *dat.*) with
der **Mitarbeiter, -**/die **Mitarbeiterin, -nen** coworker
mitbringen, brachte ... mit, mitgebracht to bring along
miteinander with one another
mitgehen, ging ... mit, *ist* mitgegangen to go with
das **Mitglied, -er** member
mitkommen, kam ... mit, *ist* mitgekommen to come with
mitmachen to participate
mitspielen to play with
der **Mitstudent, -en, -en**/die **Mitstudentin, -nen** fellow student
der **Mittag, -e** noon, midday
mitteilen to inform, tell
das **Mittelmeer** Mediterranean Sea
mitten in the middle of
die **Mitternacht** midnight
der **Mittwoch** Wednesday
die **Möbel** (*pl.*) furniture
das **Modellflugzeug, -e** model airplane
modern modern
die **Modezeitschrift, -en** fashion magazine
mogeln to cheat
mögen (mag), mochte, gemocht to like
möglich possible
der **Monat, -e** month
der **Mond, -e** moon
der **Montag** Monday
morgen tomorrow
der **Morgen, -** morning
die **Mosel** Mosel river
müde tired
der **Mund, Münder** mouth
das **Museum, Museen** museum
das **Museumsstück, -e** museum piece
die **Musik** music
müssen (muss), musste, gemusst to have to, must, be required to, need to
mutig brave, courageous
die **Mutter, Mütter** mother

nach (+ *dat.*) to, after
nach Hause [to] home (destination)
der **Nachbar, -n, -n**/die **Nachbarin, -nen** neighbor
die **Nachbarschaft, -en** neighborhood
nachdem after (*sub. conj.*)
nachdenken, dachte ... nach, nachgedacht to think about, consider
nacherzählen to retell
nachgeben (gibt ... nach), gab ... nach, nachgegeben to give in
nachher later, afterward
die **Nachlässigkeit, -en** negligence, carelessness
der **Nachmittag, -e** afternoon
der **Nachricht, -en** report; news
nachschlagen (schlägt ... nach), schlug ... nach, nachgeschlagen to look up
nächst- next
die **Nacht, Nächte** night
der **Nachttisch, -e** night table, nightstand
nackt naked
nah near, close(ly)
die **Nähe** vicinity
der **Name, -ns, -n** name
der **Narr, -en, -en** fool
die **Nation, -en** nation
die **Natur** nature
die **Nebel** fog
nebelig foggy
neben (+ *acc./dat.*) next to, alongside of, beside
der **Neckar** Neckar river
der **Neffe, -n, -n** nephew
nehmen (nimmt), nahm, genommen to take
nennen, nannte, genannt to name
neu new
neulich recently
neutral neutral
nicht not
nicht ..., sondern ... not . . . , but rather . . .
nicht nur ..., sondern auch ... not only . . . , but also . . .
die **Nichte, -n** niece
nichts nothing
nichts anderes nothing else
niedrig low
niemand no one, nobody
niemand anders no one else
nieseln to drizzle
nirgendwo nowhere
nirgendwohin [to] nowhere
noch still, yet, again
noch einmal once again
noch nicht not yet
der **Norden** north
(das) **Nordeuropa** northern Europe
(das) **Norwegen** Norway
norwegisch Norwegian
die **Note, -n** grade
die **Notiz, -en** note, notice, memorandum
null zero
die **Nummer, -n** number
nur only

ob if, whether (*sub. conj.*)
obdachlos homeless
obgleich although (*sub. conj.*)
das **Obst** fruit
obwohl although (*sub. conj.*)
oder or
der **Ofen, Öfen** oven
oft often
ohne (+ *acc.*) without
ohnmächtig unconscious
die **Oma, -s** Grandma
der **Onkel, -** uncle
der **Opa, -s** grandpa
operieren to operate (surgically)
ordnen to order, organize
die **Ordnung** order
die **Organisation, -en** organization
organisieren to organize
der **Osten** east
(das) **Ostern** Easter holiday

paar: ein paar a few
packen to pack
das **Paket, -e** package
das **Papier, -e** paper
der **Park, -s** park
die **Partei, -en** political party
die **Party, -s** party
der **Pass, Pässe** pass, passport
passieren to happen
der **Patient, -en, -en**/die **Patientin, -nen** patient
die **Pause, -n** break, pause
das **Pech** bad luck
die **Person, -en** person

pflanzen to plant
der **Philosoph, -en, -en** philosopher
die **Philosophie, -n** philosophy
die **Physik** physics
der **Pirat, -en, -en** pirate
die **Pizza, -s** pizza
der **Plan, Pläne** plan
planen to plan
der **Planet, -en, -en** planet
die **Planung** planning
die **Plastik, -en** plastic; sculpture
der **Platz, Plätze** place, seat
pleite broke, penniless
plötzlich suddenly
polieren to polish
die **Politik** politics
der **Politiker, -**/die **Politikerin, -nen** politician
die **Polizei** police (department)
der **Polizist, -en, -en**/die **Polizistin, -nen** police officer
das **Portmonee, -s** wallet
positiv positive
die **Post** mail; post office
das **Postamt, Postämter** post office
der **Präsident, -en, -en**/die **Präsidentin, -nen** president
der **Preis, -e** price; prize
der **Prinz, -en, -en** prince
privat private(ly)
pro (+ *acc.*) per, for each
probieren to try out, test
das **Problem, -e** problem, difficulty
Probleme haben mit (+ *dat.*) to have problems with
produzieren to produce
der **Professor, -en**/die **Professorin, -nen** professor
programmieren to program
das **Projekt, -e** project
protestantisch Protestant
protestieren to protest
die **Prüfung, -en** test
die **Prügelei, -en** beating
der **Psychiater, -**/die **Psychiaterin, -nen** psychiatrist
die **Psychologie** psychology
der **Pulli, -s** pullover
pünktlich punctually, on time
putzen scrub; brush
die **Putzfrau, -en** cleaning woman/lady

die **Qualität, -en** quality
die **Quantität, -en** quantity
der **Quatsch** nonsense
quatschen to speak nonsense

das **Rad, Räder** wheel; bicycle, bike
radieren to erase, rub out
(sich) **rasieren** to shave
der **Rastplatz, Rastplätze** rest stop
das **Rathaus, Rathäuser** city hall
die **Ratte, -n** rat
rauchen to smoke
reagieren to react
reagieren auf (+ *acc.*) to react to
realisieren to realize
der **Rechner, -** calculator
recht downright (*intensifier*)
recht haben to be right
die **Rede, -n** speech, talk
reden to talk, converse
das **Referat, -e** paper, report
die **Reformation, -en** reformation
die **Regel, -n** rule, guideline
der **Regen** rain
der **Regenschirm, -e** umbrella
regnen to rain
reich rich
rein pure
der **Reis** rice
die **Reise, -n** long trip, journey
reisen to travel, journey
reiten, ritt, *ist/hat* geritten to ride
die **Religion, -en** religion
rennen, rannte, *ist* gerannt to race, run
der **Rennwagen, -** race car
die **Reparatur, -en** repair
die **Republik, -en** republic
die **Residenz, -en** residence (of a prince or bishop)
restaurieren restore
restauriert restored
die **Revolution, -en** revolution
der **Rhein** Rhine river
richtig correct(ly), right
die **Rictung, -en** direction
riechen, roch, gerochen to smell
der **Ring, -e** ring
rings around
die **Rockmusik** rock music
Rom Rome
der **Roman, -e** novel
romantisch romantic
rot red
der **Rücken, -** back
der **Rucksack, Rucksäcke** rucksack, backpack
das **Ruderboot, -e** rowboat
rudern to row
rufen, rief, gerufen to call
die **Ruhe** quiet
ruhig quiet, still, at rest

der **Russe, -n, -n**/die **Russin, -nen** Russian
russisch Russian

die **Sache, -n** thing, matter, affair
sagen to say, tell
sammeln to collect
der **Samstag** Saturday
der **Sänger, -**/die **Sängerin, -nen** singer
der **Satz, Sätze** sentence
saufen (säuft), soff, gesoffen to drink to excess or like an animal
schaffen, schuf, geschaffen to create; to accomplish
sich **schämen** to be ashamed
scharf sharp; spicy
der **Schatz, Schätze** treasure
der **Scheck, -s** check
scheiden, schied, geschieden to separate
geschieden von (+ *dat.*) divorced from
scheinen, schien, geschienen to seem, appear; to shine
schenken to give (as a gift)
schicken to send
schieben, schob, geschoben to shove
schießen, schoss, geschossen to shoot
das **Schiff, -e** ship
der **Schinken** ham
die **Schlacht, -en** battle; slaughter
das **Schläfchen** nap
ein Schläfchen machen to take a nap
schlafen (schläft), schlief, geschlafen to sleep
schläfrig sleepy
schlagen (schlägt), schlug, geschlagen to strike, hit
schlampig sloppy
die **Schlange, -n** line; snake
schlecht bad
schließen, schloss, geschlossen to close
der **Schlüssel, -** key
schmecken to taste
schmeißen, schmiss, geschmissen to throw, fling
schmelzen (schmilzt), schmolz, *ist/hat* geschmolzen to melt
(sich) **schminken** to put on makeup
schmücken to decorate
schmutzig dirty, soiled

der **Schnee** snow
schneiden, schnitt, geschnitten to cut
schneien to snow
schnell fast, quick(ly)
das **Schnitzel,** - cutlet
schockierend shocking
die **Schokolade** chocolate
schon already, already for
schön beautiful, handsome, nice-looking
schräg diagonally
schreiben, schrieb, geschrieben to write
schreiben über (+ *acc.*) to write about (in depth)
die **Schreibmaschine, -n** typewriter
schreien, schrie, geschrieen to scream/cry
schreiten, schritt, *ist* geschritten to stride
der **Schuh, -e** shoe
der **Schüler,** -/die **Schülerin, -nen** pupil, student (pre-university)
der **Schuss, Schüsse** shot
schütteln to shake
schwach weak(ly)
schwarz black
(das) **Schweden** Sweden
schweigen, schwieg, geschwiegen to be silent
das **Schweinchen,** - piglet, piggy
die **Schweinerei** terrible behavior
der **Schweinestall, Schweineställe** pigsty, pig pen
die **Schweiz** Switzerland
schwer hard, difficult to do
die **Schwester, -n** sister
die **Schwierigkeit, -en** difficulty; problem
Schwierigkeiten haben mit (+ *dat.*) to have difficulty with
schwimmen, schwamm, *ist* geschwommen to swim
schwühl humid, muggy
das **Sechstel** one-sixth
der **See, -n** lake
die **See, -n** ocean
das **Segelboot, -e** sailboat
segeln to sail
das **Segelschiff, -e** sailing ship
sehen (sieht), sah, gesehen to see
sich **sehnen nach** (+ *dat.*) to long for, to have a longing for
die **Sehnsucht** longing
Sehnsucht haben nach (+ *dat.*) to have a longing for
sein his, its
sein (ist), war, ist gewesen to be
seit (+ *dat.*) since; for, since (*sub. conj.*)
seitdem since (*sub. conj.*)
die **Seite, -n** page; side
der **Sektretär, -e**/die **Sekretärin, -nen** secretary
die **Sekunde, -n** second
selb- self
selber oneself
selbst oneself; even
das **Semester,** - semester
die **Semesterferien** (*pl.*) days off during the semester; semester break
die **Semesterpause, -n** semester break
das **Seminar, -e** seminar
die **Seminararbeit, -en** term paper
senden, sandte, gesandt to send (electronically)
sentimental sentimental
servieren to serve (food)
die **Serviette, -n** napkin
der **Sessel,** - easy chair, stuffed chair
setzen to set [down]
sich **setzen** to sit down
die **Sicht** sight
das **Silber** silver
die **Sinfonie, -n** symphony
singen, sang, gesungen to sing
sinken, sank, *ist* gesunken to sink
sitzen, saß, gesessen to sit (state of sitting)
(das) **Skandinavien** Scandinavia
so so
so 'was = so etwas something like that, such a thing
sobald as soon as (*sub. conj.*)
das **Sofa, -s** sofa
der **Sohn, Söhne** son
solange as long as (*sub. conj.*)
der **Soldat, -en, -en**/die **Soldatin, -nen** soldier
sollen to be obliged/obligated to, supposed to, expected to
der **Sommer** summer
die **Sommerferien** (*pl.*) summer vacation, summer break
sondern but (*following* **nicht**)
der **Sonnabend** Saturday
sonnig sunny
sonst otherwise
der **Sonntag** Sunday
sooft as often as (*sub. conj.*)
die **Sorge, -n** care, worry
sich **Sorgen machen um** (+ *acc.*) to worry about; have worries about
sorgen to worry
sich **sorgen um** (+ *acc.*) to worry oneself about; worry about
die **Soziologie** sociology
(das) **Spanien** Spain
der **Spanier,** -/die **Spanierin, -nen** Spaniard
das **Spanisch** Spanish language
sparen to save
der **Spargel,** - asparagus
die **Spargelspitzen** (*pl.*) asparagus tips
spät late
spätestens at the latest
der **Spaten,** - spade
spazieren to stroll, walk leisurely
der **Spaziergang, Spaziergänge** walk, stroll
speichern to store (information)
spekulieren to speculate
die **Spezialität, -en** specialty
das **Spiel, -e** game
spielen to play
der **Spieler,** -/die **Spielerin, -nen** player
der **Spielplatz, Spielplätze** playground
die **Spitze, -n** point, tip
der **Sport** sport
Sport treiben to play sports
der **Sportplatz, Sportplätze** sports field
die **Sprache, -n** language
sprechen (spricht), sprach, gesprochen to speak
sprechen mit (+ *dat.*) to speak with/to
sprechen über (+ *acc.*) to speak/talk about (at length)
sprechen von (+ *dat.*) to speak of
spülen to wash dishes
spüren to feel
die **Stadt, Städte** city
die **Stadtmitte** downtown, center of the city
das **Stadtzentrum** downtown, center of the city
der **Stahl** steel
stark strong(ly)
stationieren to station
statt/anstatt (+ *gen.*) instead of
stechen (sticht), stoch, gestochen to sting
stecken to stick (into)

stehen, stand, gestanden to stand
stehlen (stiehlt), stahl, gestohlen to steal
steigen, stieg, *ist* gestiegen to climb
das **Stein, -e** stone, rock
stellen to put, place
sterben (stirbt), starb, *ist* gestorben to die
der **Stern, -e** star
das **Sternschiff, -e** starship
die **Steuererklärung, -en** tax return
stinken, stank, gestunken to stink
das **Stipendium, Stipendien** stipend
der **Stock, Stöcke** floor/story of a building
stolz auf (+ *acc.*) proud of
stören to disturb
stoßen (stößt), stieß, gestoßen to push
die **Straße, -n** street
die **Straßenlampe, -n** streetlight
streichen, strich, gestrichen to stroke, pet; to spread
(sich) **streiten, stritt, gestritten** to argue, fight (verbally)
sich **streiten über** (+ *acc.*) to argue [with each other] about
streng strict(ly)
die **Struktur, -en** structure
das **Stück, -e** piece
der **Student, -en, -en**/die **Studentin, -nen** (university) student
studieren to study, pursue a degree
das **Studium, Studien** studies (university)
der **Stuhl, Stühle** cair
die **Stunde, -n** hour
stundenlang for hours
suchen to seek, look for
(das) **Südamerika** South America
der **Süden** south
die **Suppe, -n** soup
surfen to surf
süß sweet
die **Süßigkeit, -en** candy, sweets
synchronisieren to synchronize

die **Tablette, -n** tablet
der **Tag, -e** day
die **Tageszeit, -en** part of the day
täglich daily, every day
tagsüber during the day
die **Tante, -n** aunt
die **Tasse, -n** cup
das **Tausendstel** one-thousandth
das **Taxi, -s** taxi
der **Taxifahrer, -**/die **Taxifahrerin, -nen** taxi driver
der **Tee** tea
telefonieren to telephone, call up on the phone
die **Telefonnummer, -n** telephone number
das **Teleskop, -e** telescope
der **Teller, -** plate
der **Temperaturwechsel** change in temperature
der **Teppich, -e** rug, carpet
teuer expensive
der **Teufel, -** devil
der **Text, -e** text
das **Theater, -** theater
das **Theaterstück, -e** play
das **Thema, Themen** theme, topic
die **Theorie, -n** theory
tief deep(ly)
der **Tiger, -** tiger
der **Titel, -** title
die **Tochter, Töchter** daughter
der **Tod, -e** death
tödlich deadly, fatal(ly)
toll great, fantastic
die **Tomate, -n** tomato
tot dead
töten to kill
die **Tournee, -n** tournament
tragen (trägt), trug, getragen to carry
trauen (+ *dat.*) to trust
der **Traum, Träume** dream
träumen to dream
träumen von (+ *dat.*) to dream of
traurig sad
traurig über (+ *acc.*) sad about
treffen (trifft), traf, getroffen to meet; to hit (a target)
treiben, trieb, getrieben to drive; to propel
trennen to separate
getrennt von (+ *dat.*) separated from
treten (tritt), trat, *ist/hat* getreten to step/kick
treu true, faithful
trinken, trank, getrunken to drink
trocken dry
trotz (+ *gen.*) in spite of
tschechish Czech
tüchtig hard-working
tun, tat, getan to do
die **Türkei** Turkey
die **U-Bahn, -en** subway
über (+ *acc./dat.*) above, over, across; by way of, via; in excess of; more than; about (*with verbs*)
der/die **Überlebende, -n** survivor
sich **überlegen** to consider, think about
übermorgen the day after tomorrow
übernachten to spend/stay the night
überraschend surprising
überrascht surprised
übersehen (übersieht), übersah, übersehen to overlook, forget
übersentimental overly sentimental
überzeugt convinced
überzeugt von (+ *dat.*) convinced by
übrig else; leftover
die **Übung, -en** exercise
die **Uhr, -en** clock; o'clock
um (+ *acc.*) at, around
umdrehen to turn around
umkippen to tip over
umsteigen, stieg ... um, *ist* umgestiegen to transer (train, plane)
umziehen, zog ... um, *ist* umgezogen to move (residence)
unabhängig independent(ly)
unabhängig von (+ *dat.*) independent from
unabsichtlich unintentional(ly)
unbeschreiblich indescribable, indescribably
und and
unerwartet unexpected(ly)
der **Unfall, Unfälle** accident
die **Uni, -s** university
unidentifiziert unidentified
die **Union, -en** union
die **Universität, -en** university
unnatürlich unnatural
unser our
der **Unsinn** nonsense
unter (+ *acc./dat.*) below, under, less than; underneath, beneath; among
das **Unternehemen, -** undertaking
das **Unterrichtsziel, -e** goal of instruction, instructional gòal
unterschreiben, unterschrieb, unterschrieben to sign

untersuchen to examine
der **Urlaub** vacation
Urlaub machen to take a vacation
der **Urlauber, -**/die **Urlauberin, -nen** vacationer

die **Vase, -n** vase
der **Vater, Väter** father
Vati Dad, Pop
der **Ventilator, -en** fan, ventilator
verändern to change (appearance)
verantwortlich responsible
verantwortlich für (+ *acc.*) responsible for
die **Verantwortlichkeit, -en** responsibility
verärgert annoyed
verbergen (verbirgt), verbarg, verborgen to hide, conceal
verbessern to improve
verbrauchen to consume, use up
verbrennen, verbrannte, *ist/hat* verbrannt to burn up
verbringen, verbrachte, verbracht to spend time
verderben (verdirbt), verdarb, verdorben to spoil, ruin
der **Verein, -e** club
sich **verfahren (verfährt), verfuhr, verfahren** to get lost driving
verfaulen to spoil, rot, decay, decompose
Verflucht mal! Darn it!
die **Vergangenheit** past
vergessen (vergisst), vergaß, vergessen to forget
vergesslich forgetful
vergleichen, verglich, verglichen to compare
verheiratet married
verheiratet mit (+ *dat.*) married to
das **Verkehrsmittel, -** mode/means of transportation
sich **verlaufen (verläuft), verlief, verlaufen** to get lost walking
verlegen to misplace; to postpone
verletzen to injure
verliebt in love
verliebt in (+ *acc.*) in love with
verlieren, verlor, verloren to lose
verlobt engaged
verlobt mit (+ *dat.*) engaged to
vermeiden, vermied, vermieden to avoid
vernichten to annihilate
vernünftig reasonable, rational
verrückt crazy
verrückt auf (+ *acc.*) mad/crazy about
verrückt nach (+ *dat.*) mad/crazy about
verschieben, verschob, verschoben to put off, delay
verschieden different, various
verschwinden, verschwand, *ist* verschwunden to disappear
versenken to sink
der **Versicherungsagent, -en, -en**/die **Versicherungsagentin, -nen** insurance agent
die **Verspätung, -en** delay, lateness
versprechen (verspricht), versprach, versprochen to promise
der **Vertrag, Verträge** contract
vertreiben, vertrieb, vertrieben to drive off, repel
verursachen to cause
die **Verwaltung, -en** administration
das **Verwaltungsgebäude, -** administration building
verwandt related
verwandt mit (+ *dat.*) related to
verwirrend confusing
verwöhnen to spoil, indulge (e.g., children)
verwunden to wound
verzeihen, verzieh, verziehen to forgive
der **Vetter, -** (male) cousin
viel much
viele many
das **Viertel** one-fourth; quarter
die **Viertelstunde, -n** quarter hour
die **Vitaminpille, -n** vitamin pill
das **Vögelein, -** little bird, baby bird
völlig completely, fully
von (+ *dat.*) from; of
vor (+ *acc./dat.*) in front of; before
vor kurzem a short time ago, recently
vorbeifahren (fährt ... vorbei), fuhr ... vorbei, *ist* vorbeigefahren to drive by
vorbeikommen, kam ... vorbei, *ist* vorbeigekommen to come by
vorbeilaufen (läuft ... vorbei), lief ... vorbei, *ist* vorbeigelaufen to run by
(sich) **vorbereiten** to prepare (onseself), to make ready
(sich) **vorbereiten auf** (+ *acc.*) to prepare (oneself) for
vorgehen, ging ... vor, *ist* vorgegangen to run fast (clock)
vorgestern the day before yesterday
vorhaben (hat ... vor), hatte ... vor, vorgehabt to intend
vorher before, previously
vorlesen (liest ... vor), las ... vor, vorgelesen to lecture, read aloud
die **Vorlesung, -en** lecture
der **Vormittag, -e** late morning, forenoon
der **Vorschlag, Vorschläge** suggestion
vorschlagen (schlägt ... vor), schlug ... vor, vorgeschlagen to suggest
die **Vorsicht** caution
vorsichtig careful(ly), with foresight
vorstellen to present, introduce
sich (*dat.*) **etwas vorstellen** to imagine something

wach awake
wachsen (wächst), wuchs, *ist* gewachsen to grow
wackelig wobbly
der **Wagen, -** car, auto
während (+ *gen.*) during; while, whereas (*sub. conj.)*
wahrscheinlich probably
die **Wand, Wände** wall
wandern to hike, wander
die **Wanderung, -en** hike
die **Waren** (*pl.*) wares, goods
warm warm
die **Warnung, -en** warning
warten to wait
warten auf (+ *acc.*) to wait for
(sich) **waschen (wäscht), wusch, gewaschen** to wash
das **Wasser** water
der **Wecker, -** alarm clock
den **Wecker stellen** to set the alarm clock
der **Weg, -e** way, path
wegen (+ *gen.*) because of, due to
wegfahren (fährt ... weg), fuhr ... weg, *ist* weggefahren to drive away
weggehen, ging ... weg, *ist* weggegangen to go away
weglaufen (läuft ... weg), lief ... weg, *ist* weggelaufen to run away
wegstellen to put away

wegwerfen (wirft ... weg), warf ... weg, weggeworfen to throw away
wehtun, tat weh, wehgetan to hurt, injure
weiblich female
das **Weihnachten** Christmas
der **Weihnachtsmann** Santa Claus
weil because (*sub. conj.*)
die **Weile** while, time, period
der **Wein, -e** wine
weinen to cry, weep
weinend- crying
der **Weinkeller, -** wine cellar
weiterfahren (fährt ... weiter), fuhr ... weiter, *ist* weitergefahren to travel on/further
weitergehen, ging ... weiter, *ist* weitergegangen to go on/further
weiterlesen (liest ... weiter), las ... weiter, weitergelesen to read on/further
weitermachen to carry on, continue
wenden, wandte, gewandt to turn
wenig little (quantity)
ein wenig a few, a little
wenige few
wenigstens at the least
wenn when, whenever; if (*sub. conj.*)
werden (wird), wurde, *ist* geworden to become
werfen, (wirft), warf, geworfen to throw
das **Werkzeug, -e** tool
wessen whose?
der **Westen** west
weswegen for what reason, why?
wichtig important
wieder again
wieso how come, why?
der **Wikinger, -** Viking
wild wild(ly)
windig windy
der **Winter** winter
die **Winterferien** (*pl.*) winter vacation, winter break
wirklich really
wischen to wipe
wissen (weiß), wusste, gewusst to know (factually)
der **Witz, -e** joke
woanders somewhere else
die **Woche, -n** week
das **Wochenende** weekend
wochenlang for a week
die **Wohnung, -en** apartment
wollen to desire, want to
das **Wort, Worte** (*contextual*)/**Wörter** (*non-contextual*) word
wundern to wonder
sich **wundern über** (+ *acc.*) to surprise oneself about; be surprised about
das **Wunderkind, -er** genius, wonder child, prodigy
die **Würde** worth, value

Zahl, -en number
zählen to count
zahlen to pay
der **Zahn, Zähne** tooth
der **Zahnarzt, Zahnärzte**/die **Zahnärztin, -nen** dentist
der **Zahnschmerz, -en** toothache
die **Zange, -n** pliers
das **Zehntel** one-tenth
zeichnen to draw, sketch
der **Zeigefinger, -** index finger
zeigen to show
die **Zeit, -en** time
die **Zeitschrift, -en** magazine
die **Zeitung, -en** newspaper
die **Zensur, -en** final grades
zerbrechen (zerbricht), zerbrach, zerbrochen to break into pieces
zerfallen (zerfällt), zerfiel, *ist* zerfallen to fall to pieces
zerreißen, zerriss, zerrissen to tear to pieces
zerschneiden, zerschnitt, zerschnitten to cut to pieces
zerstören to destroy
der **Zettel, -** note, short message
ziehen, zog, *ist/hat* gezogen to move/pull
ziemlich rather, pretty (*intensifier*)
das **Zimmer, -** room
der **Zimmerkollege, -n, -n**/die **Zimmerkollegin, -nen** roommate
zu (+ *dat.*) to, too
zu Besuch for a visit
zu Hause [at] home (location)
zufrieden satisfied
zufrieden mit (+ *dat.*) satisfied/pleased with
der **Zug, Züge** train
zuhören (+ *dat.*) to listen to (a person or message)
die **Zukunft** future
zumachen to close
zunehmen (nimmt ... zu), nahm ... zu, zugenommen to gain/put on weight
zurückbleiben, blieb ... zurück, *ist* zurückgeblieben to stay behind, remain
zurückbringen, brachte ... zurück, zurückgebracht to bring back, return
zurückgehen, ging ... zurück, *ist* zurückgegangen to go back, return
zurückkommen, kam ... zurück, *ist* zurückgekommen to come back, return
zurückwerfen (wirft ... zurück), warf ... zurück, zurückgeworfen to throw back
zusammenarbeiten to collaborate, work together
zusammenbinden, band ... zusammen, zusammengebunden to tie/bind together
zusammenbrechen (bricht ... zusammen), brach ... zusammen, *ist* zusammengebrochen to collapse
zusammenbringen, brachte ... zusammen, zusammengebracht to bring together, join
zusammenkommen, kam ... zusammen, *ist* zusammengekommen to come together, assemble
zusammenstellen to put/place together
der **Zuschauer, -** spectator
zuwinken to wave at/to
das **Zwanzigstel** one-twentieth
zweifeln to doubt
zweitens secondly
zwingen, zwang, gezwungen to force
zwischen (+ *acc./dat.*) between

Answer Key

Chapter 1 Present Tense

Focus on Form

2

1. fragst; fragt 2. nimmst; nehmt 3. fährst; fahrt 4. läufst; lauft 5. arbeitest; arbeitet 6. lernst; lernt 7. wendest; wendet 8. sprichst; sprecht 9. wartest; wartet 10. kommst; kommt 11. gibst; gebt 12. sagst; sagt 13. bist; seid 14. hast; habt 15. wirst; werdet

Focus on Meaning and Form

3

1. Ich kaufe ein Hemd. 2. Der Film läuft diese Woche. 3. Ich glaube das. 4. Sie ruft ihre Mutter. 5. Ich öffne die Fenster. 6. Du bist müde. 7. Ich habe viele Freunde. 8. Ich komme auch. 9. Ich lese [noch] eine Weile. 10. Wir werden dick. 11. Ich werde zu dünn. 12. Maria geht bald.

4

1. Wirst du krank? 2. Fahrt ihr nach München? 3. Hat Martina Pläne für heute Abend? 4. Gehen sie jetzt nach Hause? 5. Was machst du hier? 6. Wann enden die Frühlingsferien? 7. Wo wohnst/bleibst du diesen Sommer?

5

1. Wo ist das Buch? 2. Wohin geht ihr heute Abend? 3. Wo wohnst du? 4. Was machst du später? 5. Wann bist du zu Hause? 6. Warum machst du das immer? 7. Wer ist deine neue Freundin? 8. Wie macht man das?

Chapter 2 Present Perfect

Focus on Form

2.A

1. haben 2. ist 3. habe 4. ist 5. habe 6. hat 7. sind 8. hat 9. bin 10. hat; ist

2.B

1. habe 2. hat 3. Hast 4. hat 5. ist 6. Hast 7. habe 8. ist 9. ist 10. ist; ist

Chapter 3 Simple Past and Past Perfect

Focus on Form

2

1. Karl wartete auf seine Freundin. Karl hat auf seine Freundin gewartet. Karl hatte auf seine Freundin gewartet.
2. Maria las die Zeitung. Maria hat die Zeitung gelesen. Maria hatte die Zeitung gelesen.
3. Ich kam nicht. Ich bin nicht gekommen. Ich war nicht gekommen.
4. Wir gingen zur Uni. Wir sind zur Uni gegangen. Wir waren zur Uni gegangen.
5. Martin flog nach Rom. Martin ist nach Rom geflogen. Martin war nach Rom geflogen.
6. Wir aßen gern Wiener Schnitzel mit Spätzle. Wir haben gern Wiener Schnitzel mit Spätzle gegessen. Wir hatten gern Wiener Schnitzel mit Spätzle gegessen.
7. Ich trank ein Glas Bier. Ich habe ein Glas Bier getrunken. Ich hatte ein Glas Bier getrunken.
8. Es war kalt. Es ist kalt gewesen. Es war kalt gewesen.
9. Ihr hattet Pech. Ihr habt Pech gehabt. Ihr hattet Pech gehabt.
10. Die Kinder wurden krank. Die Kinder sind krank geworden. Die Kinder waren krank geworden.
11. Ich schrieb meinen Eltern einen Brief. Ich habe meinen Eltern einen Brief geschrieben. Ich hatte meinen Eltern einen Brief geschrieben.
12. Frau Bruns fuhr mit dem Taxi in die Stadt. Frau Bruns ist mit dem Taxi in die Stadt gefahren. Frau Bruns war mit dem Taxi in die Stadt gefahren.
13. Ich war zu Hause. Ich bin zu Hause gewesen. Ich war zu Hause gewesen.
14. Thomas sprach immer zu schnell. Thomas hat immer zu schnell gesprochen. Thomas hatte immer zu schnell gesprochen.
15. Es wurde heiß. Es ist heiß geworden. Es war heiß geworden.
16. Wir trafen unsere Freunde vor dem Kino. Wir haben unsere Freunde vor dem Kino getroffen. Wir hatten unsere Freunde vor dem Kino getroffen.
17. Ich antwortete ihnen nicht. Ich habe ihnen nicht geantwortet. Ich hatte ihnen nicht geantwortet.
18. Lerntet ihr es für die Prüfung? Habt ihr es für die Prüfung gelernt? Hattet ihr es für die Prüfung gelernt?
19. Mutti dachte immer logisch. Mutti hat immer logisch gedacht. Mutti hatte immer logisch gedacht.
20. Vati rasierte sich jeden Morgen. Vati hat sich jeden Morgen rasiert. Vati hatte sich jeden Morgen rasiert.

3

1. Nachdem ich mich geduscht hatte, habe ich mein Frühstück gegessen. *or:*
   Nachdem ich mich geduscht hatte, aß ich mein Frühstück.
2. Nachdem ich mir die Hände gewaschen hatte, habe ich ein Handtuch gesucht. *or:*
   Nachdem ich mir die Hände gewaschen hatte, suchte ich ein Handtuch.
3. Nachdem ich die Zeitung gelesen hatte, bin ich zur Uni gefahren. *or:*
   Nachdem ich die Zeitung gelesen hatte, fuhr ich zur Uni.
4. Bevor ich Musik gehört habe, hatte ich meine Hausaufgaben gemacht. *or:*
   Bevor ich Musik hörte, hatte ich meine Hausaufgaben gemacht.
5. Bevor ich ins Bett gegangen bin, hatte ich eine Weile einen Roman gelesen. *or:*
   Bevor ich ins Bett ging, hatte ich eine Weile einen Roman gelesen.

Chapter 4 Future and Future Perfect

Focus on Form

2

1. werde 2. Wirst 3. Wird 4. werden 5. werdet 6. werden 7. Wirst 8. werde 9. wird 10. werdet

3.A

1. Karl wird auf seine Freundin warten. 2. Maria wird die Zeitung lesen. 3. Ich werde später mit meinem Freund kommen. 4. Wirst du zur Uni gehen? 5. Martin und Beate werden nach Rom fliegen. 6. Wir werden Wiener Schnitzel mit Spätzle bestellen. 7. Werdet ihr ein Glas Bier trinken? 8. Es wird kalt werden. 9. Ich werde Pech haben. 10. Tina wird überrascht sein.

3.B

1. Ich werde mit meinen Eltern telefonieren. 2. Die Frau wird zwei Wochen in Heidelberg bleiben. 3. Ich werde um sieben Uhr wieder zu Hause sein. 4. Thomas wird immer lange über Politik sprechen. 5. Es wird bestimmt heiß werden. 6. Wir werden unsere Freunde vor dem Theater treffen. 7. Ich werde dem Lehrer eine Frage stellen. 8. Klaus wird morgen eine Prüfung schreiben. 9. Mutti wird immer an die Vergangenheit denken. 10. Vati wird sich rasieren.

4

gewusst haben	geworfen haben
gewaschen haben	gegeben haben
gegessen haben	getrunken haben
gestorben sein	gekommen sein
gesehen haben	geschwommen sein
geschrieben haben	gelaufen sein
gegangen sein	gefahren sein/haben

5

1. Ich werde Mutti eine schöne Bluse gekauft haben. 2. Wir werden diesen Roman für den Literaturkurs gelesen haben. 3. Die Musikstudenten werden zusammen eine Sinfonie für den Semesterabschluss komponiert haben. 4. Die Kirche wird den Obdachlosen einen Platz zum Schlafen gegeben haben. 5. Herr Mayer wird bestimmt sein letztes Geld auf das Fußballspiel gewettet haben.

Chapter 5 Imperative Mood: Commands

Focus on Form

2

1. Frag(e); Fragt 2. Nimm; Nehmt 3. Fahr; Fahrt 4. Lauf; Lauft 5. Arbeite; Arbeitet 6. Lern(e); Lernt 7. Wende; Wendet 8. Sprich; Sprecht 9. Warte; Wartet 10. Komm; Kommt 11. Gib; Gebt 12. Sag(e); Sagt 13. Sei; Seid 14. Hab; Habt 15. Werde; Werdet

Focus on Meaning and Form

3

1. Arbeite fleißig. 2. Lauf schnell. 3. Lies es jetzt. 4. Nimm das. 5. Schreib gut. 6. Mach das vorsichtig. 7. Schlaf gut. 8. Iss mehr Gemüse. 9. Trink weniger Bier. 10. Fahr sicher. 11. Fahr langsamer. 12. Sei ruhig.

Chapter 6 Verbs with Inseparable Prefixes

Focus on Form

2

1. Wir begrüßen unsere Verwandten. 2. Die Kandidaten besprechen ihre Ideen. 3. Die Kellnerin empfiehlt das Jägerschnitzel. 4. Diese Landkarte erleichtert die Planung unserer Reise. 5. Ersetzt du die Batterien? 6. Opa erzählt uns immer von dem Krieg. 7. Gefällt es dir? 8. Wem gehört das? 9. Er hinterlässt seine Familie in Bosnien. 10. Du missdeutest alles. 11. Karl verläuft sich immer in der Stadt. 12. Das verspricht er jedem Mädchen.

3

1. Die Partisanen misshandelten ihre Gefangenen. 2. Wir misstrauten dem ausländischen Verteidigungsminister. 3. Wo verbarg man das gestohlene Geld? 4. Dieses Auto verbrauchte viel Benzin. 5. Ich verbrachte den ganzen Sommer in Bulgarien. 6. Die Mutter verglich ihre Tochter mit ihrem Sohn. 7. Die Armee vernichtete den Feind in zwei großen Schlachten. 8. Der Plan entwickelte sich schnell. 9. Was geschah während deines Aufenthalts in der Schweiz? 10. Ich besuchte meine Tante in Frankfurt.

4

hat begrüßt	hat gehört
hat beantwortet	ist geschehen
hat bekommen	hat hinterlassen
hat besprochen	hat missdeutet
hat besucht	hat misshandelt
hat empfangen	hat misstraut
hat empfohlen	hat (sich) verlaufen
hat entfaltet	hat verborgen
hat erleichtert	hat verbraucht
hat ersetzt	hat verbracht
hat erzählt	hat verglichen
hat gefallen	hat versprochen

5

1. Ich habe die Frage nicht beantwortet. 2. Hast du seine Aussagen begriffen? 3. Was hast du zum Geburtstag bekommen? 4. Haben die Wikinger Amerika entdeckt? 5. Ihre Hilfe hat den Erfolg des Unternehmens ermöglicht. 6. Wir haben das Abendessen bei euch genossen. 7. Oma und Opa haben ihre Enkelkinder verwöhnt. 8. Ihr habt mich furchtbar missverstanden. 9. Warum hast du dein Aussehen so drastisch verändert? 10. Wieso bist du plötzlich verschwunden?

6

1. Jeder Student hatte seinen Aufsatz verbessert. 2. Ein Virus hatte diese Krankheit verursacht. 3. Sie hatte das Bild ihres ehemaligen Freundes zerrissen. 4. Der Koch hatte das Gemüse und das Fleisch zerschnitten. 5. Das Feuer hatte zwei Gebäude zerstört.

7

1. Wirst du die Frage nicht beantworten? 2. Wann werden wir unsere Leseaufgabe erledigen? 3. Das wird viel für uns erleichtern. 4. Die Schuhe werden Christiane sehr gefallen. 5. Ihr werdet das ohne Zweifel genießen.

8

1. Wir haben alle Fragen beantwortet. 2. Der Professor hat mir diese zwei Kurse empfohlen. 3. Al Gore hat das Internet erfunden! 4. Ich habe mich beruhigt. 5. Diese Idee hat sich ganz langsam in meinem Gehirn entwickelt. 6. So ein Spiel hat uns sehr gefallen. 7. Das ist blitzschnell und ohne Warnung geschehen. 8. Er hat mich einfach missverstanden. 9. Wir haben Ilse nicht erkannt, denn sie hatte sich sehr verändert. 10. Deine Faulheit hat deine akademischen Schwierigkeiten verursacht.

Chapter 7 Verbs with Separable Prefixes

Focus on Form

2.A

1. Jeden Abend sehe ich ein bisschen fern. 2. Endlich werden wir diesen Unsinn los. 3. Bringt ihr eure Instrumente mit? 4. Gehst du auch mit? 5. Jeder Student bereitet sich auf das Examen vor. 6. Meine Uhr geht drei Minuten vor. 7. Was hast du vor? 8. Fritz schließt sein Studium im Jahre 2010 ab. 9. Wann fängt das Konzert an? 10. Die Musikstudenten hören die Sinfonie von Mahler an.

2.B

1. Die Lehrer passen immer auf die Schüler auf. 2. Ich wache jeden Morgen um sieben Uhr auf. 3. Wie viel Geld gibst du dafür aus? 4. Unsere Kinder ziehen sich immer sehr langsam aus. 5. Viele Eltern kaufen am Samstagmorgen von neun bis Mittag ein. 6. Wie viele Gäste ladet ihr zur Party ein? 7. Wir stellen unsere Sachen jetzt weg. 8. Warum wirfst du deine alte Kleidung weg? 9. Warum bringst du es nicht zurück? 10. Die Mitglieder des Vereins kommen wegen der Tournee zusammen.

3

1. Man setzte das Spiel nach dem Gewitter fort. 2. Der Vater ließ seinen Sohn plötzlich los. 3. Alle machten mit. 4. Wir erzählten die Witze nach. 5. Andreas schlug viele Wörter im Wörterbuch nach. 6. Das Kind drehte sich blitzschnell um. 7. Die Reisenden stiegen in Berlin um. 8. Der Professor las aus seinen Notizen vor. 9. Udo fuhr sehr böse ab. 10. Klara nahm zehn Kilo ab.

4

hat abgeschnitten	hat losgelassen
hat abgeschrieben	ist losgeworden
hat angefangen	ist mitgekommen
hat angerufen	ist nachgeblieben
hat aufgepasst	hat umgedreht
hat aufgeräumt	ist umgezogen
hat ausgetauscht	hat vorgeschlagen
hat ausgezogen	hat vorgestellt
hat eingeführt	ist vorbeigekommen
hat eingeladen	hat weggeworfen
hat ferngesehen	hat zugewinkt
hat fortgesetzt	hat zusammengearbeitet

5

1. Ich habe die zwei Karten voneinander losgelöst. 2. Warum sind er und seine Söhne mitgekommen? 3. Davon hat sie uns nichts mitgeteilt. 4. Die Vase ist plötzlich umgekippt. 5. Als Kind bin ich dreimal umgezogen. 6. Klara hat zehn Kilo abgenommen. 7. Die Köchin hat die Spargelspitzen abgeschnitten. 8. Warum bist du so spät angekommen? 9. Alle Schüler haben die Bücher aufgemacht. 10. Der Junge hat sein Zimmer aufgeräumt.

6

1. Um Mitternacht hatte ich das Licht ausgemacht. 2. Wart ihr mit euren Freunden ausgegangen? 3. Der Beamte war in sein Büro eingetreten. 4. Die Chefin hatte den neuen Plan eingeführt. 5. Eine Schülerin hatte während der Klausur abgeschrieben.

7

1. Der Philosoph wird heute eine neue Interpretation der Theorie vorschlagen. 2. Wir werden der Lehrerin unsere Eltern vorstellen. 3. Karola wird später am Abend vorbeikommen. 4. Helmut wird schnell nach Hause zurückgehen. 5. Wann wirst du zurückkommen? 6. Die Kinder werden den Lehrer bestimmt auslachen.

8

1. Die Männer sind an unserem Haus vorbeigefahren. 2. Ohne ein einziges Wort zu sagen ist Hanna verärgert weggegangen. 3. Die Kinder sind von dem Fremden weggelaufen. 4. Im Hörsaal haben die Studenten dem Professor sehr genau zugehört. 5. Das Kind hat die Tür langsam und vorsichtig aufgemacht. 6. Ich habe ein bisschen zu viel abgenommen. 7. Beim Abschied hat sie mir ganz freundlich zugewinkt. 8. Wann bist du zurückgekommen? 9. Der Angler hat den kleinen Fisch ins Wasser zurückgeworfen. 10. Die Sekretärinnen haben sehr gut miteinander zusammengearbeitet.

Chapter 8 Modal Auxiliaries

Part One

Focus on Form

2

1. Wir müssen das für Montag erledigen. 2. Ich darf mit euch ins Kino gehen. 3. Kannst du mir helfen? 4. Wir sollen es auswendig für die Prüfung lernen. 5. Es soll morgen früh regnen. 6. Warum willst du ihn nicht heiraten? 7. Der Kunde muss die Rechnung bezahlen. 8. Darf man im Museum fotografieren? 9. Ich kann ein bisschen Italienisch verstehen. 10. Ich soll es niemandem sagen.

3

1. Alex konnte gut Tennis spielen. 2. Unsere Eltern wollten eine Reise nach Graz machen. 3. Man durfte da kein Bier trinken. 4. Musstest du das für den Kurs lesen? 5. Durftest du am Wochenende ausgehen? 6. Moni wollte nicht länger hier bleiben. 7. Wir konnten ihnen leider nicht helfen. 8. Solltest du das für heute erledigen? 9. Anke musste in die Stadt fahren. 10. Wir wollten eine Flasche Wein bestellen. 11. Die Kinder sollten auf Ilse warten. 12. Ich mochte das nicht. 13. Konntest du nicht später mitkommen? 14. Franz wollte dich anrufen.

Part Two

Focus on Form

2

1. Ich konnte das kaufen
   Ich habe das kaufen können.
   Ich hatte das kaufen können.
   Ich werde das kaufen können.
2. Maria wollte zur Party kommen.
   Maria hat zur Party kommen wollen.
   Maria hatte zur Party kommen wollen.
   Maria wird zur Party kommen wollen.
3. Wir mussten diese Aufgabe fehlerfrei erledigen.
   Wir haben diese Aufgabe fehlerfrei erledigen müssen.
   Wir hatten diese Aufgabe fehlerfrei erledigen müssen.
   Wir werden diese Aufgabe fehlerfrei erledigen müssen.
4. Hans durfte das nicht kaufen.
   Hans hat das nicht kaufen dürfen.
   Hans hatte das nicht kaufen dürfen.
   Hans wird das nicht kaufen dürfen.

3

1. Wir wollten Griechisch lernen. 2. Darfst du mit uns ins Kino gehen? 3. Unsere Eltern mussten nach München fahren. 4. Karl sollte das Abendessen fertig machen. 5. Wir haben unsere Hausaufgaben nicht machen können. 6. Maria hat mit Freunden ausgehen dürfen. 7. Ich hatte meine Großeltern besuchen wollen. 8. Ich werde heute zu Hause bleiben müssen. 9. Das Wetter sollte gut sein. 10. Wir werden dieses Jahr in Florida Urlaub machen können.

Chapter 9 Nouns and Case

Part One

Focus on Form

2

der Franzose
die Antwort
der Patient
die Warnung
die Woche
das Jahr
das Problemchen
das Kind
die Ärztin
die Polizei
das Mädchen
das Gold
das Stipendium
der VW
der Präsident
das Essen
der Kunde
die Grammatik
der Herbst
das Wochenende
das Auto
die Spezialität
die Straße
die Krankheit
der Regen
das Trinken
der Morgen
der Westen
die Assistentin
das B
die Operation
der Dienstag
der Abend
der Mai
der Wagen
die Freundlichkeit
die Chemie
die Freundschaft
der Ausländer
die Konditorei
der Russe
der Porsche

3

der Gummistiefel
der Lederschuh
die Semesterpause
die Strickjacke
der Trainingsanzug
die Hosentasche
der Regenmantel
das Sommersemester
der Taschenrechner
die Winterkleidung

4

Fragen
Vorlesungen
Wagen
Universitäten
Väter
Hotels
Hunde
Räder
Frauen
Gefängnisse
Studentinnen
Häuser
Pakete
Ausweise
Schecks
Ärzte
Fabriken
Schwestern
Krankheiten
Mütter
Gäste
Männer
Jahre
Mädchen
Busse
Freunde
Chancen
Romane
Stipendien
Herzen
Polizisten
Tage
Partys
Meinungen
Kinder
Bücher
Sätze
Hände
Verträge
Familien
Schuhe
Nummern
Arbeiter
Themen
Gymnasien

5

Answers will vary.

Part Two

Basic Case Affiliations

2

active subject — nominative
an/auf, hinter/vor, über/unter, in, neben, zwischen — dative/accusative
aus, außer, bei, mit, nach, seit, von, zu, gegenüber — dative
beneficiary — dative
bis, durch, für, gegen, ohne, um — accusative
direct address — nominative
direct object — accusative
duration of time — accusative
helfen, glauben, antworten, trauen — dative
indirect object — dative
noun phrase of non-specific time — accusative
noun phrase of specific measure — accusative
noun phrase of specific time — accusative
noun phrase of vague time — genitive
part of a whole — genitive
passive subject — nominative
possessor/owner — genitive
predicate adjective — nominative
predicate noun — nominative
statal subject — nominative
trotz, wegen, während, (an)statt — genitive

3

an — dative/accusative
aus — dative
bei — dative
für — accusative
hinter — dative/accusative
mit — dative
neben — dative/accusative
seit — dative
um — accusative
von — dative
zu — dative
auf — dative/accusative
außer — dative
durch — accusative
gegen — accusative
in — dative/accusative
nach — dative
ohne — accusative
über — dative/accusative
unter — dative/accusative
vor — dative/accusative
zwischen — dative/accusative

4

abschneiden — accusative
ansehen — accusative
antworten — dative
aufräumen — accusative
ausziehen — accusative
beantworten — accusative
danken — dative
einladen — accusative
empfehlen — accusative
ersetzten — accusative
folgen — dative
fortsetzen — accusative
gehören — dative
genießen — accusative
geschehen — dative
glauben — dative
helfen — dative
missverstehen — accusative
mitbringen — accusative
sehen — accusative
tragen — accusative
trauen — dative
verbrauchen — accusative
vergleichen — accusative
vorbereiten — accusative
vorstellen — accusative
wegstellen — accusative
zerschneiden — accusative
zurückgeben — accusative
zurückwerfen — accusative

Chapter 10 Articles, *der*-Words, and *ein*-Words

Part One

Focus on Form

2.A

1. der 2. dem 3. den; die 4. diesen 5. dieses 6. welchem 7. Welche 8. Diese 9. alle 10. Diese

2.B

1. der 2. aller Studenten; dem 3. dieser 4. jedes Schülers/jeder Schülerin 5. Solche 6. Diese 7. Die 8. diesen 9. Solche 10. Alle

2.C

1. Solche 2. dieser 3. der 4. Jeder; alle; der 5. des Monats 6. der; dem 7. Jedes; diesem 8. das 9. die; dieser 10. jeden

2.D

1. dieses 2. der; dem 3. diesen 4. diese 5. Manche; die 6. Alle 7. den; dieser 8. alle; den 9. jedes 10. die; die

2.E

1. allen Leuten 2. dem 3. den Kindern 4. Manche 5. den; die 6. des Semesters; den 7. des Tages 8. diesem 9. den 10. des Regens

2.F

1. Welche 2. Welches 3. Welches 4. Welche 5. Welcher 6. Welchen 7. welchem; dem/zum 8. welcher 9. Welches; Dieses; jenes 10. Welchem Jungen; die; aller

Part Two

Focus on Form

2.A

1. deine 2. meine 3. unserem 4. ein; eine 5. meinen 6. unseren Freunden 7. einem Studenten; seinen 8. keine 9. seinen 10. unsere

2.B

1. einen 2. ein 3. ein 4. (blank) 5. ein 6. ein 7. einem 8. eine 9. (blank) 10. (blank)

2.C

1. kein 2. Eine 3. einem; einer 4. keinen/keine 5. einen 6. ein 7. seinen 8. eines Filmes; eines Romans 9. meinem 10. keine

2.D

1. meiner 2. euer 3. deinen 4. seiner 5. eure 6. euren 7. ihrem 8. eure 9. Einem; einer 10. deiner; deinem; deinen

2.E

1. (blank) 2. (blank) 3. Meine; ihren 4. unserer 5. eurer 6. (blank); deiner 7. seines Filmes 8. meinen Kindern 9. deinem 10. einen; eine

2.F

1. deine 2. keine; meine 3. eine 4. euren 5. seiner; seine 6. deinem 7. unserer 8. deinen 9. euren 10. ein

2.G

1. (blank) 2. meinem 3. einen 4. Eine; einen

Supplementary Exercises

Der- and *ein*-Words Combined with Noun Endings

A

1. der 2. Ihrem 3. einen; eine 4. ein 5. einen; eine 6. welchem; welcher 7. Welche 8. Die 9. meinem; eine; einem 10. Eine

B

1. der 2. alle Kollegen 3. ihrer 4. jeden 5. Solche 6. Diese 7. Eine 8. Ein 9. Mein 10. Meine

C

1. Solche 2. dieser 3. meiner 4. Unser; alle; dieser 5. Mein; des Semesters 6. der; dem 7. ein 8. einem 9. seine 10. ein; seine

D

1. dein 2. der; ihrer 3. keinen; zum 4. diese 5. Manche; die 6. alle 7. meinen; seine 8. alle; diesen 9. kein 10. die; die

E

1. allen Leuten 2. dem 3. den; Kindern 4. Welche 5. meinen 6. des Sommers; meinen 7. des Tages 8. diesem 9. der 10. des Wetters

F

1. Welchen 2. Welches 3. Welches 4. Welche 5. Welcher 6. Welchen 7. welchem 8. welcher 9. Welches 10. Welchen Studenten; meine

G

1. dieser 2. den Schülern 3. diesen Häusern 4. ein; eine 5. der; das 6. unseren Frauen 7. jedem Jungen; seinen 8. keine 9. der 10. unsere

H

1. einen 2. ein 3. ein 4. (blank) 5. ein 6. ein 7. einem 8. eine 9. (blank); Verkehrsmitteln 10. (blank)

I

1. ein 2. Ein 3. einem; einer 4. alle 5. einen 6. ein 7. keinen Leuten 8. des Filmes; des Romans 9. der 10. eine

J

1. meiner 2. mein 3. deinen 4. seiner 5. eure 6. diesen Büchern 7. ihrem 8. diese 9. dem; der 10. deiner; deinem; deinen Geschwistern

K

1. ein 2. Jedes; diesem 3. Meine; ihren 4. unserem 5. eurer 6. Das; deiner; jenem 7. eines Romans; diesem 8. jedem; seinen 9. euren Kindern 10. einen; eine

L

1. ihre 2. diese 3. Solch eine 4. euren 5. der; alle 6. Welcher 7. Welche 8. Welcher 9. welchen Freunden 10. welchem

M

1. eine 2. (blank) 3. dem 4. deinen 5. die; ein

Chapter 11 Adjective Endings

Part One

Focus on Form

2.A

1. keinen billigen 2. ihr letzter 3. Dein grüner 4. dem letzten 5. einem anderen 6. einen armen 7. gutes 8. der alten 9. den anderen 10. keinen ausländischen

2.B

1. das andere 2. dein neues 3. dem kleinen 4. ein krankes 5. diesem neuen 6. ein altes 7. mein neues 8. ein altes 9. einem norwegischen 10. ein gutes

2.C

1. Die braune 2. eine schöne; eine 3. keine schwere 4. meiner kleinen 5. einer kleinen 6. eine deutsche 7. diese fremde 8. der neuen 9. Meine neue 10. eine alte romantische

2.D

1. seines neuen Film[e]s 2. einer großen 3. ein; klassischer italienischer 4. der langen 5. eines berühmten Politikers 6. furchtbaren Wetters 7. dieser wilden lauten 8. die alte 9. dieser kaputten 10. diese weiße

2.E

1. Liebe 2. gute 3. wenige hohe 4. schöne 5. Frisches 6. Frischer 7. teuren französischen 8. Dunkle 9. deutsche 10. schöne

2.F

1. Die ersten 2. keine deutschen 3. italienische 4. kleine 5. allen armen Leuten 6. das andere restaurierte 7. Niedrige; dieser hohen 8. der neuen 9. Unsere neuen 10. diesen alten

2.G

1. Welche alten 2. meine goldenen 3. Kaltes; einem warmen 4. kranken Leuten 5. blutroter 6. die kleinen 7. warme 8. nette freundliche 9. lieber 10. der nächsten

2.H

1. die neue 2. das grüne 3. einem amerikanischen 4. Ihr neues; großen 5. kein billiges 6. Welches neue 7. einen neuen 8. den anderen 9. euren alten 10. Welche blonden

Part Two

Focus on Form

2.A

1. andere 2. Gute 3. Dumme 4. Besonderes 5. Wichtiges 6. Nette 7. Schlechte 8. Gutes 9. Neues 10. Ähnliches

2.B

1. andere 2. Außergewöhnliches 3. Besonderes 4. neue Angestellte 5. Interessantes 6. ein alter Bekannter; einem guten 7. Gutes 8. deinem/deiner/deinen Verwandten 9. Beamte 10. eine Bekannte . . . eine

2.C

1. diesem/dieser/diesen Kranken 2. Teures 3. Viele Blinde; bedeutungsvolles 4. die/der Schöne 5. andere 6. Einfaches 7. Neues; eines Romans; den ersten 8. Interessantes 9. mögliche 10. Wichtiges

2.D

1. Einige gute 2. viele interessante 3. mehreren tschechischen 4. ausländische 5. frisches 6. alte 7. einen etwas teureren 8. einigen schwierigen 9. Mehrere sehr kleine 10. viele gute

2.E

1. Frisch gebackenes 2. gebratene 3. meine schon gewaschenen 4. steigende 5. Verletzte; keine gebrochenen 6. dasselbe 7. derselbe 8. derselben 9. denselben 10. derselben

Supplementary Exercises

A

1. mögliche 2. anderes 3. Die schwarzen 4. Die ersten 5. seines letzten Romans 6. Einige alte 7. Gebratenes 8. kein neues 9. die anderen 10. diesem/diesen Jungen

B

1. Lieber 2. Welches deutsche 3. das neue 4. viele vernünftige 5. Komisches 6. anderer 7. keine logische 8. ein ausländisches; ein japansiches 9. schöne große 10. ein Verwandter

C

1. Solch eine romantische 2. unserem alten 3. Welches blonde 4. dieser karierte 5. Wichtiges 6. dem nächsten 7. Gute 8. eine hässliche; ein formelles 9. Gewöhnliches 10. ihr letzter

D

1. gute 2. viele schwere 3. einer großen 4. kein deutsches 5. zwei gekochte 6. Billiges 7. eine braune 8. dein neues 9. meine silbernen 10. Gute

E

1. keine leichte 2. Dein schwarzer 3. viele reiche 4. ein verrückter; dieser bayrischen 5. dem kleinen Jungen 6. Dummes 7. einem russischen 8. traurige romantische 9. Heißen; einem kalten 10. alte kaputte

F

1. wenigen Leuten 2. unsere neuen 3. Außergewöhnliches 4. ein junges 5. meinem alten 6. ausländische 7. kurze 8. des langen Korridors 9. berühmte 10. kalte

G

1. Ihr neues 2. holländische 3. dem/der/den Blinden 4. dem frühesten 5. den Blonden 6. Überraschendes 7. allen 8. Verletzte; ein gebrochenes 9. unsere letzte 10. Neues

H

1. keinen billigen 2. der neuen 3. Frisches 4. frischen 5. dem/der/den armen Obdachlosen 6. einem kleinen 7. eines berühmten Historikers 8. mögliche 9. eine moderne 10. Beste

I

1. eine alte Bekannte; einer guten 2. Frische; der deutschen 3. einen alten kranken Soldaten 4. eine deutsche 5. Elegantes 6. die anderen 7. das schwere; großer 8. dieselben falschen 9. sonnigen Wetters 10. Welches neue

J

1. einige interessante 2. Interessante; diese wichtige 3. derselbe 4. diese fremde 5. einen neuen 6. gute 7. Besseres 8. einen warmen 9. meinen neuen 10. Kühle; dieser; heißen

K

1. Warmes 2. belgisches; kein deutsches 3. dieses unhöflichen Jungen 4. Diese; Gutes 5. meinen schweren 6. Helle 7. diesem/diesen Kleinen 8. meiner lieben 9. demselben Versicherungsagenten 10. deiner kranken

L

1. den anderen grauen 2. interessante freundliche 3. dem neuen 4. Positives 5. das weinende 6. eine altmodische; echtes 7. Böses; deine liebe 8. französische 9. den anderen Jungen 10. Beamter

M

1. Viele mutige 2. Meine neue 3. meine liebe 4. Unser neuer 5. dein altes 6. dieser schmutzigen 7. einem neuen italienischen 8. denselben 9. mögliche 10. reiner

Chapter 12 Comparative and Superlative Degrees

Focus on Form

2

1. leiser; am leisesten 2. dunkler; am dunkelsten 3. teurer; am teuersten 4. höher; am höchsten 5. besser; am besten 6. mehr; am meisten 7. eher; am ehesten 8. lieber; am liebsten 9. größer; am größten 10. stärker; am stärksten 11. gesünder; am gesündesten 12. näher; am nächsten

3

1. schneller als 2. am schnellsten 3. so schnell wie 4. das schnellste Auto/der schnellste Wagen 5. immer schneller 6. je schneller, desto besser 7. äußerst schnell 8. frühestens um sieben Uhr 9. spätestens um fünf Uhr 10. Die Starken sollen den Schwachen helfen. 11. Die Stärkeren sollen den Schwächeren helfen. 12. Die Stärksten sollen den Schwächsten helfen.

4.A

1. Je mehr; desto müder; 2. Das nächste 3. Die meisten Leute 4. Je leiser, desto besser. 5. immer schwerer 6. am längsten und am langsamsten 7. am schärfsten 8. größer als 9. schneller als 10. weiter als/mehr als

4.B

1. eine größere 2. das höchste 3. der schnellste 4. die verrücktesten 5. ein schärferes 6. so warm wie 7. am klärsten 8. einen wärmeren 9. dem nächsten 10. keinen intelligenteren

4.C

1. gern 2. immer hübscher/schöner 3. am kürzesten; am längsten 4. älter als 5. die dümmsten 6. noch hübscher/schöner als 7. am liebsten 8. äußerst schwer 9. lieber 10. die allerbeste/am allerbesten

Chapter 13 Pronouns

Part One

Focus on Meaning and Form

2

1. Ja, ich gebe ihr den Schlüssel. 2. Ja, er zeigt es uns. 3. Ja, er gibt ihm das Auto. 4. Ja, ich zeige sie der Frau. 5. Ja, er sagt sie uns. 6. Ja, wir kaufen ihr diese Blumen. 7. Ja, ich werfe ihn Hans. 8. Ja, er schenkt ihr Schokolade. 9. Ja, ich gebe es ihr. 10. Ja, wir sollen ihn ihnen zeigen. 11. Ja, ich schicke ihr eine Einladung. 12. Ja, sie gibt es ihrem Mann. 13. Ja, sie sagt sie mir. 14. Ja, ich kaufe es dir. 15. Ja, ich erkläre es ihnen.

3

1. Ja, ich gebe ihn ihr. 2. Ja, er zeigt es ihm. 3. Ja, er gibt es ihm. 4. Ja, ich zeige sie ihr. 5. Ja, er sagt sie ihnen. 6. Ja, wir kaufen sie ihr. 7. Ja, ich werfe ihn ihm. 8. Ja, er bringt sie ihr. 9. Ja, ich gebe es ihm. 10. Ja, wir sollen ihn ihnen zeigen. 11. Ja, ich schicke sie ihr. 12. Ja, sie gibt es ihm. 13. Ja, sie sagt sie ihm. 14. Ja, ich kaufe sie euch. 15. Ja, ich erkläre es ihr.

Part Two

Focus on Form

2.A

1. euch 2. mir 3. uns 4. dich 5. sich 6. euch 7. sich 8. mir 9. uns 10. sich

2.B

1. mir 2. sich 3. dich 4. sich 5. uns 6. sich 7. uns 8. dich 9. sich 10. euch

3

Answers will vary.

Chapter 14 Adverbs

Focus on Form

2

1. morgen 2. heute 3. vorgestern 4. morgen früh 5. heute Morgen 6. Dienstagmittag 7. heute Nachmittag 8. morgen Abend 9. übermorgen 10. heute Abend

3

1. frühmorgens 2. spätnachmittags 3. am Abend 4. spätabends 5. spätestens 6. frühestens 7. donnerstags 8. frühestens heute Abend 9. wöchentlich/jede Woche 10. jährlich/jedes Jahr 11. immer 12. fast 13. fast immer 14. nie 15. fast nie

4

1. nachts 2. abends 3. mittags 4. freitags 5. täglich 6. sonntags 7. monatlich 8. morgens 9. nachmittags 10. montags 11. wöchentlich 12. jährlich

5

1. Wir gehen jetzt nach Hause. 2. Sabine arbeitet immer zu Hause. 3. Sie sitzen lange hier. 4. Ingo macht das immer zu schnell. 5. Peter läuft morgens zur Schule. 6. Ilse fährt immer mit dem Bus zur Uni. 7. Musst du schnell nach Hause gehen? 8. Ich studiere bald in Graz. 9. Sie lernt lieber allein. 10. Kommt ihr etwas früher nach Hause?

6.A

1. nicht bald 2. nicht jährlich 3. nicht täglich 4. morgen nicht 5. jetzt nicht 6. nicht selten 7. nicht immer 8. nicht wöchentlich 9. heute nicht 10. gestern nicht 11. nicht lange 12. noch nicht

6.B

1. heute Morgen nicht 2. montags nicht 3. nicht monatlich 4. nicht viel 5. nicht allein 6. heute Abend nicht 7. abends nicht 8. nicht jährlich 9. nicht schnell 10. nicht gern

6.C

1. nicht hier 2. nicht nach rechts 3. nicht zu Hause 4. nicht sehr gut 5. normalerweise nicht 6. nicht dahin 7. nicht nach Hause 8. nicht aus Köln 9. nicht zu schnell 10. nicht dort

7

1. Wir wollen jetzt nicht hier bleiben. 2. Gehen Sie besser nicht nach rechts! 3. Ich mache das nicht oft. 4. Kommst du nicht früher? 5. Jens denkt nicht so ordentlich. 6. Die Lehrerin spricht nicht zu schnell. 7. Ich nehme den Bus nicht bald zur Uni. 8. Verstehen Sie das jetzt nicht besser? 9. Die Schüler fahren nicht nach Leipzig. 10. Der Junge schläft nicht im Klassenzimmer.

8

1. Ich bleibe bis vier Uhr an der Uni, dann gehe ich einkaufen. 2. Wir werden Milch, Brot, Fleisch und Gemüse kaufen, dann fahren wir nach Hause. 3. Lisa machte das Abendessen, dann kamen ein paar Freunde zu Besuch. 4. Wir werden alle zusammen essen, dann/danach werden wir ins Kino gehen. 5. Wir werden den neuesten Film sehen, dann/danach wollen wir in eine Kneipe gehen. 6. Ich gehe nach Hause, dann werde ich ein bisschen lesen. 7. Ich werde bestimmt von der Arbeit müde sein, dann werde ich bald einschlafen.

Chapter 15 Prepositions

Part One

Focus on Meaning

2.A

1. nach 2. Aus 3. Außer 4. mit 5. gegenüber 6. um 7. gegen/durch 8. ohne 9. zu 10. von; bis

2.B
1. bei 2. seit 3. von; bis 4. aus 5. nach 6. um 7. zu/mit/ohne 8. mit 9. für 10. entlang

2.C
1. für 2. Außer 3. bei 4. gegen 5. ohne 6. bei 7. gegenüber 8. durch 9. Seit 10. zum

Part Two

Focus on Meaning

2.A
1. unter 2. an 3. am 4. ins 5. in; auf 6. wegen 7. (an)statt 8. vor/hinter/neben/zwischen 9. ins 10. hinter

2.B
1. auf 2. in 3. an/neben/hinter/vor 4. Trotz 5. an 6. Wegen 7. Vor/An 8. über 9. außerhalb 10. diesseits

2.C
1. Während/In 2. Auf 3. an 4. Vor/Hinter/Neben 5. in 6. in 7. in 8. Trotz 9. Wegen 10. aufs

Supplementary Exercises

Focus on Meaning

1.A
1. In/Während 2. nach/bis nach 3. unter 4. bei 5. auf 6. für/ohne 7. zum 8. von; bis 9. hinter 10. diesseits

1.B
1. aufs 2. entlang 3. Aus 4. Auf 5. mit 6. an 7. seit 8. in 9. Außer 10. am

1.C
1. an 2. bei 3. von; bis 4. an/neben/hinter/vor 5. Vor/Hinter/Neben 6. Wegen 7. mit 8. ins 9. aus 10. gegen

1.D
1. gegenüber 2. in 3. auf 4. nach 5. ohne 6. an 7. Trotz 8. am 9. wegen 10. an/um

1.E
1. bei 2. in 3. An/Vor 4. durch/gegen 5. in 6. (an)statt 7. gegenüber 8. zu 9. Wegen 10. durch

1.F
1. über 2. ohne 3. neben/vor/hinter/zwischen 4. mit 5. Seit 6. Wegen 7. Auf 8. für 9. ins 10. außerhalb

Focus on Meaning and Form

2.A
1. von Bremen 2. um acht [Uhr] 3. von London nach Paris 4. nach Australien 5. zu meinem Onkel 6. auf den Tisch 7. unter den Tisch 8. bei ihren/den Eltern 9. zu Dieter 10. von der Schule nach Hause

2.B
1. auf dem Spielplatz 2. am Fenster 3. bis nächste Woche 4. für seinen/den Mantel 5. (erst) seit zwei Monaten 6. bei mir 7. bis ans Ende der Welt 8. über Köln 9. außer Betrieb 10. gegen eine Mauer

2.C
1. Aus diesem Grund 2. Neben dem Bett 3. Bei Nebel/Wegen des Nebels 4. Gegenüber vom Bahnhof/Dem Bahnhof gegenüber 5. zum Tierarzt/zur Tierärztin 6. in den Flur/den Korridor/den Gang 7. zu Fuß 8. zum letzten Mal 9. gegen sechs [Uhr] 10. bis Montag

2.D

1. nach Berlin 2. zum Friseur/Frisör 3. vor der Tür 4. zwanzig [Minuten] nach acht [Uhr] 5. zu Besuch 6. von Mai bis Oktober 7. aufs Land 8. Wort für Wort 9. bis Juli 10. Der Landkarte nach

2.E

1. durch die/deine Nase 2. des Romans 3. durch den Hinterhof/Garten 4. hinter dem Haus 5. gegen Ihre/deine/eure Methode 6. die ganze Woche hindurch 7. ins 8. im zweiten Stock 9. Durch Zufall 10. an der Ecke

2.F

1. bis zur Tür/bis an die Tür 2. aufs Bett 3. zwanzig [Minuten] vor acht [Uhr] 4. aus Gold 5. für morgen 6. aus diesem Glas 7. seit zwei Jahren 8. Wegen seines Berufs/seiner Arbeit 9. Trotz des Preises 10. außer Kontrolle

2.G

1. um die Ecke 2. aus Bayern 3. zur Arbeit/an die Arbeit 4. in die Schweiz 5. gegen sieben [Uhr] 6. außer Atem 7. Bei diesem Wetter 8. Wegen seines niedrigen Gehalts 9. an den See 10. zwischen den Häusern

2.H

1. ohne eure Jacken 2. von ihr 3. von null bis zehn/von 0 bis 10 4. zu mir 5. bei ihrer Freundin 6. Bei schönem Wetter 7. unseretwegen/wegen uns 8. gegen die Russen 9. bei der Arbeit 10. mit dem Zug

2.I

1. hinter mich; vor mich 2. an die Wand 3. mit Kartoffelsalat 4. seit vier [Uhr] 5. Außer ihm 6. Während des Semesters 7. Meiner Meinung nach 8. außer sonntags 9. nach Asien 10. aus Leder

2.J

1. unter den Tisch 2. Neben dem Bett 3. fünf nach halb drei 4. ins 5. aufs Sofa 6. Wegen seiner Arbeit/seines Jobs/seines Berufs 7. vor der Bibliothek 8. an die Wand 9. Während des Jahres 10. am Fenster

2.K

1. auf den Schreibtisch 2. in den Flur/den Gang/den Korridor 3. vor der Tür 4. hinter dem Haus 5. an der Ecke 6. Trotz des hohen Preises 7. Wegen seiner Faulheit 8. meinetwegen/wegen mir 9. an den Tisch 10. über Köln

2.L

1. in die Vereinigten Staaten/USA *or:* nach Amerika 2. Wegen des Nebels 3. auf dem Land[e] 4. im zweiten Stock 5. bis zur Tür/bis an die Tür 6. in die Türkei 7. an die Nordseeküste 8. außer Kalbsleber und Blutwurst 9. unter 2 000 Dollar 10. auf dem Spielplatz 11. gegen einen anderen Wagen/ein anderes Auto 12. Aus diesem Grund 13. über 3 000 Dollar 14. um den Tisch 15. mit dem Boot

Chapter 16 Idiomatic Use of Prepositions

Part One

Focus on Meaning

2.A

1. auf 2. mit 3. für 4. an 5. an/über 6. an/über 7. mit 8. von 9. zu 10. über

2.B

1. in 2. um 3. auf 4. auf 5. mit 6. mit 7. mit 8. von 9. auf 10. über

2.C

1. auf 2. mit 3. Mit 4. auf 5. mit/auf 6. um 7. an 8. von 9. nach 10. auf

2.D

1. mit 2. auf 3. zu 4. an 5. mit 6. von 7. über 8. bei 9. auf 10. in

2.E

1. mit 2. zu 3. von 4. auf 5. mit 6. über 7. für 8. über 9. mit 10. über

3.A

1. Antworten 2. verwandt/verlobt/verheiratet 3. gedankt 4. gearbeitet 5. denken. 6. gesprochen 7. gehandelt 8. gratulieren 9. glücklich/froh/traurig 10. hängt

3.B

1. verliebt 2. bitten 3. warten 4. stolz 5. verheiratet 6. zufrieden 7. verlobt 8. begeistert 9. hoffen 10. lacht/sprecht

3.C

1. reagiert 2. gewöhnen 3. verheiratet 4. verantwortlich 5. böse 6. bitten 7. Denkst 8. gehandelt 9. gefragt 10. stolz

3.D

1. verliebt 2. böse 3. gratulieren 4. arbeiten 5. verliebt 6. getrennt/geschieden 7. froh/glücklich 8. helfen 9. warten 10. befreundet

3.E

1. zufrieden 2. unfreundlich 3. begeistert 4. reagiert 5. sprechen/reden 6. gelacht 7. danken 8. lesen/schreiben 9. zufrieden 10. denken

Part Two

Focus on Meaning and Form

2

1. Woraus 2. Wovon 3. Mit wem 4. Mit wem 5. Mit wem 6. Womit 7. Auf wen 8. Auf wen 9. In wen 10. Worauf 11. Wofür 12. Über wen/Worüber

3

1. Hast du mit ihr gesprochen?
2. Haben wir schon mit Harald darüber gesprochen?
3. Haben Sie mit ihnen gesprochen?
4. Ist dein Vater zufrieden damit/damit zufrieden?
5. Hat der Film davon gehandelt?
6. Sind Sie auch von ihm begeistert?
7. Bist du begeistert davon/davon begeistert?
8. Kannst du deinen Vater darum bitten?
9. Hast du Oma dafür gedankt?
10. Hast du darauf geantwortet?
11. Musstest du lange darauf warten?
12. Sollen wir auf sie warten?
13. Seid ihr stolz auf ihn?
14. Bist du auch verrückt darauf/darauf verrückt?
15. Sollen wir jetzt daran arbeiten?
16. Denkst du oft daran?
17. Wart ihr froh darüber?
18. Hast du darüber gelacht?
19. Habt ihr über ihn gelacht?
20. Hast du deiner Kusine dazu gratuliert?

4

1. Womit bist du unzufrieden?
2. Mit wem bist du unzufrieden?
3. Auf wen/Mit wem bist du böse?
4. Worüber habt ihr gesprochen?
5. Wovon handelt der Film?
6. Wovon ist sie so begeistert?
7. Worum hast du deine Freundin gebeten?
8. Auf wen bist du besonders stolz?
9. Wofür soll ich dir danken?
10. Woran arbeitest du?
11. Woran denkst du?
12. Worüber lachen sie?
13. Worüber ist er so glücklich/froh?
14. Worauf wartest du?
15. Auf wen wartest du?
16. Was hast du seitdem gemacht?
17. Was hast du außerdem geschafft/erledigt?
18. Was würdest du lieber stattdessen kaufen?
19. Was würdest du deswegen ändern?
20. Wie kannst du ohne es leben?

Supplementary Exercises

Focus on Meaning

1.A

1. auf 2. über 3. zu 4. über 5. von 6. Mit 7. auf 8. um 9. für 10. auf

1.B

1. von 2. auf 3. über 4. auf 5. mit 6. auf/nach 7. mit 8. mit 9. über 10. über

1.C

1. über 2. Von 3. von 4. mit 5. mit 6. von 7. um 8. über 9. von 10. vor

1.D

1. zu 2. auf 3. an 4. auf 5. für 6. von 7. über 8. auf 9. mit 10. auf

1.E

1. von 2. über 3. über 4. nach 5. mit 6. auf 7. für 8. um 9. mit 10. nach

1.F

1. an 2. über 3. über 4. auf 5. mit

2.A

1. verrückt 2. gesprochen 3. gratulieren 4. hält 5. handelt 6. sprechen 7. interessiert 8. bitten 9. gedankt 10. antworten

2.B

1. begeistert 2. ärgerst 3. froh/glücklich 4. stolz 5. verlobt/verheiratet/befreundet/verwandt 6. verrückt 7. zufrieden 8. verwandt 9. Schreibst 10. denken

2.C

1. handelt 2. fertig 3. erstaunt 4. unabhängig 5. traurig 6. Sorgen/Kümmern 7. gelacht 8. begeistert 9. Angst 10. hoffen

2.D

1. eingeladen 2. aufpassen/warten 3. erinnern 4. streitest 5. Grund 6. erzählen 7. lesen 8. freuen 9. fertig 10. Lust

2.E

1. träumen 2. vorbereiten 3. freue 4. verrückt 5. Schwierigkeiten/Probleme 6. erkundigen 7. interessiert 8. kümmern/sorgen 9. traurig 10. befreundet

2.F

1. sehnt 2. gearbeitet 3. wundern 4. lachen 5. überzeugt

Focus on Meaning and Form

3.A

1. verrückt nach diesem Jungen/verrückt auf diesen Jungen 2. hältst; von unserem Präsidenten/unserer Präsidentin 3. auf die Rede des Kandidaten reagiert 4. sehr stolz auf unsere Tochter 5. böse auf uns/böse mit uns 6. handelt von einem jungen Mädchen in Indien 7. traurig über den/ihren verlorenen Hund 8. an deinen Beruf denken 9. Schwierigkeiten/Probleme mit dem neuen Job 10. überzeugt von ihrer Rede/von ihrer Rede überzeugt

3.B

1. verwandt mit Raimund 2. mit einem Mädchen aus Ulm verheiratet 3. verliebt in meine Mutter 4. Grund für dein/Ihr schlechtes Benehmen 5. mit ihr reden 6. Kümmern; um Ihre Familie 7. zufrieden mit deiner/Ihrer neuen Stereoanlage 8. um ein Stück Käse bitten 9. mit deinem Vater; gesprochen 10. getrennt von ihrem Mann/von ihrem Mann getrennt

3.C

1. über das Examen sprechen 2. verrückt nach dieser Person/verrückt auf diese Person 3. über seinen dummen Witz gelacht 4. nach dieser Firma erkundigen 5. über deine Jugend[zeit] erzählen 6. Interessierst; für diesen Autor/diese Autorin 7. Denkt; an eure Verwandten in der Schweiz 8. Interessiert; für Fußball 9. traurig über den Tod deiner Großmutter 10. von dem Leben des Kaisers gehandelt

3.D

1. auf die Prüfung/Klausur; vorbereitet 2. über Franz Kafka lesen 3. froh/glücklich über ihren neuen Job 4. für sein Geburtstagsgeschenk danken 5. mit ihr verlobt 6. unabhängig von deinen/euren Eltern 7. von der Revolution in Argentinien gehandelt 8. an den Termin erinnert 9. zu Ihrem Erfolg gratulieren 10. um diesen Kurs kümmern

3.E

1. über den Krieg in dem Irak 2. um Hilfe bitten 3. bei der Hausarbeit helfen 4. von diesem Konzert begeistert 5. freuen; auf unseren Urlaub 6. Schreibst; über die jetzige Situation 7. fertig mit der Zeitschrift 8. nach dir gefragt 9. Angst vor Spinnen, Ratten oder Schlangen 10. froh/glücklich über seine Note *or:* zufrieden mit seiner Note

3.F

1. von seinem Jahr in Spanien erzählt 2. traurig über das Ende des Filmes 3. auf die Kinder warten 4. hoffen auf einen Sieg 5. unzufrieden mit ihrem neuen Chef/ihrer neuen Chefin

Chapter 17 Numerals and Time Expressions

Focus on Meaning

2.A

1. heute Abend 2. nächsten/kommenden Sommer 3. letzten/vorigen/vergangenen Sonntag 4. Sonntagnachmittag oder: diesen/kommenden Sonntagnachmittag 5. heute Morgen 6. nächstes/kommendes Jahr 7. letztes/voriges/vergangenes Semester 8. nächsten/kommenden Monat 9. dieses Jahr 10. jeden Dienstag/dienstags

2.B

1. den ganzen Tag 2. in einer Stunde 3. vor zwei Tagen 4. nach einer Weile 5. eines Tages 6. heute in einem Monat 7. zweimal im Jahr/pro Jahr/jährlich 8. einmal am Tag/den Tag/täglich 9. heute in drei Tagen 10. vor zwei Jahren

2.C

1. in zehn Minuten 2. das ganze Jahr 3. eines Tages 4. morgen früh 5. heute Vormittag 6. alle drei Tage 7. um Mitternacht 8. während des Tages/tagsüber 9. eines Abends 10. die ganze Zeit

2.D

1. jeden Monat/monatlich 2. für ein Jahr 3. seit einem Jahr 4. in ein paar/mehreren/einigen Tagen 5. vor einer Stunde 6. den ganzen Abend 7. nachmittags/jeden Nachmittag 8. am Nachmittag 9. im Frühling 10. diesen/kommenden Freitag

Chapter 18 Conjunctions and Clauses

Focus on Meaning

2.A

1. Als 2. denn 3. Sobald/Als 4. wenn 5. Da 6. nachdem/weil 7. Obwohl 8. aber 9. indem 10. sondern

2.B

1. und 2. denn 3. weil 4. seit[dem]/wenn 5. dass 6. und 7. weil 8. aber 9. aber 10. als/während

2.C

1. weil 2. damit 3. während 4. warum 5. wann 6. aber 7. bis 8. dass 9. sobald 10. nachdem

2.D

1. weil 2. oder 3. damit 4. Bevor/Ehe 5. ob 6. seit[dem] 7. obwohl 8. sondern 9. Wenn 10. dass

Focus on Form

3.A

1. Ich bleibe hier und du gehst dahin.
2. Wir haben Briefmarken gesammelt, als wir Jungen waren.
3. Die Jacke ist schön, aber die Farbe gefällt mir nicht.
4. Ihr werdet das Examen bestehen können, wenn ihr genug dafür gelernt habt.
5. Man kann Gitarre schneller lernen, indem man täglich übt.
6. Es ist mir immer noch nicht klar, ob du die Theorie verstanden hast.
7. Willst du ins Kino gehen oder [willst du] ins Konzert [gehen]? Willst du ins Kino oder ins Konzert gehen?
8. Wir mussten zwei Tage länger an dem Projekt arbeiten, weil wir nicht gut haben zusammenarbeiten können.
9. Lisa hat mir schon gesagt, dass sie am Wochenende mitkommt.
10. Peter hat nicht Steak bestellt, sondern [er hat] Fisch [bestellt]. *or:*
    Peter hat nicht Steak, sondern Fisch bestellt.

3.B

1. Ich werde Sie darum bitten, wenn ich Hilfe brauche.
2. Du hast es nicht tun können, obwohl ich es dir hundertmal habe erklären müssen.
3. Wir sind schon mehrmals ins Museum gegangen, seitdem wir hier wohnen.
4. Anna konnte die Aufgabe nicht erledigen, denn sie hatte nicht genug Zeit dafür.
5. Hans musste mit dem Bus fahren, weil er seine Autoschlüssel nicht hat finden können.
6. Der Mechaniker bestellt die richtigen Ersatzteile, damit er meinen Wagen wird reparieren können.
7. Ich gehe einkaufen, bevor ich meine Mutter anrufe.
8. Warte auf mich, bitte, bis ich diesen Zettel fertig schreibe.
9. Ich bin immer schläfrig, wenn ich vor sechs Uhr morgens aufwache.
10. Ute hat nicht nur diese Hose gekauft, sondern [sie hat] auch diesen Gürtel [gekauft]. *or:*
    Ute hat nicht nur diese Hose, sondern auch diesen Gürtel gekauft.

Chapter 19 Relative Clauses and Infinitive Phrases and Constructions

Part One

Focus on Meaning and Form

2.A

1. dessen 2. das 3. dem 4. dem 5. deren 6. der 7. dem 8. dessen 9. die 10. dessen

2.B

1. die 2. deren 3. deren 4. der 5. deren 6. die 7. deren 8. der 9. der 10. dessen

2.C

1. die 2. den 3. dem 4. den 5. die 6. dessen 7. das 8. die 9. die 10. denen

2.D

1. die 2. das 3. der 4. die 5. den 6. dem 7. denen 8. den 9. das 10. den

3.A

1. Was 2. Worauf/Worüber 3. was 4. was 5. was 6. wem 7. worüber 8. was 9. was 10. was

3.B

1. wessen 2. wer 3. wessen 4. was 5. was 6. wem 7. was 8. was/wen 9. wem 10. wen

Part Two

Focus on Form

2.A

1. Anstatt zu Hause zu essen, gehen wir lieber in ein Restaurant.
2. Anstatt nach Wien zu fliegen, blieben wir eine Weile länger in München.
3. Barabara ging weg, ohne mir ihre Adresse und Telefonnummer zu geben.
4. Bergmanns Filme sind schwer zu verstehen.
5. Darf ich Sie darum bitten, Platz zu nehmen?
6. Das ist schwer zu sagen.
7. Das ist kaum zu glauben.
8. Dieser Wein ist kaum zu trinken.
9. Er bat mich, ihm zu helfen.
10. Er findet es schwer, den Film zu verstehen.

2.B

1. Sie will nicht, dass ich ihr helfe.
2. Er zeigte uns, wo wir den Wagen parken sollen.
3. Erich sagte uns, dass wir hier bleiben sollen.
4. Es hörte auf zu regnen.
5. Es ist fast unmöglich, jetzt Karten zu bekommen.
6. Es ist immer nett, Briefe von dir zu lesen.
7. Es ist Zeit, nach Hause zu gehen.
8. Es ist zu spät, heute Abend ins Kino zu gehen.
9. Ich ging in die Stadt, um schicke Kleider zu kaufen.
10. Ich habe keine Lust, Arzt zu werden.

2.C

1. Ich werde dir sagen, wen du anrufen sollst.
2. Ich sagte dir, dass du auf uns warten sollst/solltest.
3. Ich will, dass Anna auch mitkommt.
4. Ich wusste nicht, was ich sagen sollte.
5. Kannst du mir sagen, wie man das macht?
6. Karl arbeitet nachts, um mehr Geld zu verdienen.
7. Oft nimmt er den Wagen, ohne seinen Vater darum zu bitten.
8. So etwas ist eigentlich zu erwarten.
9. Ein Volkswagen ist leicht zu fahren. *or:* Volkswagen sind leicht zu fahren.
10. Willst du nicht, dass ich Sabine einlade?
11. Wir haben vor, nächstes Jahr nach Wien zu fahren.
12. Wir wissen nicht, mit wem wir sprechen sollen.
13. Wissen Sie, wohin sie gehen müssen?

Focus on Meaning and Form

3

1. Can you show us how one makes lasagna? Kannst du uns zeigen, wie man Lasagne macht?
2. Please explain to them how one fixes this engine. Bitte erklär ihnen, wie man diesen Motor repariert.
3. Show me how one corrects this mistake. Zeig mir, wie man diesen Fehler korrigiert.
4. Show us what we are supposed to do. Zeig uns, was wir machen sollen.
5. Tell me when I am supposed to begin. Sag mir, wann ich [damit] anfangen soll.
6. Tell them where they are supposed to look for it. Sag ihnen, wo sie es suchen sollen.
7. Tell him to whom he is supposed to speak. Sag ihm, mit wem er sprechen soll.
8. Tell us what we are supposed to say. Sag uns, was wir sagen sollen.
9. Request of her that she come earlier. Bitte sie darum, dass sie früher kommt. *or:* Bitte sie darum, früher zu kommen.
10. I would like that they work a bit harder on it. Ich möchte, dass sie etwas fleißiger daran arbeiten.
11. She doesn't want that you go out with him. Sie will nicht, dass du mit ihm ausgehst.
12. Toni wants that Dieter buys her a red sweater for her birthday. Toni will, dass Dieter ihr einen roten Pulli zum Geburtstag kauft.
13. We want that you invite our friends to the party. Wir wollen/möchten, dass du unsere Freunde zur Party einlädst.

4.A

1. Kannst du mir zeigen, wie man Klavier spielt?
2. Er hat mir erklärt, wie ich/man ihnen helfen kann.
3. Er will nicht, dass ich ihn frage.
4. Oft nimmt er das Auto, ohne seinen Vater darum zu bitten.
5. Er hat uns gezeigt, wie wir es richtig tun können/wie man es richtig macht.
6. Ich wusste nicht, was ich sagen sollte.
7. Ich habe keine Lust, Politiker/Politikerin zu werden.
8. Ich habe dir gesagt, dass du verschwinden sollst.
9. Ich will, dass Oma uns bald besucht.
10. Ich will dieses Wochenende ausgehen. (Remember, modal verbs use an infinitive without **zu**.)

4.B

1. Ich will, dass du dieses Wochenende mit mir ausgehst.
2. Ich bin in die Innenstadt gegangen, um einige Bücher zu kaufen.
3. Ich möchte, dass er uns eine Flasche Wein bestellt.
4. Ich möchte ein Glas Wein bestellen. (Remember, modal verbs use an infinitive without **zu**.)
5. Ich werde dir sagen, wann du es beginnen sollst/wann du damit anfangen sollst.
6. Es hörte auf zu schneien.
7. Es ist fast unmöglich, jetzt einen Flug zu besuchen.
8. Es ist immer schön, [etwas] von dir zu hören.
9. Es ist Zeit, nach Hause zu gehen.
10. Es ist zu spät, einkaufen zu gehen.

4.C

1. Kafkas Novellen sind schwer zu verstehen.
2. Gehen wir schwimmen/Lasst uns schwimmen gehen, statt in den Zoo/Tiergarten zu gehen.
3. Lisa will nicht, dass ich Rüdiger einlade.
4. Darf ich Sie bitten, nicht zu rauchen?
5. Manche Männer finden es schwer, Frauen zu verstehen. Und umgekehrt!
6. Mutti sagte [uns]/hat uns gesagt, dass wir hier bleiben sollen.

7. Sie ging, ohne ihm den Ring zurückzugeben.
8. Das ist schwer zu glauben./Das ist kaum zu glauben.
9. Wir wussten nicht, mit wem wir sprechen sollten.
10. Wir haben vor, nächsten Sommer nach Europa zu reisen.

Chapter 20 Clarifying *da*-Compounds; Extended Adjective Modifiers

Part One

Focus on Meaning

2

1. darüber 2. darauf 3. damit 4. dazu 5. davon 6. davon 7. darum 8. dafür 9. darauf 10. darauf 11. darauf/danach 12. daran 13. davon 14. darüber 15. darüber

Chapter 21 Present Subjunctive II

Part One

Focus on Meaning

2

1. If I had time, I'd go with you. 2. If you spent all your money, you'd have nothing left. 3. If you had nothing left, you couldn't go to the movies with us. 4. If you couldn't go to the movies with us, you would miss seeing the film. 5. If you missed the film, I wouldn't tell you anything about it. 6. If you lost your credit cards, you'd have big problems. 7. If I bought that, my wife would be very angry with me. 8. If I didn't know the answer, I wouldn't be able to do it. 9. If I found what I'm looking for, I'd be happy. 10. If I were depressed, I'd tend to sleep a lot.

Part Two

Focus on Form

2

2. schrieb; schriebe 3. ging; ginge 4. sagte; sagte 5. fuhr; führe 6. gab; gäbe 7. wartete; wartete 8. fand; fände 9. kam; käme 10. lief; liefe 11. tat; täte 12. dachte; dächte 13. zog; zöge 14. arbeitete; arbeitete 15. war; wäre 16. hatte; hätte 17. wurde; würde 18. fragte; fragte 19. konnte; könnte 20. musste; müsste 21. durfte; dürfte 22. sollte; sollte 23. mochte; möchte

3

1. spräche 2. schriebe 3. ginge 4. führe 5. gäbe 6. wartete 7. käme 8. täte 9. dächte 10. zöge 11. machte 12. läse 13. wäre 14. hätte 15. würde 16. könnte 17. müsste 18. dürfte 19. sollte 20. möchte

Part Three

Focus on Form

2

2. Wenn ich nicht ausgehen dürfte, [dann] müsste ich zu Hause bleiben. *or:* Wenn ich ausgehen dürfte, [dann] müsste ich nicht zu Hause bleiben.
3. Wenn ich meine Hausaufgaben machen sollte, [dann] dürfte ich nicht ins Kino gehen. *or:* Wenn ich meine Hausaufgaben nicht machen sollte, [dann] dürfte ich ins Kino gehen.
4. Wenn ich meinem Vater helfen müsste, [dann] könnte ich dir nicht helfen. *or:* Wenn ich nicht meinem Vater helfen müsste, könnte ich dir helfen.

5. Wenn ich das nicht machen wollte, [dann] würde ich es nicht machen. *or:* Wenn ich das machen wollte, [dann] würde ich es machen.
6. Wenn ich das nicht machen könnte, [dann] würde ich es nicht machen. *or:* Wenn ich es machen könnte, [dann] würde ich es machen.
7. Wenn ich alles aufräumen müsste, [dann] müsste ich den ganzen Tag zu Hause bleiben. *or:* Wenn ich nicht alles aufräumen müsste, müsste ich nicht den ganzen Tag zu Hause bleiben.
8. Wenn ich zu Hause bleiben sollte, [dann] dürfte ich nicht mit euch ins Museum gehen. *or:* Wenn ich nicht zu Hause bleiben sollte, [dann] dürfte ich mit euch ins Museum gehen.

Part Four

Focus on Form

2

1. Könnten Sie mir bitte helfen? 2. Dürfte man hier fotografieren? 3. Würden Sie mir bitte ein Glas Rotwein holen? 4. Sollten wir das für morgen machen? 5. Würden Sie das für mich machen, bitte? 6. Müsste ich das eigentlich tun? 7. Würden/Könnten Sie lauter sprechen? 8. Ich würde dir raten, das niemandem zu sagen.

Chapter 22 Past Subjunctive II

Part One

Focus on Form

2

1. If he *had caught* an earlier flight, he would have arrived on time.
2. If you *had started* work earlier, you would have finished by now.
3. If we *had studied* harder, we would have gotten better grades.
4. If I *had known* the answer, I'd have gotten a higher score.
5. If I *hadn't spent* all my money, I would have had enough for it.
6. If you *had listened* to me, you wouldn't have gotten into trouble.
7. If she *had come* earlier, she would have seen us.
8. If the mechanic *had fixed* the car, it would work right now.
9. If you *had been* here, you would have met my roommate.
10. If I *had run* just a bit faster, I would have won the race.

3

1. Wenn ich meine Familie besucht hätte, hätte ich mit Opa gesprochen.
2. Wenn ich in Berlin gewohnt hätte, hätte ich oft das Museum besucht.
3. Wenn ich bei Siemens gearbeitet hätte, hätte ich zwei Millionen Euro verdient.
4. Wenn ich mit Kolumbus gesegelt wäre, hätten wir die Neue Welt entdeckt.
5. Wenn ich ihr den Brief geschrieben hätte, hätte ich ihr die Sache nicht erwähnt.
6. Wenn er das gehört hätte, hätte er sich kaputt gelacht.
7. Wenn sie auf Hans gewartet hätte, wäre sie ungeduldig geworden.
8. Wenn wir diese Erklärung gelesen hätten, hätten wir alles viel besser verstanden.
9. Wenn ich die Rechnung bekommen hätte, hätte ich sie gleich bezahlt.
10. Wenn ich das Scheckheft gefunden hätte, wäre ich ganz glücklich geworden.

4

1. Wenn ich das gestern Abend gewusst hätte, wäre ich jetzt nicht hier.
2. Ich würde die Prüfung heute machen, wenn ich mir den Arm gestern nicht gebrochen hätte.
3. Ich hätte jetzt genug Geld für ein neues Auto, wenn ich mein Geld gespart hätte.
4. Wir wären immer noch Freunde, wenn wir miteinander in Kontakt geblieben wären.
5. Du hättest heute keine Probleme, wenn du früher fleißiger gearbeitet hättest.

Part Two

Focus on Meaning and Form

2

1. Wenn ich nur etwas Geld gehabt hätte!
2. Wenn ich nur genug Zeit gehabt hätte!
3. Wenn ich nur nicht so müde gewesen wäre!
4. Wenn ih nur nicht so viele Fehler gemacht hätte!
5. Wenn jemand/man mich als Kind nur geliebt hätte!

3

1. Ich wünschte/wollte, mein Auto wäre nicht kaputt gegangen.
2. Ich wünschte/wollte, ich hätte eine gute Note in der Prüfung verdient.
3. Ich wünschte/wollte, meine Freundin von zwei Jahren hätte mich nicht verlassen.
4. Ich wünschte/wollte, das Wetter wäre heute nicht so kalt gewesen.
5. Ich wünschte/wollte, ich hätte im Lotto gewonnen.
6. Ich wünschte/wollte, der Deutschlehrer hätte die Prüfungen nicht so streng korrigiert.
7. Ich wünschte/wollte, ich hätte das Examen bestanden.

4–6

Answers will vary.

Chapter 24 The Passive Voice

Part One

Focus on Form

2. A

1. Wirst 2. werden 3. werde 4. wird 5. wird 6. wird 7. wird

2.B

1. wurde 2. wurde 3. wurde 4. wurden 5. wurde 6. wurden 7. wurde

2.C

1. ist ... worden 2. sind ... worden 3. ist ... worden 4. sind ... worden 5. bin ... worden

2.D

1. War ... worden 2. waren ... worden 3. war ... worden

2.E

1. werden ... werden 2. wird ... werden 3. werden ... werden

3

1. Alle suchen das verlorene zweijährige Kind.

present	Das [verlorene] zweijährige Kind wird [von allen] gesucht.
past	Das [verlorene] zweijährige Kind wurde [von allen] gesucht.
pres. perf.	Das [verlorene] zweijährige Kind ist [von allen] gesucht worden.
past perf.	Das [verlorene] zweijährige Kind war [von allen] gesucht worden.
future	Das [verlorene] zweijährige Kind wird [von allen] gesucht werden.

2. Ich verkaufe das alte Auto.

present	Das alte Auto wird [von mir] verkauft.
past	Das alte Auto wurde [von mir] verkauft.
pres. perf.	Das alte Auto ist [von mir] verkauft worden.
past perf.	Das alte Auto war [von mir] verkauft worden.
future	Das alte Auto wird [von mir] verkauft werden.

3. Frau Dorner verkauft in diesem Laden Antiquitäten.

present	Antiquitäten werden in diesem Laden [von Frau Dorner] verkauft.
past	Antiquitäten wurden in diesem Laden [von Frau Dorner] verkauft.
pres. perf.	Antiquitäten sind in diesem Laden [von Frau Dorner] verkauft worden.
past perf.	Antiquitäten waren in diesem Laden [von Frau Dorner] verkauft worden.
future	Antiquitäten werden in diesem Laden [von Frau Dorner] verkauft werden.

4. Die Stadt baut hier billige Wohnungen.

present	Billige Wohnungen werden hier [von der Stadt] gebaut.
past	Billige Wohnungen wurden hier [von der Stadt] gebaut.
pres. perf.	Billige Wohnungen sind hier [von der Stadt] gebaut worden.
past perf.	Billige Wohnungen waren hier [von der Stadt] gebaut worden.
future	Billige Wohnungen werden hier [von der Stadt] gebaut werden.

5. Der Professor berät Studenten fürs nächste Semester.

present	Studenten werden vom Professor fürs nächste Semester beraten.
past	Studenten wurden vom Professor fürs nächste Semester beraten.
pres. perf.	Studenten sind vom Professor fürs nächste Semester beraten worden.
past perf.	Studenten waren vom Professor fürs nächste Semester beraten worden.
future	Studenten werden vom Professor fürs nächste Semester beraten werden.

6. Der Arzt untersucht die Patientin.

present	Die Patientin wird vom Arzt untersucht.
past	Die Patientin wurde vom Arzt untersucht.
pres. perf.	Die Patientin ist vom Arzt untersucht worden.
past perf.	Die Patientin war vom Arzt untersucht worden.
future	Die Patientin wird vom Arzt untersucht werden

Part Two

Focus on Form

2

(Agents in brackets are not necessary and would normally not be stated.)

1. Mein Zimmer muss [von mir] aufgeräumt werden.
2. Unsere Hausaufgaben sollten [von uns] gemacht werden.
3. Dieses neue Auto darf nicht gefahren werden.
4. Diese Tür soll repariert werden.
5. Zwei Konzertkarten müssen noch gekauft werden.
6. Alles sollte verbessert werden.
7. Es hat endlich getan werden dürfen.
8. Das Badezimmer muss geputzt werden.
9. Der Klempner und der Elektriker mussten angerufen werden.
10. Etwas Geld wird gespart werden können.
11. Mein Büro muss renoviert werden.
12. Eine Party soll von Sonja und Steffi geplant werden.
13. Wie soll Ihr Name geschrieben werden?

Index

A

R

S

Y

Z